Praise for INFORMATICA 1.0

"With his book, I may finally master the Internet – if I can avoid being diverted to simply relaxing with Peter Black's entertaining, erudite and thoughtful prose.

"So incredibly diverse is this book on the computer age that it would take another 380 pages to describe it. Its explanations are fascinating, its directories and guides invaluable and its essays delightful."

— Walter Cronkite

"An incandescent cavalcade of the net."

— George Gilder, *Chairman, Gilder Group*

"The best way to find the best stuff on the Net."

— Chris Kitze, *President of Xoom*

"**Informatica 1.0** is the tome that Peter Black had to write: chatty, witty, eclectic and peppered with information about today's most compelling stuff – just like Peter is. **Informatica 1.0** is less like reading a book than it is like rummaging through the attic of a really fascinating personality: Never boring, always revealing and quite often enlightening. I'm adding this one to my bookshelf under information-age survival guide."

— Fred Abatemarco, *Editor-in-Chief and President, Popular Science Magazine*

"I have never seen anything quite like **Informatica 1.0**. It is a brilliant collection of the most fascinating pieces of currently relevant information I have ever encountered. Peter Black has assembled a unique encyclopaedia of information that truly matters to today's human. Read it and avoid information age extinction."

— Tim Draper, *Senior Partner, Draper Fisher Jurvetson*

"Seems to me that **Informatica 1.0** is going to be the *Whole Earth Catalog* for the Wired generation, not just a fancy compendium of neat stuff, but a storehouse of knowledge-critical ideas and concepts that will drive us into the next millennium."

— Nat Goldhaber, *CEO of Cybergold*

INFORMATICA 1.0

ACCESS TO THE BEST TOOLS FOR MASTERING THE INFORMATION REVOLUTION

PETER McNAUGHTON BLACK

Random House
New York

INFORMATICA 1.0
ACCESS TO THE BEST TOOLS FOR MASTERING THE INFORMATION REVOLUTION

This book is available for special purchases in bulk by organizations and institutions, not for resale, at special discounts. Please direct your inquiries to the Random House Special Sales Department, toll-free 888-591-1200 or fax 212-572-4961.

Please address inquiries about electronic licensing of reference products, for use on a network or in software or on CD-ROM, to the Subsidiary Rights Department, Random House Reference & Information Publishing, fax 212-940-7370.

Visit the Random House Web site at www.randomhouse.com

Typeset by spinner28 Desktop Arts
Book design by Susan Black
Typeset and printed in the United States of America

Library of Congress Catologing-in-Publication Data

Black, Peter (Peter McNaughton), 1951-
    Informatica 1.0: the best tools for accessing and managing information /
[Peter Black]. — 1st ed.
    p. cm.
  Included bibliographical references and index.
  ISBN 0-375-70628-3
  ISBN 0-375-70637-2 (includes CD-ROM)
  1. Measuring instruments—Data processing. 2. Measuring instruments
    Automation. 3. Automatic control. I. Title.
  TA165.B53 1999
  030—dc21   99-29069
                                    CIP

First edition
0 9 8 7 6 5 4 3 2 1
September 1999
ISBN 0-375-70628-3
ISBN 0-375-70637-2 (includes CD-ROM)
New York Toronto London Sydney Auckland

INFORMATICA 1.0

Contents

The Entries

→

INFORMATICA 1.0

The Entries*continued*

II. SOURCES

→

The Entries*continued*

→

INFORMATICA 1.0

The Entries *continued*

→

INFORMATICA 1.0

The Entries *continued*

→

INFORMATICA 1.0

The Entries *continued*

ACKNOWLEDGEMENTS AND CREDITS

LAUDATE DOMINUM A QUO OMNES BENEDICTIONES EMENANT

M.M.Y., from whom I learned the value of knowledge and its source

Patti, for standing at my side through all things, good and bad.

Sean, Cassie, and Annie, for the constant inspiration only your children can provide.

Sue, for making the book look great.

The folks at Random House: Charles Levine, for taking a gamble on something that wasn't another 'me too' project; Page Edmunds for her continuing and gracious enthusiasm; Andy Ambraziejus, for managing a jigsaw puzzle of a project with permanent good humor; Pat for her fine and detailed eye; Brenda Garcia and Tracey Richards for policing the day-to-day details; Mary Beth Roche and T. J. Snyder for making sure that all this is not just a tree falling in the woods.

Publisher:	Charles Levine
Associate Publisher:	Page Edmunds
Managing Editor:	Andy Ambraziejus
Director of Production:	Pat Ehresmann
Senior Production Editor:	Joe Sora
Layout/Design:	Susan Black
Invaluable Assistance:	Tracey Richards, Mary Beth Roche, T. J. Snyder

The principle typefaces used in this book are
Rotis Serif, Rotis Semi, and Barmeno

Introduction

Devices, Programs, Publications, Places, and Web Sites That Define the American System of Innovation

The Best Tools of Sensing, Measurement, Management, and Knowledge

North America is a vast furnace, and it consumes almost half the world's raw materials. In the U.S., we have spent the better part of a generation wondering whether we are too hungry, too acquisitive, too wasteful, and too greedy.

At the same time, we have spawned an array of technologies, products, and ways of getting things done that has spread over the surface of the Earth like a wildfire.

There is a hard surface crust of cynicism about America's direction. We see vast abundance and recognize that we take it for granted. We are unnerved by the entertainments we take, as they often seem to feed unchecked appetites. The rest of the world shares the cynicism, disapproves of the appetites, and yet often enthusiastically joins in the pleasure of consumption. And what of it?

Beneath that crust of cynicism and material appetites lies something amazing and pure. It is a visceral instinct to transform the past and create something new and better. More than just that, it is a belief that there is, and will always be, something better. Here in the U.S., the peculiar chemistry of the free contest of ideas, the unfettered flow of capital, and the lionization of the individual is the recipe for something better. →

Introduction *continued*

→ We like to get the new stuff before anyone else, whether we make it ourselves, or buy it elsewhere. We crave v.1.0, but as anyone in the computer business knows, it always has problems. It is generally more expensive, more trouble, and consumes more resources. But v.1.0 has one great virtue: it leads to v.2.0.

This is what we do for the world. We are the first market for something better. We are willing to pay a premium for v.1.0, and then we drive it to v.2.0. We've been doing it for almost 200 years.

We essentially created the modern industrial manufacturing model and refined it with any number of improvements. It began with Eli Whitney and stretches to the present day. Integrated manufacturing, interchangeable parts, time and motion studies, statistical analysis, machine computation, systems analysis, information theory, mass-scale networking—were all grown here. In the meantime, we recognized the gigantic garbage pile all this has created and have spent over a quarter century figuring out how to clean it up. We are just now getting a handle on the slag piles, poisoned streams, and polluted beaches and are shipping the garbage management solutions off to everybody else.

Every time we figure something out, we package it, manufacture it cheaply, and sell it to the world. We pay the big bill for v.1.0, and in so doing build the economy of scale for the rest of the world.

That is a good and honorable thing, as long as we can and will clean up our mess. And now we have created a new kind of mess, a slag pile of data, a smog of information. Now it is time to figure out how to clean it up.

Inside here, we honor the best tools for an information society, and the best ways to sense and measure things, manage the resulting info, and refine it into practical knowledge.

This book is dedicated to the pursuit of something better. →

→ I wrote the preceding words almost a year ago, when the Random House folks asked me to explain the ethos of this book. I had originally pitched the book as *The Whole Earth Catalog*, 30 years later, without the chemical toilets and backpacking gear. They wanted me to better define what the book was about—what was the spirit behind it. Though the preceding essay reads a bit highfalutin' to me now, I'll stick with it. My intent was then, and continues to be, to portray an absolutely remarkable future, at once thrilling and a bit scary.

This is what Vannevar Bush did with his 1945 essay "As We May Think," which imagined the future with thinking machines. He timed the appearance of his thoughts to coincide with the end of World War II (he knew the atom bomb was coming and when it would likely be used), and he put those thoughts in *The Atlantic Monthly,* a place where the people he wanted to reach were likely to find them. Hence, the power elite read his piece on their porches, verandahs, and beaches that August, as they tried to figure out what the rest of the century could and should look like.

I'm hoping that you will read this book sometime before our passage into the new century, the new millennium. As for my intended audience, I would have a hard time defining a power elite to address. Everything has changed in the last bunch of years. A degree from Harvard, Yale, or Princeton doesn't carry the weight it once did. The people who make things happen don't all summer in the same place anymore. In fact, the people who count can't necessarily count on being the people who count in five years time. Maybe you are about to be one of the new ones. Hope so.

And finally, I hope the irony of calling this book *Informatica 1.0* is not lost on you. V.1.0 always stinks up the room, and I would guess that this version of *Informatica* will hold true to form. Once we get a couple of refined, elaborated, and debugged versions out, *Informatica 1.0* will look like the experimental prototype that it is. →

→ We are not going to wait for the next print version to begin work on v.2.0. Beginning in November 1999, right after Comdex, we will publish a down-loadable update to *Informatica 1.0,* filled with stuff that is new since we closed editorial on the book (June 1999) and current as of Comdex.

If you haven't bought the version of the book that comes with the CD-ROM, then you can order the disk on our Web site (*www.etronica.com*). If you have the disk, a download of the update will cost only several bucks. We'll update again and again, for the same kind of price. Kind of a magazine, but without the lag time of paper.

We'll try not to be a conduit for publicity press releases, but we won't be a *Consumer Reports* either. The charter will be to hunt for things, services, and ideas that are on their way to v.2.0—and have matured a bit. The emphasis will always be on showcasing quality, with an explanation of what we think are the criteria for quality.

If you have firsthand knowledge of something we should know about, send it on to informatica@*etronica*.com. We'll credit you at minimum and maybe find a way to compensate you for a continuing role as contributor, presuming of course that *Informatica* turns out to be a continuing operation.

Hope so. I've had a really good time getting version 1.0 together.

Peter Black
July, 1999
Pacific Palisades, CA.

What's a Metapage?

Throughout *Informatica,* certain Web sites will be referred to as "meta-pages." Since hardly anyone can agree on terminology in the world of high technology, provisional use of definitions for terms is the way to go—working definitions.

So our working definition of a metapage is a Web page that clusters links that share a focus. The beauty of the Web is that it is a web, a vast inter-twingled matrix of things, bound together by an infinite array of links. That means that any given page could have an infinite array of links, and there could be an infinite number of pages. Doesn't work out that way, though.

In practice, pages are finite in number and length and fall into two classes. One kind of page tells a story of some sort in text, graphics, sounds, video, and the like. When that kind of page loads up with links to other pages in order to tell its story, and when the links are the fundamental value of the page, then it becomes a metapage.

From www.PCWebopedia.com:

META
In computer science, a common prefix that means "about". So, for example, metadata is data that describes other data (data about data). A metalanguage is a language used to describe other languages. A metafile is a file that contains other files. The HTML META tag is used to describe the contents of a Web page.

I. hard*ware*

→

I. HARDWARE*continued*

Electronic Calipers
With Digitized Hookup
http://www.brownandsharpe.com

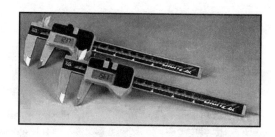

Type: Hardware

First Developed: 1998

Price: $200- $300

Key Features: Integration of the old and the new

Ages: Post-high school

Obsolescence factor: High

Further Information:

❊ *http://www.umeciv.maine.edu/ cie111/equip/dial_calipers.htm* for the University of Maine's fine tutorial on how to use a dial caliper.

❊ *http://www.fvfowler.com/ ultracal.html* for another fine electronic caliper.

Brown & Sharpe:
☎ (401) 886-2495

Whether calipers are used to measure features on something as big as a turbine engine or the size of a candy bar, it's difficult to imagine a more versatile tool. A caliper is a combination of a ruler with jaws and a measuring system.

A caliper is so simple, yet so exacting, a tool that it seems counterintuitive that it could be improved upon by attaching it to a computer. There is certainly a boatload of people who would claim that hooking one up to a computer is like retrofitting an eagle with a jet engine. In fact, the principle of SYNTHETIC APERTURE applies here: the more measurement snapshots that can be taken and digitized, the more accurate a picture of the measurement that can evolve. Brown & Sharpe has made these kinds of tools for a very long time. The company out-Germans the Germans in precision and design. You could take any one of their products, stand it up on a velvet pedestal, and simply admire it. But most savvy people put them to work, for years and years and years.

Features
- Display digits enlarged to 1/4" high for easier reading
- Automatic shut-off extends battery life to 2 years (2000 hours per year) with one lithium battery
- Measures outside, inside, depth, and steps
- Reference scale for quick confirmation
- Frame constructed from stainless steel, hardened and ground
- Tough nylon housing protects the electronic components
- Comparative measurement: Zero can be set at any point, using a standard or master part. Negative values are displayed with a minus sign
- Supplied with fitted molded case

Additional Features of the Mark 4RS only
- Data output: RS-232 Optocoupled
- Blocking of the display
- Locking of zero setting

Astroscan® 2001
Wide-Field Basic Telescope Package
http://scientifics.edsci.com/scientifics

Type: Telescope

First Developed: 1976; Edmund Scientific

Price Range: $350–$400 depending upon options

Key Features: Very simple, easy to use

Ages: Junior high, and later

Obsolescence: Low

Further Information:
✳ *http://astronomy.thelinks.com*

Contact Edmund Scientific at:
☎ (609) 573-6395

Edmund Scientific claims this is the "Easiest To Use Telescope Available," and that may not be pure hoo-hah. The thing is made of ABS plastic, so it'll take a licking and keep on ticking. It sees a very broad 3 degrees of the sky (the width of six full moons). Its rounded bubblelike body makes it easy to hold, either standing up, or cross-legged on the ground. My first telescope was a Tasco refractor. I got it in the summer of 1963, and that summer I regularly took it out on the fairway of a golf course near my family's summer home in Maine. It came in a big wooden box, and had to be unpacked and assembled. The whole process took about 20 minutes to set up, and an equal amount of time to break down, with an ample amount of opportunities to lose wing nuts in the grass at night. In the middle of that summer, there was a total eclipse, the path of which passed over the northerly coasts of Maine. My grandmother had the patience and kind-heartedness to drive me way north, and set me up on a hill with a hundred other folks. I just barely got the thing set up before the sky went dark. I wish I'd had this instead.

Deutsches Optik
http://www.deutscheoptik.com

Type: Source for fine, unique optics

First Developed: 1990

Price Range: Various prices

Key Features: Access to obscure sources for new and old devices

Ages: Post-teen

Obsolescence: Great optics never grow old

Further Information: Very interesting, quarterly catalog
☎ (619) 287-9860

My treasured and ultracool "Tanker" Binoculars

In 1991, I stumbled across an ad these guys ran in *The New Yorker*. It claimed that they had scrounged a lot of East German binoculars, manufactured for military tankers by the famous Zeiss Jena optical manufacturer (this is the Zeiss that got stuck behind the iron curtain). They said these binoculars were first rate, and at $500 were priced well below what they would cost in the West. Ruggedized, superfine optics. Flawlessly manufactured. Quite a set of claims.

They did not lie. ➔

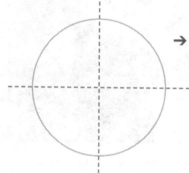

Deutsches Optik *continued*

→ I treasure this pair of binoculars, and have never found anything even close to their quality since. Sadly, Deutsches Optik ran out of these particular binoculars. But they have more gadgets from the East Germans and the Russians, and military surplus from the Brits, the Israeli Defense Force, and the Yanks. I could easily blow a lot of money with these guys. They always have thousands of binoculars, scopes, rangefinders, opera glasses, compasses, binnacles, military instruments, timepieces, books, and other unique items in stock. Only by catalog and Web site. You can tell how much these guys love what they do.

Canon Image Stabilizing Binoculars

http://www.usa.canon.com

Type: High quality optics

First Developed: 1998

Price Range: $800-$1200

Key Features: No wiggling

Ages: Post-teen

Obsolescence: Medium

Further Information:
* *http://www.birdwatching.com/ optics/binocs1table.html* (good comparison table for birding binoculars)
* *http://www.angelfire.com/ md/binoastro/* (great site for binocular astronomy)
Canon: (408) 342-2233

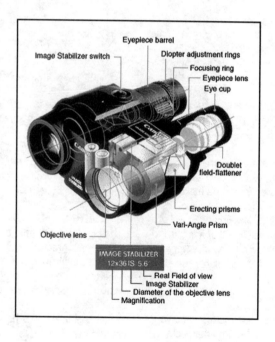

Binoculars wiggle. The longer you hold them, the more they wiggle as your muscles tire. People who can't stand this get tripods and mounts. They cast off their binoculars for spotting scopes, and end up hauling all kinds of gear around. The spontaneity of watching the night sky or birds is more than half the fun. But the wiggle is a bother. For several centuries everybody has taken the wiggle for granted. Nothing to be done about that.

Until recently.

For some years the military has given special forces and the like optics that enhance and stabilize imagery. Five years ago, such stuff started to show →

Canon Stabilizing Binoculars *continued*

→ up on the helicopters used by police and TV news, with the most notable social contribution being the high speed chase. However, Canon and Zeiss have developed good handheld binoculars with image stabilization. The Zeiss unit is north of $4000, a tad pricey for the thrill in question. The Canon devices have street prices of less than $1000, and they are a knockout. Watching anything without wiggle is an amazing experience. But, they aren't perfect.

Image made with Mavica FD91 640x480

As the little computer makes hundreds of minute optical adjustments per second, the image remains smooth, but your eye seems to have to make little adjustments as well. I find I can only use the image stabilization for short periods, else my eyes blur and tire.

FOUR BIG ISSUES WITH OPTICAL PRODUCTS

There are bazillions of fine optical products. Trying to figure out which ones are best by reading specifications is a waste of time. Manufacturing processes, optical coatings, lens sizes and speeds, telescope and binocular designs—all create an impossible set of variables to track. Forget 'em. Pay attention to these four.

1. HUMAN FATIGUE
No optical system is worth owning if it makes your eyes tired, and a great many do just that. There is only one way to test for fatigue, and that is to actually use the instrument in precisely the place and way you plan to do so. If necessary, discuss this issue with the folks you plan to buy the device from, and make arrangements to get your money back if it causes fatigue. It's easy to determine whether the device causes fatigue. It will give you a headache in short order, or you will find that it is hard to keep your attention on the object you are observing. Afterwards, fatigue will cause your eyes to be out of focus. Highly subjective, but very real.

2. RUGGEDNESS
The best device is the one that won't go bad the first time you drop it. And drop it you will, if you take it out into the backyard at night. Further, a very good device is one that resists moisture, because moisture is always a problem outdoors. For binoculars, some form of ruggedization (rubberized exterior, nitrogen-filled interior, and the like) is preferable. Often, nautical binoculars are best, because they have been designed for handling sea spray, and suffering heavy jolts and the like. Telescopes tend to be delicate, and hence the best protection is a really good carrying case—you should look at that as closely as you look at the telescope itself.

3. STABILITY
For binoculars, stability is mostly a function of the steadiness of your hand. Hence, the binocs should fit comfortably in your hands, with easy access to whatever focusing apparatus is built in. Anything boasting a magnification of 8x or more is going to need a stable mount of some sort (check to see if there is a camera-like mount on the body of the binocular), or it will need to be internally stabilized. For telescopes, the mount and its mechanical controls, electric drive, and control software are as important as the optics.

4. SIGHTING
The biggest problem in backyard astronomy—the kind that normal people practice—is finding what you are looking for. Where is Mars tonight? How do I find Betelgeuse? Once you know where it is, how do you point your instrument at it. The more powerful the device, the harder it is to really find things.

Traditional telescopes have a secondary spotting scope mounted on the barrel of the telescope. In my experience, it is impossible to keep these things properly registered. As often as not, you end up adjusting it after you already have the object sighted in the main telescope. A well-designed telescope, like the Questar or the Meade scope with the Epoch software, makes sighting easy. There are not many well-designed telescopes.

Meade ETX Astro Telescope

http://www.meade.com

Type: Hardware

First Developed: 1990s

Price Range: $500- $600

Key Features: Very portable

Ages: Post-teen

Obsolescence: Low

Further Information: Any good recent history of World War I

Meade Instruments:
☎ (714) 451-1450

This is the moderately well-funded man's Questar, mass produced without the handcrafting of the Questar. Therefore the Meade ETX doesn't have the terrific in-line sighting system of the Questar, rather, the customary, irritating sighting scope placed on the side.

All that said, it is a very fine ultraportable telescope system, with a Maksutov-Cassegrain design, following the lead of the Questar. In fact, it may very well have been designed as a mass-market knock-off of the Questar. However, in one very notable regard it is superior to the Questar: The Meade ETX has a battery-powered motor-drive system, hence automatic tracking (following the stars as the Earth rotates) even if your observing location is far from any source of external power. It also has a broad array of accessories (one of the natural benefits of broader distribution and higher numbers).

From a review of the Meade ETX Astro Telescope in *Sky & Telescope,* January 1997...

More than 20 optionally available eyepieces permit a magnification range of from 31X to more than 300X. Meade Super Plössls are excellent general-purpose eyepieces with the ETX, or use a Meade Super Wide 13.8mm, 18mm, or 24.5mm ocular for moderate–power, wide angle observing. The #126 2x Barlow Lens, a special short-focus Barlow ideally suited to the ETX system, doubles the power of any eyepiece. For terrestrial photography or for astrophotography of the moon and planets, the #64 T-Adapter threads to the telescope's rear cell and, with the appropriate T-Mount, accepts any 35mm camera with removable lens. For terrestrial observing the optional #932 45° Erecting Prism presents a convenient terrestrial observing position and correctly oriented image. The rigid, full-length ETX

Field Tripod permits standing or seated observations through the telescope.

Stellar diffraction patterns were virtually textbook-perfect... the Cassini Division in Saturn's rings popped into view despite the rings' low tilt. Epsilon Lyrae's component stars were cleanly split.... The moon was outstanding even at 75X per inch of aperture. Daytime terrestrial views were tack-sharp with rich color saturation. I could see every wisp of velvet on the antlers of a deer 50 feet away... the ETX was totally free of chromatic aberration, making this an ideal all-purpose telescope for anyone wanting to inspect eagles at 100 yards and stars at 100 light-years.

Questar

Highly Portable Astronomical Telescope

http://www.questar-corp.com/

Type: Hardware

First Developed: 1960's

Price Range: $3000–$4000

Key Features: Beautiful design and manufacture

Ages: Post-teen

Obsolescence: Low

Further Information:
✳ *http://www.scopereviews.com* for intelligent reviews of fine optical instruments

Questar Corporation
☎ (800) 247-9607

Images made with Movica FD91 640x480

Back in the 60s, the inside front cover of *Scientific American* was always graced with an ad for the Questar telescope. It vibed perfection. Small, beautiful optics, finely tooled. The design was remarkable, with the most notable feature being in-line sighting. The same eyepiece used to sight and, with the flip of a little toggle, to see the fully magnified view. Eisenhower gave them to heads of states as presidential gifties. I drooled.

But it was sooo expensive. I could only dream. Then, when I was a junior in high school, a friend of my family's, Malcolm Stuart, produced a Jerry Lewis movie with a space theme (it was called *Way Way Out*, it had a really neat moon set that I got to fool around in one of the sound stages at 20th Century Fox, but it tanked in the theaters). They bought a Questar as a prop. I begged him to bring it by our house so that I could see it.

The night he brought it by was magic. He set it up, and I saw, touched, and felt that all of the promise of the ads was fulfilled. That one night left a permanent impression. Really fine products do exist. Not everything is crappy, designed to fall apart after a few years.

It took fifteen years before I could afford to buy a Questar. I bought a used one. It showed up while I was on vacation with my family in Jackson Hole, Wyoming, one summer in the mid-80s. The Milky Way in the Grand Tetons, revealed by a Questar. Perfect.

Pixera

CS-Mount Color Digital Video Camera
with Built-In Audio

http://www.pixera.com

Type: Hardware

First Developed: 1998

Price Range: $200–$300

Key Features: Integration of the old and the new

Ages: Post-high school

Obsolescence: High

Further Information:
Contact Pixera at:
☎ (408) 341-1800

Long before there were computers and pixels, there were lenses and cameras. The C-mount evolved into a general physical standard for lens mounts. With a C-mount adapter, you could attach everything from standard lenses to telescopes and microscopes to a camera.

One of the general deficiencies of digital cameras is their lenses. Therein lies the extraordinary value of the Pixera product. You can attach it to great lenses.

Even more important, you can take telescopic or microscopic imagery with the color and precision that only a good optical system can provide, digitize it, and then submit it to the extraordinary machinations possible with good image-processing software.

Consider the Pixera if you are giving serious thought to the QUESTAR, the MEADE ETX TELESCOPE or the BROCK MAGISCOPE. Or to go the cheap, fun route, look into the INTEL PLAY X3 MICROSCOPE.

PIXERA PRODUCT DESCRIPTIONS

PXG-1100N-CS—An industry standard CS-mount interface, excellent image quality, very low power requirements and built-in audio make this compact color camera a great choice for a wide variety of industrial, security or surveillance applications. Pixera's multi-function DSP and image processing automatically controls white balance and electronic shutter. The built-in tripod screw mount and AC power adapter jack allows for constant power security/surveillance applications.

PXG-1000N-CS—The PXG-1000N-CS replaces the tripod screw mount with a battery compartment allowing for up to 5 hours of operation on just 2 AA batteries.

PAL (a European video standard—ed.) versions are available as **PXG-1100P-CS** or **PXG-1000P-CS**

ICOM PCR-1000
Computer-Controlled Wide-Band Radio
http://www.icomamerica.com

Type: Windows PC peripheral

First Developed: 1998

Price Range: $450-$500

Key Features: 100khz-1.3ghz radio (AM/FM/CW/SSB)

Ages: 10 and up

Obsolescence: Medium – 2 years (product life cycle for radios)

Further Information: Loads of Soundblaster freeware available on the Net for decoding faxes, radioteletype, and other encoded stuff. Needs a good shortwave/ UHF/VHF antenna.

A brilliant design for a computer-controlled wide-band radio receiver, with rich database capabilities (covering virtually all broadcast and public service frequencies).

When I was eleven, during a summer spent in Cincinnati, I met my first ham. As I sat next to him, he talked to people across oceans, and we listened to the news on the BBC World Service. It's 36 years later, and I've owned a boat-load of shortwave receivers and scanners that opened up a world of voices, and messages, and points of view beyond imagining.

Nothing gave a deeper sense of the chill that gripped the human spirit in Soviet Russia than listening to state-controlled Radio Moscow in the '70s and '80s. Listening to the Los Angeles fire department attack a bad brush fire was more intense than any TV news report. Hearing Richard Nixon resign late one night while I visited a mountain village in Switzerland gave me a sense of America that I have never lost (in Europe, it's hard to forget how power can change from hand to bloody hand). The cool voices of the BBC World Service ("This is London...") present a picture of the world quite different than that found in the overheated American TV broadcasts.

I've never owned a radio as terrific as the ICOM PCR-1000. Small enough to be packed in with my laptop, and with a little wire antenna, it can go anywhere. All controlled from the screen and keyboard of my computer, the accompanying software holds a vast array of frequencies for everything from aircraft in transit, to ships at sea, to the BBC. Perhaps the niftiest feature is the spectrum display, which shows (in real time, mind you) exactly where the signals are, even if they aren't in anybody's guidebook. The Net is a wonderful thing, but it doesn't take the place of those myriad live human voices passing through the airwaves. This is the original Net, and it's still a great place to go.

Guarding The Information Empire:

RADIO

In the field of human communications, radio plays a fairly unique role. It is the only medium capable of direct, personal, and immediate two-way communication anywhere. On the bands that we commonly know as AM, signals propagate via what are called ground waves during the day, a couple of hundred miles distance at the most. At night, the AM signal can move thousands of miles. I recollect a summer long ago in the Lakes District of Michigan. I was at summer camp and supposed to be asleep but rather I was vividly awake with my attention focused on the halting signal of Boston's WBZ radio station. Fading in and out, a thousand miles away, it was broadcasting the Beatles singing "Yesterday" for the first and, as far as I was concerned, last time that summer. On ensuing nights, no matter how hard I tried, I couldn't get WBZ again, and the local broadcasters were not quite as culturally advanced.

AM and shortwave signals may bounce off the ionosphere, but one cannot depend on them. The sun, thunderstorms, magnetic flux, and other transmitters act as veils on the signals. Over the years they have been observed, noted, catalogued, and charted. They are known to radiomen the way a barger knows the bottom of the Mississippi. Part of the floor plans of civilization.

Sometimes the signal itself will follow two paths and arrive sufficiently delayed on one path to distort the signal, or cancel it out altogether. This is called phase (or multipath) distortion

and as with many of the properties of radio waves, can be used both to the benefit or the detriment of the signal's distribution.

Higher frequencies, like FM and TV, are limited to line of sight. Although they can carry more information, cleaner sound, and better pictures, these brilliantly clear signals melt away as one moves over the horizon.

Conventional communications systems, most of which are run or otherwise aided by computers, are highly vulnerable. In the event of a nuclear war, one of the most likely effects would be the trashing of most of the sophisticated electronic and computer systems via an electromagnetic pulse (EMP). That is the electrical shock wave produced by an atomic blast. In these scenarios, the EMP would fry anything with transistors, blow out many common electrical appliances and just about all computers, and generally cause complete havoc. Chances are that little else but the most carefully protected communications technologies would survive.

On land the increasing use of fiber optic, instead of coaxial cable, is the technology that promises to insulate military communication systems from the EMP. But at sea, presuming the satellites are knocked out, there is only radio. Given the radio frequency turbulence that EMP would cause, any radio communications systems would have to be the most simple and sturdy to survive.

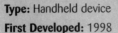

Sharp Mobilon 4600

Windows CE Handheld/Palmtop PC

http://www.sharp-usa.com/

Type: Handheld device

First Developed: 1998

Price Range: $600 ($800 with digital camera)

Key Features: Color display, integrated modem, microphone, add-on camera

Ages: College and beyond

Obsolescence: High (estimated one year)

Further Information: Windows CE based, software downloads from the Net

Sharp Electronics Corp.:
☎ (800) 993-9737

*The family in flake mode.
...a picture taken with
the Mobilon 4600*

*The digital color
camera on the
Mobilon 4600*

Windows CE handheld/palmtop PC, with stripped version of MS Office (including Outlook), and the ability to take color digital pictures.

Every time I get a smaller laptop, I find myself hungering for something that doesn't weigh even that much—a gizmo I can hide in someplace normal, not in it's own carrying case. No joy, so far.

I bought the original Mac portable (the clunker), and then the PowerBook 230. Then the 280c. Then the PowerPC upgrade. Somewhere in there I picked up a Newton with very high hopes, none fulfilled. Recently I moved to a Toshiba Portege300 (very nice), and thought I was quite happy, until I saw this Mobilon at a Computer City private trade show.

It looks perfect. I've already made the transit to Microsoft Office, and in particular Outlook for my e-mail management. This thing has a kind of freeze-dried variant of the Win95 OS and Microsoft Office—everything in tiny, discrete crystalline form called Windows CE. It's got a dandy 33.6Kbps fax-modem, a 640x200 color screen, and a keyboard designed for munchkins.

But the best part is this: you can record your voice and other stuff with the embedded microphone, and with the digital camera attachment, take pictures of just about anything, and then ship them off by e-mail.

It's the media grabbing capabilities of this device that set it apart. With a standard load of software and files (I loaded 1,900 contacts, and other stuff from Outlook 2000), it can still hold around 50 pictures.

There's some sort of a revolution in this thing. Or perhaps just another, more insidious threat to my marriage.

Rex Pro

A Palmtop PIM (Personal Information Manager)

http://www.franklin.com/rex

Type: Hardware

First Developed: 1998

Price Range: $190–$240

Key Features: This is the simplest answer

Ages: Junior high and later

Obsolescence: High

Further Information: Works with MS Schedule, Lotus Organizer, Sidekick, ACT, and if you don't already have a PIM, it comes with a good one

Contact Franklin Electronics
☎ (609) 573-6295

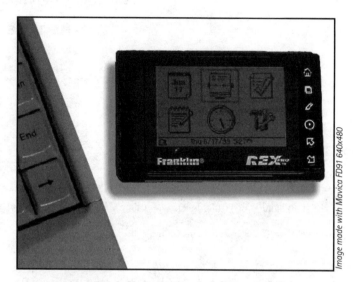

Image made with Mavica FD91 640x480

A laptop is practical in many settings, but sometimes it is downright dangerous. I've risked my life too many times, trying to boot a laptop while driving, just so I could get a phone number.

I've risked my business a couple of times, making a sales pitch with a laptop as part of the presentation, rather than standing up and just pitching. They say that the likelihood of a computer-based demo going well is inversely proportional to the importance of the demo.

The current crop of palmtops (Windows CE-based, Pilot, and others) have a great deal to offer, but they are really just stunted versions of laptops. Used as an address book, calendar and notepad, they are often overkill.

Further, the whole process of syncing your main computer's data to the palmtop computer involves cables, frustration, and (all too often) failure.

The Franklin people, long known for putting dictionaries and encyclopedias into little handheld devices, have come up with a device far better adjusted to the way a lot of people do their stuff. It's called the Rex.

Fundamentally, it is a PCMCIA Type II card with its own display screen. You stuff it into the side of a laptop, just the way you would a modem card. Once you've installed the Rex syncing software (it comes on a CD and takes about 10 minutes to install and configure), you simply click on a screen icon, and it puts all your PIM (personal information manager) data onto the Rex.

I had 1,900 contacts, and a bunch of schedules and tasks in Microsoft Outlook (the beta 2000 version). It took another 10 minutes to blow all that data into the Rex. After that, every sync session took about 30 seconds. Flawless.

This is better than a palmtop in 100 ways. The only downside that I can see is this: because it's about as big as a credit card, there's a temptation to put it into your back pocket, and it's not sturdy enough for that.

Guarding The Information Empire:

THE TIME SYSTEM

Just in case the clock at wwvh might drift a bit—lose its alignment with the real time of day—it has a little electronic chat several times a day with a GPS satellite. The satellite is part of the GPS NAVSTAR system. It belongs to a current set of 24 satellites, each orbiting the Earth twice a day at an altitude of 11,000 miles. wwvh simply double checks with NAVSTAR, when it comes into sight.

GPS itself can get out of whack a bit, so it checks itself against the primary U.S. time standard quite regularly. That standard is manufactured in Boulder, Colorado, at what used to be known as the National Bureau of Standards (NBS), but has recently, for some unfathomable reason, been rechristened the National Institute of Standards and Technology (NIST). The crucible of time is a 20-foot-long steel tube on a metal bench. Dubbed, somewhat anachronistically, NBS 6, that cesium clock plugs merrily along, measuring the passage of seconds by counting changes in the states of cesium atoms, some

9,192,631,770 of these events every second. The cesium atom is thought to be very regular and stable and thus can be relied upon to transform itself in roughly a tenth of a nanosecond. Not just like clockwork, for in this weird technology, the cesium atom *is* clockwork.

But that is not enough. Each clock in the system of atomic clocks around the world, over 220 of them, is checked. Their time signals are sent off to Paris and the Bureau International de L'heure (BIH). The miniscule differences are measured, and the recommended corrections sent out to the operators of all the other clocks. It is a fault-tolerant system, in that it relies upon no one source for its accuracy. None of that sophisticated design, however, protects it against the Y2K problem—the fact that many computer systems will not understand—mathematically—how to move from 1999 to 2000. All systems are vulnerable, to the extent that they rely upon other systems.

Oregon Scientific Atomic Clock

http://www.oregonscientific.com/

Image made with Mavica FD91 640x480

Type: Hardware

First Developed: 1997

Price Range: $60–$100

Key Features: Gets superaccurate time from WWV/WWVH

Ages: 10 and up

Obsolescence: Price/Performance Curve

Further Information: Check out Zeit for equally neat atomic clocks and wrist watches:
✱ *http://www.synctime.com/*

Oregon Scientific:
☎ (503) 639-8883

Why no one did this a long time ago escapes me. Perhaps some supercheap short-wave tuning chip made it possible just recently. No matter. Now there are clocks you can buy that you never have to set. They just pick time up out of the ether (actually from internationally broadcast time signals from WWV and WWVH). Neat.

If you worry about weather disasters, electrical power outages, earthquakes, or any of the slings and arrows nature tends to cast our way, then one of these radio-controlled clocks should be part of your emergency kit.

Orrery

From Van Cort Instruments

http://www.vancort.com/orrery.htm

Type: Hardware

First Developed: 1710

Price Range: $800

Key Features: Beautifully crafted

Ages: Junior high and later

Obsolescence: Low

Further Information: Check out orreries in great museums of science and technology, like The British Museum in London, and the American Museum in Washington D.C.

✱ *www.edsci.com*

Edmund Scientific has an array of more cheaply made orreries for schoolrooms

Van Cort Instruments:
☎ (413) 586-9800

This is a piece of hardware that is really software. The code is in the gears and the tooling, which represent the mathematics of planetary rotation. It isn't as accurate as software like WINTRAK, but it does something they can't—give a physical sense of the mechanical relationships in the solar system.

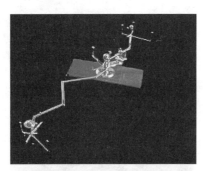

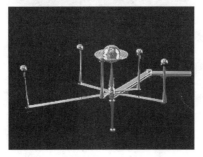

FROM THE VAN CORT WEB SITE:

This portable orrery consists of over 130 gold plated and silver plated brass parts. The earth has a triple gear driven mechanism that keeps the moon in its proper phase while it travels around the sun. The moon has a triple gear system which keeps the lit side of the moon facing the sun as it travels around the earth. All of the 130+ components are hand-made, hand assembled and fitted individually.

Saturn's arm radiates approximately 17 inches from the center of the solar system. A substantial gold plated brass disk engraved with the zodiac signs and names rests on a rectangular mahogany base (10" X 4").

The Van Cort Web site is a treasure trove of finely rendered instruments. Very East Coast things, including a set of licensed designs for items that Thomas Jefferson used and designed.

TEN RULES TO BUY BY
THE INFORMATICA GUIDE TO HARDWARE

1. Never buy version 1.0.

The integration of hardware and operating system software is extraordinarily complex, and manufacturers rarely get it right the first time. You'll save money and avoid misery if you get a slightly older, more proven model.

2. Choose a laptop over a desktop.

Laptops now feature almost all the power of desktops. They naturally integrate flat screen displays, which are much easier on the eyes. Further, all laptops have batteries, and batteries are uninterruptible power supplies. If the relative cost of the laptop vs. the desktop worries you, add the cost of a flat screen display and a UPS to the tag for the desktop, and things will even out.

3. Buy a slower processor and more RAM.

The RAM (random access memory) you buy has much more to do with the speed at which your applications (other than games and high-end graphics) run, than does the speed of the microprocessor (forget what Intel would have you believe). That is because a machine with minimal RAM will 'swap' information from RAM to the hard disk and back again contantly. Hard disks are slow access, RAM is very fast. Buying a version 2.0 laptop with a boatload of RAM is the most effective strategy.

4. Make sure the manufacturer has a good Web site for new drivers and BIOS upgrades.

Inevitably, manufacturers find flaws in the software they ship with their machines. The best of them make it very easy for you to download upgrades, and do a good job of explaining what these improvements will do, and when they will be necessary. You can check this out thoroughly before you buy the machine by cruising the Web site.

5. Get a screen that has a standard 4:3 aspect ratio.

There are many laptops that have screens that are more rectangular than the norm (they look a bit like a wide screen movie, rather than a TV screen). Stay away from them, as there are many software programs that don't handle non-standard aspect ratios well.

6. Buy from a manufacturer that will swap out for repair.

The direct sale outfits, in particular Micron, Gateway, and Dell, have terrific programs. If the machine fails while under warranty, they send you a shipping box overnight, with a prepaid shipping ticket. Off you send your ailing laptop, and in short order it comes back fixed or totally swapped out for a new. Same goes for modular components, like DVD-ROM drives. This is infinitely superior to driving the dead machine to an authorized repair shop, and being told they have a three week backlog. →

→ **(THE LAST FOUR OF THE INFORMATICA TEN RULES TO BUY HARDWARE BY...)**

7. Get lots of pre-installed software.

Microsoft Office bundled with your computer is way cheaper than Microsoft Office bought off the shelf. The same principle applies to most software you might want.

8. Make sure the port replicator is included in the deal.

Most laptops do not have all the plugs and spigots built in. Hence, to have full connectivity, it's a good idea to buy the port replicator (the thing that has all the plugs and spigots)—sometimes called a docking station when it has room for expansion cards and other internal devices. Make sure that there is an Ethernet port built into the laptop or the port replicator, because most of the future high bandwidth Internet connectivity solutions (things like DSL, digital subscriber lines) will need it.

9. Make sure the carrying case is well padded on the corners.

The biggest problem with laptops is that you can drop them. There are three solutions. The first is to get an indestructible one (see PANASONIC CF 25). The second is don't drop it in the first place (easier said than done: after all, it's a portable). The third is to carry it in a case that is very well padded in the corners (most damage to laptops happens when they are dropped on the corners—and that's the best way to destroy the flat screen display, *tres cher* to replace).

10. Get the longest-life battery available, and buy a second.

Here's the rule of thumb: Buy enough batteries to cover one full flight from New York to LA with headwinds (7 hours or so).

Kestrel 2000
Pocket Thermo-Anemometer
http://www.kestrel-instruments.com/

Type: Hardware

First Developed: 1998

Price Range: $100–$130

Key Features: Beautiful design and manufacture

Ages: Post teen

Obsolescence: Low

Further Information: For a great list of weather instrument manufacturers
✳ *http://www.ugems.psu.edu/ ~owens/WWW_Virtual_Library/ instrument.html*
For a good explanation of the Beaufort Scale for wind speed see
✳ *http://pilot.msu.edu/user/ rtsmith/wind/beauf_sc.htm*

If you have always admired those folks who have installed a wind speed device somewhere on their house (see DAVIS INSTRUMENTS WEATHER SYSTEM), this device is handy, and a lot less expensive. The Kestrel is a small electronic rotating anemometer with built-in temperature sensor. Though the little propeller that spins to measure the wind is quite sensitive, the real fun is when it spins up to measure high winds. It sings, like the ring whistles I had as a kid. The whistle's pitch increases with speed, so you can determine wind direction by pointing the Kestrel towards the highest velocity.

The combination of anemometer, precision temperature sensor, and a little microprocessor gives the instrument the intelligence to display the wind chill equivalent temperature, a function important to anyone who ever has to deal with snow and ice. ➔

APPLICATIONS OF THE KESTREL POCKET THERMO-ANEMOMETER
From a Kestrel Ad

The small robust design, high accuracy, and special functions of the Kestrel Pocket Thermo-Anemometer make it an extremely versatile instrument…

🐦 **Agriculture**–checking conditions for crop spraying or burning; checking conditions for livestock

🐦 **Automobile**–heating and air conditioning measurements

🐦 **Aviation**–gliding, hang gliding, paragliding, micro-lights, parachuting, ballooning

🐦 **Civil engineering**–site safety, working conditions

🐦 **Coastguard**–assessing conditions for survival

🐦 **Education**–air flow measurements, assessing outdoor conditions for school sports, environmental studies

🐦 **Fire fighters**–indication of fire spreading hazard

🐦 **Heating and ventilating**–air flow and temperature measurements

🐦 **Hobbyists**–model aircraft, model boats, kite flying

🐦 **Industry**–air flow and temperature measurements

🐦 **Police**–measurement of cross-winds on roads

🐦 **Outdoor activities**–archery, cycling, shooting, fishing, golf, sailing, track and field sports, camping, walking, mountaineering

🐦 **Outdoor workers**–assessing conditions

🐦 **Science**–aerodynamics, environmental science, meteorology

Kestrel Pocket Thermo-Anemometer *continued*

→ Maximum speed (in knots, miles, feet, or meters), average speed, and selection of centigrade or Fahrenheit are also provided.

One battery gives about 400 hours of operation, and it switches off automatically if no keys are pressed for 30 minutes. It's a sturdy little device, made of plastic and corrosion-resistant materials with the

electronics fully sealed. It will float if accidentally dropped into water.

There's a Kestrel 3000 that adds measurement of the water content of the air. That makes it even more interesting for people working in desert environs, or folks (like me) who live near fire danger areas.

Lowrance GlobalMap 100

GPS (Global Positioning System) Handheld with Map Data on CD-ROM

http://www.eaglegps.com/egps/guide.htm

There is no longer any particularly good reason to buy any electronic device that does not hook up to your computer. Your PC can serve as the mother lode of data, and also store data you create with whatever device you might use.

Image made with Mavica FD91 640x480

This is particularly so with handheld GPS (Global Positioning System) devices. The best of them hold map data of an array of different types—road maps, terrain and altitude data, maritime charts, and the like. But no handheld can hold as much as a CD-ROM attached to your computer.

That's why the Lowrance/Eagle system seems the best of the present lot of GPS handhelds. The accompanying IMS MapCreate CD-ROM includes all of Eagle's IMS SmartMap®, IMS WorldMap, U.S. Rural Roads, U.S. Navigation Aids, and U.S. Wrecks and Obstructions databases. With the →

Type: Hardware/software combo

First Developed: 1998

Price Range: $450

Key Features: Comes with all necessaries to connect to PC/laptop

Ages: 10 and up

Obsolescence: Medium, primarily driven by price/performance improvements

Further Information:
✳ *http://www.globe-mart.com/* for e-commerce
☎ (918) 438-8638
✳ *http://info.er.usgs.gov/factsheets/finding-your-way/finding-your-way.html* for a guide to the old way of doing things, with a map and a compass.
✳ *http://joe.mehaffey.com/* for remarkably detailed reviews and insights into the quality and features of various GPS receivers (they really like the GM100).

GlobalMap GPS Handheld *continued*

→ MapSelect and MapCreate software and a PC you have the ability to download up to two megabytes of detailed mapping info from the CD-ROM into your handheld unit. In effect, you can give the GPS unit a "local" personality.

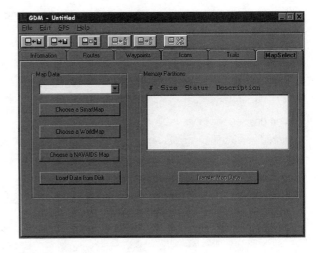

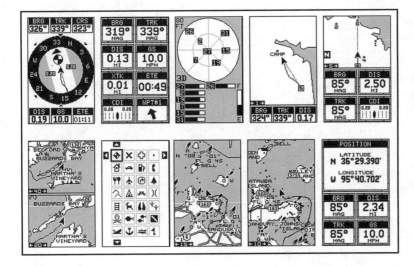

The GlobalMap 100 has a very sturdy feel to it, with about the volume you would expect a lightsaber to have. The display is easy to read, and the handheld software has a plethora of reconfigurable displays, emphasizing different combinations of the data the system can generate.

This is one of the most advanced handheld GPS devices, with the ability to monitor up to 12 GPS satellites at once. Once it has picked up enough data to fix your position (which happens rather quickly), it traces your route with remarkable precision. The level of integration of the handheld device with the PC, and the ability to precisely define the level of mapping detail are what really makes this system cook.

HARDWARE

Guarding The Information Empire:

GLOBAL POSITIONING SYSTEM (GPS)

The NAVSTAR Global Positioning System (GPS) played a decisive role in the Gulf War. Hand-held devices designed to use the satellite system to determine ground position within yards allowed tanks and APCs (armored personnel carriers) to safely navigate the featureless terrain of the Iraqi desert. The same system was used by the secret F117 stealth fighter and its supersecret companion, the TR3 stealth reconnaissance jet, to locate tiny targets in both the vast expanse of desert and the visually noisy complexity of Iraqi cities.

All navigation is based on the position of celestial objects like stars, and the relative position of certain features of the Earth. Whether marking the precise time the sun sets or the speed with which a radio signal travels its due course from Earth to satellite and back again, the precision of one's clock will ultimately determine the precision of the charted location. Each GPS satellite carries a 50 lb. atomic clock accurate to a second every 32,500 years. In the world of atomic clocks, that

kind of accuracy is relatively lightweight, so the satellite clocks rely on a standard clock maintained by the U.S. Naval Observatory, which in turn syncs with the other world clock standards. Nothing is allowed to drift.

The military designed the GPS system to be more accurate for their own use than for the public's. Clever private sector sorts have added the triangulation of conventional radio beacons to the GPS data, and have gotten the accuracy down to a matter of feet. They call it differential GPS. The mixture of mapping databases and GPS data have given regular folks the kind of fancy navigation tools that were reserved for the most advanced fighters and bombers only a decade ago. Regular folks, unhappily, include start-up guerilla and terrorist groups.

Because of the immense amount of latitude and longitude data available, on the Net in particular, anybody can find anything within 300 feet or so. Power stations, undersea cables, telephone switches, etc.

Panasonic CF-25

Laptop That Cannot Be Crushed

http://www.panasonic.com/computer/notebook/toughbook25.htm

Image made with Mavica FD91 640x480

Type: Hardware

First Developed: 1997

Price: $2,500; newer, faster models: $4700, $5,100

Key Features: Indestructible

Ages: Old enough to have or use a laptop

Obsolescence: Medium

Further Information: If you already have a laptop and need a carrying case that will ensure its survival, Codi makes the perfect solution. It has very clever systems to absorb shock, in particular on the corners where most laptops hit the ground and where the most damage is done. See

✱ *http://www.codi-inc.com*

I first saw this machine at about three in the morning at Comdex in 1997. I was waiting for my product, *Encyclopedia Electronica*, to be shown on *Good Morning America*'s review of the latest in computer stuff. Although I was focused on making sure that my product was ready to go—a live shot is rather unforgiving—I saw the ABC crew feeding a sequence of videotape back to New York, and the images were unbelievable.

A guy drops a laptop on the ground, and a HumVee drives over it. DRIVES OVER IT! Then they pick it up, turn it on, and it is none the worse for wear. It takes a licking and keep on ticking! The Panasonic guys then brought the machine out and set it up in front of the camera. Damn, it looked good. It just reeked tough. Magnesium, black, screwed together tight. A prop for a Terminator movie.

When we went on the air, the reporter—Gina Smith, an old pal and very savvy observer of things computer—started her explanation of the laptop. I could focus on what she was saying, as she had finished with my product and I was over the hump. As she runs through her spiel, I see her grab a cup of coffee and begin to talk about how the keyboard has been designed to be impervious to liquids. Then she spills the coffee on the machine. It may have looked like a mistake, but it was nothing of the sort. Pure calculation.

Now, if there is anything that will give a computer user a heart attack, it is a cascade of liquid onto the keyboard. My Mom did that to her Powerbook one time and it cost her almost $2,000. Warranties don't cover that stuff. As I watched Gina make her fake mistake, I thought I was going to die. I didn't and neither did the Panasonic laptop. Utterly amazing.

Since that time, I have dropped two laptops. Because they had plastic cases, even though they were in good, high-quality carrying cases, the plastic shattered, and the machines suffered substantial damage. Oh, how I would have liked having the CF-25. It is truly rugged, and though a bit pricey and a tad heavy, it will survive.

Davis Wireless Weather Station
Weather-Sensing Peripheral for PCs (Net-Ready)
http://www.davisnet.com/products/

Type: Hardware, standalone, and computer peripheral

First Developed: 1998

Price Range: $650–$850

Key Features: Simple installation and operation, PC and Web compatibility

Ages: High School and up

Obsolescence: Low

Further Information:
❋ *http://www.ambientsw.com/sites.htm*
for Web publishing of weather data

This is a brilliant product. It comes in two sub-assemblies: the sensor package and the monitoring station.

The toughest part of the installation is mounting the sensor package, which comes equipped with temperature gauge, anemometer (wind), wind direction sensor, rain gauge, and humidity sensor. That wasn't terribly hard, even taking into account my relatively dim-witted approach to driving nails and such. All I had to do was find a place on the roof where I could mount four quarter-inch screws, about an inch apart horizontally, and a foot apart vertically. Had I not been up to that much, the Davis people offer a free-standing tripod for the same purpose, though that needs to be bolted down or anchored with stakes.

The monitoring station is a little device about the size of a bedroom clock. It has an LCD display dedicated to the constant display of wind speed and direction, and a dizzying array of additional parameters (wind-chill factor and dew-point amongst them) either one at a time or in a constant sequence.

In a triumph of the practical application of radio, there are no wires to string from the roof to the monitoring device. The sensor package sends a constant stream of data (somewhere in the 900 Mhz range, but not in conflict with your portable phone) down to the monitoring station. It'll work up to 400 feet away. In my case, it's about 80 feet, from rooftop to ground floor office.

If that were all it did, the system would be terrific. There is more, however, and the added value is in cyberspace. Through a Davis Instruments add-on package called WeatherLink, you can hook this whole system into your computer, which then will take over the monitoring activities and maintain a database of all the weather data, performing all sorts of analysis and graphing. →

Images made with Mavica FD91 640x480

Davis Wireless Weather Station *continued*

→ But it gets even better. You can put all this stuff up on a Web site. If you've always wondered exactly why you might want to exploit your Internet service provider's offer to give you your own free Web site, then here's a decent reason. Become part of a network of people who run weather monitoring stations around the world. Too cool.

Although I haven't seen it, the Davis people are about to release a set of software add-ons and utilities that will make setting up a weather Web site straightforward. The WeatherLink Toolbox, together with a WeatherLink data logger and software package, will let you set up the Web site with preconfigured templates, which even allow the addition of a Java applet that will scroll a ticker-tape display of current data, and drop in a Netcam if you so desire.

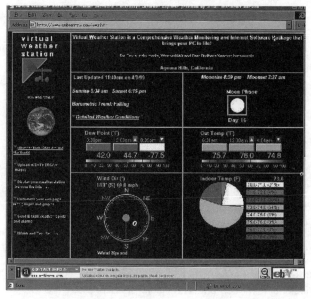

A screen dump from a weather monitoring Web site in Agoura Hills, just north of Los Angeles, California

ELECTRONIC WEATHER STATIONS FROM THE DAVIS WEB SITE:

As the Internet grows larger, more people are developing solutions to enhance Web sites. In our case, having electronic weather stations connected to the Internet is a capability that many people have been asking for. This type of connectivity can be a great tool for enhancing corporate or non-profit Web sites. The potential of this type of connectivity is also great, for educational use, remote monitoring of environmentally sensitive equipment, and long-term remote monitoring of weather conditions.

In most cases these solutions require some type of Web server based on the TCP/IP networking protocol. Setting up a Web server is not as complicated as one might think, especially for organizations that already have an established IP network. Web servers can run on just about any type of platform from Windows 95 and Macintosh to Windows NT and UNIX-based servers. Most Web server programs are available for free.

Web Server Software

➡ **Windows 95/98 Personal Web Server:** Avalible from Microsoft

➡ **Windows NT Workstation:** Pear Web Server (Included)

➡ **Windows NT Server:** Internet Information Server 3.0 or 4.0

➡ **Macintosh:** MacHTTP 2.2

➡ **Linux and BSD (UNIX):** Apache Web Server

Davis Wireless Weather Station *continued*

PERCHING ABOVE A PATAGONIAN GLACIER

A testimonial from
the Davis Weather Instruments Web site

March 1999—As most of you know by now, we love it when our stations travel to far off lands or engage in groundbreaking research. Out of the blue, Keri Pashuk wrote in to tell us of a station doing both in the Patagonian Canals of South America. What follows is the story she told us, pieced together from several different e-mails and one amazing phone call.

"We learned about the Davis Weather Stations firsthand, when we were down in the Patagonian Canals last April. We had kayaked in to Seno Exmouth to meet up with our friend Charlie Porter, who was there aboard his sailing vessel, *Gondwana.* Charlie was collecting glacial data from the longest and fastest moving glacier in South America, Pia XI (pronounced PEEA OWNSAY).

"Greg [Landreth] and I were Charlie's pack horses (Greg more than I), and we transported all the necessary steam drills and weather equipment up to 3,500 feet, just below the icecap. We were camped out on a rocky ridge about 100 feet down from the Davis weather station. That night, our tents were almost blown off the ridge. With the wind not succeeding in extracting us from our precarious perch, the rain had a go and tried to flood us off the mountain. The next morning, after the wind calmed enough to climb the 100 feet to the weather station, we discovered that the winds had exceeded 70 knots (80 mph) the night before!

"After being encouraged back to sea level by the weather, we followed Charlie to the end of Seno Exmouth where a finger of Pia XI was cascading and advancing into the mouth of the fjord. We had to hike in through mud-flooded forests and wade through gelid glacial waters, which were rushing past at thigh height.

"This glacier was discovered to be advancing. You could almost see it move. Standing next to the push moraine, where trees were being bulldozed over, rocks tumbled forward apparently for no reason other than the glacier's advancement. The glacier in its present location is not shown on any of the maps or charts for the area. Charlie's discovery entitled him to name the glacier 'Dacrydium Glacier' after a miniature tree that graces the surrounding slopes."

Intel Play X3™ Microscope
A PC-Ready Imaging System for Kids
http://www.intel.com/pressroom/archive/releases/toy20399.htm

Type: Hardware

First Developed: 1999

Price Range: $100

Key Features: Classic kid stuff, made computer savvy

Ages: They say 5–12, but older kids will find a lot of hip uses for this

Obsolescence: High

Further Information: Check out Edmund Scientific for a great array of microscope samples
✽ *www.edsci.com*

The early press releases from Intel suggested that the Intel lab engineers thought this was a neat gadget. Not surprising—there is something magical about capturing images of things and then getting a computer to alter and improve the image. People who know how to use Photoshop (a ground-breaking image manipulation program that transformed graphic arts in the 1990s) have been delighted by its image filtering and manipulation tricks for years.

Edges can be found where the picture was fuzzy before. Colors can be used to show the differences between things. This is all standard stuff in the world of satellite reconnaissance, graphic arts, and the sciences. It's a new world, however, for kids (and normal adults).

Imagine heightening the contrast of a moth's wings to see the structures. Imagine colorizing the flora found in water, so the little bugs don't look like little see-throughs but really stand out.

Essentially, it isn't just a microscope, but a child's first remote sensing and image processing platform. The microscope can also be lifted off its base so children can aim it at all kinds of stuff (I can imagine the sun being the end of the useful life of the system). The software included with the microscope allows children to capture video and still images, as well as create time-lapse movies, which they can share by printing, e-mailing, or creating an on-screen show.

Tesla Coil

From Edmund Scientific

http://scientifics.edsci.com/

Image made with Movica FD91 640x480

Type: Hardware

First Developed: 1886

Price Range: $150–$200

Key Features: Very simple way to look into the heart of the universe

Ages: Junior high, and later

Obsolescence: Low

Further Information: *Tesla: Man Out of Time,* by Margaret Cheney

Edmund Scientific for supplies
☎ (609) 573-6295

Here's a news flash you may have missed: we don't understand everything. The pablum that human knowledge is expanding at an exponential rate is silly. Human-generated data may be expanding at that rate, but real knowledge comes hard and slow.

Case in point: electricity. We've found a lot of ways to put it to use, but we still don't fully understand it. There was a man at the end of the 19th century who seemed to have a grasp of it. His name was Nikola Tesla, and he —not Edison—is responsible for the fundamental design of the AC system of electrical distribution the world uses today.

That was only the beginning for Tesla. He is generally acknowledged to have done the first practical work on radio. He figured out the fundamentals of fluorescent lighting, remote control of machines, and some say the Russians and the Americans have spent a lot of time and money developing his ideas about particle-beam weapons.

His most ambitious work appears to have revolved around the distribution of electricity without wires. He did a number of spooky experiments in Colorado Springs, Colorado, around the turn of the century, using gigantic coils. He lost his financial backing from J.P. Morgan, who felt that it would be uneconomic to try to replace Tesla's successful system of distribution, AC electricity. All that is left now is Tesla's somewhat cryptic lab notes.

The Tesla coil is still one of the most startling devices you can operate. It creates lightning in the laboratory. The first one most people ever saw was in the original Frankenstein movie. You can buy one—a small one—from Edmund Scientific.

When you crank it up, it fills the air with visible, glowing, sparking energy. But you can feel and smell it too. It's a fine reminder that we have not plumbed the depths of material creation, that there is more to know, and that sometimes we lose knowledge, rather than constantly gaining it.

BedLounge
A Chair for Your Bed

http://www.cequal.com/

Type: Hardware

First Developed: 1998

Price Range: $100

Key Features: Practical design, highly survivable in a home environment

Ages: Only for grown-ups. Please.

Obsolescence factor: Low

Further Information:
❋ *http://www.ahcp.com/ lumbar.htm*
...for other interesting back support pillows and the like

I doubt that anyone has done the research, but it's probably safe to say that—with the advent of the portable computer—a vast amount of work gets done in bed (the locus of the "Home Office" for millions of people).

However, bed is a lousy place to sit. Pillows settle and compress as you lie on them. Shortly, your back is bent out of its natural "S" curve into a hunchback-like "C." I'm not certain what the resulting malady is called, but it is bound to give carpal tunnel syndrome a run for its money.

Millions of people with poor posture, diminished lung capacity, and lousy digestion (so what's new?). Recognizing the forthcoming disaster, a Dr. Robert Swezey of UCLA Medical School did a little engineering and came up with this piece of furniture. It's damned sturdy, and the cover can be removed and washed. It's got little pockets for sundry crud.

It's comfortable, no doubt, as I often have to pry mine away from my children. It makes hours of bed-borne computing tolerable. Highly recommended.

A FEW CHOICE DETAILS ON THE FABULOUS BEDLOUNGE

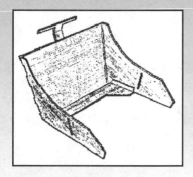

❋ INTERNAL FRAME

Ultra-light weight Feature. The foundation around which the BedLounge is built is a marvel of engineering. A rigid, ultra-lightweight, hollow plastic frame. No fasteners, no adhesives or glues, no rivets hold this frame together, just well placed weld points. There is nothing to come apart, break, separate, or unravel. This keeps its weight to an absolute minimum. Though it is feather-light, it is rugged too.

In fact, made entirely of polypropylene it is very nearly indestructible. Its made to be tossed off your bed, bounced off the floor repeatedly—without harm. Its also about as ecological as can be, composed entirely of post-consumer recycled plastic. →

A Few Choice Details on the Fabulous Bed Lounge *continued*

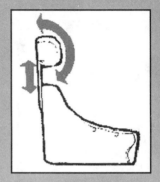

→ ✿ **THE HEADREST PILLOW**

Tilting Feature. Your head and neck naturally tilt together, upward and downward, through an arc. The Headrest Pillow rotates through a full 90°. It tracks or follows your head and neck's position as you move from reading to watching TV (or anywhere in-between). It has earned a patent for its unique ability to move and adapt in this manner. It maintains a gentle, nestling support to your neck and head.

Height Setting Feature. The Headrest Pillow is adjustable in height. The Headrest Pillow is made to be positioned to your proper neck height, to your exact support and comfort level. It remains at this height by means of a specifically designed friction fitting. Its height can be changed with a simple up or down movement.

A further unique feature of the Headrest Pillow is its elliptical shape. Look at it from a side view. When rotated to set on its longer side, the Headrest Pillow's oblong shape permits a greater surface contact for optimal head/neck/shoulder support. When positioned to its shorter side, the Headrest Pillow comfortably cradles your head and neck.

✿ **THE BEDLOUNGE ARM RESTS**

The BedLounge Arm Rests support the upper body and distribute the weight load of your body, helping to reduce the strain on your head, neck, and shoulders. They help support the lower back, as well. Using the BedLounge Arm Rests significantly reduces the weight of your neck and shoulders as well as the pressure on your back's discs.

Pivoting Arm Rest Feature. Built into the frame are "living hinges" which allow the arms of your BedLounge to effortlessly pivot back and forth—and to automatically return back into place.

The "living hinges" let the arms of your BedLounge hug you, giving you that perfect enveloping fit. They swing aside for easy access—in and out of bed. The BedLounge Arm Rests adjust gently inwards, as well. This allows you to adapt the width of the BedLounge to your own individual body type. You get the snug, embracing support your body needs and wants. You get a "custom fit" seat every time you use it.

Roomy Storage Pocket Feature. The BedLounge Arms Rests each have a buttoned pocket. In them you can store magazines, channel changers, baby bottles, reading glasses, pens, pencils, calculator, the Sunday *Times*—whatever you need is right at your side.

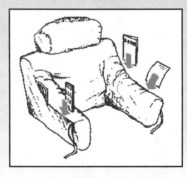

✿ **THE REMOVABLE OUTER SLIPCOVER**

Built into and running the full length of the arms of the BedLounge, are side pockets. The cover of the BedLounge is 100 percent breathable, natural cotton. It is removable. It is washable.

The cover is tailored and detailed, like a fine garment. Notice how it is sleek and taut across the exterior surfaces, accentuating the clean, contemporary lines of the BedLounge's form. On the seating surfaces where your body rests, it is soft, lush, and inviting. The Headrest Pillow's gentle creases compliment the pillowy, organic contours of the BedLounge.

Logitech Wheel Mouse
Pointing Device for Laptops
http://www.logitech.com

Type: Hardware

First Developed: 1997

Price Range: $30–40

Key Features: The simple answer is often the best, this is the simple answer

Ages: Junior high and later

Obsolescence: Medium

Further Information: See the material on Douglas Englebart in *The History of Hypermedia and the Internet.*

✣ *http://www.netvalley.com/ netvalley/intvalxan.html*

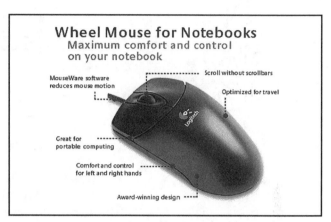

Douglas Englebart was one of the people inspired by Vannevar Bush (see ENDLESS FRONTIER). Englebart developed an engineer's obsession for the man-machine interface.

What he invented was the mouse. There was already a device used in advanced workstations called a trackball. Englebart upended it, so that it moved with your hand—the trackball caused you to move your hand in a bunch of inefficient gyrations. The mouse just went where your hand wanted it to go.

The people at the Xerox Palo Alto Research Center (PARC) really liked it, and made it an intergral part of the Xerox Alto system. It worked seamlessly with the rest of the hardware, the operating system, and the applications.

When Steve Jobs of Apple saw the Alto, he found the essence of what was necessary to craft a computer for consumers. Along with the first graphic user interface (GUI), he brought along the mouse. It first showed up with the late, not very lamented LISA (a version 1.0 if there ever was one).

The mouse hung around for the Mac, and the rest (Windows included) is computer history.

The mouse has not aged gracefully. It is fundamentally ill-suited for use with laptops—a fact that laptop designers recognized early on. Their answers, the trackpad (yuck) and the little button in the middle of the keyboard (double, nay, triple yuck) are now commonplace.

Far better is a little device called the Logitech Wheel Mouse. It is made by Logitech, which also makes a very good line of mice and trackballs. The Wheel Mouse is designed to sit by your laptop keyboard, if you wish.

The Wheel Mouse is at its best when it resting in the cup of your hand. The footprint is 2.5" up and down, and a little more than an inch side to side. Your thumb rolls the ball, and your index finger clicks. The connecting cable is mercifully short—roughly two feet. It really does the trick, and packs easily into a laptop case.

It is also relatively easy to maintain, in particular when cleaning out the mung (dust, grease, eyelashes, cookie crumbs, and the like) that inevitably collect in devices such as this.

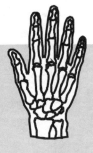

TEN RULES TO BUY BY
THE INFORMATICA GUIDE TO PALMTOPS

1. Never buy V. 1.0.

V. 1.0 of every piece of hardware ever made, throughout history, without exception, stinks up the room. Let someone else guide the manufacturer up the learning curve. If the product has been around for six months or so, make sure and check whether the one you are buying has the latest firmware (software encoded on a chip inside) revision—these are digital devices, and V. 2.0 is often defined by a firmware revision. Even better, get a device whose firmware can be upgraded over the Net. Check the sales and support Web site for the manufacturer to see how well they are prepared to handle these kinds of improvements.

2. Make sure it works with your PIM (personal information manager).

The biggest investment you are likely to have is the time you have spent inputting your contact data. If the device you buy doesn't export that contact data (as well as calendar, tasks, and notes) with no trouble at all, it is not worth buying.

3. The screen should be easily legible.

The ability to use the device without ruining your eyes is as critical as it is when buying an optical instrument (see FOUR BIG ISSUES WITH OPTICAL PRODUCTS). Check it out—not only in lighting conditions approximating those of your home and your office, but also in the car. Try reading a phone number at 35 miles per hour as the definitive test. If you crash or kill someone (or take your eyes off the road long enough to make that possible), the device has failed.

4. The battery should last a long time.

Just being rechargeable doesn't cut the mustard. Nobody gets to recharge on a plane or in a business meeting. The best devices have both a long-life battery (measured in months), and a fail-safe backup battery.

5. Buy small or buy big but don't buy in-between.

Unless you represent the Lollipop Guild, most of the tiny keyboards are ridiculously impractical. Better off getting a small device (see REX PRO) with no keyboard or a larger device (see MOBILON TRIPAD) with a grown-up sized keyboard. →

→ (THE LAST FIVE OF THE INFORMATICA TEN RULES TO BUY PALMTOPS BY...)

6. Get the one with lots of memory.

Most of the products come with a low-memory version and a high memory version. Always get more memory. If it's a really useful device, you'll find a way to fill it up.

7. Make sure there is a good replacement policy.

Palmtops are, by definition, small enough to fit in your hand. Hence, you will drop them. You will sit on them and find other unique ways to smash them as well. I have a friend whose dog actually ate his PALM PILOT. He wrote the president of the company to get a replacement (he included the chewed Pilot), and they thought it was a hoot. He got his replacement, but I don't think this is standard policy. Franklin has a $75.00 replacement policy for the REX PRO, no questions asked. That's the correct kind of policy.

8. Syncing with your computer should be simple and fast.

Spending time configuring your PC for the syncing process is inevitable, but you should do it only once. After that, it should be "plug and play." No update sync should take longer than a few minutes. One of the best guarantors of speedy syncing is a speedy connection. Direct, as in the case of the REX PRO when inserted into the PCMCIA port, is ideal. Next best would be by USB (Universal Serial Bus). Next best is serial cable. Last is infrared which—though it certainly is something that seems very fancy—is often plagued by interruptions and software glitches.

9. If you are counting on handwriting recognition, don't.

Along with "the check's in the mail," handwriting recognition has made the assertion "it's gotten much better" one of the great lies of the late 20th century. The present devices don't recognize your handwriting—you recognize and try to adapt to their notion of written characters. That is why you see keyboards for the Palm Pilot that are bigger than the Palm Pilot itself. Use it, have fun, just don't count on it.

10. Choose features with care.

There are some very good add-on features. The SHARP TRIPAD and Vadem Clio have really neat manipulable screens. The SHARP MOBILON 4600 has a fine add-on digital camera. Some devices have cellular modems. Give some real thought to how you expect to use the device and choose accordingly. Keep in mind that the neatest features are the ones most likely to obsolesce fast.

Zip Express

Laptop Adapter for Zip Drives

http://www.microtech-pc.com/

Type: Hardware

First Developed: 1998

Price Range: $100

Key Features: Practical design, and you don't have to buy a new Zip drive.

Ages: Would you give a perfectly good laptop to a kid?

Obsolescence factor: Low

Further Information:
❋ *www.iomega.com/*
for all things related to Zip drives.

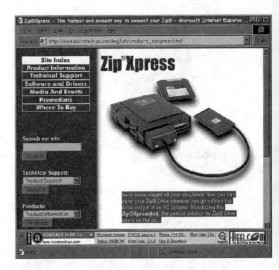

Once you grasp the gestalt of portable computers, you become a little bit like Colin Fletcher, the author of a wonderful book called *THE COMPLETE WALKER*. He was devoted to hiking and backpacking, and the book was half lovely recollections of hiking ventures, and half an obsessive meditation on paring every ounce off of the total weight of the stuff that had to be put into a backpack.

I now feel the same way about digital accoutrements. When it came to the task of hanging a Zip drive off of my laptop, I did not want to remove any of the other devices to make a place for it (there are replacement Zip drive modules for most of the major portables), nor did I want to haul a parallel Zip drive around with me, replete with AC converter.

The answer was the Zip Express. You can take a normal parallel or SCSI Zip drive (if this jargon is getting to you, see ACRONYM FINDER), remove the AC adapter, and plug this device into a PCMCIA slot. It provides both a data connection and the AC necessary to power the Zip drive. This is really a good idea, and well implemented.

The transfers are fast, the PCMCIA card can be hot-swapped in and out of the laptop whenever you like, and you get to ditch the AC adapter. Heaven. (Note: as I correct this entry in early May, the Microtech people have replaced this with a new product that uses the USB port, instead of the PCMCIA slot—an even smarter idea).

Jotto Desk

Work Surface for Your Car

http://www.jottodesk.com/

Type: Hardware

First Developed: 1998

Price Range: $150

Key Features: Practical, proven design

Ages: Old enough to drive

Obsolescence: Low

Further Information:
✳ *www.gps4fun.com/* Adventure GPS and
✳ *www.delorme.com* are good places to buy a Jotto Desk.

I constantly juggle electronic devices in my car. After years of futzing with a cell phone, I decided to have a floor unit mounted in my car. I have never regretted it. Keeping my eyes on the road and my hands on the wheel seems to be a fairly sensible strategy.

My electronic gadgets still fight for my attention, and juggling them while driving is just plain dangerous. I see mobile desks, portfolios, and all kinds of devices designed to solve this problem in catalogs all the time. None of them fits the bill.

The ideal device would have to be rock solid, so everything doesn't go flying when I brake, and aimed at me, for when I have to turn (my torso, not my vehicle) to get at it. In other words, just like the set-ups you see in police cars equipped with mobile terminals.

The Jotto Desk was invented by a deputy sheriff in northwest Arkansas. The company has a special line of ergonomic writing and notebook computer desks for police cars. I think of my car as a patrol vehicle, and this product is perfect for my purposes. They also make tall ones for RVs and dual-surface ones for handling lots of gadgets. All in all, the mother lode of car-desks.

The Jotto Desk combines a lockdown mechanism for your laptop and an articulated swing arm designed (they say) to meet the "rugged demands of public safety." If I'm not diddling with a laptop at 65 miles per hour, I believe I make a valuable contribution to public safety.

Simpson Machine Tool Company #1 Odd Jobs Tool

Web Site for Low Technology, High Quality

http://www.smtco.com/index.html

Type: Basic tool

First Developed: 1998

Price Range: $50–$70

Key Features: Made to last, and as such a standard for hi-tech products

Ages: 10 and up

Obsolescence: Low

Further Information:
❋ *http://www.vancort.com/tj.htm*
Van Cort's Web site for other fine reproductions

There are some things that cannot be done with electronics and software. It is instructive to know where the boundaries are. Basic woodworking defines one of those boundaries.

Several years ago, we were feeling flush and rebuilt our house. The most fascinating part of it all was watching the craftsmen do their work. The bricklayer made stunning use of a simple trowel. The plumber did beautiful things with copper pipes.

The leading players, however, were the woodworkers. Their killer act was the framing—putting up the superstructure of the house. Their tools were very simple—nails, hammers, levels, and the like. Most of the tools were linear descendants of the #1 Odd Jobs tool.

This new version is cast in solid manganese bronze, machined to ±.0015 inches on all sides, with an angle variation of less than 1"—a truly precise instrument. The Simpson Machine Tool Company #1 Odd Jobs includes a 6" brass-lined solid maple ruler, the scribe/screwdriver, and a thumbscrew.

Simpson's pride and joy. The #1 Odd Jobs

The Simpson people clearly love making these things. The heft and certainty of this device bespeaks something fundamental, even timeless. This kind of thing is worth having around. →

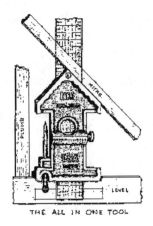

THE ALL IN ONE TOOL

→ Machined From Solid Manganese Bronze

→ Inside Mitre & Try Square

→ Scribe/Screwdriver/Locking Screw

→ Mortise Scribe & Layout Tool

→ Depth Gauge

→ 6" Brass Lined Laser Engraved Maple Ruler (12" Optional)

→ Threaded Centering Pin For Laying Out Circles & Arcs

→ A Beam Compass

→ View Level From Both Sides

Simpson Machine Tool Company *continued*

"At SMTC (Simpson Machine Tool Company) we take great pride in re-creating high-quality tools that, historically, were great favorites of discerning cabinet and furniture makers. With today's greater emphasis on quality workmanship done by hand, these tools bring back an age of woodworking satisfaction only experienced in a bygone era. In order to enhance this experience, SMTC has re-created these tools with improved materials, precise machining, and redimensioning to meet the demands of today's woodworker. Much attention has also been given to their aesthetic value. The fit, finish, and feel is incredible. Though beautiful in their own right, they are first and foremost built to work hard, day in and day out. They have been re-created utilizing virtually indestructible manganese bronze, the best tools, and high-carbon steels and brass."

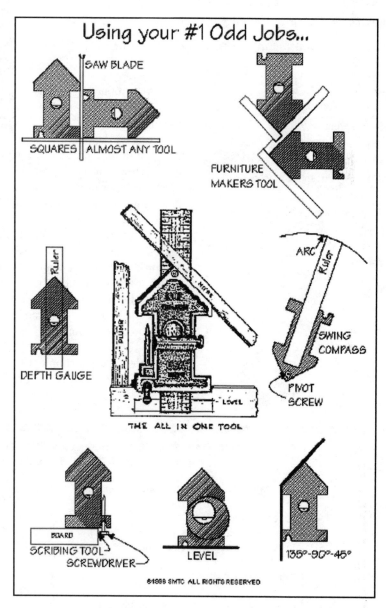

1,001 Uses for the Odd Jobs: Exactly what can't it do?

Panasonic Datalink KX-TCL100

900 MHz Cordless Phone for Laptops

http://www.panasonic.com/PCEC/telecommunication/

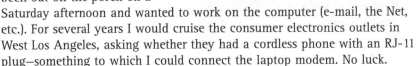

Type: Hardware

First Developed: 1998

Price Range: $200

Key Features: A cordless phone for your modem

Ages: Old enough to have or use a laptop

Obsolescence: Medium

Further Information: See...
❋ *www.powerexperts.com/ solar.htm*
...for solar panel chargers for laptops and peripherals

This is a product I wanted long before it existed. Any number of times I have been out on the porch on a Saturday afternoon and wanted to work on the computer (e-mail, the Net, etc.). For several years I would cruise the consumer electronics outlets in West Los Angeles, asking whether they had a cordless phone with an RJ-11 plug—something to which I could connect the laptop modem. No luck.

Finally, by cruising the Panasonic Web site, I found the Datalink. Not much fanfare, but it sounded right (see the table of features below). I had to special order it from the store I went to. Once I got it, after charging the batteries, it started up perfectly. From a base station upstairs (I put it upstairs because for the most part I will be receiving, rather than sending, and the higher the antenna, the broader the reach), I could use it on the front and back porch downstairs.

This little device is simple, easy to use, and makes a laptop truly portable, at least in the confines of your house and its environs.

THE PANASONIC CORDLESS PHONE FOR LAPTOPS: WHAT MAKES IT SO DARN COOL?

- Perfect accessory for use with notebook computers

- Wireless phone connection for easy and convenient hookup of computer modems, DSS® TV systems, TV Internet set-top boxes, or other single-line devices

- 10-channel auto scanning

- V.34 data and v.17 fax transmission capable. Can handle fax and data speeds of up to and including 28.8 Kbps

- Easy-to-use two-piece system consists of a pocket-sized base unit and portable unit

- Docking recharger built into base unit

- Simplified controls including multi-color LED and low-battery warning beep

- 2.5 day battery standby/2.5 hour "talk" time

- Use wherever a phone line is needed

Panasonic Telenium EB-P55S

Hybrid Cordless and Cellular Phone

http://www.panasonic.com/PCEC/telecommunication/

Type: Hardware

First Developed: 1998

Price Range: $180–$200

Key Features: Cordless/Mobile in the same package

Ages: Old enough to have a phone

Obsolescence: Medium

Further Information: See...
✼ *http://www.agcs.com/ ingage/acre*
...for more information on authorization and call-routing equipment (ACRE)

The Telenium, like the PANASONIC DATALINK, is a simple product, designed to solve an obvious and universal problem. Everybody has to switch phones when they leave home. Set down the cordless, pick up the mobile. Two phones, easy to forget to switch. Pain in the butt.

The Telenium has both cordless and mobile designed in. When you get about 1,000 feet from home (less if there are buildings, hills or other obstructions in the way), the cordless connection to the base station disappears and the mobile phone kicks in. It's that simple. Simple products, well-designed are good and rare—literally. This is one of them.

◄► CRITIC COMMENTARIES

From a review in *Fortune* magazine of the Panasonic Hybrid Cordless and Cell Phone:

Dual-mode operation is a great convenience. But the Telenium really earns its keep if your phone company offers a service called ACRE (short for authorization and call-routing equipment). ACRE transfers cellphone calls to your normal phone line if your cell phone is off the air. Since you pay nothing to receive a call on your regular line but have to cough up at least 10 cents a minute for cellular time, ACRE can save a bundle. Normally you must remember to call the phone company and turn it on. But that's no problem with the Telenium—it automatically initiates the service whenever you slip it into the base unit. The result is as close as you can get to a single phone number that follows you everywhere—at the cheapest possible rate.

What if you and your spouse each want a cell phone? The Telenium allows up to three different handsets to be registered to a single base unit. (Each handset must have its own cellular number; a base unit can handle only one regular phone number.)

RealZV Card and TV Tuner

http://www.softechmedia.com/

Type: Hardware

First Developed: 1998

Price range: $250

Key Features: Turns your laptop into a flatscreen TV.

Ages: Old enough to have a laptop

Obsolescence: Medium

Further Information:
http://www.informationfactory. com/tp18.htm
for a bit of background on video monitors and the like

Images made with Mavica FD91 640x480

This is a product I wanted before it existed. Flat screens give true colors, are easy on the eyes, and come built into laptop computers. I want a flat-screen portable TV. Ergo, I want a laptop that tunes TV stations. No such animal.

For a while, I cruised the computer stores and asked. No dice. Then one came along (nameless), and it did the trick, but it could deliver only a real, thirty frame-per-second TV signal in a quarter screen. I wanted it to fill the screen. Hence, my quest went on.

Finally, in the fall of 1998, a Korean firm called Softech launched a product that filled most of the bill. It's a PCMCIA card (hence it fits into standard slots on most laptops) which connects into a little exterior module (small enough to fit in your laptop's carrying case). The exterior module, in turn, has antennas, a video input spigot, and a cable input. So far, perfect. I can just take it out and turn it on (presuming there is a strong enough signal—not true in airports and big metal buildings, for the most part). Or I can connect it to a VCR or a DVD player. Or I can connect it to the cable TV system. Very nice.

The software allows me to select which input I like and puts up a video screen that can be tiny or fill up the laptop's screen. This is made possible by my laptop's ZV (zoom video) PCMCIA port. Effectively, that means that all the pixels can be schpritzed directly to the screen. Full screen, 30 frames-per-second. I can get really good TV screen shots, snapped in real time.

It all works pretty well. There are a couple of software glitches with my laptop, but they are not enough to really bother me. The design of the software is good, flexible, and doesn't occupy an inordinate amount of screen space. The soft documentation has some of the peculiar syntax and grammar I associate with English written by Asian engineers, but it is passable.

Now my laptop is a TV. I like it. →

RealZV Card and TV Tuner *continued*

From the SOFTECH Web Site:

RealZV™ PC Card/TV Tuner converts your notebook PC into a camcorder monitor. By connecting a video camera, even an inexpensive analog one, you are now ready for video teleconferencing. RealZV™ comes with a PCMCIA card that functions as a motion/still video capture card including audio. This would eliminate a need for costly digital camcorders or digital cameras for your multimedia projects. RealZV™ converts your PC to a mobile TV ready for various sources, using the standard RCA jack, including cable, digital satellite, laser disk, and VHS. On top of that it can accept Super VHS input

Features:

- High quality full motion picture video (30 frames per second)
- Playback and record from VCR, LDP, camcorder, or Super VHS
- Video overlay/capture
- Video e-mail
- Video clip production

- YUV 4:2:2 format
- 640x480 to 1028x768 graphic mode with overlay
- NTSC/PAL/SECAM video system support
- Super caption
- Software control for color, tint, bright, and contrast
- Built-in speaker, video-in, and stereo audio-in
- VHF (2-13), UHF (14-69), cable (1, 14-125) channels

Sony VAIO 505
Slim Laptop Computer
http://www.ita.sel.sony.com/

Image made with Mavica FD91 640x480

The VAIO 505, simply stated, redefined what a portable computer could be. Light, tough (with a magnesium, not plastic case), and fast, the 505 left the competitors in shock. It took six months for most of them to respond—an eternity in the time cycles of computer equipment. →

Type: Hardware

First Developed: 1998

Price Range: $2,000–$2,500

Key Features: Tiny, light, with a magnesium case

Ages: All

Obsolescence: Medium

Further Information:
✳ *http://home.att.net/ ~epbrown01/sony505.html* for a fine, personal Web site devoted to the 505 and in particular to the optimized performance thereof

Sony VAIO Laptop *continued*

Image made with Mavica FD91 640x480

→ It is a real PC, though when compared with the Sharp Tripad *(left)* it occupies just about the same space and has about the same heft. Its keyboard is more than good enough, and the screen is fine and bright. Clearly it is a first step for Sony, but the form factor works and the company is sticking with it. The early ones had 233 MHz processors, and Sony has constantly upgraded performance since.

This machine marks one more step in a progression that began with the IBM 5100, continued through the Osborne, the Mac Powerbooks, and on. It is the exemplar of today's state of the art.

Sony VAIO PGC-C1X Picturebook
Full-Fledged Windows 98 Computer with Built-in Digital Camera
http://www.sony.com/clubvaio

Type: Hardware

First Developed: 1999

Price Range: $2,300

Key Features: Win 98 subnotebook with built-in digital camera

Ages: 12 and up

Obsolescence: Medium—2 years (product life cycle for notebook computers), Head-turning design; tiny size; lets you feel like a spy. See SHARP MOBILON 4600.

One of the "coolest" subnotebook PCs out there, with stunning styling, a tiny footprint, a great price, and—get this—a built-in digital camera.

Anyone who climbs on planes as much as I do knows that the pace of improvement in notebook computers is extraordinary and that trying to keep up with the guy in the next seat is a hopeless effort. The latest source of jealousy (at least until I get one) was the new Sony VAIO C1, which I saw on a recent flight to New York.

By far the most head-turning feature of the VAIO is its built-in digital camera, a minuscule device at the top of the screen, smaller than a quarter. It swivels 360°, so you're not just taking pictures of yourself all day, and downloads quickly and easily to the 4.3 GB hard drive, eliminating the need for complicated memory cards. The VAIO comes with a full suite of photo manipulation utilities. →

Sony VAIO Picturebook *continued*

→ The VAIO is a tiny package: 9.5" by 5.5" by 1.5", weighing less than 2.5 lbs. But it carries all the features of its much larger brethren, although both the floppy and optional CD-ROM drive are external. The screen is sensational, despite having dimensions slightly different from a normal PC monitor; the stick-like mouse is terrific, and the entire package is clad in eye-catching brushed magnesium. It runs Windows 98, not Windows CE like some similarly sized subnotebooks, and is equipped with a respectable Intel Pentium 266 MHz processor and 64 MB of RAM on the base model.

The digerati have taken to mocking Sony's line of notebooks (or at least their name), referring to them as the "EIEIO" (as in "Old McDonald had a farm..."). Methinks it's jealousy.

HP CDWriter 7500e/7510e
A Convenient, External CD Reader and Writer for PCs
http://www.hpcdwriter.com

A terrific way to create audio and video CDs and store and share large amounts of data, all with one simple device.

Anyone who's been around computers for a while has inevitably hit some sort of storage problem—running out of hard disk space, wanting to store a file on a floppy and finding the file to be too large, losing files if a hard disk crashes. As files have grown, what with audio and video clips becoming more common and data files growing ever larger, companies have come up with all sorts of ways to try to meet these needs, none entirely satisfactory.

The closest I've seen to a great solution are these drives from HP. Both plug into a parallel port on your computer and will create, erase, and re-create CDs on widely available blank disks (the 7510e comes with more software). They're easy to install and can be up and running about five minutes after you get them home. Whatever you create can be read by a standard CD-ROM drive, a near-ubiquitous feature of computers—meaning you can take →

Type: Hardware

First Developed: 1995 (this model in 1997)

Price Range: $350 plus $1–$5 per disk

Key Features: 650MB of audio, video, or data storage per removable disk

Ages: 6 and up

Obsolescence: Low–2002 or so before the mass scale adoption of DVD+RW drives

Further Information: A very cost-efficient way to store and share large amounts of data, if you're patient about performance

HP CDWriter continued

→ your disks around with you to grandma's. Each disk stores 650 MB of data, about 400 floppies or 6 Iomega Zip disks worth.

If you're going to write on a disk only once (say, to archive stuff off your hard drive, or to send a disk to someone else), the CD-R disks cost $1 each. The rewritable disks (CD-RW) are a little more expensive (somewhere near $5 right now) but plummeting in price—and they can be reused up to a thousand times. A word of caution: Even with the HP software, these

drives can seem a little slow. To write the full 650 MB to a disk takes about 35 minutes. You'll seldom want to save that much data at one go, and if you were swapping in 400 floppies, it would take significantly longer—but I've found my fingers drumming on my desk waiting for the saving to complete. Some improvements are possible by buying the internal version of the drive, but the installation challenges can be significant for newbies.

—*Ravi Desai*

Intelogis Passport

Home Networking System

http://www.intelogis.com/

Type: Hardware/software

First Developed: 1997

Price Range: $180–$200 for a basic kit (2 PCs and one printer)

Key Features: Simple system using AC wall plugs for home networking

Ages: Post-high school

Obsolescence: High

Further Information:
❋ *www.homepna.org*
for more on using phone wiring for networking and
❋ *www.diamondmm.com* for more on a good wireless solution

A lot of homes have more than one PC, and a lot more will as the prices of PCs drop. It's inevitable that folks would want to lash their PCs together, not so much for file sharing and passing little messages to one another, but so that everyone at home could share one printer, and maybe even have common fast access to the Net. Larry Magid of the *Los Angeles Times* likes to call this sort of thing a HAN (Home Area Network).

My neighbor, Dave Cipriano, had ISDN put in his house. He did it primarily because he is one of the leading voices in L.A. (he works for CBS and Fox—"Tonight, a totally new Simpsons!"). The ISDN line allows him to do voice work from a little studio in his home. But it also allows him to have a fast pipe to the Internet for his household.

Several years ago he spent a healthy amount of money, though less than $1,000, to install Ethernet wiring throughout his house. I thought that was neat, but the price tag was a tad steep for me. →

ntelogis Passport Home Networking *continued*

➔ Recently, while browsing Staples, I discovered the Passport system. Designed by a spin-off group of engineers from a major computer networking company, the Passport system is made to exploit the electrical wiring in your home to connect your PCs. This is a very good idea, for very practical reasons.

Rewiring your home is expensive and complex, and who knows whether the cable installed today will be good enough for whatever you want to do five years from now. Using the phone wiring is a slick idea (an approach endorsed by Intel with their Anypoint system), but it is not always convenient to put a PC next to a phone jack.

Wireless is an attractive approach, but even in the confined space of a home, there can be dead spaces for radio signals (remember those times when your mobile phone surprises you with a surge of static?). Also, I'm not thrilled at the idea of further permeating my home with VHF radio signals.

AC plugs are everywhere, and hence pose the least impediment to putting your PCs where you want them. Much better. Of course, there are two worries. First, am I going to electrocute myself putting this system in? Second, is my electrical wiring good enough to sustain this system?

I decided to give the Passport system a try. First off, the hardware for the system installs very easily. Oversized two-prong plugs go into AC wall sockets. They look like white, bloated AC adapters. They are big enough to cover two side-by-side plugs, but hang nicely out of the bottom plug of a two-plug AC wall plug.

Image made with Mavica FD91 640x480

The Passport Network Connector. Installed in only 20 minutes, weeks after the original system, it worked fine.

Once the plug is in (there's one kind for printers and one kind for PCs), a conventional cable connects the Passport AC adapter to the parallel port on the PC or printer. A little green light flickers on top of the Passport adapter once it is plugged in correctly. The kit also comes with several power strips, designed to condition the power delivered to your PCs and printers. This part of the installation is a no-brainer.

Now comes the installation of the software. This part is a bit hairy. The documentation is clear, but I *always* get nervous about installing new drivers and the like on a PC. The kit comes with a CD-ROM that is designed to automatically install the drivers, and so it does, but not without giving me a serious set of butterflies. The software is designed to do everything automatically, but it brings up a host of Windows dialogue boxes (none of which are you supposed to futz with) without letting you know that you should just cool your jets. During the process I had to insert the Windows 95 CD-ROM—that was a bit unnerving (swapping disks in the middle of an automated process scares me). ➔

Intelogis Passport Home Networking *continued*

→ Once done, the system started up with an application called the Passport Administrator. It allowed me to verify that the other PCs were seeing my PC, and me them. At every PC, I had to run the Administrator in order to set up the use of the LaserJet printer (that meant having the printer drivers for the LaserJet installed on each of the machines, an additional, but unavoidable hassle).

Once that was done, the system worked. We all can print (no more sneakernet–carrying floppy disks around to print out homework and school reports) off the same printer. Then came the really big one, shared access to the Internet.

I had our phone company install a DSL (see INFORMATICA GUIDE TO BANDWIDTH) some months back, and I had been using it for a while with my computer alone. Everybody else in the house was dialing up over conventional phone lines for access to the Net and AOL. We have been spending up to $150 a month for dial-up, because ATT WorldNet doesn't have a nontoll local access number for our area (this is in West Los Angeles, near Santa Monica—are these guys nuts?). I wanted *out* of that.

In theory, I could take the PC with the DSL, and set it up to pass along the DSL access to all the other PCs on the Passport network. No toll charges for phone-based dial-up access. Direct access to AOL. Everybody gets fast e-mail, Internet, and AOL downloads. Smaller bills. Too good to be true.

It required setting up a proxy server on the DSL-connected PC. In human language, that means getting that PC to share the DSL service with all the other PCs over the local network. I discovered that the Intelogis people had just converted to a new proxy server setup package made by aVirt *(www.avirt.com)*, having for a while used an early system called WinProxy, which the support guy said had proven too complex.

I downloaded the new installer with the aVirt proxy server, from the Intelogis Web site in short order (remember, I have DSL) and installed it. Instead of subjecting me to the usual misery, it flew through the install with a set of sensible, reasonably explained default settings, and that was it. Once with the proxy server software for the machine with DSL. Once for every other PC with the client software. Each and every PC, simple and fast.

Each and every PC connected to the Net. Voila. Every machine fast, every machine printing to the same printer. It took a bit of phone support to make AOL work via direct access (something that I think should have been made a default in the installation), and then that was cooking too. →

No more sneakernet–carrying floppy disks around to print out homework and school reports..

Intelogis Passport Home Networking *continued*

→ This is really great stuff. I'm certain that it has deficiencies (when I tried to set a laptop up on the Passport Net upstairs, it didn't seem to connect, but that may have been a problem with that particular PC). It will stretch a maximum of a quarter mile, or as far as the transformer to which your power system is connected. If you share power with others (as in an apartment building), you'll want to set up the security system the Passport people have provided, at minimum (see AtGuard and Intruder Alert '99 for more protection). As it stands, this is a great, flexible solution. It works at a speed of roughly 350Kbps, which is a bit more than the speed of the DSL line that I have coming into my home (256Kbps or effectively 8-10 times the speed of a 56Kbps modem). The Intelogis folks are talking about bumping that up to 1Mbps (three times as fast), but for now, I don't need that. Nor will most people.

Freeplay Hand-Cranked Radio
A Survivable AM/FM/Shortwave Radio
http://www.freeplay.net/swradio.htm

Type: Hardware

First Developed: 1998

Price Range: $100, with shortwave antenna for $20

Key Features: Tough and survivable

Ages: Junior high and beyond

Obsolescence: Low

Further Information:
✳ *http://www.baproducts.com/sm837d.htm*
for another hand-crank radio, with more frequency coverage, including NOAA weather reports, but requiring more cranking to get the same duration of play

Here in California, we are a bit paranoid about the lights going out. I remember the morning of the 1994 earthquake, before the sun had come up, looking down the Santa Monica coastline and seeing no lights at all. Spooky.

Folks who have been through tornadoes, floods, hurricanes, and the like tend to have the same feelings and like to have a few survivables around. One of the handiest, most valuable survivables is a radio. Radio stations survive disasters better than TV stations do: there are more of them, plus AM and shortwave signals go over far longer distances than TV signals.

Batteries, however, don't last very long. Solar-powered devices depend upon sunlight. Nighttime, smoke, and clouds defeat them. Hence the value of a hand-cranked radio.

Dimensions	U.S.	Metric
Height	10"	245 mm
Length	13.5"	345 mm
Depth	5.5"	140 mm
Weight	6lbs 3oz	2.8 kg

Baygen is a South African company that has advanced the state of the art to the point where thirty seconds of cranking yields forty minutes of play. This particular radio comes with AM, FM, and shortwave. They throw an AC adapter in and will provide an optional shortwave antenna (though any decent stretch of unshielded wire will do quite nicely as a shortwave antenna). The body of the device is made of ABS plastic (just like the Kestrel), and hence can be knocked around quite a bit. This is a fine product, worth keeping handy, just in case (Baygen makes a crank lantern with a xenon bulb, as well). Of the materials used in this radio, 147 of the 149 parts are totally recyclable.

Lego Mindstorms

Legos Designed to Function as a Peripheral to Your PC

http://www.legomindstorms.com/

Type: Hardware

First Developed: 1998

Price Range: $200, with add-on kits around $50

Key Features: Integration of the old and the new

Ages: Junior high and beyond

Obsolescence: Low

Further Information:

✱ *http://www.msichicago.org/ exhibit/lego/msilego.html* for the home page of the Chicago Museum of Science and Industry's Lego Mindstorm Workshops. The Media Lab Web site can be found at

✱ *http://www.media.mit.edu* and it hosts a nice techie metapage with weird things to see and do on the Web.

If ever there were a product designed by Poindexters for Poindexters, this is it. When Lego saw the possibility of their age-old toy franchise threatened by computers and game software, they hustled on over to the Massachusetts Institute of Technology and its famed Media Lab.

The match was a natural, because, when all is said and done, both were devoted to toys. In their more formal decalaration of common intent, this is the way they put it: "The best way to learn is by doing. You can't just give children knowledge; you must help them build their own theories and marry new information to their views." Very geek.

The Lego Group began working with M.I.T. in 1984 to link computer programming language to Lego® bricks, with the notion that the Media Lab people were at the hairy edge of AI (artificial intelligence) technologies and would be able to build a product line that wouldn't be obsolete the day it came out.

Lego Mindstorms is a new (1998) brand built from the products and programming language Lego and M.I.T. developed. With Mindstorms, kids over age twelve can build and program robotic inventions of their own design. The Robotics Invention System, the core Lego Mindstorms set, includes the RCX, a fully programmable microcomputer. In addition to the RCX, the Robotics Invention System includes programming software on CD-ROM, two motors, two touch sensors, one light sensor, a building guide, and over 700 Lego building pieces. →

Lego Mindstorms continued

→ The system needs a PC, and comes with a boatload of specialized software on a CD-ROM. The disk provides users with basic training on using the RCX and working with RCX code, a simple (they claim) programming language (part of the fancy stuff they developed with the Massachusetts Institute of Technology). RCX code is a visual programming environment that allows kids to drag, drop, and stack commands and bits of code. The CD-ROM includes training missions geared to help kids learn how to build, program, and test their robots with guided assistance.

Once you have a program put together, the code is downloaded from the PC to the RCX module via an infrared hookup. Very slick—program at the desk, play on the floor.

Though this is not for the faint of heart, if you or your kids are of the pocket-protector persuasion, this is for you.

WaveCom Senior
Home Wireless Computer Link System
http://www.rflinktech.com/

I truly hate wires, and my wife hates them worse. Whether for computers, audio, or video, they muck up the house. Further, they require me to bend into positions my body is not designed for.

I haven't figured out a way to get rid of them all together. For computers, the PASSPORT system is a terrific way to network without exposed wires. There is an array of wireless solutions for audio, the most practical of which seem to be headphones. Video is a different story. There is so much raw data necessary for video that moving it over the air is a challenge.

A Taiwanese company called RF-Link came up with the WaveCom devices in 1997, and they have made their way into a variety of TV-oriented →

Type: Hardware

First Developed: 1997

Price Range: $120–$150 for a basic kit (transmitter and receiver)

Key Features: Great for having the VCR/DVD near you

Ages: Post-high school

Obsolescence: Medium

Further Information:
✳ *http://www.tscm.com/ bugfrqmfr.html*
for background on what frequencies are used for bugging and who makes the equipment

✳ *http://www.transmitter.com/ what.html*
for background on radio frequencies and how they are put to use; written by Doug Lung, a very experienced television engineer

Wavecom Home Wireless Computer Link *continued*

→ systems. Hi-Val bundled them with its first DVD-ROM kits. Cable companies offer them as add-ons, as do DSS providers.

The 2.4 GHz Wavecom signal penetrates walls, doors, ceilings, and floors, up to 300 feet away. That means that people can mount surveillance cameras at their front gate or door and such.

RF Link Technology Inc.	
2.453 GHz	WaveCom Wireless Video System–Channel A
2.473 GHz	WaveCom Wireless Video System–Channel B
60-72 MHz	Video/RF Output from 2.4 GHz Module

In fact, The WaveCom video systems are commonly modified, repackaged, and sold by "spy shops" and private investigators as an eavesdropping device. The signature of such a device is operation between 2.10 GHz and 2.85 GHz with a slightly modified negative sync pulse on the video signal.

Magna-Lite
Illuminated Pocket Magnifier
http://www.magna-lite.com/

Type: Hardware
First Developed: 1996
Price Range: $10–$20
Key Features: Handy
Ages: All
Obsolescence: Low
Further Information:
❋ *www.edsci.com*
for an extraordinary collection of loupes and magnifiers of high quality

...with tweezers!

Ever need to see something up really close and for some strange reason (could it be we are getting older? ...nah!) things are a little blurry? Or you're in your car and hopelessly lost, and the map you're trying to read is making your head spin? Trying to read the fine print in *TV Guide* and suffering from terminal squinting? Or perhaps you just got a yen to repair your own watch.

These simple little pocket magnifier/flashlights are pretty good solutions for such problems. Low-tech, utilitarian, and useful in many ways. I keep one on the bed table, and it comes in handy just often enough to stay out of the drawer.

Each of the five models available has a plastic lens and comes with an on/off switch that can be locked in the "on" position, which is pretty handy. You have several optical powers to choose from, and even one with a sharp tweezer attachment. That one, in particular, is good if you spend much time fiddling with dandy electronic devices and loose screws and other detritus of high technology.

Sony FD91 Mavica
An Advanced Digital Camera
http://www.sony.com

Self Portrai

Type: Hardware

First Developed: 1998

Price Range: $900

Key Features: Use of floppy disks for storage and image stabilization system

Ages: Junior high and later

Obsolescence: High

Further Information:

❋ *http://www.hyperzine.com/* for good summary of current state of digital photography and imaging and

❋ *http://www.shortcourses.com/* for digital photography education site

The Sony Mavica Digital Camera is a splendid example of a highly evolved product. It traces its conceptual lineage back to the Polaroid Land Camera of the late 1950s. The business was (and is) that of instant photography, which then was accomplished with a very smelly assembly of chemicals, rollers, and special papers and film. But it worked, and it was the rage in its time.

Original Polaroid Land Camera From the collection at All American Hero, purveyors of vintage Americana in Santa Monica, CA (310) 395-4452

Polaroid Spectra System

Polaroid, over a period of four decades, took instant photography as far as it could go, effectively ending the technical arc with the Spectra system. Clearly, Polaroid fell victim to marketing myopia (see VALUE MIGRATION); apparently it never saw the digital revolution coming.

Sony, by the same token, has done a remarkable job of exploiting its product lineage and the disparate technologies of the recent past. The FD91 is a beautifully rendered hybrid of several products from the early and mid nineties.

One of the progenitors of the FD91 is the first Mavica system, which was designed for professional video use (the most notable instance of which was CBS News' use of Mavica still cameras in Tienanmen Square in 1989, with the little cameras used where video cameras—at the time still bulky—could not be). →

Images made with Mavica FD91 640x480

Mavica Digital Camera *continued*

→ The first Mavica system used little nonstandard disks, around which elaborate video-compatible disk playback systems were built. The good thing was the image quality; the bad thing was the output standard, NTSC video. Nobody really wanted to look at their still pictures on a TV screen.

Mavica disk media, old and new

The other progenitor was the array of dandy HI8 video cameras of the mid-90s. With these, Sony perfected such features as image-stabilized lens systems, digitally controlled system parameters, and small flat screen viewers.

Sony Hi8 Video Camera with Image Stabilization

Following the best of the SKUNK WORKS rules, Sony assembled the best from their rich kit of design features and matured technologies and melded them together in the FD91, itself a v. 2.0 of the present generation of Mavica cameras.

The single best feature of this camera is the use of the standard floppy disk for storage, and browser-compatible HTML and JPG files for the indexing and review of the pictures. Instead of fiddling with nonstandard flash memory cards and readers, the medium of exchange is one of the most widely available on Earth. A conventional disk will hold 30 or so images at a standard 640x480 resolution.

The camera is equipped with an optical zoom based on a fine, clean lens system. The lens is mechanically stabilized so when the zoom is in tight, you can still get a decent, unblurred

image. The flat-screen LCD switches back and forth with an eyepiece—the eyepiece primarily for situations where ambient light drowns out the LCD flat screen. The camera is menu driven, with most of the things you want to twiddle operated off the screen.

The battery will run for 70 plus minutes and cover hundreds of pictures. The images can be bumped up to higher resolution (1,024x768) with a resulting reduction in the number of images that can fit on one disk. Some people think the FD-91 runs counter to the trend. It is a larger device, not a tinier one. But it fits well in the hand, and because of the lens pointing the FD-91 is natural and intuitive.

Images made with Mavica FD91 640x480

Mavica Digital Camera continued

IMAGE QUALITY

A quick comparison of resolutions

No one would expect any of these devices to compare properly, as they are all designed to do different things. The digital camera add-on to the Mobilon 4600 is an incidental feature, rather than a reason for being. It is a practical convenience, and fine if treated as such.

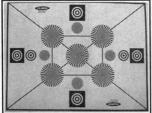
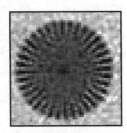

Sharp 4600 (640x480)   *Detail*

*(Note: less light sensitivity, roughly comparable to
FD91 at 640x480 in resolving detail,
plus noticeable lens distortion)*

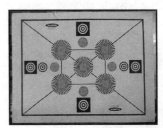
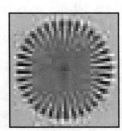

FD91 (640x480)   *Detail*

(Note: less lens distortion than 4600)

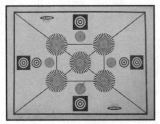
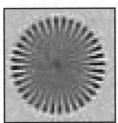

FD91 (640x480 fine)   *Detail*

(Note: fine mode yields slight improvement in detail)

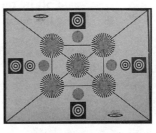
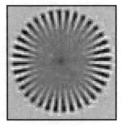

FD91 (1024x768)   *Detail*

*(Note: higher resolution improves
resolution substantially)*

*Capshare scan of detail
(Note: exceptionally fine resolution)*

Electric Cars

http://evworld.com/weblinks.html

1999 EV1

http://www.gmev.com

General Motors is running a very clever promotion for their electric automobile. The headline is Car version 2.0. For years, people have been yammering about wanting a good electric car. None appeared for quite some time, and there were dark mutterings about the big car companies having all the technology necessary but being paid off by the oil companies.

Gas Version 2.0

electric car. GM, several Japanese firms, and an array of fringish entrepreneurs have come up with deliverables.

Anyone who has owned laptops over the last decade and has watched how battery technology has improved from the poor state it was in at the beginning of the '90s will have no trouble believing that there has been nothing approaching good technology until recently. I, for one, am pleased that the car companies waited a bit. I have vivid recollections of the Mac Powerbook whose battery spontaneously combusted. I don't fancy that experience in an enclosed cabin on the freeway.

By the same token, I devoutly wish to stop going to gas stations. It appears that I shall shortly have my wish. The California and Arizona state governments have established very difficult emissions requirements and thus set the economic premises for the

The GM EV1 can be seen zipping around Los Angeles of late. The company only leases it, and it comes with its own charger. There are supposedly charging stations all around Southern California, run by Southern California Edison. The car itself looks a little like an incidental design from Fritz Lang's Metropolis, all smooth and faux future. It's peppy, however (0–60 in nine seconds and a claimed max speed of over 180 mph, though regulated down to 80 mph).

It doesn't have a vast range, about 60–80 miles between charges with the lead batteries and 110 or so with the newer Nickel-Metal Hydride batteries, and you can't swap the batteries like you would in a laptop, as half the car is batteries. It takes two to three hours to charge with the big chargers, and 13 hours with the portable plug-in charger. You can charge it in the rain, as the transfer is through induction rather than the contact of metal leads. Kind of a commuter vehicle, but not for a trip to Wyoming.

The great thing is that it has no emissions, and the cost of electricity is about one third that of gas.

Images made with Movica FD91 640x480

→

Electric Cars continued

Toyota RAV4 EV
An Electric Station Wagon
http://www.toyota.com

An electric wagon with a 126-mile range and both inductive and conductive charging. No consumer availability as yet. Toyota is also working on hybrids that use electricity and/or gasoline and/or methanol.

The Gizmo
An Electric Covered Three-wheeled Motorcycle
http://www.nevco.com

This one is simple and peculiar. You get in/on by lifting the cover and settling in. It'll go 20 miles in city driving, at a max of 40 mph. The brakes are hand actuated, and from the looks of it, wisdom dictates staying on the side streets.

Nissan Altra EV
An Electric Station Wagon
http://www.nissan~na.com

Nissan plans a wagon for 2000; it uses Lithium-Ion batteries, jointly developed by Nissan and Sony. It'll hold four people and baggage and go 120 miles at a 75 mph maximum speed. And it looks like a normal car. No word on price as yet.

The Sparrow
An Electric Covered Three-wheeled Motorcycle
http://www.ev-sparrow.com

Another single-person vehicle, this time with doors and a single piece exterior shell. It takes roughly six hours to charge off a wall socket, but two hours with a 220 volt source. It'll go up to 65 mph,

and stretch out to 50 miles or so. If the marketing hustle is correct—97 percent of commuters travel 18 miles or less to work, and the vast majority drive alone—then this vehicle makes sense. I wouldn't take this one on the freeway either, but I wouldn't commute by conventional motorcycle. Maybe it's just me.

HP CapShare 910

Handheld Scanner

http://www.capshare.hp.com/

Image made with Mavica FD91 640x480

Type: Hardware

First Developed: 1998

Price Range: $699

Key Features: Lightweight, easily transported, easily used

Ages: Junior high and later

Obsolescence: Medium

Further Information:
✳ *http://www.jetsend.hp.com/ developer/WhatIs.html* for an explanation of HP's plans for enhancing infrared communication between devices. Very slick.

The CapShare must have been a very difficult device for HP to bring to market. It doesn't fit into any established product category and doesn't do what any other device does. The marketing materials take great pains to explain that it is not a handheld scanner (of course it is, and a very good one).

Sometimes the transit from v.1.0 of a technology to v.2.0 requires an utter transformation. v.1.0 in this case is the scanner. It has taken an array of forms in the first generation, from flatbed scanners to little desktop devices that suck a single piece of paper through. Inevitably, because of wires and design, the source document had to be brought to the machine. Practically, that's bass ackwards. You discover printed stuff in unexpected places, and you can't always take it with. You want the scanner to move, not the document. This obvious insight was overwhelmed by the inadequacy of the first generation of the technology.

So a bunch of mad Englishmen (HP researchers in the U.K.) leapt out of the box and created this handy, dandy device. Suffice to say, it works. All you do is click a button and drag it in a U pattern over the document, taking care that the two paths down and up overlap about a half inch. Then, either via infrared or serial cable, you spritz the data back to the PC, where it can be stored as an Adobe Acrobat compatible PDF file, or a TIFF (graphic image) file.

Then, if you've got a decent OCR package, you can turn the graphic into editable text. Bingo. Just what I needed for this book. Moreover, extraordinarily practical for a boatload of folks. →

CapShare Handheld Scanner *continued*

➔ When I first cracked the box, I was disconcerted to see there was no manual (kind of silly, because that's the way we have arranged things with our Encyclopedia Electronica DVD-ROM, no docs other than voiceovers embedded in the application itself). There is only a getting started card and a CD-ROM. The getting started card was enough. The CD was brilliant, an excellent use of standard PC media to convey the necessary info. The first part is a set of animations with voice-overs that make the CapShare an easy thing to understand. Then there is a simple mechanism for installing the software. All of this stuff occupies about 20 minutes worth of fiddling. Well done.

You can capture a page in six seconds and store up to 50 letter-size documents in black and white. And, you can send these documents directly to a printer (IR-enabled printers only) for an immediate hard copy, or to a notebook PC, desktop PC, HP hand-held PC running Windows CE 2.0, or smart wireless handheld device (such as the Nokia Communicator), where they can be shared with anyone from anywhere. That's the HP market prattle from the Web site, and it's all true.

Even better, the software was immediately updatable, both the application on the PC and the firmware in the device itself. The only false note was struck when I had to register (a prerequisite for the downloading of new stuff), which required ten minutes of answering marketers' questions. That kind of invasive, time-wasting stuff is one of the downfalls of the Net.

Paper has not gone away since the advent of the PC. I read more stuff now—on paper—than I ever did before. Having this thing around as an artificial enhancement to my memory is a godsend.

Comments from MSNBC's Gary Krakow on the CapShare Handheld Scanner

When I first read about this device, I thought to myself, "So what?" Then I got to see one in action. Just like Palm Pilots revolutionized the PDA industry, HP's CapShare 910 will revolutionize the way we use information scanners. Hand scanners, in particular.

I should have known better. HP refuses to call it a hand scanner. They say it's an information appliance. That's because it not only scans, but can also save what it scans (up to 50 pages worth) and then send it to a computer, printer or even cellular phone via infrared port or serial cable. The CapShare is aimed at mobile professionals who need to capture, store, and share paper documents easily while away from their office. I believe anybody who sees one in action will want one.

Brock Magiscope
Rugged Practical Microscope
http://www.magiscope.com

Type: Hardware

First Developed: 1997

Price Range: $150

Key Features: Tough, high quality construction

Ages: 10 and above

Obsolescence: Low

Further Information:
❖ *http://letsgetgrowing.com/ pages/lenses.html* for a fine Web site devoted to school equipment and supplies, and
❖ *http://www.indigo.com/* for more great educational products

This seems to be an industrial grade microscope. The kind of equipment you see in school labs, hands-on exhibits at museums and the like. The manufacturer says it is built to last generations and warrants the device for ten years!

They use good solid optics; real lenses—not plastic—full size lab grade, achromatic objectives produce images of fine color, contrast, and clarity. The scope has one moving part, solid cast aluminum with a brass focusing mechanism. The eyepieces and objective lenses are interchangeable, with choices running from 20x magnification to 400x.

The design allows the examination of anything up to 2 inches thick. That combined with the construction makes this an excellent device to haul off into the places where the specimens naturally occur—your backyard, the woods, etc. The light source is ambient light, which is delivered via a waveguide to backlight the specimen, rather than some sort of electrical bulb.

Sharp Mobilon TriPad PV-6000
Windows CE Computer
http://www.sharp-usa.com

Image made with Mavica FD91 640x480

Type: Hardware

First Developed: 1998

Price Range: $900

Key Features: Really thoughtful design

Ages: Junior high and later

Obsolescence: Medium

Further Information:
❖ *http://www.cnet.com/Content/ Gadgets/Special/WinCE/* for the scuttlebutt on CE
and
❖ *http://www.microsoft.com/ windowsce/default.asp* for the Microsoft corporate line.

Normally, you wouldn't talk about the AC adapter of a product. In the case of the TriPad (which is pretty much the same thing as the Vadem Clio), the AC adapter is emblematic of the attention to detail and design in this product.

I hate AC adapters. Manufacturers use them because they are then relieved of the hassle of passing the devices through government safety tests, which can cause months of delays. The AC adapters are easy, cheap ways of wiggling out of a problem. But they create a big problem for the buyer. ➔

Sharp Tripad Windows CE Computer *continued*

→ Those rotten little adapters always take up more than one space in a wall socket. They are in the way, and for years I have wondered why nobody redesigned them to be practical. Somebody did, finally, and here's what it looks like.

Lots of room to move here. This isn't where the thinking stopped. The TriPad physical design can take three forms, because of the brilliantly designed cantilevered arms upon which the 640x480 9.4" screen is mounted. Normal configuration, as seen here, is like a conventional laptop, but because the screen is slightly offset forward, it can actually be used in a steerage class seat on an airplane—most laptops don't work that way, in particular when the passenger in front of you tilts the seat back. That alone might be enough. Mode B makes it even better.

The thing can be set up in an A-frame configuration, and then the touch screen used for a business presentation. Not for a roomful of people, but good enough to satisfy four or five at a small conference table. There are limitations to the design. It doesn't have a monitor or video output, so you can't drive a large-screen display—but then again, that's not the point. Also, you can't create new Powerpoint presentations, only download one you have created on your main PC. Then again, that's also not the point.

Lastly, it can be set up as a flat-screen device (keyboard hidden) and carried around as if it were a notepad. The device is pretty rugged (though nothing like the PANASONIC CF-25), with a superstructure made of metal, not plastic. The 16 mb memory is good enough for quite a bit. I downloaded 1,800 contacts and a full schedule from my main Outlook system on a PC, and there was quite a bit of room left over. I suspect a graphics heavy Powerpoint file might push things enough to make the 32 mb upgrade necessary.

It weighs a bit more than the VAIO 505, at 3 lbs. 4 oz. with battery and 3 lbs. 7 oz. if you add the included AC adapter. However, unlike the VAIO, whose screen weighs more than the keyboard and hence tends to fall backwards, the TriPad is well balanced. The battery life is about 12 hours, which is quite enough to cover a day of travel and presentations. Carrying the thing is very nice, as it bulges slightly at the bottom and thus fits the contour of your hand.

The keyboard has a nice feel, but it's a tad small for me (but then I have bigger than normal hands). The microphone and power switch are located on the right side of the screen. Other ports and compartments are on the base unit, with the AC, serial, infrared, and RJ-11 jack on the left side and the PC Card slot →

Sharp Tripad Windows CE Computer *continued*

→ on the right. There is a little light on the front edge that indicates power status and blinks when you've got an appointment coming up. Very thoughtful.

With the Clio, Vadem bundles Paragraph's handwriting recognition software Calligrapher 5.2, Bsquare bFAX Pro, and Vadem ViewFinder Intelligent Viewer and Finder Utility. Calligrapher is particularly useful when using Microsoft's new InkWriter, which senses

a handwriting recognition engine and makes using the Clio in tablet mode a natural extension of the device.

Sharp's software bundle includes Sharp's own PC File Viewer, Bsquare's backup utility bUseful, Citrix ICA Client, and Proxim Driver for Wireless LAN PC Card. Really good, practical design is rare. The TriPad has a healthy measure of the right stuff.

Excalibur Ivan

Intelligent Chess Board

http://www.planetbig.com/services/excabur/ivan.htm

Type: Hardware
First Developed: 1998
Price Range: $110–$120
Key Features: Smarter than me
Ages: All
Obsolescence: Low
Further Information:
✳ *http://www.cs.berkeley.edu/ ~russell/ai.html*
for a fine metapage devoted to artificial intelligence sites on the Web

The front line of the battle to achieve something close to human intelligence has often been on the chess board. The last 20 years have been peppered with stories of face-offs between man and machine with rooks and pawns.

The advent of decent computer graphics on personal computers—first on the Mac, then migrating to PCs—led to an array of neat chess games. The one I liked the best was one on the Mac where the opposing pieces actually beat the pawns up.

None of these games ever did much of a job of teaching me chess. In the last few years, the productization of chess has changed course. Now the chess board, instead of being virtually realized on a screen, has been made intelligent on its own terms. It will talk to you, train you, scold you for stupid moves, and cackle when it takes you down.

Olympus D1000

Digital Recorder with Speech Converter

http://www.olympusamerica.com/

Type: Hardware and software

First Developed: 1998

Price Range: $200

Key Features: It actually works

Ages: All

Obsolescence: High

Further Information:
✳ *http://www.dyslexic.com/ dictcomp.htm*
for an extraordinarily detailed, practical comparison of PC-based voice recognition solutions, albeit a bit skewed to the point of view of the dyslexic

Although we take them for granted, the keyboard and the mouse are not a natural way to communicate, record your thoughts, and investigate things. They are simply old habits we are stuck with, as we have nothing better with which to replace them.

In a few years, they will seem as crude and painful as Civil War surgical instruments. When we want to point at things we will point at them (as can be done now with the SHARP TRIPAD), when we want to describe things, we will describe things. Period. →

D1000
World's First Digital Voice Recorder
With Miniature Card Removable Media

FROM DYSLEXIC.COM ON SPEECH RECOGNITION SOFTWARE:

So, in brief, if you have the commitment and can get through the training process. Naturally Speaking may be the better bet. For more casual users and people with reading and short-term memory problems, Via Voice may be a better choice, and (it) certainly performs well by any standards.

The current version of Voice Xpress does not seem to have caught up with the others yet and deserves to be cheaper. Recognition does not seem as good, whether out of the box or after training. The correction process is less helpful and slower. The Natural Language control system, nice in theory, needs more development in practice. You cannot listen to what you actually said, to

remind yourself, which we would regard as practically essential for serious use. The help system and integration with Word 97 are good. But Microsoft has an investment in L&H, who bought Kurzweil's dictation, so this is the system to watch.

A final factor is that different people and different computers sometimes get inexplicably different results from what it would be reasonable to expect, even when you have taken all the best information into account. So it makes sense to buy from someone who will support you in any problems and allow you to change your mind if you or your computer don't get on well with a particular system.

Olympus Digital Recorder *continued*

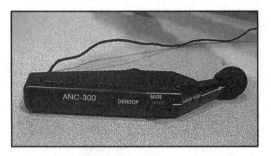

→ The speech recognition part of it is almost there. The IBM Via Voice technology is pretty much finished. It hears your voice and over time learns your style. You have to be a bit careful, but then again, that kind of care is often necessary when talking to people.

The problem is in the recording technology. The Olympus D1000 and its recent successors do a smart job of recording your voice digitally and integrate cleanly with the Via Voice software. But you must close-mike yourself and avoid noisy environments. IBM has just begun to ship a mike with Via Voice that combines two opposed directional microphones. The electronics inside the mike compare the two signals, keep the common signal (your voice) and cancel out the differential signal [the different background noises coming from opposite directions (see SYNTHETIC APERTURE)].

This stuff is good enough for use in the office. Pretty soon it will be good enough to allow you to throw away your keyboard.

Samson Overbed Table

Hospital Furniture for the Home Office Upstairs

http://www.medlineplace.com

Type: Hardware
First Developed: Long ago
Price Range: $120–$150
Key Features: Institutional furniture, ugly but very solid
Ages: All
Obsolescence: Low
Further Information:
✳ *http://uhs.berkeley.edu/ Facstaff/Ergonomics/* for UC Berkeley's computer ergonomics page,
✳ *http://www-ehs.ucsd.edu/ vdtwork.htm* for the same from UC San Diego, and
✳ *http://ergonomics.ucla.edu/* for UCLA's take

If laptops were really laptops, things would be easier. Typing on a machine that rests on the top of your legs can be rather precarious. Things can get really frightening when you are trying to work on your bed. Reach for the phone and you can dump $2,000 worth of high tech on the floor. Cats leap, children bounce, coffee spills. Yikes.

When I saw bedside worktables in several catalogs, I thought I had found the answer. I bought one of them and learned that it was designed with a three-point base, equipped with rotating casters. Turns out that's a very tippy design. After the first time the thing almost went over with my laptop, I consigned it to my home office, next to the chair, stabilized next to a bookshelf.

It occurred to me that I had seen very sturdy institutional bedside tables in hospitals, and so I scouted a medical supply store near my home and found →

Samson Overbed Table *continued*

→ just the thing. The Samson Overbed Table is absolutely stable, with a four-point base equipped with really good casters. The **H** shape of the base makes it almost impossible to tip the thing over.

The 18" by 32" surface is big enough for a laptop and all of the sundry crud I am likely to collect in a work session. It can be adjusted to a detented slant position in both directions (which I like as it aims the keyboard up at my palms). The surface itself can be raised and lowered to accommodate an array of bed heights. In all, the Samson is built solid, designed in a very practical fashion.

My guess is that hospitals are careful not to buy furniture that can tip over, spill things, and threaten to hurt people. They also like it to last forever. I can't think of a better set of criteria for choosing something you are going to use as a work surface at home.

EMPEG

Linux-Powered Car Radio
http://www.empeg.com

Type: Hardware
First Developed: 1999
Price Range: $999
Key Features: Plays MP3 music files
Ages: 16 and up
Obsolescence: Medium
Further Information:
✳ *http://www.crunch.co.uk/*
for a U.K. supplier of downloaded MP3 files

True geeks can cruise through "meat-space" while listening to MP3 tunes that they've downloaded from the Net into their car radios, which happen to be running Linux.

The Empeg car radio system delivers 35 hours of continuous music uploaded via a serial connection or an infrared device. Future enhancements will allow users to log-on to the system and will potentially interface with GPS units and develop custom software applications.

Featured on SLASHDOT, this has to be one of the most anticipated geek toys of the year and the penetration of devices like this into the consumer market could have a profound impact on the music industry.

—Matt Devost

Linux–Powered Car Radio *continued*

From the Empeg Car Radio Web Site

- Euro-DIN sized unit (approximately 6"x7"x2"): the unit is pull-out, for security and loading of new tunes.
- Up to 28.2Gb of disk storage, with approximately 17 hours of CD-quality stereo audio per Gb.
- MPEG 1 layer 3 and MPEG 2 decoding with the full range of supported bitrates.
- FM Stereo RDS tuner, with station name and Radiotext display Quad oversampling and interpolating 18-bit DACs.
- Gold plated docking and audio connectors.
- Gold plated 4 volt line outputs (front and rear pairs) for connection to in-car amplifiers.
- Gold plated stereo 1 volt/4 volt line inputs for existing head units.
- Gold plated 1 volt line outputs on the unit itself for home-hifi hookup.
- 5 band individual equaliser for each channel (4 of them!).
- Bass, treble, loudness, balance and fader controls.
- Auxiliary power out, for amplifier/antenna switching on power on/off.
- Credit-card sized IR remote control.
- High quality stainless steel casing.

- Blue display as standard: options for amber and green illumination for a small extra charge.
- Anodised aluminium carry handle.
- Home power supply for in-home use (100-240 volts, autoranging, supplied with appropriate IEC mains lead).
- PC download and categorisation software (empeg emplode).
- Full manual & installation instructions.
- FCC and CE approved.

Family Radios

Neighborhood Walkie Talkie

http://www.mot.com/LMPS/RPG/NA/portables/talkabout/

Type: Handheld communications device

First Developed: 1998

Price Range: FRS $200-$200 per pair, GMRS $300-$400 per pair.

Key Features: Simple to use, clear signal

Ages: From grade school on up

Obsolescence: Medium (estimated 3 years)

Further Information:
✳ *http://www.dougweb.com/ frslinks.html*
and
✳ *http://members.tripod.com/ ~jwilkers/frspage.html*
for good Family Radio information and product comparisons

When were kids, we dreamed about owning the Dick Tracy wristwatch radio. It didn't exist. (Dick Tracy and his radio were only real in the newspaper comics, next to "Beetle Bailey" and "Peanuts.") Then, when I was about twelve, some toy company came up with a real wristwatch radio (actually, the mike and speaker were on the wrist, and the electronics had to hang off your belt.) It was plastic—and in those days plastic was bad—it had a useful range of about 50 feet, and it sucked the life out of batteries posthaste. But it was big time fun.

CB (citizens band) radio became a craze about a decade later but was co-opted by truckers. The assigned frequencies of CB were at the very top end of the shortwave portion of the spectrum and hence didn't do very well in the fidelity department and were very distorted and scratchy.

It's a quarter century later, and electronics have evolved from Cro-Magnon to Renaissance. Several years ago, the FCC set aside another part of the spectrum up near the region used by police and news organizations. They called it family radio, and it has taken off.

There are over 20 companies that make family radios now, and they are all pretty good. Some, however, have broken out of the realm of design for geeks. Motorola, in particular, has developed some very sophisticated products (see Frank Tyneski's sidebar on the design of the TalkAbouts).

These radios are good for neighborhood communications, with a line of site range of two miles. The distance degrades when building and hills get in the way. In our neighborhood, we first saw them at use when some kids enhanced a game of Ditch with the FRS radios they had just gotten for Christmas. The use expanded to car caravans on weekend trips. Stories abound of people using them for camping, biking, hiking, visits to the mall, amusement parks (very good for keeping track of separated groups at Disneyland), and even Neighborhood Watch.

The Motorola TalkAbouts are among the most widely available, and they feature a nicad rechargeable battery pack and charger—a particularly important feature if you hate buying replacement AA batteries ➔

Family Radios *continued*

→ and throwing dead ones away. The nicads will hang on for a max of 10 hours in light use, and a couple of hours if you are talking constantly.

There are neat peripherals for these devices, as well. Notable is the headset, the microphone for which is voice-activated. I've seen groups of bikers on LA's Pacific Coast highway equipped with these.

There are FCC-mandated rules for the FRS radios, and all the manufacturers follows them:

Radios for the Family Radio Service:

✱ Are limited to one-half watt of effective radiated power. (The CB folks used to amp up their transmitters and walk all over everybody else. That doesn't happen here.)

✱ May not have removable antennas nor can the antenna that came with the radio be replaced or modified with any type of antenna other than the type it was designed to use.

✱ May not connect to external antennas to increase the range of operation. (The antennas are either built-in, or connect with nonstandard plugs, such that you cannot circumvent the rules via a quick visit to RadioShack.)

Some folks can't abide the two-mile distance. For them, Motorola has an extended-range version (which requires that you apply for a license from the FCC—trivial paperwork), based on General Mobile Radio Service (GMRS) frequencies. These are called the TalkAbout Distance radios.

The Distance radios have a little more than twice the power and share some frequencies with FRS radios (see table). I heard a story from a retailer about a fellow who bought the FRS radios for his paintball team. He came back a year later and bought the

TalkAbout Plus 200, 250 SLK Channel	Frequency MHz	TalkAbout Distance/DPS Sport 10X Channel
1	462.5625	1
2	462.5875	2
3	462.6125	3
4	462.6375	4
5	462.6625	5
6	462.6875	6
7	462.7125	7
8	467.5625	N/A
9	467.5875	N/A
10	467.6125	N/A
11	467.6375	N/A
12	467.6625	N/A
13	467.6875	N/A
14	467.7125	N/A
N/A	462.575	A–8
N/A	462.625	B–9
N/A	462.675	C–10
N/A	Scan	S–Distance & DPS Only

Distance radios, having suffered for the limited range. In our use of the FRS and the GMRS around our place, it became clear that the FRS radios are well-suited to the bounds of the neighborhood and that's it. The Distance radios, though less fancy in design, fulfilled all expectations for extended range. They are worth the additional money, if certainty of communication is important.

→

Family Radios *continued*

Terrain	TalkAbout Plus Sport 7/7X	TalkAbout Distance/DPS Sport 10X
Outside, Clear Flat Terrain	1.5 to 2 miles	3 to 4 miles
Suburban Neighborhoods	1 to 1.5 miles	1.5 to 2 miles
Urban Areas	1/2 to 1 mile	1 to 1.5 miles
Inside Buildings or Malls	1/2 mile or 5 floors	1.5 miles or 10 to 20 floors
Between Buildings or Houses	1/8 to 1/2 mile	1/2 to 2 miles
Woodlands, Moderate Vegetation	1 to 1.5 miles	1.5 to 2 miles
Woodlands, Thick Vegetation	1/2 to 1 mile	1 to 1.5 miles

Distance Radio

Image made with Mavica FD91 640x480

GMRS Interstitial and FRS Frequencies		FRS Only Frequencies	
Channel Designation	Frequency	Channel Designation	Frequency
1	462.5625*	8	467.5625
2	462.5875	9	467.5875
3	462.6125	10	467.6125
4	462.6375	11	467.6375
5	462.6625	12	467.6625
6	462.6875	13	467.6875
7	462.7125	14	467.7125

Many users of the Family Radio Service use channel 1 for general calling and move off to channels 2 through 14 for conversations. This channel is the most frequently used of all the FRS channels as Radio Shack markets their popular single-channel units only on that frequency.

→

Family Radios *continued*

CREATING THE
MOTOROLA TALKABOUT TWO-WAY RADIO

By Frank Tyneski

Designing a "consumer" two-way radio was clearly a new opportunity for us. Our team was composed of well-established designers specializing in commercial two-way radios, and each one of us had a history of making contributions toward the development of Motorola's commercial radio products, including designing radios for public safety officials and military personnel. We also shared a proud corporate heritage; Motorola's corporate culture ran deep into the core of our work.

The task at hand was to first take a mental departure from our expected product design concepts and begin thinking about creating a "fun" radio product designed solely for consumer use. This was quite a challenge for the group as we were all accustomed to designing products for more serious purposes.

The team involved knew that designing a consumer two-way radio required a different kind of think-

ing—truly out of the box ideas. It would be the only way we could own the category in a sea of other intriguing consumer electronics. Most important, it would take a

Image made with Movica FD91 640x480

brave business team to believe in us, despite our constant ability to make them uncomfortable during the concept phases. One vice president even said when viewing the final design "you're either bold or crazy." We replied that it was important to be both.

Exercising our design freedom far beyond the utility of the device was also important to the design process. TalkAbout consumer radios

had to be optimized for fun and usability rather than for mission-type, critical tasks in hostile environments. We realized we had the freedom to reinvent the look and feel of the typical two-way radio. We knew that cheap radios purposely emulate the look of our commercial radios but are intended as children's role-playing toys with no practical communications utility. We discovered that consumers associated inexpensive toy radios with "walkie-talkies." With this understanding, we realized the traditional form factor might be perceived as an expensive toy rather than a real communication device.

The project's concept was beginning to come together, and we concluded that an appliance that's fun, playful, and easy to use while still exuding the traditional, durable Motorola quality was going to be the basis for a great product. A benefit of collaborating with the mechanical design team was that its core competency was based on creating extremely robust →

Family Radios *continued*

→ products that wouldn't be compromised when designing for consumer markets.

Our competition in consumer electronics had their strengths in points of distribution and methods of low-cost production—often at the expense of quality. We knew we were competing in the marketplace with other exciting consumer products and that our competition wasn't just other two-way radio manufacturers.

With this information in hand, we asked ourselves, "if I had $100, what would I buy?" Each of us answered differently: Nike shoes, Rollerblades, Casio G-Shock watch, CDs and so on. Next, designers in the group were given the money to go and buy these items for the purpose of a "design dissection." It proved to be a justifiable expense. When the products were scattered across our conference table, it made for a colorful battle for our eyes' desire. With all these different products, the amazing thing was that all of the objects shared one common denominator: *emotion*. In some cases, emotion influenced our purchasing decision beyond the utility of the device. Each of these products exuded excitement and a distinct product personality appropriate for their intended use. It became obvious to us that today's successful products convey emotion and excitement, coupled with quality construction and ease of use. Next, we created image boards by cutting out inspiring images of other products and lifestyles with a multitude of colors and textures. (The idea of creating image boards is not new; in fact many design studios practice this technique as a stereotypical way of defining consumer values and product associations.) Our image board included images of off-road Jeeps, suspension mountain bikes, skis, snowboards, and young families. During this process, our studio was littered with popular magazines and catalogs, making it hard not to focus on what we were trying to accomplish.

Unfortunately, the pressure was on; we knew our time was limited and we had only a few weeks to conceive a design that could proudly occupy a space represented by a large collage of really exciting outdoor products. It required an "all hands on deck" design effort to come up with a real winner in such short order. We concluded that the defining criteria for the product design would need to include a distinct form factor with a unique product character that immediately communicated its use to the consumer. The final product miraculously went from concept to shipment out the door within six months and ultimately created the launch of a brand new product category.

Designed for fun and rugged and reliable use, Motorola's TalkAbout radios now dominate the consumer two-way radio category. Today, the TalkAbout business is three years old and it's one of the highest pre-tax profit centers within Motorola. In 1998, the TalkAbout was recognized with one of the highest honors in the business—a Gold Award for Design Excellence from the Industrial Design Society of America.

Frank Tyneski is the guy who designed the TalkAbout, and has been lauded for the design ever since.

Sony ICFSC1-PC

Computer-Controlled Radio Scanner

http://www.sony.com

Type: Windows PC peripheral scanner

First Developed: 1998

Price Range: $300–$400

Key Features: VHF and UHF coverage in FM and AM modes. Windows software, with serial cable connection

Ages: 10 and up

Obsolescence: Medium—2 years (product life cycle for radios)

Further Information:
❖ *http://www.strongsignals.net/ htm/antenna.htm*
Good background on scanners and how to use them

Image made with Mavica FD91 640x480

In some ways this product is very much like the ICOM PCR-1000 and PCR-100. It is a fine radio, designed to be controlled by a PC. Unlike the ICOMs it does not cover the short-wave spectrum; hence some of the fun of radio monitoring is lost. No BBC and the like.

In one gigantic respect it is superior—it is battery operated, and it stores the frequencies in its own on-board memory. In this respect, it is like the Eagle/Lowrance GPS handheld receiver, which can operate on its own, without requiring the processor and memory of a PC.

The PC serves as a master operations console and a storage bin for multiple (if you wish) frequency databases. Any one set of frequencies can be downloaded to the scanner and then the scanner can be unhooked and operate wherever you wish.

Essentially, the PC imparts a personality to the radio, adjusted to your whims. Want to go out to sea and monitor all the marine frequencies? Zap, it's a marine radio. Going to an airshow? Zap, it's ready to monitor the action in all relevant frequencies.

In a very real sense, the radio becomes a satellite processor to the main PC, assimilating information when hooked up and capable of harvesting information (newly discovered active frequencies) while away.

This is a model for many of the devices we will see in the future, from TVs to toasters (imagine an English muffin database). Very much fun.

Suncatcher Solar Panel

A Portable Power Source for Portable Devices

http://www.powerexperts.com/

Type: Hardware

First Developed: 1997

Price Range: $400

Key Features: A way of disconnecting from the power grid

Ages: Old enough to have a battery-operated device

Obsolescence: Medium

Further Information:
✳ *http://www.solar-electric.com/* for a large selection of solar and wind power systems

Portable computers are portable, kind of. Whenever you are away from an AC outlet, you are counting the minutes until you are out of business. For airplane flights, you are stuck (hence our recommendations in the *Informatica* TOP TEN RULES FOR BUYING A COMPUTER to make sure you have enough batteries—fully charged—to last a flight from New York to LA). But everywhere else, from Everest to Palm Springs, there are other options.

One of life's joys is to set up the laptop outside and whack out some work. As I write this entry, I am doing just that, without the irritation of worrying about when the battery will run out. That neat trick is performed by hooking up the Suncatcher to my laptop. The Suncatcher is a nicely engineered set of two solar panels bound into a sturdy, ballistic nylon carrying sleeve (something of the form factor of a small artist's portfolio). In all, it weighs about six pounds.

The Radio Shack adaptor

Inside is a connector designed to be the equivalent of the cigarette lighter in your car. In order to hook the thing directly into the laptop, I needed the car adaptor. Instead of getting the Toshiba-manufactured system, I went to RadioShack and got the all-purpose version (cat no. 273-1825). Hence, I can hook up my laptop, but I can also hook up things like the ICOM PCR-1000 or the SONY ICFSC1-PC. Virtually anything that runs off a car lighter can be driven by this device.

This appeals to me on two levels. First, it extends the freedom of portability by one great measure. No matter where I am, I can charge by day and work in the evening. Second, if we get another earthquake in LA, or even a significant power outage, with the Suncatcher and the RadioShack adapter, I'm in business either by running it off the car or by running it off the sun.

I am told by the manufacturer that "fast-charge" systems—such as the one used in the PANASONIC CF-25—don't work well with the Suncatcher. But my system—a Toshiba Tecra 750DVD—works just dandy.

→

Suncatcher Solar Panel *continued*

ABOUT THE SUNCATCHER SOLAR PANEL

From the Powerline Web site...

❋ **Heavy-duty solar power charging system**—our "Explorer Grade" model. Runs or recharges most available mobile devices with power from the sun!

❋ **Provides a solar charging station for use with over 350 portable computers**—not to mention many other devices, such as powered coolers, cellular phones, camcorders, radio equipment, or just about anything that runs off rechargeable batteries.

❋ **Assists the internal battery of your portable computer**, adding many hours to your normal run time from a charged internal battery (runs many devices, not just extends).

❋ **Recharges the internal battery of your computer or device.** Also capable of running an external charger for your batteries.

❋ **Product comes with female "cigarette lighter" output socket**—plug any device into it that you would normally plug into your automobile's cigarette lighter.

❋ **Precisely regulated power supply**, which ensures that no incoming voltage will exceed manufacturer's specs (when used with manufacturer-approved cigarette lighter adapter).

❋ **Accessories available to recharge your automobile's battery** (sold separately, order #A0015), or recharge AAA, AA, C, or D cell batteries (sold separately, order #A0003).

❋ **Utilizes the best solar cells available**—Polycrystalline cells, with an expected life span of at least 20 years.

❋ **Full one-year warranty** and unconditional 30-day, money-back guarantee.

Go mobile, stay mobile!

SafeSun

Handheld Sun/UV Sensor

http://www.safesun.com

Type: Hardware

First Developed: 1998

Price Range: $100

Key Features: Small, simple, efficient

Ages: All

Obsolescence: Low

Further Information:
✴ *http://www.safesun.com/uv_map.html*
A great metapage devoted to government UV and sun exposure maps for the U.S., Australia, and others.

From www.safesun.com:

A Technological Breakthrough

The sensitivity of human skin varies among different types of UV (UVA, UVB). This sensitivity is described by a worldwide accepted standard—the Erythemal Response Spectrum. SafeSun is the only consumer-targeted device based on this standard.

Other consumer-focused products are not based on the Erythemal Response Spectrum. This makes their readings misleading and even dangerous to use.

Until now, the only way to precisely measure the "skin burning intensity" of UV light was with expensive and cumbersome scientific instruments.

In the past few years, unhappily, we have known several people who have died of melanoma. Having grown up in Los Angeles, and having spent countless hours on the beach, this is unnerving. Worse, I have kids now, and my wife is fair-skinned. My son, Sean, is fair-skinned as well.

In recent years, we have taken to slathering vast amounts of sunblock on, and it does seems to do the trick, but who knows? It occurred to me that there must be some little device I could find to sense how bad the sun was on any given day. It didn't take much time before I discovered SafeSun on the Net.

It is about the size of the KESTREL, and it seems to me to be the KESTREL's natural companion. I gather from talking to the SafeSun folks that there are substantive scientific debates with regard to how to measure the sun's radiation and what constitutes too much. They have made the SafeSun a very simple device, however it is hard for me to believe that it could not function as a very adequate rough indicator.

You set it up for the right time of day (it has a clock), the level of sunblock you are using, and the relative sensitivity of your skin. After that, you just put it out in the sun when you are in the sun. It shows a real-time display of the UV levels, and calculates how close you are to overdosing. When it hits 100 percent, it beeps and then flashes a warning.

One weekend in Palm Springs, even though the temperature was the same on Saturday and Sunday, the UV levels were quite different. Hence, I was able to pace my exposure on the basis of something more than whether I felt like my skin was burning. I do like empiricism. This is a damn good device, very well constructed, and worth keeping around if you spend a lot of time on the slopes, on the beach, or in the desert.

Earthmate

Peripheral GPS (Global Positioning System) Receiver

http://www.delorme.com/earthmate/

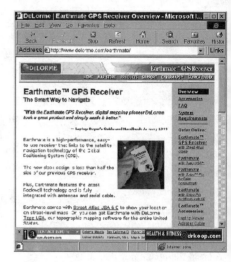

Type: Hardware, augmented by software

First Developed: 1998

Price Range: $159

Key Features: Small, and more impressive the stronger the computer to which it is attached.

Ages: All

Obsolescence: Low

Further Information:
✳ *http://www.expediamaps.com/* for Microsoft's map on the Net

Delorme is a fine mapmaking company based in Yarmouth, Maine, just a few miles south of Freeport, the home of L. L. Bean. For years it published fine mapbooks, and in the early '80s started to develop digital maps. Today, the company is a leading supplier of CD and DVD map systems, competing with and sometimes running rings around the likes of Microsoft.

DeLorme has also developed an exceptional GPS receiving instrument, about the size of a pack of cigarettes, and designed to function as a peripheral to a computer. As such, the Earthmate is quite different from the hand-held GPS receivers available elsewhere. It cannot function on its own. Rather, it needs the machine intelligence of a PC, preferably a fully loaded laptop PC portable, to do its stuff.

Image made with Mavica FD91 640x480

When used with a Windows CE device, as pictured here, it is not at its best. This is not due to any deficiency on the part of the Earthmate, but rather to the weaknesses of the CE devices. They do not have enough processor power and memory to fully support what can be done with the map data and imagery DeLorme can supply. All that can be downloaded are fixed, static images of maps, over which the Earthmate's position can be plotted.

On a PC, however, digital map data of the most robust sort—even 3-D data of the kind provided by DeLorme's TOPO USA software product—can be employed. That means you can choose the details you want to see. That means you can zoom in and out, with the imagery reconstituted for maximum effect. Further, the laptop can plot a course and give you spoken instructions on where to turn and the like. Amazing.

Palm Pilot

Palmtop Computing for the Masses

http://palmpilot.3com.com/

Type: Hardware

First Developed: 1996

Price Range: $200–$500

Key Features: Regrooves your personal tires

Ages: 16 and up

Obsolescence: Medium

Further Information:
❋ *http://ftp.nchu.edu.tw/LDP/ HOWTO/PalmOS-HOWTO-5.html*
for a short history of the early Palm Pilots, and
❋ *http://members.aol.com/ StanBoyd3/palmpage.htm*
and
❋ *http://www2.southwind.net/ ~miked/pilot/pilot.html*
for personal Palm Pilot metapages

Digital Life Improvement?

All geeks or quasi-geeks harbor dark, unspoken thoughts that life isn't really any better now that we've granted so much control to our computers.

But there is one computer—a little one—that truly can make life better, especially if you're chronically unorganized, as I am. This one moved me up one or two planes in quality of life. It even made me more virtuous.

I was a chronic birthdays forgetter. The truth was that I didn't have most of them memorized at all. It was a nightmare.

But the Palm Pilot (latest versions simply called Palm III and Palm V) actually changed me and made me a better person.

I took the time to add all important birth dates to the Palm's calendar and set the device to warn me a full week before each one. Presto! Everyone gets a card or gift, on time!

That function alone was enough for me to pack my Palm. It beats my old Filofax hands down for the amount of information it stores and the useful functions it performs. It has all my 1,000 names, addresses, and phone numbers, searchable by keyword. And I found a great piece of software I downloaded from the Internet to keep track of my athletic training program.

My next version was the Palm VII. I was always a less-is-more kind of guy, but I've played with the prototype. It won me over the instant its wireless Web connection gave me a choice of Italian restaurants a few blocks from me—and did so in less than 15 seconds. (It also found a friend's phone number in Seattle in 10 seconds.) This simple, cheap Web functionality coupled with all the other reasons I've always loved my Palm will keep me a loyal Palm aficionado for a long time to come.

—*Tom Bradford*

(Editor's Note: recent reviews of the Palm Pilot VII indicate that the on-line wireless services are very pricey—beware.)

II. SOURCES

→

II. SOURCES *continued*

→

II. SOURCES *continued*

→

II. SOURCES *continued*

History of Internet and WWW

The Roads and Crossroads of Internet History
Created by Gregory R. Gromov
http://www.netvalley.com/netvalley/intvalxan.html

Type: Web site

First Developed: 1998, Internet Valley

Price Range: Connect time

Key Features: Deeply "intertwingled"

Ages: Post-high school

Obsolescence: Low.

Further Information: another, somewhat less robust, but very fine history of the World Wide Web.
❋ *http://hoshi.cic.sfu.ca/*
~ guay/Paradigm/History.html

If the utter chaos of the Internet bothers you; if the dog's breakfast of design of most Web sites hurts your eyeballs, this Web site is not for you.

However, if you believe, as Ted Nelson has said, that "everything is deeply intertwingled"; if you are thrilled by the unstructured array of forces that have yielded the Internet; if you love the idea of hypertext, and find clicking on random buttons good practice for the serendipitous discovery of unexpected stuff (in other words, if you are an undiagnosed sufferer from a slight case of attention deficit disorder), this one is for you.

It binds Eisenhower to the Internet, Vannevar Bush to Ted Nelson, the interstate highway system to *Star Trek,* bomb shelters to TCP/IP. It tells the story of the development of the Net, and the parallel development of the new way of communication that the Net has spawned.

Only TV can really show the history of TV. The best histories of cinema I have ever seen are done on film. It stands to reason that the very best way to tell the history of the Net is to do it in hypertext on the Net.

ANCIENT HYPERLINKS

We imagine that hyperlinks and the like are great innovations of the modern day. In fact, they are an artifact of the technology of the modern day, but they are not an innovation.

In ancient India, the fabric of the culture was preserved, not through text, but rather through memory. Families preserved vast chunks of the Vedas, Upanishads, and other such bodies of knowledge, by memorization.

The combination of melody, meter, and an array of subtle linguistic tricks embedded in the material aided in the performance of magnificent mnemonic feats (bodies of material the size and complexity of a modern dictionary, memorized by individuals perfectly, and passed on by generation after generation without any change).

If you don't think humans can remember that much, inventory the number of pop tunes you can remember—music, beat, lyrics, guitar licks, keyboard riffs, etc. Melody, meter, and tone are very powerful mnemonic devices when combined.

In order to explain and expand upon the content and composition of the remembered material, the Indians used a system called Bhashya. Literally, illumination.

Bhashya would take a brief, aphoristic excerpt from the body of a work and break the highly organized text into its linguistic components. Each word would be treated separately and expanded into a sentence, often using the linguistic roots of the word to throw light on its meaning by reference.

The same thing can be done with certain English words. For example, The meaning of the word *order* is brought into further relief by noting that it comes from the same linguistic root as *right*.

Often a word or phrase would naturally resonate with a similar word or phrase existing elsewhere in the memorized material—(Aha, that sounds like...)—much like starting a speech on civil rights by using the phrase, "life, liberty, and the pursuit of happiness." There is an immediate connect.

So a three word aphorism might yield a three sentence Bhashya, which might in turn yield another similarly expanded Bhashya of multiple paragraphs.

We've got a great example of Bhashya in pop music: The Do Re Mi song from *The Sound of Music*. First, you have the musical aphorism: Do Re Mi Fa So La Ti....

The Bhashya goes like this:

> Do: a deer, a female deer,
> Re: a drop of golden sun...

Basic text, broken into components, each component amplified, brought into relief...

This is true hypertext, not constrained by the linearity of typography, but by the immediate presence of all relevant knowledge, with resonant material brought to the forefront of consciousness by Bhashya (illumination).

The great thing about the Net is that it is nonlinear, and the more links there are, the less are there discernable hard boundaries between chunks of knowledge. However, a trusted source of Bhashya, someone who creates the illumination, is very valuable. A Yahoo without Bhashya (links organized within a robust, but simple classification system) is simply a vast flood of data, without context, heart, soul.

That's why encyclopedias are needed (perhaps many), and that's why human guides are needed—stewards whose responsibility it is to lead you down a particular path.

This is ancient stuff, ripe to be rediscovered.

Mediametrix

Rating Web Site Traffic

http://www.mediametrix.com/TopRankings/TopRankings.html

Type: Web site

First Developed: 1998

Price: Connect time, and lots of money for detailed reports

Key Features: It's what everybody pays attention to

Ages: 10 and up

Obsolescence factor: Medium

Further Information:

✳ *www.netratings.com*

This is the service owned by the Nielsen people, now playing second fiddle to Mediametrix

✳ *http://searchenginewatch.com/ reports/mediametrix.html*

This site rates the search engines

✳ *http://www.rubicon.com/ turnpike/demogrph.html*

…for an excellent Metapage devoted to demographics.

Recently, the Net has been overwhelmed by marketeers. Their only objective is to get and keep eyeballs. It's a horse race, and the race is being called by a company called Mediametrix.

Web people watch these numbers just like the TV people watch Nielsen ratings numbers. Fortunes rise and fall, initial public offerings float or sink, portals become side doors, all based on the numbers.

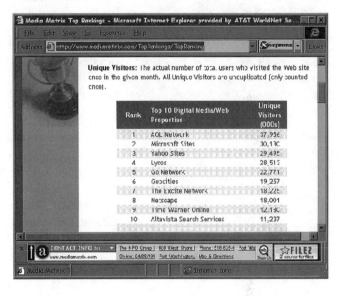

(Like CNN and ESPN), **Shopping** sites (like Amazon), **Web Directories** (like Infospace), **Education** sites (the ones that end in .edu), and **Government** sites (the ones that end in .gov).

In the old media, the numbers were guarded secrets. On the Net, you get to know. Sometimes what you get to know is surprising.

Mediametrix counts Unique Visitors: The actual number of total users who visited the Web site once in the given month. All Unique Visitors are unduplicated (only counted once).

The categories are **Top Digital Media/Web Properties** (people like to call these portals today, but by the time you read this, they may like to call them something else as business models for the Internet change every 10 days or so), **Domains** (places like Yahoo), **News and Entertainment sites**

Recently, near the top of the biggest e-commerce sites (places like Amazon.com and AOL) is a place called bluemountainarts.com. It's an electronic greetings card site, and its design looks like a five-and-dime shop on the wrong side of town. But it's drawing a big crowd, with its folksy, free samples. Go figure.

How Stuff Works

http://www.howstuffworks.com/

Type: Web site

First Developed: Started halfway through 1998

Price Range: Connect time

Key Features: Excellent integration of text, animation, and hypermedia

Ages: 10 and up

Obsolescence: Low

Further Information:
❋ *http://www.bygpub.com/ books/tg2rw/tg2rwbooktoc.htm* leads you to the author's book, *The Teenager's Guide to the Real World* This Web site's company is BYG Publishing, Inc.:
☎ (919) 269-5880

Some folks think this is the finest site on the Web.

It boasts an array of articles devoted to explaining the workings of common things, and does the job with good humor, good writing, simple but effective animations, and really good lists of relevant links.

For decades there have been books devoted to the subject—great compendiums of text and graphics. They tend to fall into two categories: dense or whimsical. I always want to own these books, but I never find them readable.

This is a good place to go instead. The fellow who crafts this site started it on a whim. There are reports that he was offered a six-figure sum to buy the site. He turned it down, and instead turns out a new entry every week. It's a labor of love, and you can tell. In case you still want a book, this site keeps a very good list of *How Things Work*-style books. But they all pale in comparison.

Binocular Astronomy

http://www.angelfire.com/md/binoastro/

The sky goes everywhere with you. Optical devices are not so accommodating. Hauling a telescope out into the backyard can be a pain. Taking it on vacation or any kind of traveling is too much hassle. Binoculars, however, can go everywhere. Binocs make for the best astronomy.

The broad field of view, the ability to locate what you are looking for quickly, and the ability to ponder the extraordinary depth of space beat telescopes hands down. This Web site is not professional, nor is the content. Happily, the attitude is not professional either.

This guy just utterly loves the night sky, and has that kind of insight into how to make the experience of looking at it magic.

Type: Web site source

First Developed: 1998

Price Range: Connect time

Key Features: Very focused, by an enthusiast

Ages: All

Obsolescence: Low

Further Information:
❋ *http://www.starchair.com/* (an Australian company that makes an expensive, Star-Wars-like mechanical chair just for backyard astronomers)
❋ *http://astronomymall.com/ regular/ products/virgo/* (well-designed, pricey binocular tripods, built to let you sit in any chair and have the binocs rest, properly oriented, right before your eyes) *See photo, right.*

Internet Traffic Report

Summary of Global Activity

http://www.internettrafficreport.com/

Type: Web site

First Developed: 1996

Price Range: Connect time

Key Features: Clear, comprehensible graphics

Ages: Post-high school

Obsolescence: Medium

Further Information:
✳ *http://www.cybergeography.org/atlas/atlas.html*
Visit the Atlas of Cyberspace for other ways to sense the status of the Net. Internet Traffic Report site is by Andover Advanced Technologies:
☎ (978) 635-5300

Sometimes it's fun to see what's going on in cyberspace. Here is a simple summary of the global performance of the Net. Continent by continent, this site shows how fast things are moving, how much data is being sent to Venus, rather than its intended destination, and what the response time seems to be.

It must have been very interesting to see the traffic report the day the Starr Report was released.

It will also be very interesting to see the stats on New Year's Eve 2000. Scope it out.

BINOCULAR ASTRONOMY
Looking at the world through Web-colored binoculars: A fanciful shot from www.angelfire.com.

Viral Marketing

http://www.drapervc.com/ViralMarketing.html

Type: Web document

First Developed: 1997

Price Range: Connect time

Key Features: Heavy on Silicon Valley-speak, but heavily admired in the cybercommunity

Ages: High school and later

Obsolescence: Medium

Further Information:
✱ *http://www.hotmail.com/*
(This is Draper's first big viral marketing win that has become a classic e-business start-up example)

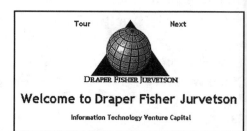

"Viral marketing" is the current Internet marketing buzzword. The guys purveying it have had a venture capital hot streak of humongous proportions. Everybody's paying attention.

Here's the opening paragraph of the essay Tim Draper and Steve Jurvetson published on their venture capital firm's Web site:

> *A lot of the energy behind the Internet is the ability for everyone to be a publisher. Consequently, we are in a land grab for precious spectrum—people's attention. Attention is finite. Rising above the noise of a thousand voices requires creativity. Shouting is not very creative. Just hanging up a Web shingle and hoping for visitors is not very creative. Rather, new companies can structure their businesses in a way that allows them to grow like a virus and lock out the existing bricks and mortar competitors through innovative pricing and exploitation of these competitors' legacy, distribution channel conflict.*

These guys should also get the award for the most distasteful/compelling analogy as well. To wit:

> *Digital viruses can spread internationally more rapidly than biological viruses that rely on the physical proximity of hosts for their spread—via a sneeze or handshake.*

Setting aside the disgusting simile, there is a fundamental insight here, and it has a great deal to do with Internet time, where days are weeks, months are years, and the speed of ideas is the speed of light.

VIRAL MARKETING

Written by Steve Jurvetson and Tim Draper, updated October 1998. The original version was published in the Netscape M-Files, November 1997.

A lot of the energy behind the Internet is the ability for everyone to be a publisher. Consequently, we are in a land grab for a precious spectrum, people's attention. Attention is finite. Rising above the noise of a thousand voices requires creativity. Shouting is not very creative. Just hanging up a Web shingle and hoping for visitors is not very creative. Rather, new companies can structure their businesses in a way that allows them to grow like a virus and lock out the existing bricks-and-mortar competitors through innovative pricing and exploitation of these competitors' legacy, distribution channel conflict.

In 1996, Sabeer Bhatia and Jack Smith pioneered a great new product category —free Web-based e-mail. But many great ideas and great products have withered on the vine. The special catalyst for Hotmail's torrid growth is what we at Draper Fisher Jurvetson have come to call "Viral Marketing"—not because any traditional viruses are involved, but because of the pattern of rapid adoption through word-of-mouth networks. Viral Marketing powerfully compounds the benefits of a first-mover advantage. And it's something we eagerly look for when evaluating any Internet start-up company. As a founding investor in Hotmail and a member of their board of directors, we think Hotmail is a great case study on the impact of the Viral Marketing strategy over its full life cycle.

Hotmail's Amazing Growth

* Hotmail grew a subscriber base more rapidly than any company in the history of the world …faster than any new on-line, Internet, or print publication ever.

* Hotmail is the largest e-mail provider in the world.

* In its first 1.5 years, Hotmail signed up over 12 million subscribers.

* A traditional print publication would hope to reach a total of 100,000 subscribers within a few years of launch. Hotmail signs up more than 150,000 subscribers every day, seven days a week.

* Every Hotmail subscriber, without exception, has filled out a detailed demographic and psychographic profile including occupation and salary. This is an unprecedented supply of personal information.

* Yet, from company launch to 12 million users, Hotmail spent less than $500K on marketing, advertising and promotion. This compares to over $20 million spent on advertising, and brand promotion by Juno, Hotmail's closest competitor with a fraction of the users.

Elements of Viral Marketing

The Hotmail adoption pattern is that of a virus—with spatial and network locality. People typically send e-mails to their associates and friends; many of them are geographically close, and others are scattered around with clusters in areas of high Internet connectivity. We would notice the first user from a university town or from India, and then the number of subscribers from that region would rapidly proliferate. The beauty of it is that none of this required any marketing dollars. Customers do the selling.

Digital viruses can spread internationally more rapidly than biological viruses that rely on the physical proximity of hosts for their spread—via a sneeze or handshake. Hotmail is the largest e-mail provider in Sweden and India despite the fact that they have done no marketing of any sort in these countries. It's a happy day when you discover your business has displaced several entrenched competitors to become the market share leader in a country you have never visited. What's more, Hotmail is used in over 220 countries, despite the limitation that it is only available in English.

Viral Broadcasts

A sneeze releases two million aerosol particles. In the digital domain, this can get very interesting. For example, Tumbleweed Software enables secure e-mail delivery of documents or newsletters to a huge numbers of recipients. Every recipient also gets a Web link to the enabling Tumbleweed service. So when a single new customer starts to use Tumbleweed, thousands of potential new customers receive the Tumbleweed pitch.

The power of this approach has been demonstrated in the junk e-mail domain. Have you ever gotten one of those e-mail chain letters that urge you to forward it to as many people as possible? Often shrouded with a bogus virus warning or a charitable cause, these messages rapidly spread thoughout the globe until people have received multiple copies. →

Viral Marketing *continued*

→ These junk e-mails are like digital graffiti in that the people that create them want their "tag" or message to be seen by as many people as possible. Traditional graffiti "artists" choose targets like trains and buses to maximize their exposure. Similarly, many computer virus authors are seeking to promote their name, and they seek maximum exposure—on the PC. You don't see many viruses on niche computer platforms (as the Macintosh market share has dwindled, so too have the number of new Mac viruses). This personal quest for fame, while annoying, is not too different from the desire of many businesses for brand awareness.

A good virus will look for prolific hosts (such as students) and tie to their high-frequency social interactions (such as e-mail and messaging). Viral Marketing is most powerful when it taps into the breadth of its customers' weak connections to others. Tapping the customer's entire address book is more valuable than just reaching their best friend.

Viral Marketing Strategies
The Internet is a wonderful substrate or petri dish for the proliferation and replication of intellectual property. A good idea can spread more quickly over the Internet than has ever been possible before in the physical world, where manufacturing and distribution fundamentally limit the rate of product adoption. Especially in the Internet era, a company's competitiveness seems to depend on its velocity of thought and action.

Hyper-Growth
An interesting side effect of geometric growth is that by the time a virus spreads to the point of being an epidemic, its growth curve relative to a new entrant is somewhat daunting. Hotmail was doubling in size each month, but it took several months to reach one million users. Until then, they were under the radar screen of many potential competitors and acquirers. By the time the industry came to realize that free Web-based e-mail was indeed a hot idea, Hotmail was adding one million new subscribers per month, and that growth rate was accelerating. A new fast follower would start small and have to grow for several months to reach one million subscribers. But in that same time, Hotmail would have grown to 10 million subscribers. So although Hotmail's followers grew geometrically as well, the absolute difference in subscriber bases widened every month (while the ratio remained approximately constant).

Absolute size matters. One significant effect of Hotmail's absolute size is that their efficiencies of scale allowed them to be the lowest-cost e-mail provider on the planet. Server utilization and bandwidth pricing improved with growth. Also, the perceived gorilla in a category tends to get the dominant share of the business and financial partnerships.

A challenge for the hypergrowth gorilla is scalability. On a technology level, server scalability is a critical concern. Fortunately, companies like Hotmail are turning software into a service. What were sold as e-mail servers and clients are now offered as a Web-based service where the customer need only have a standard Web browser. This makes product upgrades a lot easier; Hotmail can upgrade its server software several times a month without involving, or in many cases even notifying, its large customer base. The customer still uses the same browser.

But once one problem is solved, hypergrowth tends to uncover new scalability bottlenecks. Often the young Internet company finds that its growth is constrained by its ability to hire good people. This is why many of these companies try to engineer around people-intensive elements of their business.

Where might this all lead? We are still looking for the emergent intelligence of the hive. An ant colony exhibits a higher order of intelligence than that of its individual members. We don't look at a neuron and think of it as being very smart. In many ways, we are the neurons on the Net, and the network applications that take advantage of that collective intelligence have not been developed yet. The Santa Fe Institute argues that computer viruses are a form of artificial life. Perhaps viral marketing can also find an evolutionary form.

But in the meantime, the Hotmail juggernaut just keeps on growing—quietly and consistently—on its own momentum. Hotmail now has over 30 million subscribers.[*] As a technological dislocation, we believe that the Internet provides an unfair competitive advantage to nimble startup companies. A good idea can spread like wildfire if its business model maps to the medium. Viral Marketing adds fuel to the fire.

At press time, the number of members Microsoft (the new owner of Hotmail) claims is 35 million, with 125,000 new members each day.

Netcopter

Report on ISPs (Internet Service Providers)

http://www.netcopter.com/Netcopter

Type: Web site

First Developed: 1998

Price Range: Connect time

Key Features: Real, embarrassing data on the big guys.

Ages: Post-high school

Obsolescence: Low.

Further Information:
❊ *http://www.mids.org/weather/*
The Internet Weather Report, a set of maps indicating the status of the Net.
Netcopter is from Clearlink:
☎ (415) 505-4800

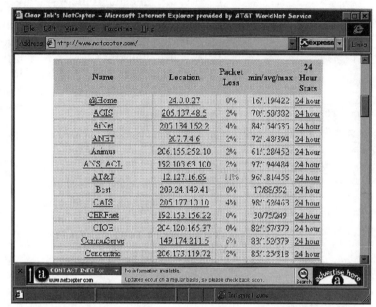

Here's the first screen they want you to see on Netcopter, a Web site which reports the reliability of the major Internet Service Providers.

The folks at Clearlink who provide the Netcopter page tell you right up front:

> *This page is not an indication that one Internet Service Provider is superior to another. Rather, it is intended to be an indication of Internet health from the perspective of OUR connection here at Clearlink at a given moment.*
> *Specifically, if there are problems within GTE Internetworking or at an exchange point where GTE Internetworking connects to another network, packet loss can occur.*

The Netcopter page is lousy with copyright notices, as well. This level of paranoia can mean only one thing: These guys have found out that some big names are doing a rotten job!

They have made it possible for us poor schlubs to know who, what, and where. In response, Netcopter/Clearlink has undoubtedly received a bunch of nasty letters with big logos, or strong legal mastheads.

Sure is nice that they didn't disappear. One of the great features of the Net is the cojones often shown by some of its netizens.

MP3.com

Digital Audio

http://www.MP3.com

Type: Web site

First Developed: 1998

Price Range: Connect time

Key Features: The granddaddy of MP3 sites

Ages: From first computer use

Obsolescence: Medium.

Further Information: Other notable MP3 sites (according to Rolling Stone Magazine) are:

✤ *www.goodnoise.com*
✤ *www.mp3place.net*
✤ *www.audiodreams.com,*
✤ *www.mp3web.com*
✤ *www.audible.com*

and for generic search for MP3 files on the web,

✤ *www.mp3search.lycos.com.*

Also:

✤ *www.rioreport.com*

from Diamond, the people who developed the portable MP3 player. MP3.com Web site is from Filez

☎ (619) 453-2845

In 1997, I sat in on meetings between the computer industry and the home video industry. The Hollywood people were scared to death that their copyrights (they think of themselves as being in the copyright business) would be ruined if the digital files on movie DVDs, and particularly movie DVD-ROMs, were not equipped with some sort of solid copy protection technology. The Silicon Valley people could care less (feeling that all content is fair game), but they wanted movies to play on their computers. These meetings were intense, often strained. So much was as stake. But they all ultimately agreed, and the copyrights are safe. You cannot, without the aid of some world-class cryptanalysts, crack the movies that come on DVD.

However, the horse was out of the barn long ago when it came to recorded music, and there is digital hell to pay now. It appears in the form of MP3, which is nothing more than a way of encoding digital audio in such a fashion that it can be downloaded quickly over the Net.

Kaboom. There is an array of sites where you can download the software you need for playback; the software you need for recording what you already have on audio CDs, tapes, cassettes, and vinyl records; and legal or illegal MP3 files. This allows mass copyright violation. Mass value migration (see the entry on the book by the same name). Mass marketing myopia. Mass dislocation. The 1998 Full Employment Act for Litigators.

Watch the fun. It won't end for a long time.

FROM A NOTE BY MICHAEL, a somewhat mysterious voice on the MP3 site

Q: If the music industry gets behind their own technology like the Madison Project, they could obliterate MP3. Does that concern you?

A: In spite of the fact the industry has launched negative PR campaigns and lawsuits while pressuring organizations to exclude MP3 and block advertisers from supporting MP3, the movement thrives. A long list of software vendors, including some of the biggest in the world like Microsoft, either already support MP3 or soon will. Computer peripheral companies such as Diamond Multimedia and Creative Labs are supporting MP3. A growing list of consumer electronic giants like Samsung and others that we cannot disclose are prepping MP3 playback devices. Most importantly, consumers are lining up squarely behind MP3. To summarize, MP3 has experienced its current growth with incredible resistance from the industry. I don't believe they could erect any new barriers that will prevent MP3 from moving forward. →

XOOM

Web Portal

http://xoom.com

Type: Web portal

First Developed: 1997

Price Range: Connect time

Key Features: Lots of stickiness, lots of community, lots of business savvy

Ages: High school and later

Obsolescence: Medium

Further Information: Watch what Chris Kitze does. He has a very good record in high tech.

WEB PORTAL: A *Web site or service that offers a broad array of resources and services, such as e-mail, forums, search engines, and on-line shopping malls. The first Web portals were online services, such as AOL, that provided access to the Web, but by now most of the traditional search engines have transformed themselves into Web portals to attract and keep a larger audience.*

— *from PC Webopaedia*

Xoom is a Web portal, on-line since the end of 1996. Two years and Xoom goes public, making its founders filthy rich (on paper, we must remind ourselves, on paper). Ever wonder what one of these guys used as their rules for success. At right are the rules (circa February 1999), courtesy of Chris Kitze, one of the Xoom founders.

THE RULES OF MAKING MONEY ON THE WEB

by Chris Kitze, Xoom Co-founder

1. Don't worry about making money right away (I know this sounds counter-intuitive).
2. Make everything free.
3. Build traffic.
4. Use viral marketing (see VIRAL MARKETING), so that every time someone uses the service, they tell someone else about it.
5. Find sponsors.
6. Embed e-commerce opportunities.
7. Capture membership info (this is where the real value of a service comes in).
8. Use the service to qualify people to receive some kind of offer (or better yet, multiple offers).
9. DON'T SELL PHYSICAL GOODS YOURSELF!!! (This is the best way to slow yourself down).

The rules may have changed by the time you read this, but think of it as a snapshot of reality, a firsthand report from the frontlines, at a critical juncture in the history of the Net.

→ FROM A NOTE BY MICHAEL (continued)

Q: But with the music industry's massive back catalog, don't they have the upper hand in the long run?

A: There are two distinct viewpoints on this issue. The first is the music traditionalist who believes that those with the gold (read: content) make the rules. For the last 50 years or so, this has been the case and many believe it will hold true. Others have a more Internet mindset and believe that the consumer is king. The Internet gives consumers the ultimate control because they can take their business elsewhere with a click of the mouse. This empowerment energizes consumers and tilts the scales in their direction. Over time this will surely shape up to be the defining battle which will set the course of music for the next hundred years. Only time will tell who the victor will be.

Reel 3-D

Stereoscopic Photography Web Site

http://stereoscopy.com/reel3d/

Type: Source (catalog and Web site)

First Developed: 1978

Price Range: Products vary from very little to quite a bit

Key Features: Stereoscopic photo systems from ancient to modern

Ages: 10 and up

Obsolescence: Low

Further Information: Web site references an array of additional sources of info on stereoscopic and 3-D imagery.

Contact:
P.O. Box 2368
Culver City, CA 90231
United States of America

e-mail: Reel3D@aol.com

For all the interest in holography and virtual reality, not many of the present-day computer technologies that fake reality can come close to the impact of a real photographic image. Photos generally are flat and static, but we are used to them and accept their limitations because they look real.

Moving pictures really make a difference, but even they don't quite get it. Hence the spectacular experiments in cinema over the years: anamorphic wide-screen displays started in the late '20s with a fine black-and-white film by 20th Century Fox, *The Big Trail* (starring a young John Wayne). Later came Cinerama (with even wider screens), and more recently IMAX (with the biggest screens to date, see *http://www.imax.com*).

But nothing comes close to good stereoscopic photography for 3-D verisimilitude, and amazingly enough, it's been going on since the Civil War. Matthew Brady made a bunch of them, and there were companies in the late 19th century that made a business of publishing them. During the heyday of stereoscopic photography, photographers were sent on assigment around the globe, capturing historical gems from China to Alaska. The surviving libraries range from erotica to a rich library devoted to the history of California.

Enthusiasts continued to take stereoscopic pictures through this century. One of them was silent movie star Harold Lloyd, who took stereoscopic pictures of Marilyn Monroe. Today there are very good 3-D (though non-digital) camera and viewing systems. The catalog from Reel 3-D Enterprises is a great place to brief yourself on what's there.

For an even more spectacular visual experience of the digital kind, see IPIX 360° DIGITAL PICTURES.

IPIX

360° Digital Pictures

http://www.ipix.com/

Type: Web technology

First Developed: 1996

Price Range: Connect time

Key Features: Takes you there

Ages: 10 and up

Obsolescence: Medium–2 years

Further Information: A nice, fast internet connect would be handy, as IPIX files are fairly big (200-300KB over the Net). Contact IPIX at: Interactive Pictures Corporation 1009 Commerce Park Drive Oak Ridge, Tennessee 37830

☎ 1.888.909.IPIX

☎ (423) 482-3000

fax: (423) 482-5447

My father took me to Gettysburg when I was twelve, and I remember two things vividly. First was that you could feel the anguish and pain of the battle. I've since found that to be true at other battlefields, whether in the U.S. (Manassas), or Europe (Verdun and Normandy can overwhelm you).

The other vivid Gettysburg memory was the Cyclorama (*http://www.nps.gov/gett/gettcyclo.htm*). The basic notion of a cyclorama is to paint a big picture on the interior of a cylindrical building, to give a sense of the scope of some great event. Attempts at this sort of thing stretch back for centuries.

The tapestry at Bayeux (*http://www.reading.gov.uk/museum/bayeux.htm*)—just a few miles from the Normandy invasion beaches—strives to capture the battle of Hastings, as I suppose cave paintings and the artwork on the interiors of ancient Egyptian crypts strove to communicate something of their times. They are interesting to look at, but they don't really give you a terrific sense of place. Stereoscopic photography is much better (see REEL 3-D).

But nothing comes close to the effect of a very recent technology developed by Interactive Pictures Corporation. These are digital pictures crafted to present all 360 degrees of a view, in all directions. The only way you can see an IPIX is to log onto a Web site with some IPIX built in, or get a piece of software that uses them.

Instead of an image laid out on the interior of a cylinder (as with early attempts at immersive photography by Apple with Quicktime VR and Microsoft with Windows Surround Video), IPIX are images laid out on the interior of a sphere. You can see the sky, you can see the ground, you can see all around.

They are proliferating like a virus on the Internet, and the best way to find them is to search on IPIX with a good search engine, or go to the IPIX Web site for links to other Web sites that use them.

Ellis Island

Museum and Multimedia Exhibit

http://www.ellisisland.org

Immigrants on line to be checked in at Ellis Island

Type: Museum and related Web site

First Developed: 1995

Price Range: $30 boat ride; $5 for the movie

Key Features: The Great Hall where the immigrants were vetted

Ages: 10 and up

Obsolescence: None

Further Information: Skip the long wait for access to the interior of the Statue of Liberty, and spend more time on Ellis Island.
✳ *www.ellisisland.com*
(the site hosted by Aramark, the authorized Ellis Park concessionaire)

There are places you can go in the world that are revered as holy: Lourdes for Catholics. Mt. Kailash for Hindus. Mecca for the faithful in the world of Islam.

For Americans, who have made a point of keeping religion out of their republic's hair, there is no such thing as a holy place. But if liberty were a faith, Ellis Island would be one of the first destinations for the faithful.

You reach Ellis Island on the second half of the boat ride to the Statue of Liberty in New York Harbor. You arrive at this skimpy piece of land just as many of our grand- and great-grandparents might have—save for the vermin, seasickness, and utter terror that they might be refused entry after months, perhaps years, of struggling to get to America.

As with any great memorial, you can almost hear the voices, almost sense the anxieties, almost reach out and touch the ghosts inhabiting this great gateway to the New World. Where memory and imagination fail, there are exhibits, displays, and a documentary which stands out in my mind as the finest, most haunting I have ever seen (produced by a master of the art, Charles Guggenheim).

The Obsolete Computer Museum
Web Site Devoted to Long-Dead Computers
http://www.ncsc.dni.us/fun/user/tcc/cmuseum/cmuseum.htm

Obsolete Computer Museum

Type: Web site

First Developed: 1996

Price Range: Connect time

Key Features: Good, big pictures

Ages: 10 and up

Obsolescence: This is dedicated to obsolescence

Further Information: The Boston Computer Museum
✻ *http://www.tcm.org/*
and the American Museum in Washington, D.C., for good static displays of old personal computers.

There's a new discussion about "The First Time," though it hasn't made it to the women's magazines, as yet. It's the first time you messed with a computer. An entertaining variant of the discussion is the first time your computer crashed and ate your data (something no one forgets).

My first time was with the IBM 370 in the summer of 1972, with punched cards and all. One summer evening in 1972, all of the punch card data we had entered for weeks seemed to disappear. It actually turned to garbage in a diagonal effect across the surface of a page of the print-out. The programmer

was ready to kill himself. He thought he had left the storage tapes on a heater. It turned out that IBM had released a bad version of the operating system. Imagine that. (I am reminded of a classic Ted Nelson quote about IBM, "Obsolete power corrupts obsoletely.")

The first real computer I owned was an Apple II, and I got it before they had a disk drive. You had to load programs from a cassette player. I bought it at The Computer Store in Santa Monica (the first retail computer store), about a month after I read a book called *The Home Computer Revolution* by Ted Nelson (see COMPUTER LIB/DREAM MACHINES). Little did I know. This Web site has pictures of just about every machine I ever owned or lusted after. Put together by curator Tom Carlson at the National Center for State Courts Technology Lab (?), it is an entirely homegrown site, but wonderful. This one is a stroll down memory lane of the first and strangest order. Check out, in particular, what the first portables looked like (Kaypro, Osborne, IBM 5100).

Below, some samples from the museum.

The Osborne 1
One of the first portables. The tiny screen measures 3.55" x 2.63"! Owned by R. Kuhlenschmidt of Pacific Palisades, CA

The Apple] [+
The twin drives each hold around 140k–160k. Hefty! Owned by Don Miller of Williamsburg, VA

The IBM 5100 Personal
...er, Portable... Computer
Note the tape drive. In 1976, it cost $14,275. Owned by G. Berg of Newburgh, NY

Exploratorium Museum of San Francisco

http://www.exploratorium.com/

Type: Exhibition/Museum/Web site

First Developed: 1969

Price: Connect time for virtual, $6-$12 for a physical visit

Key Features: Takes you there

Ages: 10 and up

Obsolescence: Medium—2 years

Further Information: Visit this Web site for a terrific listing of museums and exhibits:
❋ *http://www.icom.org/vlmp/*

Prince Albert, Queen Victoria's consort, threw a World's Fair in Hyde Park, London, in 1851. It was held at the legendary Crystal Palace. He called it "the Great Exhibition of the Industries of All Nations." Over six million people attended the exhibition.

When it closed down, the British Museum of Science and Industry (*http://wwmice.cs.ucl.ac.uk/local/museums/BritishMuseum.html*) picked up the mantle with terrific exhibits and hands on demos. The Germans took notice, and duplicated the success in a spectacular fashion in the form of the Deutsches Museum (*http://www.deutsches-museum.de/e_index.htm*). Both are still open and terrific, deserving of an in-person or on-line visit.

The fellow who started the Exploratorium in the Palace of Fine Arts in San Francisco—University of Colorado physics professor Frank Oppenheimer—was in Europe in 1965, where he visited science museums such as the one in South Kensington, London, and the Deutsches Museum in Munich. He took his inspiration from those places, and took it to the next level. The participatory exhibits—the hands-on stuff—are what characterize the place. Other terrific exemplars of the form are the American Museum in Washington and the California Museum of Science and Technology in Downtown Los Angeles.

Many of the exhibitors are moving their action to the Web, and San Francisco's exploratorium seems to have done a good job there, as well. But the physical institution is where the term "hands-on" counts. The Exploratorium has over 650 interactive exhibits that attracted more than 600,000 visitors in 1998. Very worthwhile.

Over 6 million visited the Web site in 1998, and that tells the story of the future of hands-on.

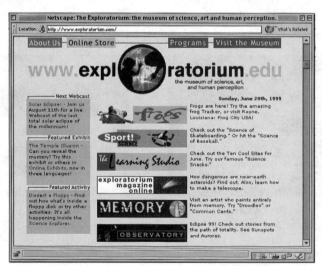

FUN AT THE EXPLORATORIUM
Activities for the Millennium, from the Exploratorium Web Site

BEHIND THE SCREEN
October 1999–January 2000

From 19th century pre-cinema toys to state-of-the-art digital technology, the science of the moving image is explored in all its depth and breadth. Learn the science behind how we perceive moving images, and create your own animated sequences. In a modern TV control room, find out how editors work to combine live and recorded images to tell a story.

Discover how sound editors mix and manipulate dialogue, music, ambient sounds, and effects to create the aural texture of a scene, then stand behind a microphone to dub your own voice into *Jerry Maguire* or *My Fair Lady.* Find out just how digital special effects artists created the dinosaurs in *Jurassic Park,* or use the Magic Mirror to try on some famous costumes from films and television.

OUR BODIES, OUR FACSIMILES
Spring, 2000

Examine how our conceptions of the body have evolved over time and in response to the development of more powerful and complex imaging technologies.

SEEING
Fall, 2000

Learning to See integrates physics, biology, culture, and technology, to investigate the ways in which seeing is influenced by the world inside us and the world around us.

THE EXPLAINER PROGRAM
Community involvement since 1969

The Explainer Program is one of the most exciting programs at the Exploratorium. It focuses on Bay Area youth between the ages of 15 and 20.

The Explainer program makes students part of the museum staff, giving them the important responsibility of being our primary point of contact with

the general public. In keeping with the Exploratorium's philosophy, participants build their own skills while learning to help others. Approximately 2000 students have participated in the program since its inception in 1969, when the Exploratorium first opened to the public.

Three groups of Explainers fill thirty paid positions each year. Each Explainer group participates in over seventy hours of training conducted by museum staff and visiting professionals. Besides explaining exhibits to the public, the Explainers are responsible for opening and closing the museum, helping maintain exhibits, and interacting with visitors in a variety of ways. Explainers also perform public demonstrations, including cow's eye dissections and helium-neon-laser presentations.

The Explainer program provides an interactive social environment, rich in science and the arts, in which students can explore phenomena and learn about themselves and others as they provide the museum with a young, energetic floor staff. Candidates for the Explainer program are not required to be knowledgeable, or even interested, in science. The directors look for the "spark" that indicates a student has the potential to learn and an interest in interacting with others. Some are skilled in interpersonal relations; others have more science background. Explainers have come to us in wheelchairs. Some have had hearing, physical, and visual impairments; others have had reading, speaking, and other learning disorders. Student diversity is one of the great strengths of the program.

Explainers are trained in a wide variety of subjects and are given a great deal of responsibility for handling complex public interactions and museum operations. The program offers students much more than job training. It also offers them a means by which they can recognize their own value as contributing members of a group, whose opinions are taken seriously and whose needs are respected.

Terrorism Research Center
Web Site Review of Policy and Suggested Policy
http://www.terrorism.com

> "Terrorism is the unlawful use of force or violence against persons or property to intimidate or coerce a government, the civilian population, or any segment thereof, in furtherance of political or social objectives."
>
> —FBI definition

A wealth of resources and community space for terrorism, information warfare, and other homeland defense issues. Features a Calendar of Significant Events that lists troublesome dates for international travelers and focus areas on homeland defense, infrastructure protection, and chem/bio terrorism. This information, provided for free, costs thousands of dollars if you acquire it through commercial security organizations. Also features an interactive community of diverse personalities, from science fiction authors like Bruce Sterling to actual members of special forces and counterterrorism groups.

Type: Web site

First Developed: 1997

Price Range: Connect time

Key Features: Various articles and resources built around the theme of Infowar

Ages: Post-teen

Obsolescence: Speedy, but constantly updated

Further Information:
✳ *http://www.wired.com/wired/archive/1.03/1.3_softkill.html* (the original *Wired* magazine article on the subject)
also, see
✳ *http://ww.infowar.com*

At 400,000 hits a month, it isn't one of the busiest sites on the Net but it's one of the top five destinations for terrorism, information warfare, and infrastructure defense issues and is often cited by CNN, *The Washington Post*, and an assortment of academic and professional Web sites.

—*Matt Devost*

There is an entirely new kind of warfare on the horizon (see MELISSA'S LESSON*) that promises to level the playing field between big, rich countries (read: the U.S.), and small countries with limited resources (read: just about everybody else; see sidebars at right).*

This asymmetric warfare takes a bunch of different forms, and no one has settled on a name for it. Some of the contenders are cyberwar, infowar, infrastructure warfare, I-war, and such.

Anyone can play, from nation-states to Ibn Bin Lauden. All it takes is money and smart people to target the communications, and other nerve centers on which an advanced post-industrial nation depends. Read all about it, here and at Infowar.com.

→

→ Terrorism Research Center *continued*

TOP TEN U.S. INFRASTRUCTURE WARFARE TARGETS

✳ **Funds Transfer Systems**—in Culpepper, Virginia, several electronic switches handle federal and commercial funds transfers and transactions.

✳ **Internet**—Subject to both cyber and "bricks and mortar" attack.

✳ **Phone Systems**—Electronic Switching Systems (ESS) subject to hackers with techniques well documented at an array of sites in the Internet, and in such magazines as *2600*.

✳ **Alaska Pipeline**—Carries 10 percent of domestic oil for the U.S.

✳ **Time Distribution System**—all major systems depend upon accurate time, from stoplights to air traffic control.

✳ **Panama Canal**—still immensely important in the transport of raw materials and goods, and the transit of all U.S. Navy ships, save the carriers.

✳ **Worldwide Military Command and Control System (WWMCCS)**—particularly susceptible to soft attack, as demonstrated by Eligible Receiver (see MELISSA'S LESSON).

✳ **Natural Gas Pipeline system**—once crashed, would take months to restore.

✳ **Electric Power Grid**—highly interdependent, as demonstrated when the 1994 LA earthquake crashed systems all the way up to Idaho.

✳ **National Photographic Interpretation Center (NPIC)**—a ten-minute walk from the U.S. capitol, this is the repository and processing facility for all of the government's photographic intelligence.

Guarding The Information Empire:
ASYMMETRIC WARFARE

The Japanese attack on Port Arthur, China in 1905 was the first example of modern "asymmetric warfare." The initial attack on the Russian Pacific fleet at anchor in Port Arthur was made by a ridiculously small force of torpedo boats. Using surprise and pure audacity, the Japanese sank most of the fleet in port. The ships were not destroyed for the most part, simply disabled temporarily while at anchor in the harbor. The wreckage of the ships, as can be seen in photographs taken at the time, made the port itself fundamentally useless. The effect was not destroying a navy, but rather rendering it temporarily inactive and unrecoverable. The attack was on infrastructure.

The Japanese did not seek to destroy the fleet, merely to put it out of action for a decisive period of time. In so doing they echoed the tactical observation of Napoleon Bonaparte waiting on the cliffs of Boulogne across from England one century before, "Give me six hours control of the strait of Dover and I will gain mastery of the world."

After the Japanese attack on Port Arthur, the Russian Baltic fleet took months to steam south into the Atlantic, round the treacherous Cape Horn, coal at Cam Ranh Bay, Viet Nam, then as now a Soviet naval base, and arrive at the straits of Tsushima for the second, decisive and conventional battle with the Japanese fleet. That second Russian fleet was defeated by its own exhaustion.

A modern attack on a navy carrier group might involve the localized projection of force by aircraft, missiles, and undersea weapons. The expenditure in planning, logistics and equipment, not to mention human lives would be horrifying. In the present day, such an attack →

Asymmetric Warfare *continued*

→ would likely be considered too expensive, too uncertain and too risky. A subtler, though no less effective attack would be one which disabled the carrier group's ability to project force in a coordinated and decisive manner at the right time. An effective attack on their time systems might help do just that.

Imagine a small naval force seeking to secure the Straits of Malacca immediately prior to a takeover of Singapore. The task would be to reduce the risk of a larger naval force in the immediate area retaining control of the Straits, and thus prohibiting the takeover. A coordinated program of throwing the local time sources out of sync, wide-band jamming to forestall accurate communications, and other tactical moves against the infrastructure of communications and decision making could delay the speedy and accurate projection of force just long enough to achieve tactical success. Navigation systems would go down not only for ships, but also for the targeting of smart weapons. Secure communications would be impeded, leading to missed and garbled messages, hence confusion at sea.

All that would be necessary is ten of the right hackers, and a couple of million dollars. This may seem an absurd claim, but the fundamental reality of this kind of threat was confirmed in 1997 during a military exercise called Eligible Receiver. A team of NSA and Air Force hackers were given twenty days and the task of destroying the military command, control, and communications systems in the Pacific. After four days the exercise was brought to an early halt. The team had come so close to achieving the goal that further progress was deemed dangerous.

The lesson is simple. Victory can come from stunning an adversary at the right time. The inherent weaknesses in his own system will do the rest of the work. Just such stunning attacks on the soft empire are not only possible today, but a likely future exercise in geopolitical power.

From THE MAN WHO PHOTOGRAPHED THE WORLD, *Burton Holmes' striking photograph of the sinking of the Russian fleet by Japanese forces at Port Arthur, China*

Infowar Web Site

Created by Winn Schwartau

http://www.infowar.com

Type: Web site

First Developed: 1996

Price Range: Connect time

Key Features: Very rich in links

Ages: Post-high school

Obsolescence: Low

Further Information:
✳ *http://www.cert.org/advisories/CA-99-02-Trojan-Horses.html*
✳ *http://www.av.ibm.com/ Inside TheLab/Bookshelf/ ScientificPapers/ Gordon/ HH.html.*

Infowar.Com, Ltd
☎ (727) 556-0833

Winn Schwartau was a paranoid several years back, when he warned of information warfare. He was a loon when he and his friends started screaming about the Y2K problem.

He's no longer considered loony or paranoid. In fact, his Infowar conferences have become critical gatherings for the loosely bound network of people in government, industry, and the sciences who have set about the task of preparing for these troubles. His Web site is an always current, richly varied, very well-informed compendium of material on hackers, crackers, viral attacks, cyberterrorism, Trojan horses, plus the weakness and stupidity of government agencies and software vendors in the face of increasing threats to the cyberinfrastructure. Schwartau posts new stuff almost every day.

This is testimony to his being on top of things, but also a warning: There are new things to be on top of virtually every day. Apparently, the policy wonks in the Clinton administration are taking the threat seriously. The 1999 Clinton budget asks for over $2 billion to prepare for terrorism and protect critical infrastructure. Unfortunately, none of the money has been allocated yet.

3/2/99
Hackers* Reportedly Seize British Military Satellite

[This may or may not be true. Highly speculative. This story has not been verified.]

LONDON (Reuters) - Hackers have seized control of one of Britain's military communication satellites and issued blackmail threats, *The Sunday Business* newspaper reported.

The paper, quoting security sources, said the intruders altered the course of one of Britain's four satellites, which are used by defense planners and military forces around the world.

The sources said the satellite's course was changed just over two weeks ago. The hackers then issued a blackmail threat, demanding money to stop interfering with the satellite.

"This is a nightmare scenario," said one intelligence source. Military strategists said that if Britain were to come under nuclear attack, an aggressor would first interfere with military communications systems.

"This is not just a case of computer nerds mucking about. This is very, very serious and the blackmail threat has made it even more serious," one security source said.

Police said they would not comment as the investigation was at too sensitive a stage. The Ministry of Defense made no comment.

*[sic. Should be "crackers." —Ed.]

National Cryptologic Museum and Web Site

http://www.nsa.gov:8080/museum/

Type: Museum and related Web site

First Developed: 1995

Price Range: $0

Key Features: The neatest secrets

Ages: 10 and up

Obsolescence: None

Further Information: Read *The Puzzle Palace* by James Bamford before you go, to amp up the experience

No secrets on Earth are protected with as much judicious care as the codes and ciphers used for secret communication. The NSA (National Security Agency)—home of America's code–makers and codebreakers—is suspected of being the most expensive government agency of them all.

Yet America's codebreakers, and their associated quiet eyes and ears (often referred to obliquely as "national technical means") have a long, fascinating, and somewhat bizarre history. Only ten years ago, there were only a small number of books that told some of the story (*The Puzzle Palace, The American Black Chamber, The Codebreakers*), and a handful of publishers that risked putting out the more abstruse stuff (such as The Aegean Press).

Several years ago, just after the end of the Cold War, the NSA utterly blew the minds of everyone familiar with this hidden universe by creating a museum. "Open to the Public!" Check out the Web site, and see the picture of the senior intelligence officer from the former Soviet Union standing in the reception hall of the museum. The look on his face speaks volumes about how amazing it is that this museum exists at all.

A personal visit is much better than a visit to the Web site. There, explained and displayed, are devices which people gave their lives to protect. This is the stuff that led to the joke, "If I told you, I'd have to kill you." Some of the devices are no more than ten years old (for example, the NSA's first CRAY computer, and the legendary Thinking Machine, the massively parallel processing supercomputer).

Even more astonishing is the museum store, where you can get crypto game and puzzle books for the kids, and (honest to God) an NSA windbreaker. I wear mine constantly. It freaks people out big time.

The Cray XMP

SRI VALS

Values and Lifestyles Marketing Survey

http://future.sri.com/vals/valsindex.html

Reach the Consumers Who Drive Your Business

Type: Aggregation Web site

First Developed: 1978

Price: Freebie

Key Features: One stop shop for searching strategies and insights

Ages: 10 to the end

Obsolescence factor: High

Further Information:
✳ *http://www.knowthis.com/research/companies/psychographic.htm*
Stanford Research Institute
☎ (650) 859-6073

Who are you?

There are a lot of folks who think they know. Every time you get a piece of junk mail, it's because a marketeer somewhere thinks he knows what you want. Every TV ad that airs, every radio spot that runs, every Internet banner ad that flashes—they all are there because somebody thinks they've got your number.

Stanford Research Institute has made a bunch of companies believers in their system of categorizing consumers, called VALS. VALS™ (Values and Lifestyles) categorizes U.S. adult consumers into mutually exclusive groups based on their psychology and several key demographics.

The SRI folks claim VALS is unique because it highlights factors that motivate consumer buying behavior. Lots of marketers use the system, hence it is more than interesting to scope out the Web-based survey SRI runs. Answer the questions, and the system tells you who you are—at least in the eyes of the people who use the VALS system.

They think they know...
☞ Who you are
☞ What you buy and do
☞ Where you live
☞ How to get in touch with you
☞ Why you act the way you do

They aren't the only ones. Claritas has a whole system based on zip codes. Yankelovich has its system. Everybody's got a system. Question is, *do* they have your number? →

SRI VALS Values and Lifestyles *continued*

STANFORD RESEARCH INSTITUTE
VALUES AND LIFESTYLES CONSUMER CATEGORIES
(SRI VALS)

→ ■ **Actualizers**

Actualizers are successful, sophisticated, active, "take-charge" people with high self-esteem and abundant resources. They are interested in growth and seek to develop, explore, and express themselves in a variety of ways—sometimes guided by principle, and sometimes by a desire to have an effect, to make a change.

Image is important to Actualizers, not as evidence of status or power but as an expression of their taste, independence, and character. Actualizers are among the established and emerging leaders in business and government, yet they continue to seek challenges. They have a wide range of interests, are concerned with social issues, and are open to change. Their lives are characterized by richness and diversity. Their possessions and recreation reflect a cultivated taste for the finer things in life.

ACTUALIZERS — High Resources
FULFILLEDS ACHIEVERS EXPERIENCERS
BELIEVERS STRIVERS MAKERS
STRUGGLERS — Low Resources

© 1997 SRI Consulting. All rights reserved. Unauthorized reproduction prohibited.

■ **Fulfilleds**

Fulfilleds are mature, satisfied, comfortable, reflective people who value order, knowledge, and responsibility. Most are well educated and in (or recently retired from) professional occupations. They are well-informed about world and national events and are alert to opportunities to broaden their knowledge. Content with their career, families, and station in life, their leisure activities tend to center around the home.

Fulfilleds have a moderate respect for the status quo institutions of authority and social decorum, but are open-minded to new ideas and social change. Fulfilleds tend to base their decisions on firmly held principles and consequently appear calm and self-assured. While their incomes allow them many choices, Fulfilleds are conservative, practical consumers; they look for durability, functionality and value in the products they buy.

■ **Achievers**

Achievers are successful career- and work-oriented people who like to, and generally do, feel in control of their lives. They value consensus, predictability, and stability over risk, intimacy and self-discovery. They are deeply committed to work and family. Work provides them with a sense of duty, material rewards, and prestige. Their social lives reflect this focus and are structured around family, church, and career.

Achievers live conventional lives, are politically conservative, and respect authority and the status quo. Image is important to them; they favor established, prestige products and services that demonstrate success to their peers.

■ **Experiencers**

Experiencers are young, vital, enthusiastic, impulsive, and rebellious. They seek variety and excitement, savoring the new, the offbeat, and the risky. Still in the process of formulating life values and patterns of behavior, they quickly become enthusiastic about new possibilities, but are equally quick to cool. At this stage in their lives, they are politically uncommitted, uninformed, and highly ambivalent about what they believe. →

SRI VALS Values and Lifestyles *continued*

→ Experiencers combine an abstract disdain for conformity with an outsider's awe of others' wealth, prestige, and power. Their energy finds an outlet in exercise, sports, outdoor recreation, and social activities. Experiencers are avid consumers and spend much of their income on clothing, fast food, music, movies, and video.

■ Believers

Believers are conservative, conventional people with concrete beliefs based on traditional, established codes: family, church, community, and the nation. Many Believers express moral codes that are deeply rooted and literally interpreted. They follow established routines organized in large part →

Various Other Actualizer-Related Products and Activities

These categories represent a sample of some consumer activities that involve Actualizers either markedly more (high index) or less (low index) than the population at large.

Category	Index
Membership in Arts Association	382
Visit Art Museum in Past Year	302
Cross Country Skiing Past Year	291
Own Elect. Expresso/Capuccino Maker	268
Give Dinner Party 1/Month or More	240
Foreign Travel in Past 3 years	240
Cruise Ship Vacation in Past 3 Years	230
Swim 20+ days in Past Year	218
Own Import/Foreign Car	202
Bought Custom-Made Furniture Past Year	195
Own Hot Tub/Spa	189
Play Golf	175
Own Personal Computer at Home	175
Bought Sheet Music	168

Various Other Fulfilled-Related Products and Activities

These categories represent a sample of some consumer activities that involve Fulfilleds either markedly more (high index) or less (low index) than the population at large.

Category	Index
Swimming Pool/In Ground	197
Own Spreadsheet Software	192
Membership in Church Board	184
Stayed in Ski Resort in Last 12 Mo's	179
Own Station Wagon	179
Own Piano	176
Ordered Trees, Plants, Seeds by Mail	175
Belong to a Book Club	173
Own Backpacking Equipment	172
Own Binoculars	172
Woodworking in Last 12 Months	168
Own Shower Massager	154
Foreign Travel in Last 3 years	148
Have Automatic Garage Door Opener	132

Magazines and Newspapers Popular with Actualizers

Item	Index
Conde Nast Traveler	539
Scientific American	463
Audubon	413
Tennis	405
Sky Magazine (Delta Air)	402
Barron's	387
New Yorker	375
Travel & Leisure	374
N.Y. Times Daily Edition	368
National Geographic Traveler	340

Magazines and Newspapers Popular with Fulfilleds

Item	Index
Kiplinger's Personal Finance	251
The New Yorker	248
Smithsonian	242
Money	242
Wall Street Journal	206
National Geographic	198
Travel & Leisure	197
Country Living	193
Popular Science	189
Golf Magazine	182
New York Times Magazine	177

SRI VALS Values and Lifestyles *continued*

→ around home, family, and social or religious organizations to which they belong.

As consumers, Believers are conservative and predictable, favoring American products and established brands. Their income, education, and energy are modest but sufficient to meet their needs.

■ Strivers

Strivers seek motivation, self-definition, and approval from the world around them. They are striving to find a secure place in life. Unsure of themselves and low on economic, social, and psychological resources, Strivers are concerned about the opinions and approval of others.

Money defines success for Strivers, who don't have enough of it, and often feel that life has given them a raw deal. Strivers are impulsive and easily bored. Many of them seek to be stylish. They emulate those who own more impressive possessions, but what they wish to obtain is often beyond their reach.

■ Makers

Makers are practical people who have constructive skills and value self-sufficiency. They live within a traditional context of family, practical work, and physical recreation and have little interest in what lies outside that context. Makers experience the world by working on it—building a house, raising children, fixing a car, or canning vegetables—and have enough skill, income, and energy to carry out their projects successfully. Makers are politically conservative, suspicious of new ideas, respectful of government authority and organized labor, but resentful of government intrusion on individual rights. They are unimpressed by material possessions other than those with a practical or functional purpose (such as tools, utility vehicles, and fishing equipment.)

■ Strugglers

Struggler lives are constricted. Chronically poor, ill-educated, low-skilled, without strong social bonds, elderly and concerned about their health, they are often resigned and passive. Because they are limited by the need to meet the urgent needs of the present moment, they do not show a strong self-orientation. Their chief concerns are for security and safety.

Strugglers are cautious consumers. They represent a very modest market for most products and services, but are loyal to favorite brands.

Home page for
the Human Genome Project
(story opposite page)

GenBank (The Human Genome Project)

National Library of Medicine

http://www.ncbi.nlm.nih.gov/Entrez/index.html

"Science has 'explained' nothing; the more we know the more fantastic the world becomes and the profounder the surrounding darkness."

—Aldous Huxley, *Along the Road* (1925)

Type: Web site

First Developed: 1990

Price Range: Connect time

Key Features: You can look into the smoking pit

Ages: 10 and up

Obsolescence factor: Low

Further Information:

❋ *http://www.ornl.gov/ TechResources/Human_Genome/ home.html*
The Human Genome Project government site.
National Library of Medecine:
☎ (301) 496-9300

This is the entry port to the database that holds as much as man knows about his own genetic structure. Abandon all hope, all ye who enter here. The search for the secrets of the human gene is a combination of the Tower of Babel Project (now discontinued) and the California Gold Rush (now being re-enacted).

The byproducts may range from something close to divine knowledge, to hellish weapons, gigantic profits for companies that can fix all manner of human afflictions, and the temptation to play God in places where human beings have not recently demonstrated anywhere near enough wisdom and restraint.

Genbank is a product of the U.S. Human Genome Project. Begun in 1990, it is a 15-year effort coordinated by the U.S. Department of Energy and the National Institutes of Health to:

■ Identify all the estimated 80,000 genes in human DNA.

■ Determine the sequences of the 3 billion chemical bases that make up human DNA, store this information in databases, and develop tools for data analysis.

To help achieve these goals, researchers also are studying the genetic makeup of several nonhuman organisms. These include the common human gut bacterium *Escherichia coli*, the fruit fly, and the laboratory mouse. Look out for *E. coli,* because it has recently proven that it can be the host for an array of diseases.

The fact that the Human Genome Project makes no mention of the potentially hellish side of this stuff—the weapons—is an indication of the hubris that infects the people involved.

WHAT'S A GENOME?
AND WHY IS IT IMPORTANT?

❋ A genome is all the DNA in an organism, including its genes. Genes carry information for making all the proteins required by all organisms. These proteins determine, among other things, how the organism looks, how well its body metabolizes food or fights infection, and sometimes even how it behaves.

❋ DNA is made up of four similar chemicals (called bases and abbreviated A, T, C, and G) that are repeated millions or billions of times throughout a genome. The human genome, for example, has 3 billion pairs of bases.

❋ The particular order of As, Ts, Cs, and Gs is extremely important. The order underlies all of life's diversity, even dictating whether an organism is human or another species such as yeast, rice, or fruit fly, all of which have their own genomes and are themselves the focus of genome projects. Because all organisms are related through similarities in DNA sequences, insights gained from nonhuman genomes often lead to new knowledge about human biology.

PC Webopedia

http://www.pcwebopedia.com/

Type: Web site

First Developed: 1997

Price Range: Connect time

Key Features: An excellent example of what reference should be on the Web

Ages: 15 and up

Obsolescence: Low

Further Information:
✱ *http://www.webreference.com*

It appears that high technology has written the Full Employment Act for Lexicographers. The number of new words crafted and coined every year is astounding. This particular Web site does a more than credible job of keeping current.

Of particular interest are the top 15 most popular terms listed, and the 10 newest terms added. This place is just fascinating, and it does a fine job of work with long-standing terms as well. All the definitions are extensively hyperlinked, and enhanced with a boatload of references.

Originally assembled by Robert E. Margolis, a technical writing consultant.

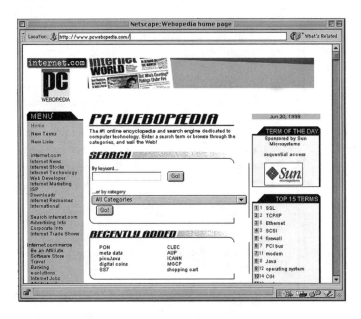

Tree of Life
Global Net-Based Distributed Database on Life
http://phylogeny.arizona.edu/tree/phylogeny.html

Type: Hierarchical, branched system of links corresponding to phylogenetic systems (ways of organizing organisms)

First Developed: 1996

Price Range: Connect Time

Key Features: Well thought-out Hyper library

Ages: 10 and up

Obsolescence: Low

Further Information: For a drier, academic treatment of the same subject (in other words, life) go to Harvard's Phylogenetic Web site ✳ *http://herbaria.harvard.edu/ treebase/index.html*
TreeBASE is a relational database being developed to manage and explore information on phylogenetic relationships, clearly by geeks who have little sense of what fun this all is—while the Tree of Life people clearly do.

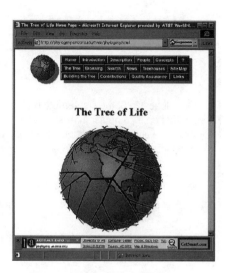

The Tree of Life is a collection of over a thousand Web pages containing information about the diversity of life. The pages are housed on 20 computers in four countries, and are authored by biologists from around the world. It is a vigorous attempt to lash together a loosely related group of phylogenetic sites into a database of globally "distributed" intelligence.

Each page contains information about one group of organisms (for example, the *Coleoptera* page gives information about all beetles; the *Salticidae* page about jumping spiders; the *Cephalopoda* page about squids, octopi, and related mollusks; and the *Fungi* page about fungi).

The pages are linked in the form of the evolutionary tree of organisms. Inevitably, this site is heavy on hierarchical structure (trunk to branches, to sub-branches, etc.) For example, the links from the page on frogs leads to pages on individual families of frogs, and eventually up to some individual species of frogs.

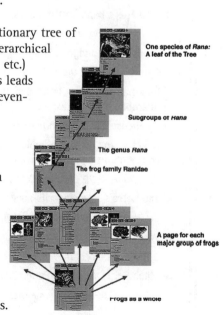

One species of *Rana:* A leaf of the Tree

Subgroups of *Rana*

The genus *Rana*

The frog family Ranidae

A page for each major group of frogs

Frogs as a whole

Here's where God and Web designers seem to be in utter agreement. Living things evolve from living things, and evolution yields complexity. The first glimmerings of the Tree of Life began sometime in the late '80s, when one of the designers flashed on the value of using hypermedia to expose nature's organization. He tried to do it on the Macintosh, but grew tired.

In 1993 he and his brother started again, this time on the Net. The really clever notion was having the Tree of Life distributed around the world, with different branches residing on different computers, and with a worldwide collection of experts authoring informative pages on their particular specialties.

→

Tree of Life Net Database *continued*

THE CRAYFISH PAGES

On 1 June 1995, the first remote branch of the Tree was added, the crayfish pages by Keith Crandall (U. Texas). These files resided on a computer in Austin, Texas. Since then, a number of remote branches have been added. The branches of the Tree that were authored by people other than the originals, which were attached to the Tree when the Tree was first formally announced (5 January 1996), are as follows. (Some of these contain no more than a branch, others are fairly complete.)

❖ **Keith Crandall's crayfish pages.**

First attached 1 June 1995; pages housed at the University of Texas, Austin.

❖ **Peter Beerli's Western Palearctic water frogs.**

13 June 1995; University of Washington.

❖ **Scott Stockwell's scorpion pages.**

16 June 1995; Smithsonian Institution.

❖ **John Lundberg's Chordata, Vertebrata, and fish pages.**

4 July 1995; at the home site.

❖ **John Friel's banjo catfish pages.**

5 July 1995; Florida State University.

❖ **James Albert and John Lundberg's electric fish.**

2 August 1995; at the home site.

❖ **Jonathan Browne, Clarke Scholtz, et al.'s Scarabaeoidea pages.**

24 August 1995; at the home site.

❖ **David Stern's pages on aphids and related insects with contributions by Nancy Moran.**

26 October 1995; Churchill College, Cambridge, England.

❖ **Tim Berra's salamanderfish page.**

20 December 1995; at the home site.

❖ **W.E. Hall's featherwing beetles page.**

2 January 1996; at the home site.

❖ **Mitch Sogin and David Patterson's basal eukaryote pages.**

3 January 1996; at the home site.

❖ **David Cannatella, Lori Bockstanz, et al.'s frog pages.**

3 January 1996; University of Texas at Austin. The addition of the branch turned Peter Beerli's pages into the first doubly-remote site (that is, a branch of the Tree on a computer other than the home computer that is connected not to the home site but to another remote site).

❖ **Allan Larson's salamander pages.**

3 January 1996; at the home site.

❖ **Michel Laurin's Terrestrial Vertebrates and Amniotes pages.**

4 January 1996; at the home site.

❖ **Rick McCourt et al.'s Green Plant pages**

4 January 1996; at the home site.

❖ **Michael Donoghue's angiosperm pages**

4 January 1996; at the home site.

❖ **Kenneth Sytsma and Jeffrey Hapeman's Myrtales pages**

4 January 1996; at the home site.

On 5 January 1996, when the Tree of Life project was first formally announced, the Tree itself contained 948 Web pages, housed in seven computers on two continents. Now its thousands of pages are housed all over the Net, and who knows how many braches there will be by the time you read this.

Tree of Life Net Database *continued*

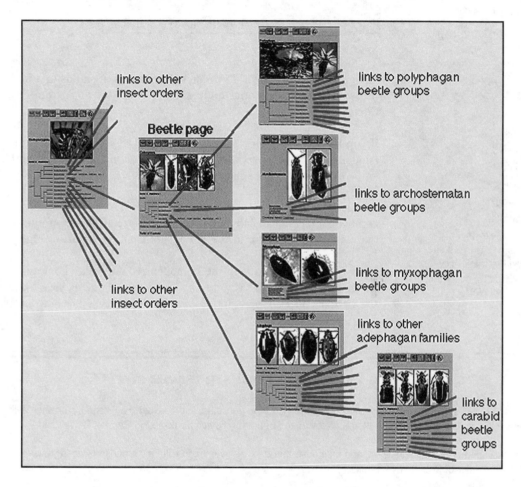

The root page of the entire Tree is housed on the home computer in Tucson, Arizona. The project is distributed across various computers (Web sites), so that any one computer will house only a portion of the Tree's branches. Towards the tips of the tree we envisage many hundreds of sites maintaining phylogenetic and other information concerning specific groups of organisms. And throughout, there would be links to other information on the Internet for that group.

Foyle's
Great British Bookstore
http://foylebooks.com/

Type: Bookstore

First Developed: 1904

Price Range: Round-trip air fare to London

Key Features: Endlessly well-stocked

Ages: 10 and up

Obsolescence: High

Further Information:
❊ *www.amazon.co.uk*
check out Amazon's UK Web site (recommended by Charles Levine of Random House: "…it's becoming a favorite with U.S. book sleuths.")

Foyle's is one of the world's greatest bookstores. It stands in a building all its own, four or five stories high, about 10 minutes' walk from Picadilly Circus in London.

If you like books, Foyle's is adequate reason to schedule a round trip to London. And if you live in or around London, you are that much closer to an incomparable book store experience.

Because it is in Britain, and not in the States, you will discover a cornocopia of English-language volumes (especially from around the world) that will never show up in the States, not even on Amazon.com.

There is nothing like this in the homogenized American book market. As I looked today, Foyle's is vectoring its Web site to a new Foyle's e-commerce site. Perhaps they are planning to become the British Amazon.com. I hope so.

FROM THE FOYLE'S BOOKSTORE WEB SITE

Foyle is a name that has a long relationship with bookselling and the public. In 1904, Gilbert Foyle and his brother William founded W&G Foyle in London, building it into the much-loved and honoured Foyles Bookshop in Charing Cross Road.

Gilbert and William were pioneers in 1904, and their adventurous spirit lives on in Gilbert's grandson Robert, third-generation bookseller and founder of Robert Foyle Books.

Like his grandfather before him, Robert and his team aim to provide speedy, reliable service, offering British books to the world through this efficient and convenient Web-based search, order, and delivery system.

You can still walk into Foyle's Bookshop in London, or you can take a look at Robert Foyle Books online bookshop. Both companies work independently of each other and no business connection exists now, but the family name continues to be synonymous with quality books and quality service.

Robert Foyle Books—good service from a name you can trust.

The Map Shop
U.K.-Based Retail Resource
http://www.themapshop.co.uk/

Type: Web site

First Developed: 1997

Price Range: Freebie

Key Features: One-stop shop for non-American mapping products

Ages: 10 and up

Obsolescence: Low

Further Information:
✱ *http://www.jpmaps.co.uk/*
Jonathan Potter is a fine source for antique and associated products such as globes.

The English are sailors by nature, and most of their history is—in one way or another—bound to the sea. As a result, they are fascinated with navigation, and that means maps.

In the States we have the National Geographic Society, and Rand McNally as classic sources of maps. Delorme and others have put the whole of the U.S. into digital form, and offered it up on DVD-ROMs and the Net. We also have satellite imagery from the USGS, the Russians (see TERRASERVER), and the DOD's National Imagery and Mapping Agency (NIMA).

Maps, however, often reflect cultural prejudices, and the U.S. has its share. ABC News can give a skewed view of the world today, when compared to the more worldly view presented by the BBC. For the same reasons you might want to listen to the BBC now and then, you might want to patronize a good British map retailer.

The Map Shop is just such a terrific source, filled with all kinds of European products—from British Ordnance survey maps of the English terrain to French products. Good maps of the third world are often more easily found here than in the States.

NPR Web Site
Web Site for National Public Radio
http://www.npr.org/programs/

Type: Aggregation Web site

First Developed: 1993

Price Range: Connect time

Key Features: Good broadcasting, easy on the nerves, nutritious for the head

Ages: College and up

Obsolescence: Medium

Further Information:
✱ *http://www.bbc.co.uk/ worldservice/*
for live and archived broadcasts of the BBC World Service

For a lot of baby boomers, Rush Limbaugh and Howard Stern are part of each morning's thrills. In the afternoon, after suffering the slings and arrows of the day, instead of such high-octane stuff, we find the comforting, dulcet tones of NPR just the thing.

Often enough, however, blown schedules cause me to miss NPR. Everything NPR broadcasts now gets encoded for playback with RealAudio (an audio decoding technology which is available for free over the Net at *www.realaudio.com*) and archived on the NPR site. Hence the stuff I regret the most missing on radio can be time-shifted. →

NPR Web Site *continued*

→ The archives for "All Things Considered," for example, go back to 1995.

While so much on the radio is vulgar, visceral stuff, this is the other kind of radio. And you can get it anytime you want. The NPR system even allows you to search for topics, so if you hear about a great broadcast, you can probably track it down by a keyword search on the NPR site.

AskJeeves

Search Site Using Natural Language Query

http://www.askjeeves.com/

Type: Search Web site

First Developed: 1998

Price Range: Connect time

Key Features: Natural language query, and real time display of incoming queries

Ages: 10 and up

Obsolescence: Medium

Further Information:
✻ *http://www.metaspy.com/spy/ filtered_b.html?shadow = 92180124.488*
For more insight into what people are searching on at this very moment, check out the "Metaspy" territory of the
✻ *www.go2net.com* search site

People have been trying to make searching easy long before the Internet reared its peculiar head. The obvious solution is to make the computer understand the same questions you might ask a teacher or a librarian.

Back in the early days of CD-ROM publishing (1990 and on), when big loads of data became publishable, "natural language query" came out of the lab, and started to show up in software. The problem was (and remains) this: The software was always looking for a kind of normalized English language—without idioms or slang. So you had to learn to use a new kind of carefully phrased English.

In the newer versions, as can be found in the latest version of Microsoft Access and the AskJeeves service over the Net, the problem is much the same. The English language is still fluid and complex, while software development techniques aren't nimble enough to keep up.

Still, for simple kinds of questions, Askjeeves.com can be helpful. Something like "Where is the state of Kansas?" will work fine. Try "How high did the Zeppelin fly?" and you may get a lot of peculiar responses. →

AskJeeves Search Site *continued*

→ It's also quite a bit of fun to check out the live display of the queries coming in at the moment on the Ask Jeeves site, as well as the list they maintain of the most popular queries, simply as an index to what is shooting through people's minds.

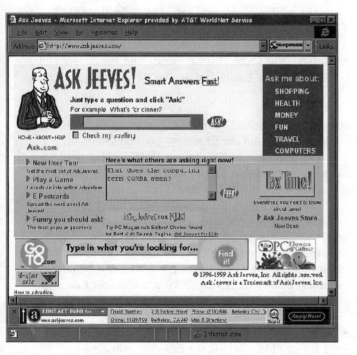

A RANDOM SAMPLING OF QUESTIONS FOR MR. JEEVES

These were the questions most frequently asked of Jeeves in the month of February 1999.

Find your favorite.

? Where can I find information about the Y2k problem?

? Where can I find a Spanish language dictionary online?

? Where can I find my horoscope?

? How can I find the right career?

? Where can I find desktop wallpaper online?

? Where can I find the Simpsons online?

? Where is the NASA Web site?

? Where can I find Nike online?

? Where can I find Yellow Pages online?

? Where can I find desktop themes for Windows?

? What is a blue moon?

? What is internic?

? Where can I find free greeting cards online?

? Where can I find information about soccer?

? Where can I learn about Chinese New Year?

? Who is Jeeves?

Character Counts

Web Site for Non-Religious Organization Devoted to Ethics

http://www.charactercounts.org/

Type: Web site

First Developed: 1997

Price Range: Connect time

Key Features: Simple commitment to good values

Ages: 10 and up

Obsolescence: Low

Further Information:
❋ *http://www.pbs.org/adventures/*
For something along the same vein, but oriented toward small children, a children's story site, drawn from William Bennett's kids version of the *Book of Virtues.*
also, The Josephson Institute of Ethics site:
❋ *http://www.josephsoninstitute.org*

This is the most encouraging site on the Net. It's not religious. It's not loony. There's no end-of-the-world rhetoric. There's no political agenda that I can discern. There is, however, an unyielding dedication to doing the right thing, and describing the principals that define the right thing.

This site holds the promise of things to come for which I dearly wish. I have children, and like any parent, I anguish over what evils and temptations they will be exposed to as they grow up and away from home. I see the vulgar, degraded behavior of some of their friends and the people and notions they are exposed to in the media and on the Net. I worry that is all they'll get.

But it is not and here is proof. Michael Josephson, the guy who founded the Josephson Institute of Ethics and the Character Counts! Coalition, is a lawyer and academic who made his money, got out, and decided to put his life to some better use. He worried that people were losing track of simple non-denominational values that are the glue that binds civilization together.

The program is founded on simple premises: "Effective character education is based on core ethical values rooted in democratic society, in particular, respect, responsibility, trustworthiness, justice and fairness, caring, and civic virtue and citizenship." Sounds a bit like the Boy and Girl Scouts. If I didn't have kids, I would probably think this all very unhip. But I do and it's not.

His foundation has programs in hundreds of schools, and people seem to flock to it. The part of the site I like best is the immense compendium of quotes from all manner and sort of people, living and dead. You can even download a big file, filled with the quotes.

Words to Live By:
The basic concepts that constitute Josephson's "Six Pillars of Character": Trustworthiness, Respect, Responsibility, Fairness, Caring, Citizenship. Details on each can be found at:
❋ *http://charactercounts.org/defsix.htm*

→

Character Counts *continued*

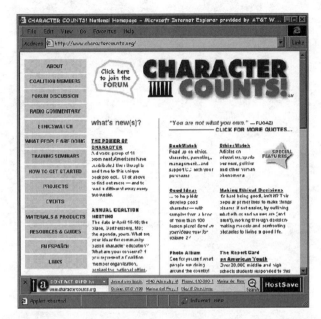

"The true test of civilization is not the census, nor the size of cities, nor the crops—no, but the kind of man the country turns out."

—*Ralph Waldo Emerson, 19th-century American essayist, public philosopher, and poet*

"Character cannot be developed in ease and quiet. Only through experience of trial and suffering can the soul be strengthened, vision cleared, ambition inspired, and success achieved."

—*Helen Keller, 20th-century American social activist, public speaker, and author*

"The measure of a man's character is what he would do if he knew he never would be found out."

—*Baron Thomas Babington Macauley, early 19th-century English historian*

"The proper time to influence the character of a child is about a hundred years before he's born."

—*William M. Inge, 20th-Century American playwright*

A STORY...
that the founder of Character Counts, Michael Josephson, told on the radio in LA:

A southern woman—I'll call her Lila—told me of an incident with her grandfather when she was only five. She was at his house all dressed up in a white dress with crinoline and gloves, proud as she could be. Her granddaddy told her she could go into the kitchen and get herself a special cookie. Next to the cookies was a stack of quarters. Lila, sure that no one was looking, took a quarter. When she returned with her cookie, her granddaddy asked her to show him her gloves. She held out only her left hand and he said, "Show me the other hand." When she revealed the quarter, she saw the disappointment in her granddaddy's eyes. Still, he "hugged her up" and said, "Darlin', you can have anything in the world that I have, but it breaks my heart that you would ever steal it."

Few things have as large an impact on shaping the values of a child as the sting of shame lovingly administered. It helps define right from wrong and gives a powerful emotional dimension to issues of ethics and character. In Lila's case, clearly expressed disappointment was enough—sometimes it takes more. How many of you remember experimenting with shoplifting only to be forced by a parent to return the stolen item and apologize?

You see, in those days, parents weren't too worried about ruining their kids' self-esteem by making moral judgments. They were more worried that anything short of unequivocal firmness would seem to condone dishonorable conduct. Modern parents who lack the wisdom or will to hold their children firmly accountable for their choices fail their children and endanger society.

THE VIRTUES PROJECT
A Web site devoted to Values

http://www.virtuesproject.com/

Like CHARACTER COUNTS, this is the work of an empassioned individual—Linda Popov. I heard of this because of a stray e-mail that appeared one day. The method of distribution reminds me of the use of audio cassettes in the 1970s, and faxes in the eighties. They fomented revolutions. I hear a vast amount about the bad stuff on the Net. Here's a bit of good stuff.

Plugging The Hole In The Moral Ozone

In the 1990s, a tragic succession of copycat killing sprees, in which children have been both the victims and the perpetrators, stunned America. We have had to face the fact that too many of our children are technical wizards and moral incompetents. Staring at the hole in the moral ozone, it is easy to give in to a numbing helplessness, but we dare not go back to sleep.

We can heal the virus of violence claiming our children by taking shared responsibility—responding ably. How often we have heard the African proverb that it takes a village to raise a child. As never before, we need to cultivate a village mind.

There are four gifts a village offers its children: kinship, friendship, mentorship and worship. If we are to save our children, we need to love them better. We need to fill the vacuum of virtue. According to all the world's spiritual traditions, the purpose of life is to cultivate our virtues—our love, our service, our kindness, our idealism.

There are steps to take, strategies that can save our children, say Linda Kavelin Popov and Dr. Dan Popov, cofounders of The Virtues Project and coauthors of *The Family Virtues Guide: Simple Ways to Bring Out the Best in Our Children*

and Ourselves. The Virtues Project was honored by the United Nations in 1994 as a model global program for families of all cultures.

The Strategies
The five strategies of The Virtues Project offer a more intimate form of kinship and mentorship, to bring out the best in our children and ourselves.

1. Speak the Language of Virtues: Replace shaming by naming virtues and empowering children to act on their virtues.

2. Recognize Teachable Moments: Turn stumbling blocks into stepping stones, by seeing the countless daily happenings as opportunities to cultivate virtues.

3. Set Clear Boundaries: Have ground rules based on virtues, with educative consequences. "We treat people, bodies, feelings, and things with respect." Apply restorative justice in our homes and schools.

4. Honor the Spirit: Address the need for meaning with routines of reverence, share family stories, give children something to believe in.

5. Offer the Art of Spiritual Companioning: Listen, deeply present, and support children and others to honor their feelings and help them make moral choices

May 5, 1999

CONTACT:
Linda Kavelin Popov
Tel: (250) 537-1978; Fax: (250) 537-4647
e-mail: lkp@virtuesproject.com
Web site: www.virtuesproject.com

Reference Desk

A Metapage Devoted to Reference Sources

http://www.refdesk.com

Type: Metasite

First Developed: 1990s

Price Range: Connect time

Key Features: A huge number of links, arranged by subject and cross-indexed by pages like My Virtual Newspaper, My Virtual Encyclopedia, and First Things First. Searchable.

Ages: All

Obsolescence: Low

One of the most explosive Web sites in the past few years has got to be *http://www.drudgereport.com* where fedora-sporting Matt Drudge has been re-inventing Walter Winchell in a digital age. Many people don't realize that one of the most useful Web sites is The Virtual Reference Desk by Bob Drudge, Matt's father.

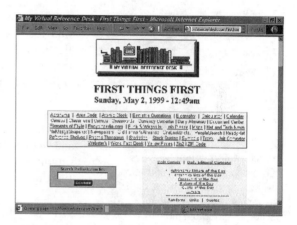

The only way to describe Refdesk is a "labor of love." It's not graphics-heavy, doesn't have any Shockwave or Java apps... what it has are links, thousands and thousands of links. Atomic Clocks to the Useless Facts page, *The New York Times* to *The Bahrain Tribune,* the Bermuda Stock Exchange to 200 Letters for Job Hunters.

It's simple, it loads fast and the links work. The uniqueness is in the sheer size of the lists and the clear care and attention that have been put into their choice and arrangement. It's about as good an example as there is on the Web of what the individual can accomplish.

Molecular Expressions
Web Archive for Micrographic Imagery
http://micro.magnet.fsu.edu/index.html

Buckyball thin film on silver

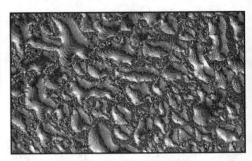

Type: Web image archive

First Developed: 1997

Price Range: Connect time

Key Features: Meant to be a promotional site, but rich with startling images

Ages: 10 and up

Obsolescence: Low

Further Information: Bill Gates' Corbis library keeps a good selection of microscopic images on hand as well (search on the word "microscopic" from within the site) ✥*http://www.corbis.com/image*

As much fun as it is to play with a microscope and samples of hair, blood, dust, and other things around the house, it's often hard to find and mount samples of the objects you'd really like to check out.

This site has most everything you might want already handy in digitized form. Although this site is built around the promotion of a book and the licensing of images for commercial use, it is overflowing with stunning images. Everything here is done with an optical microscope, and the digitizations are first rate.

Of particular interest are the images in the Silicon Zoo, all drawn from the artwork etched on the surfaces of computer chips. The Molecular Expressions Photo Gallery contains hundreds of examples of full-color photomicrographs (photographs taken through a microscope).

Each of the small images on the site is actually a link to a larger version of the image. This site is a very cheap way to avoid buying a microscope for your kids, and an equally entertaining way to pass a few hours on the Net, or to come up with a new image for the wallpaper on your computer screen.

From the Molecular Expressions Web site, an image of an HP chip design.

"Normally when we think about computer chips, the last thing that comes to mind is the inherent beauty of nature's vast wilderness. You can imagine our surprise when we stumbled across this silicon rendition of Colorado's Maroon Bells-Snowmass Wilderness Area on a Hewlett-Packard integrated circuit."

—Caption from Molecular Expressions Web Site image of an HP chip design

Molecular Expressions *continued*

MOLECULAR EXPRESSIONS IMAGE LIBRARIES
from micro.magnet.fsu.edu

AIDS THERAPEUTICS—Some images of hope for this dreadful disease.

AMINO ACIDS—The building blocks of proteins.

ANTIBIOTICS—Fungi are helping us kill bacteria.

ANTICANCER AGENTS—Good drugs for some bad diseases.

THE ARCHAEOLOGICAL COLLECTION—Ancient relics found in archeological digs.

AUSTRALIA—Photomicrographs from the land down under.

BEER—See what some of your favorite beverages look like under the microscope.

BIRTHSTONES—Check out the beautiful minerals that make birthstones.

BUCKYBALLS—The newly discovered third form of naturally occurring carbon.

CHIPSHOTS—Surface features of integrated circuits.

CHOLESTEROL—Beautiful shots of the artery-clogging steroid.

COCKTAILS—It's time for happy hour.

COMPUTER PARTS—Hard Disks, CD-ROMS, and other computer innards.

THE CRIME COLLECTION—Items used in crimes and law enforcement.

DINOSAUR BONES—Beautiful fossilized relics from these ancient reptiles.

DNA—Views of the genetic material.

DYES—Essential materials of the textile and printing industries.

THE EDUCATION COLLECTION—Things you use in school.

ENDORPHINS—Neural hormones for that all-natural high.

FATTY ACIDS—A close-up view of these essential biochemicals.

FEATHERS—These masterfully-crafted structures allow birds to fly.

FLAVORS—Chemicals used to make food taste good.

FRAGRANCES—Things that make you smell good.

HORMONES—See where many of your problems stem from.

ICE CREAM—The Ben and Jerry's Collection.

LIQUID CRYSTALS—The fourth state of matter.

MAGNETIC THIN FILMS—New technologies that provide more bytes.

METEORITES—Rocks from outer space.

MICROSCAPES—Multiple-exposure micrographic landscapes.

MINERALS—Essential salts.

MITOSIS—The process whereby cells divide.

MOON ROCKS—Remnants of the successful Apollo missions.

NEUROTRANSMITTERS—Chemicals that allow your brain cells to communicate.

NUCLEOTIDES—Much more than simply building blocks for RNA and DNA.

THE OCEAN SPRAY COLLECTION—Unique products from a unique company.

PEROVSKITES—The basis for high-temperature superconducting ceramics.

PESTICIDES—Drugs for Bugs.

PHARMACEUTICALS—Drugs for people.

PHYTOCHEMICALS—Drugs in the food we eat.

POLYMERS—Very long-chain molecules.

PRECIOUS METALS AND GEMS—Diamonds are a girl's best friend.

PROSTAGLANDINS—Bioactive lipids.

PROTEINS—The molecules that make up cells and enzymes.

THE RELIGION COLLECTION—From religions around the world.

SILICON ZOO—We've caged the creatures found on silicon computer chips.

SOFT DRINKS—Cool tools for a POP culture.

THE SPORTS COLLECTION—Football, baseball, and basketball—something for everyone.

SUGARS—Pour some sugar on me.

SUPERCONDUCTORS—A new revolution in the making.

SUPERLATTICES—Tomorrow's semiconductors today.

VEGETABLES—We're running the garden on the microscope.

VITAMINS—Our favorite essentials.

WINE—Is it red wine with fish or white wine with veal?

Concordance of Great Books

Cross-Referenced Digital Library of Great English Literature

http://www.concordance.com/

Type: Specialized search engine

First Developed: June 1998

Price Range: Connect time

Key Features: Full indexing of great books

Ages: 10 to the end

Obsolescence factor: Low

Further Information:
✳ *http://www.gutenberg.net/* for Project Gutenberg

William A. Williams Jr. is the Internet's sultan of citation—the man who posted The Concordance of Great Books on the Net. You can read the books straight through (Does anybody really want to read this stuff on a computer screen?), or you can track things down (Does anybody besides a Shakespeare fan know what a *bodkin* is?).

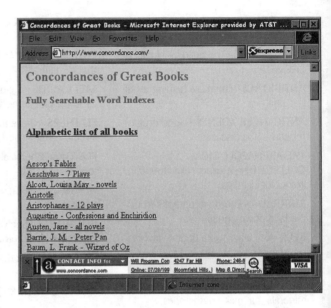

Williams is a Mormon, and he got a Mormon-like bug in his bonnet when chatting with a friend about the lineage of uses of words in the Bible and the Book of Mormon. He taught himself how to write code, and built his own search engine. He borrowed heavily from PROJECT GUTENBERG and others for source material, but the real value he has added is the indexing. *The New York Times* reports that based on the average number of hits per day, the most popular stops on the site are Mark Twain (about 18 hits), Charles Dickens (24), Jane Austen (11), the L.D.S. (Church of Jesus Christ of Latter-day Saints) Research page (13), and the Bible (5). Euripides has also racked up a fair number of visits. Kenneth W. Starr has fared less well, and Williams is thinking of dropping his report for lack of interest.

Concordance of Great Books *continued*

ON-LINE AT CONCORDANCE.COM
from www.concordance.com

Aesop's Fables
Aeschylus—7 Plays
Alcott, Louisa May—novels
Aristotle
Aristophanes—12 plays
Augustine—Confessions and Enchiridion
Austen, Jane—all novels
Barrie, J. M.—Peter Pan
Baum, L. Frank—Wizard of Oz
Bible
Beowulf
Bierce, Ambrose (wonderful satire!)
Blake, William—selected poetry
Brontë sisters—novels
Bunyan, John—Pilgrim's Progress
Byron, Lord
Carroll, Lewis—Alice in Wonderland, Through the Looking Glass
Cervantes—Don Quixote
Chaucer—Canterbury Tales
Chesterton, G. K.
Children's: Fairy Tales, Lewis Carroll's Alice and Looking-Glass, Aesop's Fables, Beatrix Potter
Civil War Books
Collins, Willkie: Moonstone, Woman in White
Cooper, James Fenimore—novels
Devotional: Cloud of Unknowing, Eddy—Science and Health (See St. Augustine separately)
Dante—Divine Comedy
Defoe, Daniel
Dickens, Charles—19 works
Dickinson, Emily—selected poetry
Dostoevsky
Dumas—novels
Eliot, George (Mary Ann Evans)
Epictetus
Emerson, Ralph Waldo
Euripides—21 plays
Exotic Literature

Fairy Tale Books (Red, Blue, Violet, Yellow combined)—Andrew Lang
Federalist Papers—Alex. Hamilton, et. al.
French and Spanish: Cervantes—Don Quixote, Hugo—Les Miserables
Gibbon—Decline and Fall of the Roman Empire
Gilbert/Sullivan—plays
Grant, U.S.—personal memoirs
Hardy, Thomas
Hawthorne
Herodotus
Historical books: Federalist Papers, Livy, Josephus, J & S Tanner
Homer—Works
Hugo, Victor—Les Miserables
Hume, David
Infidels Paradise: Ingersoll, Hobbes, Voltaire
James, Henry
James, William
Johnson, Samuel
Jonson, Ben
Joyce, James—novels
Kant—Critique of Pure Reason, Practical Reason, Judgment
Kempis, Thomas A.—Imitation of Christ
Kipling—novels and poems
The Holy Quran, translated by Maulvi Sher Ali
Lawrence, D. H.
L.D.S. Research: 1830 BoM, J.&S. Tanner, Papyrus, Bible, Spalding, View of Heb, Josephus
Lewis, Sinclair
Livy—History of Rome
London, Jack—novels
Longfellow
Melville
Milton
Montaigne—Essays
More, Sir Thomas
Nietzsche

Nostrodamus
Ovid
Plato—Dialogues
Plotinus
Poe, Edgar Allan
Potter, Beatrix—children's stories
Plutarch's Lives
Riley, James Whitcombe
Scott, Sir Walter—10 major works plus a biography
Scriptures: Bible, Apocrypha, Koran, Bhagavad-Gita, Tao Te Chung, Confucius
Shakespeare—Works
Sherlock Holmes—complete works combined, 4 novels—Doyle, A. Conan
Sophocles
Starr Report, White House Rebuttal, Clinton Grand Jury Testimony
Stevenson, Robert Louis—6 books
Stowe, Harriet Beecher
Sun-Tzu—The Art of War
Swift, Jonathan
Tacitus—Histories
Tennyson, Alfred Lord
Thackeray, William Makepeace
Thoreau, Henry David
Tolstoy, Leo—novels
Thucydides—Histories
Trollope, Anthony
Mark Twain: Tom Sawyer, Huck Finn, Puddinhead Wilson
Jules Verne—novels
Virgil—Aeneid
Wells, H. G.
Wallace, Lew—Ben Hur
White, Ellen
Wilde, Oscar
Whitman, Walt
Zola, Emile

Electronic Zoo

Resource Web Site for Links to Web Zoos

http://netvet.wustl.edu/E-ZOO.HTM

Type: Resource Web site

First Developed: 1997

Price Range: Connect time

Key Features: Simple commitment to good values

Ages: 10 and up

Obsolescence: Low

Further Information: For a quick text overview of many of the resources of NetVet, see
✳ *http://netvet.wustl.edu/ vetmed/*
at the World Wide Web Virtual Library

There's a St. Louis veterinarian who has crafted a work of love and obsession (as are so many of the best things on the Net). This one is all about animals.

The Electronic Zoo (linked from NetVet) originates from the vivid imagination and late night Websurfing of Dr. Ken Boschert, a veterinarian at Washington University's Division of Comparative Medicine, located in St. Louis, Missouri.

Dr. Boschert seems to spend his evenings tracking the best of net sites and resources—both professional and fun—on things animal. He keeps a pretty good what's new list, and a good "Pick of the Litter" selection. You can almost smell the mustiness of a vet's office, and hear the virtual squeaks, squacks, yelps, and whines.

It's not fancy and the graphics are crude, but it has the stuff.

Project Gutenberg

Web-Based Library of World Literature

http://www.gutenberg.net/

Type: Digital Library of Alexandria

First Developed: 1971

Price range: Connect time

Key Features: Great literature in ASCII

Ages: 10 and up

Obsolescence factor: Low

Further Information:
✳ *ftp://metalab.unc.edu/pub/ docs/books/gutenberg/*
is an FTP (File Transfer Protocol) site for Gutenberg e-texts at Cal Berkeley.

The idea here is that any text, once digitized, is likely to go anywhere. Electronic texts (e-texts) created by Project Gutenberg are made available in the simplest, easiest to use forms available. That means plain ASCII text files (what a PC calls a .TXT file). No layout, no typography. Pure words (they do take italics, underlines, and bolds and capitalize them).

Project Gutenberg began in 1971 when Michael Hart was given an operator's account with $100,000,000 of computer time in it by the operators of the Xerox Sigma V mainframe at the Materials Research Lab at the University of Illinois. →

Project Gutenberg *continued*

→ Hart decided there was nothing he could do, in the way of "normal computing," that would repay the huge value of the computer time he had been given... so he had to create $100,000,000 worth of value in some other manner. He decided the greatest value created by computers would not be computing, but would be the storage, retrieval, and searching of what was stored in our libraries.

He typed in the "Declaration of Independence" and tried to send it to everyone on the networks at the time, thus creating an early version of what would later be called a virus. Project Gutenberg was thus born as Hart figured he had "earned" the $100,000,000 because a copy of the Declaration of Independence would eventually be an electronic fixture in the computer libraries of 100,000,000 of the computer users of the future.

He has earned much more since. →

THE PROJECT GUTENBERG PHILOSOPHY

The Project Gutenberg Philosophy is to make information, books and other materials available to the general public in forms a vast majority of the computers, programs and people can easily read, use, quote, and search.

This has several ramifications:

❶ The Project Gutenberg texts should cost so little that no one will really care how much they cost. They should be a general size that fits on the standard media of the time...

❷ The Project Gutenberg texts should be so easily used that no one should ever have to care about how to use, read, quote and search them...

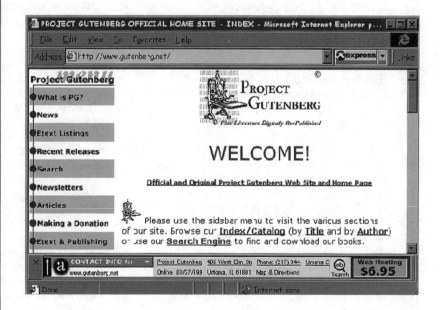

Project Gutenberg *continued*

PLANNED ADDITIONS FOR OCTOBER, 1999
from www.gutenberg.net

Oct 1999 On War, by Carl von Clausewitz [Volume 1]
[CvC #1][1onwrxxx.xxx]1946

Oct 1999 Egmont, by Johann Wolfgang Von Goethe
[Goethe #2][egmntxxx.xxx]1945

Oct 1999 The Witch, et. al, by Anton Chekhov
[Chekhov#14-28][witchxxx.xxx]1944

The stories contained in addition are:

Oct 1999 The Peasant Wives, by Anton Chekhov
[witchxxx.xxx]1944

Oct 1999 The Post, by Anton Chekhov
[witchxxx.xxx]1944

Oct 1999 The New Villa, by Anton Chekhov
[witchxxx.xxx]1944

Oct 1999 Agafya, by Anton Chekhov
[witchxxx.xxx]1944

Oct 1999 At Christmas Time, by Anton Chekhov
[witchxxx.xxx]1944

Oct 1999 Gusev, by Anton Chekhov
[witchxxx.xxx]1944

Oct 1999 The Student, by Anton Chekhov
[witchxxx.xxx]1944

Oct 1999 In The Ravine, by Anton Chekhov
[witchxxx.xxx]1944

Oct 1999 The Huntsman, by Anton Chekhov
[witchxxx.xxx]1944

Oct 1999 Happiness, by Anton Chekhov
[witchxxx.xxx]1944

Oct 1999 A Malefactor, by Anton Chekhov
[witchxxx.xxx]1944

Oct 1999 Peasants, by Anton Chekhov
[witchxxx.xxx]1944

Oct 1999 Louis Lambert, by Honore de Balzac
[de Balzac #86][lmbrtxxx.xxx]1943

Oct 1999 Rise and Fall of Cesar Birotteau, by Honore de
Balzac [HdB85][rfbrtxxx.xxx]1942

Oct 1999 Letters of Two Brides, by Honore de Balzac
[HdB#84][l2brdxxx.xxx]1941

Oct 1999 Christ in Flanders, by Honore de Balzac
[Balzac#83][flndrxxx.xxx]1940

Oct 1999 A Gentleman of France, by Stanley Weyman
[Weyman#2][gntfrxxx.xxx]1939

Oct 1999 Resurrection, by Leo Tolstoy
[Leo Tolstoi] [LT #6][resurxxx.xxx]1938

Oct 1999 The Second Jungle Book, by Rudyard Kipling
[RK #6][2jngbxxx.xxx]1937

Oct 1999 Letters from England, by Elizabeth Davis Bancroft
[ltengxxx.xxx]1936

Oct 1999 Adventures of Major Gahagan, by Thackaray
[W.M.T.8][majghxxx.xxx]1935

Oct 1999 Songs of Innocence and Experience, by Wm. Blake
[2][sinexxxx.xxx]1934

Oct 1999 The Great Hoggarty Diamond, by Thackeray
[W.M.T.7][gthgdxxx.xxx]1933

Oct 1999 Early Kings of Norway, by Thomas Carlyle
[T.C. #6][knrwyxxx.xxx]1932

Oct 1999 The Zeppelin's Passenger,
by E. Phillips Oppenheim
[zplnpxxx.xxx]1931

Oct 1999 Penguin Island, by Anatole France
[pngwnxxx.xxx]1930

Oct 1999 School For Scandal, by Richard Brinsley Sheridan
[scndlxxx.xxx]1929

Oct 1999 Elinor Wyllys, by Susan Fenimore Cooper
[Volume 2] [1wyllxxx.xxx]1928

Oct 1999 Elinor Wyllys, by Susan Fenimore Cooper
[Volume 1] [1wyllxxx.xxx]1927

Oct 1999 Elinor Wyllys, by Amabel Penfeather
[Volume 2] [2wyllxxx.xxx]1928

Oct 1999 Elinor Wyllys, by Amabel Penfeather
[Volume 1] [1wyllxxx.xxx]1927

Oct 1999 Grandfather's Chair, by Nathaniel Hawthorne
[NH #8][gfchrxxx.xxx]1926

Oct 1999 Droll Stories [V. 1], by Honore de Balzac
[HdB #82][1drllxxx.xxx]1925

Oct 1999 Many Voices, by E. Nesbit
[Poems] [E. Nesbit #8][mnyvcxxx.xxx]1924

→

Project Gutenberg *continued*

➔ **Planned Additions** (continued)

Oct 1999 The Poisoned Pen by, Arthur B. Reeve
[tppenxxx.xxx]1923

Oct 1999 Deirdre of the Sorrows, by J. M. Synge
[Synge #7][drdrexxx.xxx]1922

Oct 1999 The Chouans, by Honore de Balzac
[de Balzac #81] [chounxxx.xxx]1921

Oct 1999 Billy Baxter's Letters, By William J. Kountz, Jr.
[bbxtlxxx.xxx]1920

Oct 1999 Ballads, by Horatio Alger, Jr.
[H. Alger Jr. #10][blldsxxx.xxx]1919

Oct 1999 Long Odds, by H. Rider Haggard
[H. R. Haggard #8][loddsxxx.xxx]1918

Oct 1999 The Queen of Hearts, by Wilkie Collins
[Collins#21][qnhrtxxx.xxx]1917

Oct 1999 The Great Stone Face, et. al. by Nathaniel
Hawthorne
[totwmxxx.xxx]1916; Includes The Great Stone Face
and other Tales from the White Mountains

Oct 1999 Sketches From Memory, by Nathaniel
Hawthorne [#7] [totwmxxx.xxx]1916

Oct 1999 The Great Carbuncle, by Nathaniel Hawthorne
[#6] [totwmxxx.xxx]1916

Oct 1999 The Ambitious Guest, by Nathaniel Hawthorne
[#5] [totwmxxx.xxx]1916

Oct 1999 The Great Stone Face, by Nathaniel Hawthorne
[#4] [totwmxxx.xxx]1916

Oct 1999 Second Thoughts of An Idle Fellow, by Jerome
[#14][scthkxxx.xxx]1915

Oct 1999 [Reserved for The Titanic
[xxx.xxx]1914*

Oct 1999 The Drums Of Jeopardy, by Harold MacGrath
[jprdyxxx.xxx]1913

Oct 1999 The Muse of the Department, by de Balzac
[HdB #80][msdptxxx.xxx]1912

Oct 1999 Concerning Christian Liberty, by Martin Luther
[#6][clbtyxxx.xxx]1911

Centers for Disease Control Web Site
U.S. Government Research Center for Disease and Epidemics
http://www.cdc.gov/

Type: Web site

First Developed: 1996

Price Range: Connect time

Key Features: The most advanced info on mortality and morbidity in the world

Ages: High school and beyond

Obsolescence: Low

Further Information: See THE COBRA EVENT and GENBANK

Hollywood loves this place. No wonder, because some of the most dramatic activities in the world go on here. The people at CDC look after evidence of biological warfare activities, the appearance of new diseases (like HIV and legionnaires'), and the control of old ones (Ebola, Marburg, and hemorrhagic fever).

There are many sub-groupings of CDC reflected off the main site. One of the most interesting is the National Center for Infectious Diseases (NCID). There is an encyclopedia of all those diseases, with excellent descriptive material on display.

The travel information section is a rich source of info on emerging disease threats throughout the world and on the readiness of inoculations and vaccines.

All in all a fascinating site, where the appearance of one of those little NEW! logos on any page sends a shiver up my spine. ➔

Centers for Disease Control Web Site *continued*

DISEASE INFORMATION
Viral Hemorrhagic Fevers:
Fact Sheets from www.cdc.gov

EBOLA HEMORRHAGIC FEVER

What is Ebola hemorrhagic fever?
Ebola hemorrhagic fever is a severe, often-fatal disease in humans and nonhuman primates (monkeys and chimpanzees) that has appeared sporadically since its initial recognition in 1976.

The disease is caused by infection with Ebola virus, named after a river in the Democratic Republic of the Congo (formerly Zaire) in Africa, where it was first recognized. The virus is one of two members of a family of RNA viruses called the Filoviridae. Three of the four species of Ebola virus identified so far have caused disease in humans: Ebola-Zaire, Ebola-Sudan, and Ebola-Ivory Coast. The fourth, Ebola-Reston, has caused disease in nonhuman primates, but not in humans.

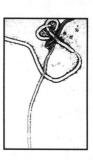

Electron micrograph of Ebola virus.
Courtesy Centers for Disease Control and Prevention

Where is Ebola virus found in nature?
The exact origin, locations, and natural habitat (known as the "natural reservoir") of Ebola virus remain unknown. However, on the basis of available evidence and the nature of similar viruses, researchers believe that the virus is zoonotic (animal-borne) and is normally maintained in an animal host that is native to the African continent. A similar host is probably associated with the Ebola-Reston species isolated from infected cynomologous monkeys that were imported to the United States and Italy from the Philippines. The virus is not known to be native to other continents, such as North America.

Where do cases of Ebola hemorrhagic fever occur?
Confirmed cases of Ebola hemorrhagic fever have been reported in the Democratic Republic of the Congo, Gabon, Sudan, and the Ivory Coast. An individual with serologic evidence of infection but showing no apparent illness has been reported in Liberia, and a laboratory worker in England became ill as a result of an accidental needle-stick. No case of the disease in humans has ever been reported in the United States. Ebola-Reston virus caused severe illness and death in monkeys imported to research facilities in the United States and Italy from the Philippines; during these outbreaks, several research workers became infected with the virus but did not become ill.

Ebola hemorrhagic fever typically appears in sporadic outbreaks, usually spread within a health-care setting (a situation known as amplification). It is likely that sporadic, isolated cases occur as well but go unrecognized. A table showing a chronological list of known cases and outbreaks is available.

How is Ebola virus spread?
Infection with Ebola virus in humans is incidental—humans do not "carry" the virus. Because the natural reservoir of the virus is unknown, the manner in which the virus first appears in a human at the start of an outbreak has not been determined. However, researchers have hypothesized that the first patient becomes infected through contact with an infected animal.

After the first case–patient in an outbreak setting (often called the index case) is infected—humans can transmit the virus to each other in several ways. People can be →

Centers for Disease Control Web Site *continued*

Fact Sheets from www.cdc.gov *continued*

→ exposed to Ebola virus from direct contact with the blood and/or secretions of an infected person. This is why the virus has often been spread through the families and friends of infected persons: in the course of feeding, holding, or otherwise caring for them, family members and friends would come into close contact with such secretions. People can also be exposed to Ebola virus through contact with objects, such as needles, that have been contaminated with infected secretions.

Nosocomial transmission has been associated frequently with Ebola outbreaks. It includes both types of transmission described above, but it is used to describe the spread of disease in a healthcare setting such as a clinic or hospital. In African health-care facilities, patients are often cared for without the use of a mask, gown, or gloves, and exposure to the virus has occurred when health-care workers treated individuals with Ebola hemorrhagic fever without wearing these types of protective clothing. In addition, when needles or syringes are used, they may not be of the disposable type, or may not have been sterilized, but only rinsed before reinsertion into multi-use vials of medicine. If needles or syringes become contaminated with the virus and are then reused, numbers of people can become infected.
The Ebola-Reston virus species that appeared in a primate

research facility in Virginia may have been transmitted from monkey to monkey through the air in the facility. While all Ebola virus species have displayed the ability to be spread through airborne particles (aerosols) under research conditions, this type of spread has not been documented among humans in a real-world setting, such as a hospital or household.

Ebola hemorrhagic fever prevention poster used in the Kikwit outbreak

What are the symptoms of Ebola hemorrhagic fever?

The signs and symptoms of Ebola hemorrhagic fever are not the same for all patients. The table below outlines symptoms of the disease, according to the frequency with which they have been reported in known cases.

Time Frame		Symptoms that occur in most Ebola patients		Symptoms that occur in some Ebola patients
Within a few days of becoming infected with the virus:	⫸	High fever, headache, muscle aches, stomach pain, fatigue, diarrhea	⫸	Sore throat, hiccups, rash, red and itchy eyes, vomiting blood, bloody diarrhea
Within one week of becoming infected with the virus:	⫸	Chest pain, shock, and death	⫸	Blindness, bleeding

Ideatree
Web Site Devoted to Ideas
http://www.ideatree.com

Type: Source of Pure Ideas
First Developed: 1997
Price Range: Free
Key Features: Broadly relevant
Ages: Post high school
Obsolescence: Low
Further Information: Check out
❋ *http://www.mou.org/index.html*

Noise. Entropy. Chaos. Catastrophe. Phase Transition. Fractals. Wavelets. Complexity. Dynamic Systems. Coherence. The first time I heard most of these terms, I was attending summer courses run by the Maharishi Mahesh Yogi, for people who practiced Transcendental Meditation. He brought in physicists, mathematicians, and medical experts to draw extraordinarily abstract analogies between these cutting-edge scientific concepts and ancient Hindu philosophies and scriptures.

It may have been easy to blow the minds of young sixties meditators (many of whom were just a few months high and dry of the drug culture), but he had the same effect on the scientists and professionals. Outsiders, like parents and journalists, tended to treat all this as flaky, if not entirely loony. Since that time, applying such abstractions to all kinds of everyday stuff has transited from weird to fashionable and then to commonplace.

The Ideatree is a terrific Web site that clusters lots of essays and free-form HTML presentations on such scientific abstractions, often with yeasty sixties-style musings on the analogies to the real world. My favorite essays on the site are on the subjects of change (catastrophe theory, chaos, dynamic systems) and noise (information theory and the like).

NOISE

Too much change, too much information, too much chaos, too much noise. All ways of saying the same thing. All part of the stuff that causes stress and fatigue. Backs break, bridges fail, cars crash, people can't handle it any more, and they freak.

Then again, put someone in an anechoic chamber—an echoless, noiseless room—and they will eventually lose it. A certain measure of noise, background noise, is necessary for one to stay sane. Babbling brooks, the hum of the kitchen refrigerator, wind blowing through the hay, the pitter-patter of little feet.

The mathematical manipulation of signal and noise lies at the core of moving data and managing error correction (see Surge Networks), and is the essence of code-making and code-breaking (see Silicon Dreams, written by Robert Lucky). A quote from a terrific article found on the Ideatree site (www.ideatree.com):

> The mathematical ground for this growing view comes from Chaos Theory and the Complexity work which appended itself thereto. "Chaos," mathematicians proclaim, "is nothing more or less than differential equations which feed back on themselves. 'Noise,' therefore, is computable, and therefore, usable." And so on. Thus, "noise" is drug, clawing and screaming, down into science itself. One wonders if it will ever re-emerge into the fullness of reality.

TEN RULES TO BUY BY
THE INFORMATICA GUIDE TO BANDWIDTH

1. Buy fast access, both ways.

Although you may think you only want fast downloads, eventually you will want fast uploads for videoconferencing and e-mail. You may not have a choice between DSL (digital subscriber line), cable modem and ISDN (integrated services digital network) in your area. Take what you can get, but get it fast.

2. Get DSL.

DSL doesn't require any new wiring, and lives on top of an existing telephone line. You will get telephone company quality service, not cable company service. There are several levels of bandwidth—incoming and outgoing, and the speeds are relatively constant. Get DSL now, because the equipment can become fully subscribed, and until such time as there is new equipment installed, service providers will have to put a moratorium on new accounts.

3. If you can't get DSL, get cable modem.

Cable modem can be very fast, but it depends upon existing cable wiring. It is very sensitive to bad wiring (including splitters—those little devices that divide the cable signal into two or more signals). Cable modem speed degrades when more people are hooked up in your local circuit. Cable modem security is less than ideal, and people on your circuit can get into your system (somewhat like the party lines of old telephone systems). Cable modem support and repair are provided by cable companies. Nuff said.

4. If you can't get cable modem, get ISDN.

ISDN is fast, but it requires special cabling, both to your house and then to your computer. Pricing is complex, and no one ever explains it without being confusing. It is the old way of doing things, and unless you do professional audio work, it is the least preferred means of getting good bandwidth into your home.

5. If you can't get high bandwidth, get local access without toll charges.

Local dial-up access (from the likes of Earthlink, ATT, Mindspring and AOL) is almost always $25 or less per month. However, if the call to the dial-up access number is a toll call, yout telephone charges may be 7 to 15 times as much.

6. Don't sign a long-term contract.

Prices are constantly in decline for high bandwidth services, and the necessary equipment is always getting smaller and cheaper. The services themselves get faster and more efficient. A long-term high bandwidth contract is as dumb as a long-term cell phone commitment. In other words, don't commit to anything longer than 12 months, at most. →

→ **(THE LAST FOUR OF THE INFORMATICA TEN RULES TO BUY BANDWIDTH BY...)**

7. Stay away from AOL e-mail.

AOL e-mail is the stinker of the industry. None of the existing e-mail programs can pick up AOL e-mail, only the AOL program itself can do that. Also, AOL will not automatically transfer your incoming mail to another account. This severely limits your ability to exploit the fast e-mail pickup you might otherwise have through high bandwidth. It also inhibits your ability to move your e-mail account elsewhere.

8. Don't buy equipment... rent.

Don't let any high bandwidth supplier talk you into buying modems and the like. Either make it part of the monthly charges, or get it for free (through special promotional offers, which are very common).

9. Trust, but verify.

The speed of the high bandwidth service can vary, and sometimes degrades over time. Use a software sensor (like the Internet Packet Speed sensor in the Norton Utilities, or a program like VISUALROUTE 4.0) to watch what the constant speed of your service is. If it isn't up to snuff, complain to the provider. Sometimes they have not noticed the degradation, and you will get better service if you ask for better service.

10. Pay attention to security.

Cable, and to a lesser extent DSL, make your machine vulnerable to cracking. Use something like ATGUARD or INTRUDER ALERT to set up a local firewall.

HACKER *vs.* CRACKER:

Crackers are individuals whose sole aim is to break into secure systems for the purpose of stealing and corrupting data. Hackers are more interested in gaining knowledge about computer systems and possibly using this knowledge for playful pranks. Although hackers still argue that there's a big difference between what they do and what crackers do, the mass media have failed to understand the distinction, so the two terms — "hack" and "crack" — are often used interchangeably.

FIREWALL:

A system designed to prevent unauthorized access to or from a private network. Firewalls can be implemented in both hardware and software, or a combination of both. Firewalls are frequently used to prevent unauthorized Internet users from accessing private networks connected to the Internet, especially intranets. All messages entering or leaving the intranet pass through the firewall, which examines each message and blocks those that do not meet the specified security criteria.

—Definitions from Random House Webster's Computer & Internet Dictionary

Intellicast Weather

Accuweather Forecast on the Net

http://www.intellicast.com/weather/usa

Type: Weather info metasite

First Developed: 1998

Price Range: Connect time

Key Features: One stop shop for weather forecasts

Ages: 10 and up

Obsolescence: Low

Further Information:
✳ *www.weather.com*
for The Weather Channel's home page:
✳ *http://www.nws.noaa.gov/*
for National Weather Service's home page:
✳ *http://www.fnmoc.navy.mil/*
for the US Navy's weather page.

For years WSI (Weather Services International) has provided weather status and forecasts to you from the boonies of Massachusetts, but you never knew it because the reports always seem to be coming from your local radio or TV news broadcast.

Syndicated and packaged for local consumption, the reports are often tagged with the brand name Accuweather. Why is there is any demand for this at all, when the U.S. government National Weather Service (see below) does a reasonable job of predicting the weather, and then proliferating its reports in an array of forms?

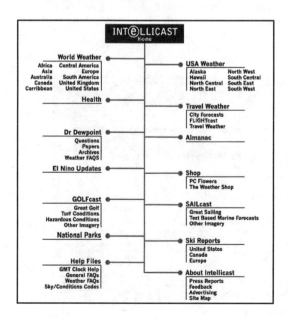

It seems to all come down to packaging (soap in a generic box is less marketable than Dove). WSI has done a great job of packaging weather on its Intellicast site. It is better and more convenient than the weather reports you'll find on CNN and MSNBC. Consistently ranked among the top 100 Web sites by Relevant Knowledge (see MEDIAMETRIX), Intellicast sets a fine standard for quality, in-depth coverage of world weather.

WWV/WWVH (NIST)

Source for Accurate Time

http://www.boulder.nist.gov/timefreq/wwv/wwv.html

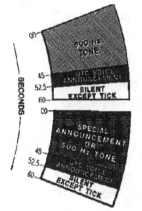

Type: Radio Broadcast

First Developed: 1923

Price Range: Already paid for

Key Features: Ubiquitous

Ages: 10 and up

Obsolescence: Never

Further Information:

❋ *http://www.bldrdoc.gov/ timefreq/pubs/sp432/s_wwv.htm* for NIST's explanation of the radio stations;

❋ *http://www4.nas.edu/beyond/ beyonddiscovery.nsf/ DocumentFrameset?OpenForm &TheGlobalPositi* for an explanation of the role of atomic clocks in the Global Positioning System (GPS);

❋ *http://www.tmoj.jpn.hp.com/ tmo/pia/broadcast/PIAProd/Not es/English/5965-9782E.html* for a Hewlett Packard explanation of how the time system works.

Here's the place whence comes time on the radio. There are others, of course, but this is the place the U.S. government funds in order to distribute time to the public. WWV/WWVH can be heard at 5,000 MHz, 10,000 MHz, and 15,000 MHz on virtually any shortwave radio, anywhere in the Western Hemisphere and the Pacific.

The clock it uses is a cigar-shaped device, about seven feet long, and one foot in diameter. It watches cesium atoms resonate (9,192,631,770 times a second), a standard for time accuracy that was set by international agreement in 1967. The clock costs about $200,000,000.

The signal drives electrical power grids, TV networks, and the new radio-controlled clocks. And a bazillion other important things. It is part of a very large network of some 230 atomic clocks which feed their "product" into the Bureau International de l'Heure (BIH) in Paris. There the signal is vetted, and miniscule corrections are recommended for each clock.

But you get it for free.

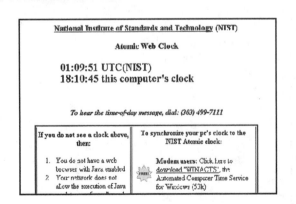

Guarding The Information Empire:

HOW LONG IS A NANOSECOND?

The product that WWVH delivers appears in deceptively simple garb. Every minute of every hour of every day a pleasant woman's voice reports something like this, "At the tone, eight hours thirty-seven minutes, coordinated universal time." Then, at the moment the new second begins, the obligatory beep, followed by another 50 seconds worth of electronic ticks. At the beginning of every hour, instead of the stroke of a bell, a 1500hz tone—roughly the pitch of a child's whistle—runs for 0.8 seconds.

All of this is hyperaccurate. Not just one clock, but an interlocking network of clocks—a system—insures that no individual clock can be far off. Although these clocks are very good, it's just possible that one might drift off a bit, perhaps to the extent of several nanoseconds. That is an infinitesimally small period of time—so small as to be hard to explain. The Navy's recently deceased Grace Hopper, the woman who some say invented computer programming, used to carry around about a foot-long stretch of string, referring to it as her own personal nanosecond: That, she explained, was the distance light traveled in a billionth of a second. Since it's hard to comprehend how fast light travels, this explanation falls a bit short.

Perhaps another way to imagine what a nanosecond means is to consider a television picture. Thirty times a second a new picture is constructed on the screen. At that rate, the individual pictures don't flicker, but rather meld together into a moving picture for our eyes. If you wiggle your finger in front of a TV, you can just barely begin to observe the difference between one of the pictures and the next. To construct each one of those pictures, something called a "flying spot" travels left to right across the screen at a slight diagonal. It is a beam of focused electronic energy causing the phosphors on the screen to glow.

When it reaches the right edge of the TV screen, after having drawn its line of varying degrees of light, it leaps back to the left to start again. After doing this over 250 times in the space of a 30th of a second, enough to create a stack of these horizontal lines, from top to bottom, the picture is complete. Then it is all left to fade away, and the flying spot shoots to the top left of the screen to start again.

Imagine how fast, then, that flying spot is moving across the TV screen. Now imagine a single letter from a sentence about the size that the warning "void where prohibited by law" appears at the bottom of the screen on a commercial. If you were to take the distance between the sides of the letter "i" in the word "void," and consider the time it would take for the flying spot to make its way across that tiny little void, you would just about have 200 nanoseconds. 200 billionths of a second. 0.02 milliseconds. An eternity for some of the more sensitive systems of modern technology. An error of incalculable proportions.

Satellite Imagery from USGS

U.S. Government Site for Access to Geo-Imagery

http://mapping.usgs.gov/www/products/1product.html

Type: E-commerce from the government

First Developed: 1997

Price Range: Varies (well under $100 per image)

Key Features: Very wide coverage

Ages: 10 and up

Obsolescence factor: Low

Further Information: Check out unclassified military reconnaissance images offered by USGS. Consider TERRASERVER as an alternative source
❋ *http://www.terraserver.com*

Pictures of where you live, from way up high!

Virtually every inch of urban/suburban/exurban America has been photographed from above. Every bureaucrat and policy wonk trades in this stuff to figure out everything from how to redistrict (the artful, bureaucratic term for gerrymandering) to where your plumbing should go.

Maybe you can't put terrain data or millimeter wave surveys to practical use, but having a nice picture of the neighborhood—from straight up above—is kind of fun. The U.S. Geological Survey archives this kind of stuff, and they'll make a beautiful picture for very few bucks.

From the Web site: Indianapolis Motor Speedway in Indiana. The track is 2.5 miles around. This track is home to the Indianapolis 500 in May and NASCAR's Brickyard 400 in August. Note the golf course inside the track.

SATELLITE IMAGES AND SATELLITE-DERIVED DATA

Products archived and available through the USGS with substantial coverage of the United States include:

■ **Satellite Photographs**
From NASA.

■ **Digital Satellite Images**
Products include Advanced Very-High Resolution Radiometer (AVHRR) images and Land Satellite (LANDSAT) Thematic Mapper (TM) and Multispectral Scanner (MSS) digital data.

■ **Photo Products Derived from Airborne and Satellite Sensor Data**
These include color and black-and-white photographic products generated from Advanced Very High Resolution Radiometer (AVHRR), Side-Looking Airborne Radar (SLAR), Land Satellite (LANDSAT), and Systeme Probatoire d'Observation de la Terre (SPOT) imagery digital data.

Terraserver

http://www.terraserver.com

Type: Search engine from Bill Gates and an array of collaborators

First Developed: 1998

Price: Connect time, or $10–$20 for downloads and printouts

Key Features: Limited coverage

Ages: 10 and up

Obsolescence: Low

Further Information:
❋ *http://www.spin-2.com/*
Visit the SPIN-2 Website, and see how the Russians market their technology
❋ *http://www.expediamaps.com/ PlaceFinder.asp*
Microsoft's conventional Internet map system

This is a Web site hooked up to a dedicated search engine, designed to explore terabytes worth of satellite imagery of the earth. Lots of pictures of where you live, from way high. Unlike the USGS, the search is in real time, even though the imagery may be as much as a decade old.

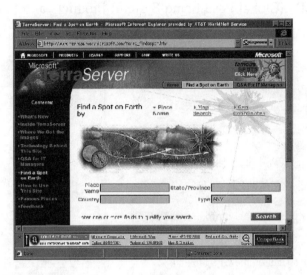

More pictures of where you live, from way up high!

It's fast, but the images are only in black-and-white. It's extraordinarily detailed, but the coverage is spotty. I tried to get my home in west Los Angeles (no dice), my family's summer spot in Maine (no dice), and the National Security Agency in Maryland (no dice, big surprise).

I did get beautiful images of Jackson Hole, Wyoming. It seems to be an ongoing project, and hence likely to expand its coverage. And it's financed by some big guns, so maybe it will stick around.

Lastly, it combines both SPIN-2 Russian satellite imagery and stuff from the USGS, so you've got to believe they have the NSA. What's the big secret?

Joe Mehaffey and Jack Yeazel's GPS Information Web Site

GPS (Global Positioning System) Products and Service Web Site

http://joe.mehaffey.com/

Type: Web site

First Developed: 1996

Price Range: Connect time

Key Features: Clear, comprehensible graphics

Ages: Post-high school

Obsolescence: Medium

Further Information:

✳ *http://www.laafb.af.mil/SMC/CZ/homepage/* for the U.S. Department of Defense's master Web site on the GPS program.

✳ *gopher://unbmvs1.csd.unb.ca/hPUB.CANSPACE.GPS.INTERNET.SERVICES.HTML* for a fine list of GPS related links.

✳ *http://milhouse.jpl.nasa.gov/* The Southern California Integrated GPS Network, an array of GPS sensors laid out to determine earth movement that might presage earthquake activity.

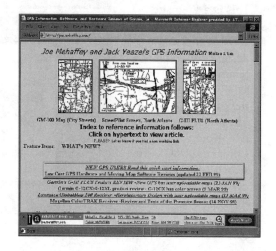

The GPS (Global Positioning System) is one of the great technological achievements of the 20th century. Though it was made by the U.S. military for the U.S. military, enabling hyperprecise targeting of weapons and sensors, and equally precise tracking of U.S. men and material, the feds decided to open it up to civilian use.

The result has been a transformation in everything from trucking to hiking to fishing. The cost of GPS devices has dropped like a stone, and they are increasingly integrated with computer graphics maps and other kinds of data.

The military system was designed to be accurate within inches, and the civilian system was supposed to be far cruder. Those clever civvies have figured out how to combine GPS data with conventional navigational aids (like Loran), and what is called 'differential' GPS yields fixes almost as precise as the military.

When anything evolves this fast, it is tough to keep track of it. It takes obsessive, heavy duty, major geek kinds of attention, and the guys who run this site have the tickets. There is no better site on the Web for understanding GPS and figuring out what are the best products to buy. →

From the Dept. of Defense's GPS Web site:

The NAVSTAR Global Positioning System is managed by the NAVSTAR GPS Joint Program Office at the Space and Missile Systems Center, Los Angeles Air Force Base, Calif.

NAVSTAR GPS is a space-based radio-positioning system consisting of a constellation of 24 orbiting satellites that provide navigation and timing information to military and civilian users worldwide. In addition to the satellites, the system consists of a worldwide satellite control network and GPS receiver units that pick up signals from the satellites and translate them into position information.

Delta II expendable launch vehicles are used to launch the GPS satellites from Cape Canaveral Air Station, Fla., into circular orbits of nearly 11,000 nautical miles.

GPS provides the following:

- 24-hour, worldwide service

- Extremely accurate, three-dimensional location information (providing latitude, longitude, and altitude readings)

- Extremely accurate velocity information

- Precise timing services

- A worldwide common grid that is easily converted to any local grid

- Continuous real-time information

- Accessibility to an unlimited number of worldwide users

- Civilian user support at a slightly less accurate level [...*than the military gets—Ed.*]

GPS satellites orbit the earth every 12 hours, emitting continuous navigation signals on two different L-band frequencies. The signals are so accurate, time can be figured to within a millionth of a second, velocity can be figured to within a fraction of a mile per hour, and location can be figured to within feet.

GPS significantly outperforms other position and navigation systems, and it does so with greater accuracy and at a lower cost. Such endeavors as mapping, aerial refueling, rendezvous operations, geodetic surveying, and search and rescue operations have all benefited greatly from GPS's accuracy.

GPS was put to the test during Operations Desert Shield and Desert Storm, where coalition forces relied heavily on GPS to navigate the featureless desert of Southwest Asia. Forward air controllers, pilots, tank drivers, ground troops, and even cooks used the system so successfully that many U.S. defense officials cited GPS as a key to victory.

The GPS worldwide satellite control system consists of five monitor stations and four ground antennas. The monitor stations use GPS receivers to passively track the navigation signals of all the satellites. Information from the monitor stations is then processed at the master control stations, operated by the 2nd Space Operations Squadron at Falcon Air Force Base, Colo., and used to update the satellites' navigation messages.

Updated navigation information is sent to the GPS satellites from the Master Control Station at Falcon Air Force Base through ground antennas using an S-band signal. The ground antennas are also used to transmit commands to satellites and to receive the satellites' state-of-the-art telemetry data.

As a service to GPS users, the Department of Transportation has established the "Navigation Information Service" (formerly "GPS Information Service") as a point of contact for civil GPS users. Operated and maintained by the United States Coast Guard, the NIS can be reached at (703) 313-5900 Monday through Friday from 8 A.M. to 4 P.M. Eastern time.

SATELLITE CHARACTERISTICS

Weight (in orbit) **Block IIA**—2,175 pounds

Orbit altitude—10,988 nautical miles

Power source—solar panels generating 700 watts

Launch vehicle—Delta II

Dimensions—5 feet wide, 17.5 feet long (including wing span)

Design life—7.5 years

Cartographic Reference Resources

Metasite for Mapping Links

http://www.lib.utexas.edu/Libs/PCL/Map_collection/Cartographic_reference.html

Type: Web site

First Developed: 1996

Price Range: Connect time

Key Features: Well chosen links

Ages: High school and beyond

Obsolescence: Medium

Further Information:

❋ *http://mapweb.parc.xerox.com/map*
The Xerox Parc Map viewer, one of the original Net atlases, and still one of the best.

❋ *http://www.geo.ed.ac.uk/quakexe/quakes*
World-Wide Earthquake Locator: Global Earthquake Report is an equally interesting combination of remote sensing, calculation, and graphics over the Web.

This is not a fancy site, by a long shot. But it is the richest source of good cartographic and mapping sites that I have found.

There are an infinite number of great things you can do with maps, and with the addition of computing and graphics, the variety is startling. Just visiting the first level of the sites listed here is a fine Sunday afternoon vacation.

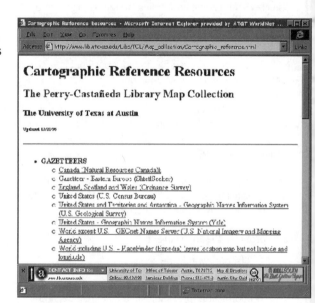

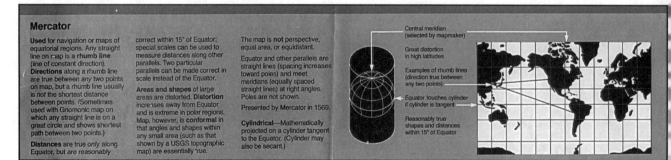

From the Cartographic Reference Web site: A description of the Mercator projection

TheTrip

Air Flight Tracking

http://www.thetrip.com/usertools/flighttracking/

Type: Web site

First Developed: 1998

Price Range: Connect time

Key Features: Amazing integration of the FAA's remote sensing and data management capabilities

Ages: 10 and up

Obsolescence: Medium

Further Information:
✳ *http://e-flight.com/*
Great site for people who hate flying. Reports on near misses and pilot errors provide ample support for paranoia

COOKIE:

*A message given
to a Web browser
by a Web server, to
identify users and possibly
prepare customized Web
pages for them.*

*— Definition from
Random House Webster's
Computer & Internet
Dictionary*

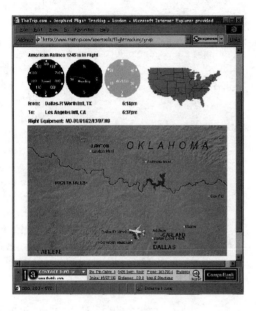

My sister and I had to travel a lot when we were kids. With parents divorced and living in different cities, every summer meant a plane flight from Los Angeles to Cincinnati, and back.

Several of the flights were scary, one with a flaming engine, one with a bomb scare. Neither my Mom nor my Dad ever sent us skying away without a frightened glitter in their eyes.

Now that I'm a parent, I know the feeling. Sending any loved one off on a plane trip is scary, but I've recently found a palliative, TheTrip.com.

Nominally, this site is set up to be a cyber travel agent. I suppose it does that, but I don't know. The only reason I ever come here is when I have a family member on a plane. The site has a little service called flight tracking.

Enter the airline and the flight number, and it reaches into the noumenon (actually the FAA radar data), and determines the position, speed and altitude of any flight. TheTrip flight tracker continuously plots the position of the plane over a map of the US. If you wish, you can watch the whole flight crawl across the surface of the Earth. Sometimes I do.

TheTrip will e-mail up to three dear ones, indicating when a flight has landed. A couple of cookies are a small price to pay for this kind of peace of mind.

Cloak and Dagger Books

http://www.halcyon.com/dagger/

Type: Source

First Developed: 1980s

Price: From a few dollars up to several hundred, depending upon the rarity of the book.

Key Features: Very well informed

Ages: 10 and up

Obsolescence factor: Low

Back in the eighties there was a wonderfully peculiar bookstore called the National Intelligence Book Center. It was hidden on the sixth floor of a nondescript building on K Street in Washington, D.C.. You had to check your stuff (weapons? sensors?) in lockers at the door and be buzzed in by someone who looked at you from behind bulletproof glass. It was weird, but it felt like it was for real. In the early ninties, the NIBC closed down, and Elizabeth Bancroft, the woman who appeared to be NIBC's proprietor, started a newsletter called *Surveillant*.

A quirky, immensely intelligent review of everything published on espionage, *Surveillant* was the best way to keep current with the rapidly changing and hard-to-track world of security and intelligence literature. Especially when most of these titles are never carried by local bookshops or reviewed by magazines or newspapers.

Culled from hundreds of special sources, foreign databases, publisher catalogs, reference periodicals, journals, and news and insider tips both foreign and domestic, *Surveillant* detailed new books, the latest U.S. government documents on security and intelligence, many supplied with special phone numbers so you can obtain free copies, new video and audio tapes and computer programs, forthcoming books, banned (or about-to-be) books, and tradecraft rarities. Now *Surveillant* has suspended publication, and

Here's a book that Surveillant *recommended and* Cloak and Dagger *sells...*

WAR SECRETS IN THE ETHER
by Wilhelm F. Flicke
[Aegean Park Press, PO Box 2837, Laguna Hills, CA 92654, Voice: 800-736-3587; 714-586-8811; Fax 714-586-8269, US]; 1994 reprint; ISBN: 0-89412-233-9; Aegean Order No. M-2; 234 pages; $26.80 pb.

Shortly after WWII, the U.S. Government commissioned Wilhelm F. Flicke, because of his "inside" knowledge of German radio-espionage and "code-breaking" efforts, to write *War Secrets in the Ether*. Translated from the German by Ray W. Pettengill for the National Security Agency in 1953, the contents of this work remained classified until the late 1970s. It was originally reprinted by Aegean Park Press as two volumes in 1977 and now, in this edition, has been combined as one. Flicke tells the story of German successes in reading the secret codes of both enemies and friends. Historians have long pondered how General Rommel knew in advance the moves of the British army in North Africa. Flicke reveals the reason: the Germans had broken the U.S. secret code between Cairo and Washington.

the best resource for these sorts of things is the Cloak and Dagger Bookstore in Bedford, New Hampshire.

When I first visited there, proprietor Dan Halperin had one room filled with books, mostly used and rare. Now his house—every room of it—is filled up: 12,000 books, and he has started to track and carry the new publications.

He carries material you are unlikely to find at Amazon or Barnes & Noble. That's why Hollywood types looking for good story ideas and the details of intelligence tradecraft regularly get shipments from Cloak and Dagger. →

Cloak and Dagger Books *continued*

➔ The Cloak and Dagger Web site is not a direct-order e-commerce site. You have to order a book the old fashioned way, by phone, fax, or e-mail. But the site has a set of text files listing all the books, ready for downloading. If you don't know precisely what you're looking for, these files are better for browsing than any of the search facilities on Amazon and B&N.

SAMPLE LINKS FROM THE CLOAK & DAGGER BOOKS SITE
How user friendly is this!

➡ Download our zipped catalog sorted by authors (243k)

➡ Download our self-extracting archive catalog sorted by authors (259k)

➡ Download our plain text archive catalog sorted by authors (463k)

➡ Download our zipped catalog sorted by titles (335k)

➡ Download our self-extracting archive catalog sorted by titles (351k)

➡ Download our complete, zipped, annotated, descriptive catalog in DBase IV format (298k)

➡ Download our complete, self-extracting, annotated, descriptive catalog in DBase IV format (314k)

EXCERPTS FROM "THE CATHEDRAL AND THE BAZAAR"
on the Open Source Software Revolution, from www.tuxedo.org

Eric Raymond is the most noted Net spokesman for Open Source Software, a non-profit, collaborative technique of software development which has yielded the widely admired, much-adopted LINUX operating system. His essay on Linux, and the Open Source system of making software, is legendary. The Linux system has caused tremors at Microsoft headquarters, and this essay is something of a Declaration of Independence in the software world. Here follow excerpts from a recent issue of "The Cathedral and the Bazaar" (which Eric Raymond constantly improves and republishes on his Web site: http://www.tuxedo.org/ ~ esr)

Linux is subversive. Who would have thought even five years ago that a world-class operating system could coalesce as if by magic out of part-time hacking by several thousand developers scattered all over the planet, connected only by the tenuous strands of the Internet?

Certainly not I.

Linux overturned much of what I thought I knew. I had been preaching the Unix gospel of small tools, rapid prototyping and evolutionary programming for years. But I also believed there was a certain critical complexity above which a more centralized, a priori approach was required. I believed that the most important software (operating systems and really large tools like Emacs) needed to be built like cathedrals, carefully crafted by individual wizards or small bands of mages working in splendid isolation, with no beta to be released before its time.

Linus Torvalds's style of development—release early and often, delegate everything you can, be open to the point of promiscuity—came as a surprise. No quiet, reverent cathedral-building here. Rather, the Linux community seemed to resemble a great babbling bazaar of differing agendas and approaches (aptly symbolized by the Linux archive sites, who'd take submissions from anyone) out of which a coherent and stable system could seemingly emerge only by a succession of miracles.

The fact that this bazaar style seemed to work, and work well, came as a distinct shock. As I learned my way around, I worked hard not just at individual projects, but also at trying to understand why the Linux world not only didn't fly apart in confusion but seemed to go from strength to strength at a speed barely imaginable to cathedral-builders.

Raymond's Methods (drawn from his open source development of an e-mail application called Fetchmail)

1. I released early and often (almost never less often than every ten days; during periods of intense development, once a day).

2. I grew my beta list by adding to it everyone who contacted me about fetchmail.

3. I sent chatty announcements to the beta list whenever I released, encouraging people to participate.

4. And I listened to my beta testers, polling them about design decisions and stroking them whenever they sent in patches and feedback.

The payoff from these simple measures was immediate. From the beginning of the project, I got bug reports of a quality most developers would kill for, often with good fixes attached. I got thoughtful criticism, I got fan mail, I got intelligent feature suggestions.

Which leads to: →

The Cathedral and the Bazaar *continued*

1. Every good work of software starts by scratching a developer's personal itch.

2. Good programmers know what to write. Great ones know what to rewrite (and reuse).

3. "Plan to throw one away; you will, anyhow." (Fred Brooks, *The Mythical Man-Month*, Chapter 11)

4. If you have the right attitude, interesting problems will find you.

5. When you lose interest in a program, your last duty to it is to hand it off to a competent successor.

6. Treating your users as co-developers is your least-hassle route to rapid code improvement and effective debugging.

7. Release early. Release often. And listen to your customers.

8. Given a large enough beta-tester and co-developer base, almost every problem will be characterized quickly and the fix obvious to someone.

9. Smart data structures and dumb code works a lot better than the other way around.

10. If you treat your beta-testers as if they're your most valuable resource, they will respond by becoming your most valuable resource.

11. The next best thing to having good ideas is recognizing good ideas from your users. Sometimes the latter is better.

12. Often, the most striking and innovative solutions come from realizing that your concept of the problem was wrong.

13. "Perfection (in design) is achieved not when there is nothing more to add, but rather when there is nothing more to take away."

14. Any tool should be useful in the expected way, but a *great* tool lends itself to uses you never expected.

15. When writing gateway software of any kind, take pains to disturb the data stream as little as possible—and *never* throw away information unless the recipient forces you to!

16. When your language is nowhere near Turing-complete, syntactic sugar can be your friend.

17. A security system is only as secure as its secret. Beware of pseudo-secrets.

18. To solve an interesting problem, start by finding a problem that is interesting to you.

19. Provided the development coordinator has a medium at least as good as the Internet, and knows how to lead without coercion, many heads are inevitably better than one.

I think the future of free software will increasingly belong to people who know how to play Linus's game, people who leave behind the cathedral and embrace the bazaar. This is not to say that individual vision and brilliance will no longer matter; rather, I think that the cutting edge of free software will belong to people who start from individual vision and brilliance, then amplify it through the effective construction of voluntary communities of interest.

And perhaps not only the future of free software. No commercial developer can match the pool of talent the Linux community can bring to bear on a problem. Very few could afford even to hire the more than two hundred people who have contributed to fetchmail!

Perhaps in the end the free-software culture will triumph not because cooperation is morally right or software ``hoarding'' is morally wrong (assuming you believe the latter, which neither Linus nor I do), but simply because the commercial world cannot win an evolutionary arms race with free-software communities that can put orders of magnitude more skilled time into a problem.

● ● ● ● ● ● ● ● ● ● ● ● ● ● ● ● ● ●

Open Source Software

Web Site Devoted to the Open Source Movement

http://www.opensource.org/

Type: Software

First Developed: 1990s

Price Range: Nothing

Key Features: Free

Ages: Post-teen

Obsolescence: Likely never

Further Information:

❋ *http://www.earthspace.net/ ~esr/faqs/linus*
for a backgrounder on Linux, and:
❋ *http://www.sciam.com/1999/ 0399issue/0399cyber.html*
for a *Scientific American* article on Open Source stuff.

In 1975, Bill Gates wrote a letter to members of the Homebrew Computer Club in the Bay Area, scolding them for freely making copies of software (Microsoft Basic, in particular). At the time, snatching other people's software from freebie libraries and repackaging it for sale was also common practice. How could programmers afford to write good code, Gates asked, if they couldn't get paid for it?

A quarter of a century later, Gates has proven beyond a shadow of a doubt that Microsoft can create mediocre code for a lot of money. Amazingly, another bunch of folks have proven that a completely different approach—one that threatens the very core of Microsoft's business—can work just as well.

The approach holds a lot in common with Amish barn-raising. A community of interested people works up a product that nobody owns, and so nobody charges money for it. The leading offering in this domain is something called LINUX, and it is an operating system that can effectively replace Microsoft's offering, Windows NT. The programmers I know say that NT can be expected to crash about once a week. They say that LINUX almost never crashes.

People all around the word, connected by the Net, fix bugs in LINUX. The fixes are made almost as soon as the bug is discovered (imagine that with a Microsoft product). It is very hard to imagine today how this approach might be applied to a program like Quicken or Microsoft Word. After all, the people who use Quicken are not people who have coding talents. The people who use LINUX by and large do have those talents.

But if there ever were a way to cut Gates down to size, this is probably it. Maybe Ted Nelson is right, "Obsolete power corrupts obsoletely." →

→ From www.pcwebpoedia.com

OPEN SOURCE

Open Source Software is a movement, not a thing. It is the result of efforts by Internet-linked bands of programmers, who publish their source code, and then let everybody have a whack at making it better. The most significant outcome, so far, is LINUX. Short for Open Software Foundation, now part of The Open Group.

LINUX

Pronounced lee-nucks, A freely-distributable implementation of UNIX that runs on a number of hardware platforms, including Intel and Motorola microprocessors. It was developed mainly by Linus Torvalds. Because it's free, and because it runs on many platforms, including PCs, Macintoshes, and Amigas, Linux has become extremely popular over the last couple years. Another popular, free version of UNIX that runs on Intel microprocessors is FreeBSD.

THE OPEN GROUP HOME PAGE

The Open Group is an international consortium of vendors, ISVs and end-user customers from industry, government, and academia. Their home page provides links to information on open systems, a software mall, organization overviews, news, events, research, and technical focus areas. Updated on Jun 5, 1998.

THE MICROSOFT HALLOWEEN DOCUMENT: CLOSED WINDOWS vs. OPEN SOURCE SOFTWARE

The Halloween Document is a Microsoft internal memo that was published on the Net right after Halloween 1998. It was entitled, "Open Source Software A (New?) Development Methodology."

Eric Raymond is the most noted Net spokesman for Open Source Software, a non-profit, collaborative technique of software development which has yielded the widely admired, much-adopted LINUX operating system. Following are his comments on the Halloween Document:

The body of the Halloween Document is an internal strategy memorandum on Microsoft's possible responses to the Linux/Open Source phenomenon. Microsoft has publicly acknowledged that this memorandum is authentic, but dismissed it as a mere engineering study that does not define Microsoft policy. However, the list of collaborators mentioned at the end includes some people who are known to be key players at Microsoft, and the document reads as though the research effort had the cooperation of top management; it may even have been commissioned as a policy white paper for Bill Gates's attention (the author seems to have expected that Gates would read it).

Either way, it provides us with a very valuable look past Microsoft's dismissive marketing spin about Open Source at what the company is actually thinking—which, as you'll see, is an odd combination of astuteness and institutional myopia. →

The Halloween Document *continued*

KEY QUOTES FROM THE MICROSOFT HALLOWEEN DOCUMENT
(Plain English Translations by *Informatica* Editors)

HD: OSS (Open Source Software) poses a direct, short-term revenue and platform threat to Microsoft, particularly in server space. Additionally, the intrinsic parallelism and free idea exchange in OSS has benefits that are not replicable with our current licensing model and therefore present a long-term developer mind share threat.	**English Translation:** People hate our despotic style, and if they can ditch us, they will.
HD: Recent case studies (the Internet) provide very dramatic evidence… that commercial quality can be achieved/exceeded by OSS projects.	**English Translation:** They can make better, more stable software than we do.
HD: …to understand how to compete against OSS, we must target a process rather than a company.	**English Translation:** They are coming at us from all sides—we're being pecked to death by ducks.
HD: OSS is long-term credible… FUD tactics can not be used to combat it.	**English Translation:** FUD = Fear, Uncertainty and Doubt (the originator of this competitive approach in the computer industry was IBM) won't work. No matter how much we ignore, dismiss, or disinform about this stuff, it's going to come back and bite us.
HD: Linux and other OSS advocates are making a progressively more credible argument that OSS software is at least as robust—if not more—than commercial alternatives. The Internet provides an ideal, high-visibility showcase for the OSS world.	**English Translation:** Windows NT crashes on the average of once a week while Linux never crashes—such is the perception of people in the computer business.
HD: Linux has been deployed in mission critical, commercial environments with an excellent pool of public testimonials. …Linux outperforms many other UNIXes …Linux is on track to eventually own the x86 UNIX market…	**English Translation:** Uh oh. It's really good.
HD: Linux can win as long as services/protocols are commodities.	**English Translation:** If we can't get people to do it our way, we are in deep trouble.
HD: OSS projects have been able to gain a foothold in many server applications because of the wide utility of highly commoditized, simple protocols. By extending these protocols and developing new protocols, we can deny OSS projects entry into the market.	**English Translation:** Maybe we can copy it, and call it our own.
HD: The ability of the OSS process to collect and harness the collective IQ of thousands of individuals across the Internet is simply amazing. More importantly, OSS evangelization scales with the size of the Internet much faster than our own evangelization efforts appear to scale.	**English Translation:** They're smarter than we are.

Rush Limbaugh read this speech by Charlton Heston on his radio program, and then refused to tell people how he found it on the Net. He said if he could find it, so could everybody else, and that people should be prepared to learn on their own. He got 10,000 e-mails complaining about his unhelpful attitude.

Three days later, Metaspy, a subsidiary service of Go2net which reports the top 10 search terms of the past several days (www.go2net.com) showed the words "Harvard" and "speech" to be among the top ten search terms (Harvard was up 795%). The interaction of conventional broadcast media and the Internet has an unknown and unpredictable power.

Will views ridiculed by conventional media work themselves around and find favor with the people? Will the media intermediaries disappear? How silly do you find Charlton Heston, and his ideas?

On the day of the Limbaugh reading of the speech, it existed on one Web site: *http://www.law. harvard.edu/News/Charlton_ Heston_speech.html*

A month later (April 18, 1999), it has proliferated to at least nine more sites (search on Infoseek), with many more indicated by searches with other search engines. Try searching with this text string ("Winning the Cultural War"), when you read this article. See how many you can find.

"WINNING THE CULTURE WAR"

Some Excerpts from the Speech by Charlton Heston That Sent Them Searching the Net

...Dedicating the memorial at Gettysburg, Abraham Lincoln said of America, "We are now engaged in a great Civil War, testing whether this nation or any nation so conceived and so dedicated can long endure."

Those words are true again. I believe that we are again engaged in a great civil war, a cultural war that's about to hijack your birthright to think and say what resides in your heart. I fear you no longer trust the pulsing lifeblood of liberty inside you... the stuff that made this country rise from wilderness into the miracle that it is....I've come to understand that a cultural war is raging across our land, in which, with Orwellian fervor, certain acceptable thoughts and speech are mandated.

Telling us what to think has evolved into telling us what to say, so telling us what to do can't be far behind. Before you claim to be a champion of free thought, tell me: Why did political correctness originate on America's campuses? And why do you continue to tolerate it? Why do you, who're supposed to debate ideas, surrender to their suppression?

When a mugger sues his elderly victim for defending herself... jam the switchboard of the district attorney's office. When your university is pressured to lower standards until 80 percent of the students graduate with honors... choke the halls of the board of regents. When someone you elected is seduced by political power and betrays you... petition them, oust them, banish them....

When told how to think or what to say or how to behave, we don't. We disobey social protocol that stifles and stigmatizes personal freedom....

Who will guard the raw material of unfettered ideas, if not you?

S U R G E
of Activity on the Net

It turns out that the Net is more like an aircraft carrier than a highway. Highways are defined by a constant flow of traffic, and aircraft carriers handle surges of activity. Highways are analog. Aircraft carriers are binary, operating in on or off mode.

The problem is this: the people who run the Net are telephone people, and the telephone system runs like a highway. Traffic ebbs and flows in an analog sort of fashion. The worst of it comes on Mother's Day, or in moments of national crisis, but those surges are the exception. The telephone people understand analog traffic flow and have for almost a century.

Just as the 20th century began, a fellow named Erlang decided to do a time and motion study (see SYNTHETIC APERTURE) on folks operating a telephone switchboard in a small town. Erlang's resulting formula holds that there is an average length for phone calls and a mean traffic rate (see A CARTOON GUIDE TO STATISTICS). Just as the 20th century is drawing to a close, the telephone people are discovering that Erlang's formula (and queing theory and all the fancy algorithms that have been built into telephone switching systems) doesn't apply to digital stuff.

"Erlang's formula started to break down when computers started talking to computers," says Robert Calderbank, VP Information Sciences Research at AT&T

Labs, "When fax machines and computers started using the Network, instead of just people, the statistics of the traffic started to change."

Traffic on the Net comes in spikes, much as action on an aircraft carrier comes in surges. The Navy has had 50 years to learn how to manage surges. The phone carriers have only just discovered spikes, and they haven't figured out how to handle them yet. This is the reason why performance on the Net has periods of exceptional degradation. Dial-up access numbers give busy signals, mail servers don't serve mail, Domain Name Servers (DNS) can't recognize URLs.

The essence of the problem is that voice traffic, though it may vary in length, doesn't vary that much. Digital traffic varies as much as six times more in length—everything from chat room messages to digitized video. Further, all computers use "caching" to store and forward chunks of data, amplifying the burst effect.

The AT&T people are diddling with techniques of analysis far more sophisticated than simple time-and-motion studies. They have, for example, noticed that the bursts of traffic on the Net form patterns, which repeat themselves in large and small scale. Hence they are looking at them as fractals. Further, they are breaking the patterns down using wavelet decomposition. All

of these techniques are built around the premise of removing noise from the immense traffic data they mine and refining it into usable information (see SILICON DREAMS).

It appears that there will be some other discoveries too. Aircraft carriers and the Net are man-made systems, and hence their surges are "designed in." It's very likely that the Net can be deconstructed and optimized, just as the Navy has done with carrier operations for 50 years.

Both aircraft carriers and the Net were originally designed to accommodate the conditions of war. Long periods of utter boredom, broken by short periods of frantic activity. The Net exhibits its outages in response to external stimuli, just as an aircraft carrier does. Flights of planes and weapons off carriers are called packages. The Net carries packets. Perhaps some of the improvement in the Net's performance will come from the planning of packages.

For example, when the Starr report was released on the Net, the spikes in activity and downloading causes spot performance degradation all over the Net. The same thing happened on the night of the Oscars in 1999, when people from all over the world were going to the Net for Oscar promotions, games, live video feeds, reportage, and the like.

Those are predictable stimuli—others aren't. Case in point: Right before the →

Net Surge *continued*

→ academy awards, Rush Limbaugh—a political radio personality with tens of millions of listeners—read a fiery speech by Charlton Heston—a famous actor and conservative political figure—given at Harvard in the previous month. The speech had been posted on a few small sites, but not drawn much attention.

Limbaugh read the speech on the air, said he had found it on the Net, and then refused to give a Web address for it. He declared that people should learn how to find things on the Net, just like he did. The result was almost 10,000 angry e-mails to Limbaugh, On the Net, the few sites that held the speech were overwhelmed with demand, and the major search engines spiked on keywords like *Harvard* (up 700 percent at one search engine), *speech* and *Heston*.

The resulting Net traffic could have been dramatically reduced had there been more sites with the speech posted, had the search engines pre-searched for the speech and sensed which were the best sites to find it, and had the speech itself been tagged with data that made it easier to find.

None of these "packaging techniques" fall into the natural charter or expertise of the phone companies. They require dealing with traffic on the basis of its content, rather than as data.

Search Engine Watch
Web Site Devoted to Search Engines on the Net
http://www.searchenginewatch.com/

Type: Aggregation Web site

First Developed: 1998

Price Range: Freebie

Key Features: One stop shop for searching strategies and insights

Ages: 10 and up

Obsolescence: High, but constantly refreshed

Further Information:
✳ *http://www.oclc.org/oclc/fp/fptxthm.htm*
the Web site for the Dewey decimal system, includes a Dewey decimal system screen saver.
Search Engine Watch/ Mecklermedia
☎ (203) 341-2828

The Web is a like town with 500,000 radio stations. Because we are humans, we have room in our heads for about 10 presets, just like our car radios.

We need help to find the rest. Librarians have fiddled with searching and finding for eons. There used to be a narrow discipline within library science called ontology—the study of categories. Until about five years ago, the most famous ontologist was Melvil Dewey (the guy who crafted the Dewey decimal classification system we used in library filing systems).

Today, places like Yahoo and Excite employ hundreds of ontologists, all in service of the task of making things findable on the Net. But they aren't, and searching—though it accounts for somewhere north of 70 percent of all the traffic on the net—is still tough. Ask anyone who has gotten hundreds of thousands of hits off an Alta Vista search.

But there are tricks (see SYNTHETIC APERTURE), and there are new search engines coming on line all the time (see INFERENCE FIND and GOOGLE). Most of these are tracked by a very good Web magazine called Search Engine Watch.

Though some of it is written in geek-talk, a lot of what it offers is very practical, highly useful stuff. →

Search Engine Watch *continued*

A HANDY CHART FROM THE SEARCH ENGINE WATCH WEB SITE

SECTION	DESIGNED FOR	DESCRIPTION
A Webmaster's Guide To Search Engines	Webmasters	This section explains how search engines find and rank Web pages, with an emphasis on what webmasters can do to improve how search engines list their Web sites.
Search Engines Facts And Fun	Search Engine Users	This section provides background about search engines, tips on how to use them better, some history, and even a game to test your search engine knowledge.
Search Engine Status Reports	Anyone	This section provides some insight on how search engines are performing in different areas. Check out some of the material, and make note of reports you want to keep an eye on.
Search Engine Resources	Anyone	A collection of links to search engine related resources across the Web.
Search Engine Report Mailing List	Anyone	It's free, and it will keep you updated on the latest search engine news.

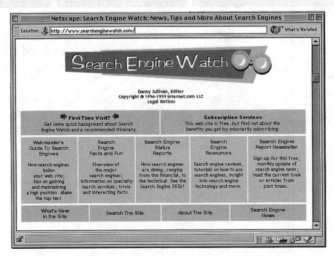

SYNTHETIC APERTURE

The Secret to Finding Things on the Net

The trend in fancy telescopes is to have a lot of little ones rather than one big one. The idea is to composite all the little pictures together to create an image of detail and accuracy far greater than what could be achieved by the biggest telescope that could be built. And it works.

For years the American intelligence agencies have been putting this trick to work, in particular with photoreconnaissance. A satellite will take a picture from many miles above the Earth. On its own, the accuracy might be enough to read a license plate on a car bumper (pretty amazing, in and of itself).

With the advent of big computing, it became possible to merge the information of two, or three, or many photos into one very high-resolution image. How good can it get? They don't talk about it much. In fact, they don't talk about synthetic aperture much. But a rough guess would be that, under good conditions, they can read a hand of cards, or the print on a document.

That, of course, is synthetic aperture in space. It works in time, as well. In Washington, D.C., there is a building on the far edge of the Washington Navy Yard. It's called the National Photographic and Interpretation Center (see more at the *Federation of American Scientists* Web site) and it is very well-protected. Some of the building looks normal, but about a third of it looks like a heating plant. In fact, it's refrigeration—not for the supercomputers in the basement, but rather for the supermemory.

They keep a digitized version of every reconnaissance picture taken since World War II, and the computers can build a time-lapse movie of most of the strategically important places in the world. They bend and stretch the photos so they match up, and then they witness the construction of new roads, the depletion of raw materials, the deployment of resources, etc. Synthetic aperture in time.

The fundamental idea here is that two or more samples of the same thing improve your information. CBS News requires two independent and unbiased sources for a story (at least they did). Employers like multiple references on a résumé. Time and motion studies weren't effective until the motion picture camera made it easy to "sample" an event many times over with a constant, predictable time base.

The Net is a gigantic sensing machine, and the power to create synthetic aperture when tracking down info is immense. The simplest way to do it is to use a Boolean ANDed search with the search engines (like Yahoo, Excite, and Alta Vista).

Instead of using one word (the equivalent of taking one picture of the Net from a particular angle), you use two words (the equivalent of taking two pictures and merging their info into one higher resolution picture). This ANDing throws away info that is not relevant to both search terms.

For example: searching on the word *blackbird* might yield tens of thousands of hits when searching Alta Vista, with results ranging from rock bands, to birds, to consulting firms, to airplanes. Search on *blackbird* AND *reconnaissance,* and the number of "hits" reduces by two orders of magnitude (from 6,000 to 60 hits) and almost all of the referenced Web sites (the "hits") deal with the famous SR-71 spy plane (known as the Blackbird).

Although the search engines vary a bit in how they want to see the query constructed, most of them are happy with a search that looks something like this:

+blackbird +reconnaissance

The effect of this is to indicate (with the pluses) that both the words *blackbird* and *reconnaissance* MUST occur in the verbiage of the Web page, and that the word *blackbird* is more important than *reconnaissance* (because it comes first in the query): hence pages with more occurrences of the word *blackbird* will be sorted first in the resulting list.

When the Charlton Heston speech at Harvard was hard to find (see SURGE), all I had to do was query Alta Vista as follows +Heston +Harvard +Speech. The Web site with the full text of the speech was returned at the top of the list.

Google

Importance Engine

http://www.google.com/

Type: Advanced search engine

First Developed: 1998

Price Range: Freebie

Key Features: Very fast, and simple

Ages: 10 and up

Obsolescence: High

Further Information: Similar approach from:
* *http://www.directhit.com/*
☎ **Google:** (650) 723-3154

In the real world, were you to try to find out something important, you might seek the opinion of a trusted, important person. Or perhaps you would canvass several such folks, to see whether they agreed upon the answer.

Therein lies the fundamental premise of some of the most advanced new search technologies for the World Wide Web, led by Google. Each one of these pieces of software employs a "magic bullet" algorithm—a set of rules for search and analysis employed in its programming which crawls through millions of Internet pages, looks at the links they have and what they are talking about, and concludes which pages are the best to go to to find information on a given subject.

Here's what such software does: prioritizes the hits they return, on the basis of their set of rules for importance, credibility, or popularity.

Here's what these programs don't do as yet: figure out what you are really interested in. Are you talking about Blackbird the thrush, the reconnaissance plane, the rock group, or the software technology?

Google also saves (in computer parlance, caches) a lot of the most commonly accessed pages, so you can get them quicker. IBM has developed something along these lines, with emphasis on "credibility," but there is no place to go on the Web to see this as yet.

Another Internet search engine, DirectHit, fancies itself a popularity engine, and tracks the sites that people actually select from the search results lists generated on places like Yahoo, HotBot, and Excite. By analyzing the activity of millions of previous Internet searchers, DirectHit determines the most popular sites for search requests.

Inference Find

Metasearch Engine

http://www.inference.com/infind/

Type: Web site with metasearch engine

First Developed: 1998

Price Range: Connect time

Key Features: Very fast and well organized

Ages: 10 and up

Obsolescence: Medium

Further Information: Similar value from *Sherlock* on the Mac, and *Copernic* which works as an application for Win 95/98 machines
✳ *http://www.copernic.com*
See also *Infoseek Express,* a downloadable application at
✳ *http://www.infoseek.com*
and
✳ *http://www.dogpile.com*

Now here's a hot idea, and it's called "metasearch"—a search engine that uses other search engines, and then whittles down their results to a manageable set of options.

The Inference Find Web site calls out—in parallel—WebCrawler, Yahoo, Lycos, Alta Vista, InfoSeek, and Excite, merges the results, removes redundancies, and clusters the results into neat understandable groupings. You can quickly see which documents are relevant and which are irrelevant.

Inference Find describes itself as an "Intelligent Massively Fast Parallel Web Search."

For example, if you search for "The David Letterman Show" with Inference Find, you can quickly see those pages that come from CBS's official site and those pages posted by fans. With any other search engine these results are intermixed, and you'd have to manually scan through hundreds of items to determine which is which.

It doesn't always get it right, and the results can be peculiar (search on blackbird and stealth, and see what comes up). But it's pretty damn good.

IN SEARCH OF...

...The Ten Commandments? The Net features a plethora of search engines, each boasting their own special way of providing you with the info you seek. The following pages illustrate the way some of the major ones do their stuff in helping you to find what you are (and aren't) after.

A GOOGLE SEARCH ON "10 COMMANDMENTS"

At least 643 matches for 10 Commandments showing results 1-10. Search took 1.04 seconds.

➤ 54% www.visdesigns.com/design/ commandments.html *No Phrase Match*

➤ 34% **The DOS 10 Commandments**
...Humor: The Dos 10 Commandments The DOS 10...www.infidels.org/misc/humor/dos_10_commandments.html Cached (fast!) 4k Phrase Match

➤ 41% **10 Commandments Project: Publishing the Ten Commandments in as many different**
...Steward's Guidelines The 10 Commandments Project A Wise Steward......Sin? Then Who Can Be Saved? 10 Commandments Project Goal: To... (13 more) home.sprynet.com/sprynet/ WiseStewards/10comm.htm Cached (fast!) 16k Phrase Match

➤ 38% **CEI: Ten Thousand Commandments**
...THOUSAND COMMANDMENTS A Policymaker's Snapshot of the Federal Regulatory......1996 edition of "Ten Thousand Commandments": Regulation costs more than... www.cei.org/ essays/crews1.html Cached (fast!) 4k No Phrase Match

➤ 38% **10 Commandments of Good Historical Writing by Theron F. Schlabach**
...Ten Commandments of Good Historical Writing by Theron F. Schlabach With... www.bluffton.edu/~schlabachg/ courses/10commnd.htm Cached (fast!) 11k Phrase Match

➤ 27% **FoRK Archive: Re: 10 Commandments of FoRKposting.**
...Re: 10 Commandments of FoRKposting. CobraBoy... Previous message: I Find Karma: "10 Commandments of FoRKposting."... (11 more) xent.ics.uci.edu/FoRK-archive/ spring97/0273.html Cached (fast!) 5k Phrase Match

➤ 27% **FoRK Archive: 10 Commandments of FoRKposting.**
... 10 Commandments of FoRKposting. I Find Karma... Next message: CobraBoy: "Re: 10 Commandments of FoRKposting."... (17 more) xent.ics.uci.edu/FoRK-archive/ spring97/0272.html Cached (fast!) 6k Phrase Match

➤ 42% **The Ten Commandments for C Programmers (Annotated Edition)**
...The Ten Commandments for C Programmers (Annotated Edition) by Henry...so hard as the belittlers claimeth. 10 Thou shalt foreswear, renounce,...www.lysator.liu.se/c/ten-commandments.html Cached (fast!) 17k No Phrase Match

➤ 48% **The Ten Commandments for Sending E-Mail**
...Suffer The Consequences!!! The 10 Commandments for Sending E-Mail...Actually, there's more than 10 Commandments. But it's a great... (2 more) www.owt.com/dircon/ten.htm Cached (fast!) 26k Phrase Match

➤ 30% **Werbal: Advertising Agency - The 10 Commandments**
...our up-to-date homepage. The 10 Commandments for Successful...provide a nice link to a page about 10 design mistakes for beginners. The... (1 more) www.werbal.ch/english/10commandments.html Cached (fast!) 10k Phrase Match

In Search of... *continued*

AN INFERENCE FIND SEARCH ON "10 COMMANDMENTS"

Misc. Commercial Sites

➥ 10 Commandments #5 Exegitical Outlines

➥ 10 Commandments of PC Ownership

➥ Christian P. Bellingrath, M.B.A. - Senior Consultant for E-C...

➥ comedycity.com 10 commandments of Golf!

➥ Cyberfile.com

➥ Darts - The Scorekeepers "10 Commandments" - CYBER/DARTS

➥ Darts - The Scorekeepers "10 Commandments" - CY...

➥ God loves you do u love him???

➥ Grace Gospel Worship Center Homepage

➥ Knight Air Homepage

➥ MuseNet Home Page

➥ Rush Limbaugh articles and resources on the 'net

➥ Sales and Bargains - SampleSale Sales in Cities

➥ Sasha's Wild Page

➥ Susan Boyd Home Page

➥ Ten Commandments of HTML FAQ

➥ The Christian faith

➥ Title:Seventh Day Sabbath Truth

➥ Transverse Myelitis Internet Club List: Fwd: (TIE)The 10 commandments of an MSer

➥ Travel Survival Guide

Misc. Internet Provider Sites

➥ 1 Way Only–Salvation

➥ Are You Going to Heaven or Hell?

➥ Karate Philosophy in Montana

➥ Newsletter

➥ Steve Pribut's Chess Page

➥ The Wizard of Odds

➥ www.british-israel.net

Misc. European Sites

➥ Morten's Backgammon Page

➥ The 10 Commandments of Backgammon

➥ The 10 Commandments of HTML Credits

Misc. North American Sites

➥ The 10 Commandments of Motorcoaching

➥ The Law of Christ superior to Law of Moses

Misc. Educational Institution Sites

➥ Religion and the 10 Commandments

➥ The 10 Commandments and the Supreme Court Building

Misc. Asian Commercial Sites

➥ Untitled

Misc. Australian Sites

➥ 10 Commandments religious pictures and Australian rock music

Misc. Israeli Commercial Sites

➥ TORAS ERETZ YISRAEL

Misc. Non-Profit Sites

➥ THIRD HEAVEN MINISTRIES

Misc. Sites

➥ Directory topics

➥ Infoseek web search results

In Search of... *continued*

A DIRECT HIT SEARCH ON "10 COMMANDMENTS"

1. Ten Commandments Image and Sound
IMAGE AND SOUND Click picture to capture both Image and Sound BACK TO TEN COMMANDMENTS...
http://www.prophecysite.com/tenimage.htm

2. 10 Commandments
[AmericanNet.com] [SuperShops][Software][Events][Books-Music][Contest][Opportunity][Classifieds][I-CAN][Chat][Newsworthy][Bulletin Board]
http://www.americannet.com/10_commandments.htm

3. Commandments, The Laws of God
Commandments, "The Laws of God" THE TWO GREAT COMMANDMENTS You shall love the Lord your God with your whole heart, and with your whole soul, and with your whole mind...
http://www.prayerbook.com/commandme.htm

4. poster art: Ten Indian Commandments II poster
Text reads as follows: "Remain Close to the Great Spirit. Show great Respect for your fellow beings. Give Assistance and Kindness where-ever needed. Be...
http://art-posters.net/Indian2.htm

5. The Ten Commandments
The Ten Commandments: The Ten Commandments have be delivered again to the world through The Miracle of Saint Joseph. The following Revelations are excerpts in...
http://www.themiracleofstjoseph.org/10cmds.htm

6. Bible Studies
The Angels God's Word is Truth: What is the Truth to be Learned from Nature? What is the Truth about the Bible? What is the Truth about God and the Origin of...
http://www.christianinconnect.com/BibStud.htm

7. The Ten Commandments Project
Important Links: Operation Save Our Nation The National Clergy Council Judge Moore's Home Page Please contact us at: Operation Save Our Nation 601...
http://www.tencommands.org/

8. 10 Commandments for Sabbatarians and 7th day Adventists
10 Commandments for Sabbatarians! Thou Shalt not divide the first covenant up into moral and ceremonial laws! Thou shalt not arbitrarily switch the definition of terms like...
http://www.bible.ca/7-10forSDAs.htm

9. SOFTSEEK.COM - Ten Commandments Screen Saver by Ray Landreau
is a slide show screen saver that displays an image of Jesus and each of the ten commandments. SOFTSEEK.COM—The Source for Shareware, Freeware and Evaluation Software...
http://192.41.3.165/Desktop_Enhancements/Screen_Savers/Religion/F_17775_index.html

10. NAFFS Home
NAFFS HOME MEMBER ENTRANCE SEARCH WRITE US Please visit our sponsor. MARK YOUR CALENDARS!!! NAFFS Technical Meeting April 20 9 a.m. - Noon New Jersey Expo Center Edison, N.J.
http://www.naffs.org/index.htm

In Search of... *continued*

AN EXCITE SEARCH ON THE "10 COMMANDMENTS"

Top 10 matches. [6154492 hits. About Your Results] Show: Titles   List by Web site

➤ 72% **Edu_Admin_Discussion: 10 Commandments for School Leaders**: jg36

(Jay_P_GOLDMAN@UMAIL.UMD.EDU) Tue, 22 Dec 1998 14:29:00 EST Each year at its national convention, the American Association of School Administrators debuts a new novelty T-shirt bearing a Top 10 list.
http://www.design.ncisc.org/~edad-l/current/0246.html (*Search for more documents like this one*)

➤ 69% **Ten Rules**: I get a lot of statements from people like, "You can't keep all ten commandments." or, "Do you keep all ten commandments?" or, "We can't keep all ten commandments." The question one should ask is, "Do you break a commandment now and then?" I would admit that yes, I do.
http://www.cyberport.com/~ev/10rules.html (*Search for more documents like this one*)

➤ 69% **Hist-games mailing list archive: Re: hist-games: 10 Commandments game**   David Salley

(salley@niktow.canisius.edu) Wed, 30 Jul 97 08:15:58 EDT > What was that game the Egyptian princess was playing in the > movie: "the 10 Commandments"?
http://www.pbm.com/~lindahl/hist-games/archive/0023.html (*Search for more documents like this one*)

➤ 69% **10 Reasons To Restore The 10 Commandments**: A Christian guide to the Charlotte Metro Area including local news, ministries, family information, events, entertainment, education, churches, businesses, bookstores, classifieds, childcare, shopping and dinning.
http://www.cityguides.net/charlotte/command.htm (*Search for more documents like this one*)

➤69% **Edu_Admin_Discussion: Re: 10 Commandments for School Leaders**: This is a multi-part message in MIME format.
————FD6568560B9014FB60AC48E0 Content-Type: text/plain; charset=us-ascii Content-Transfer-Encoding: 7bit
http://www.design.ncisc.org/~edad-l/current/0247.html *Search for more documents like this one*

➤ 68% **Biblical Study Paper** - The 10 Commandments–Biblical Study Paper * "The Commandments of God" Copyright & Copy; 1995 by Greg Thomas * This biblical study paper was created for the personal study of the author.
http://junior.apk.net/~glt/10commst.html (*Search for more documents like this one*)

➤ 68% **"Ten Commandments of Weight Loss"**: HealthWorld Online–Ten Commandments of Weight Loss Emily Kane ND The 10 COMMANDMENTS of WEIGHT LOSS please affix with thy most favorite refrigerator magnet 1) Thou shalt honor thy health and good spirits above all else. 2) Thou shalt not go on crash diets; there lieth the way of madness. 3) Thou shalt not clean thy neighbor's plate. 4) Thou shalt not eat when thine eye lusteth but when thy stomach doth...
http://aanp.net/articles.lay/ART.TenCom.EK.html (*Search for more documents like this one*)

➤ 68% **Sales and Bargains**: SampleSale Sales in Cities–SampleSale Home Page–Your place on the Internet for sample sales, clothes, apparel, accessories, outlet centers, bargain sales, discount sales and designer sales in New York City, Los Angeles, San Francisco, Boston, Chicago, Washington DC and Miami.
http://www.samplesale.com/ (*Search for more documents like this one*)

➤ 68% **MuseNet Home Page**: MuseNet is the original Contact Organization for musicians who have an E-Mail address. It's An Internet Funnel for Professional Musicians.
http://www.musenet.com/ (*Search for more documents like this one*)

➤ 68% **Only Ten? Key 5**: Key #5 Only Ten? Just about everyone today is familar with the 10 Commandments. Many Christians hold the 10 as their standard of measure. We are taught over and over to keep the 10 commandments.
http://pweb.netcom.com/~samson4/key5.html (*Search for more documents like this one*)

Copernic

Software for Searching the Net

http://www.copernic.com

Type: Browser Enhancement Software

First Developed: 1997

Price Range: Free, or $29.95 for the tricked out version

Key Features: Fine Interface, book search

Ages: 18 and up

Obsolescence: Medium

Further Information:
Infoseek offers something similar called Infoseek Express at
✱ *http://express.infoseek.com/ subdocuments/expressdetails.html*

I've been using Copernic for the better part of a year, but I had decided it was a better footnote to one of the entries on metasearch Web sites (INFERENCE FIND), and it really didn't merit an entry of its own. That was before I downloaded the most recent version. Whoa!

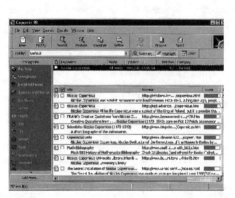

The new version, in addition to performing excellent metasearches on many of the most popular search engines and then putting together a good, ordered summary page (all that stuff it did before), now has crossed the threshold into major indispensability.

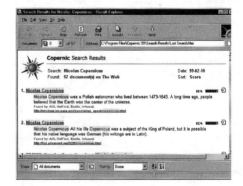

They have done two things that make the software righteous (at least these are the two that appeal to me, there are a boatload of features). First, they have attached Copernic to IE4.0, in the manner of ALEXA. This option, once chosen, binds Copernic to the Search button in the browser, so that every search is a metasearch.

The other innovation is a targeted metasearch for books, exploiting Amazon.com, Barnes&Noble.com, and several others. These folks are very smart, and this is—even in its shareware version—a spectacular piece of software.

Northern Light

A Web Site with Search and Library Services

http://www.northernlight.com

Type: Web site

First Developed: 1995; Northern Light Technologies, LLC

Price Range: Free search, $4.95 a month to subscribe, $1–$5 per article.

Key Features: High speed search, high quality content

Ages: Adult

Obsolescence: Low

Internet Search Engines and the Percentage of Searchable Net They Cover:

Northern Light	16.0
Snap	15.5
Alta Vista	15.5
Hot Bot	11.3
Microsoft	8.5
Infoseek	8.0
Google	7.8
Yahoo	7.4
Excite	5.6
Lycos	2.5
Euroseek	2.2

—NEC Research Institute

One of the fundamental realities of using the Internet as a search tool is Robert Heinlein's motto—TANSTAAFL (There Ain't No Such Thing As A Free Lunch). People really do excellent work only when they are paid, and most Internet search engines are free and point you to free sites where you generally get what you pay for. The alternative, at least in corporations, is Nexis-Lexis, which has access to just about everything but which can quickly turn into a significant budget item with just a few searches.

Northern Light is an alternative. The search engine is free and has both a WWW search and a "Special Collection" search. The Web search seems at least up to HotBot standards (at least that's my impression) and, of course, any World Wide Web locations are available free of charge.

The real value appears in The Northern Light Special Collection™, an online business library comprising 5,400 trusted, full-text journals, books, magazines, newswires, and reference sources. The breadth of information available in the Special Collection is unique to Northern Light, and includes a wide range of diverse sources such as *American Banker, ENR: Engineering News Record, The Lancet, PR Newswire,* and ABC, NPR, and Fox News Transcripts.

This is all a la carte. If you want an article, you pay from one to five dollars, which is charged to a credit card account. About half the time, just reading the free synopsis of the article is enough and when you do purchase one, it's worth the money. I have found it lightning-fast, even over a slow connection, and very thorough.

—Terry Irving

Acronym Finder

Web-Based Database of Acronyms

http://www.mtnds.com/af/

Type: Web site

First Developed: 1996

Price Range: Connect time

Key Features: Clear, comprehensible graphics

Ages: Post–high school

Obsolescence: Medium

Further Information:
❋ *http://wombat.doc.ic.ac.uk/foldoc/index.html*
The Free On-Line Dictionary of Computing.

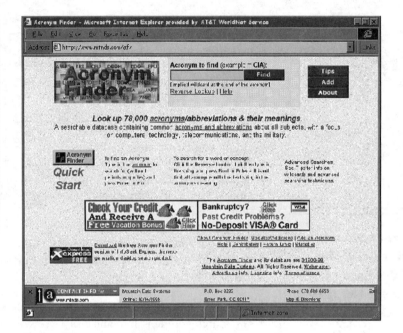

We seem to live in a world where nobody takes enough time to explain anything to anybody, and everyone is trying to cut corners in communication. Hence, technical communication tends to be a Cobb salad made of characters.

I found this dandy site when I was trying to decode some impenetrable military terms. It was referenced by a hacker who had assembled a robust list of words, code words, and acronyms none of us normal people are supposed to know. Every one I checked had an entry here. Invaluable.

→

→ Acronym Finder *continued*

From the Acronym Finder Web site...
WHAT'S AN ACRONYM?

Here's an example of an acronym:

North **A**tlantic **T**reaty **O**rganization = **NATO**

Technically, an acronym is defined as a (pronounceable) word formed from each of the first letters of the descriptive phrase, but throughout this site and its database we use a broader definition, which includes abbreviations or "initial-izations." It is our opinion that the distinction between acronym and abbreviation has already blurred to the point that it's no longer worth making. **Please don't write us to point this out.**

Though you sometimes see acronyms written with periods after each letter (e.g., **U.S.A.**), that form isn't used here. When entering search terms, don't include the periods (unless the acronym normally contains a period, i.e., **X.25**). ACRONYM is an acronym, too. Want to see a nested acronym? The term "SRK" contains *three levels* of "nested" acronyms (this is not made up).

Your search for ACRONYM returned 13 acronyms:

Acronym	Meaning
ACRONYM	A Clever Re-Organization Nudges Your Memory :-)
ACRONYM	A Completely Random Order Never Yields Meaning
ACRONYM	A Contrived Reduction Of Nomenclature Yielding Mnemonics :-)
ACRONYM	A Cryptic Reminder Of Names You Meet :-)
ACRONYM	Abbreviated Coded Rendition Of Name Yielding Meaning :-)
ACRONYM	Academy's Choice Reading, One Newspaper for You and Me (Newspaper of IMSA)
ACRONYM	Alphabetic Collocation Reducing Or Numbing Your Memory
ACRONYM	Alphabetically Coded Reminder Of Names You Misremember
ACRONYM	American Committee Really Out to Numb Your Mind :-)
ACRONYM	Association for the Conservation of Really Old New York Matrons :-)
ACRONYM	Association for the Creation of Rare and Outré Names for Young Men :-)
ACRONYMS	A Cryptic Rendition Of Names You Might See :-)
ACRONYMS	Abbreviated Capitalized Real-time Organizational Neological Yeomanlike Memory Surrogates :-)

Computer Emergency Response Team (CERT)

U.S. Government-Funded Research Center

http://www.cert.org/

Type: Web site

First Developed: 1988

Price Range: Connect time

Key Features: The most advanced info on computer mortality and morbidity in the world

Ages: High school and beyond

Obsolescence: Low

Further Information: See *The Cuckoo's Nest* by Clifford Stoll, and
❋ *http://www.disa.mil/ disahomejs.html*
for insight into how the military is handling these matters.

This is the Centers for Disease Control (CDC) for computer systems. Hollywood hasn't discovered this place yet (perhaps if Leonardo DiCaprio doesn't bathe for a while, the movie industry will invent geek chic, and CERT will end up in movies), but there is very dramatic stuff going on here.

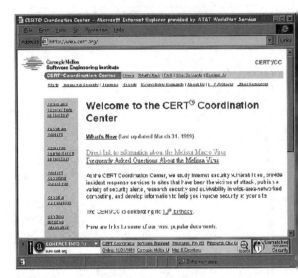

This is the place where computer viruses, worms, logic bombs, and other attempts to damage computers and crash networks are sensed and counter-attacks launched. This place is something like a digital fire department. When the sirens go off, more than likely millions of people will be affected. This site is a place where headlines are made and "ghost stories" debunked. There is no more authoritative place to go when you hear rumors of a computer virus.

From the CERT Web site:

It has now been 10 years since a Cornell University graduate student let loose the notorious "Morris Worm" that brought down much of the Internet and demonstrated the growing network's susceptibility to attack. Once a group of researchers drawn from government and the academic community successfully contained the worm, the National Computer Security Center (part of the National Security Agency), initiated a series of meetings to discuss preventing and responding to such occurrences in the future.

Shortly thereafter, the Defense Advanced Research Projects Agency (DARPA) announced its intention to fund development of the CERT® Coordination Center (CERT/CC). DARPA chose the Software Engineering Institute (SEI) on the campus of Carnegie Mellon University, in Pittsburgh, Penn, as the new center's home. The SEI was charged with establishing a capability to quickly and effectively coordinate communication among experts during security emergencies in order to prevent future incidents and building awareness of security issues across the Internet community. ➔

Raging Bull

Web Site Financial Reportage

http://www.ragingbull.com

Type: Web site

First Developed: 1998

Price Range: Connect time

Key Features: Screens allowing extensive personalization and filtering of other posts

Ages: Junior high and up

Obsolescence: A bear market, or imitation by competitors

The smartest of the Internet financial bulletin boards out there, although still somewhat prone to hype and rumor.

A few years ago, I would have been hard-pressed to name ten people I knew who traded stocks every single day. Now I can name hundreds of them, ranging from grandmothers to fresh college grads, from the very rich to people who borrow on their credit cards to do it. As this pool of people has grown, so has their tendency to interact on Internet bulletin boards, such as the Motley Fool, Yahoo Finance, and Silicon Investor. Unfortunately (for them and us), these bulletin boards are so prone to rumor, hype, and silly juvenilia that they are useless for all but the most patient investor. →

→ **...from the CERT Web site** *(continued)*

Since its inception in 1988, the CERT/CC has responded to more than 14,000 security incidents that have affected over 200,000 sites in the Department of Defense, other federal agencies, and the private sector. Consequently, the time to resolve computer security incidents and repair computer system vulnerabilities has decreased. Adoption of practices developed by the CERT/CC has improved resistance to attacks on networked computers and improved protection of the information stored on or transmitted by those computers.

Even so, as the Internet and other national information infrastructures become larger, more complex, and more interdependent, the frequency and severity of unauthorized intrusions into systems connected to these networks will increase. Today, as the CERT/CC begins its second decade of operations, the number of computer security incidents continues to grow as fast as the number of hosts on the Internet: from 80,000 hosts in 1988 to 29 million hosts today, with expected growth to 100 million by the year 2000.

Raging Bull *continued*

→ Raging Bull, although just as unmoderated as all the others, adds nice features to permit a more intelligent dialogue between its members. In particular, it allows you to set up personalized pages (by stock), which filter in posts from your "Favorite Members"; it also permits you to set up an "Ignore" function for postings from those members whom you can't stand. Any regular readers of bulletin boards know that there are specific participants with consistent insight and others deserving of the abuse they receive.

Raging Bull has 100,000 members already, but they are consistently more serious-minded than those at the other sites, and significantly less inclined toward the "You are an IDIOT" comments that are rampant elsewhere on the Web. The typical Raging Bull post is longer, more thoughtful, and more based on fact than those I have seen anywhere else.

All of that having been said, many believe that bulletin boards do more harm than good: They create a hair-trigger mentality among their participants and accelerate the spread of misinformation. Take them—Raging Bull included—with a pinch of salt.

—*Ravi Desai*

Fund Alarm
Web Site Devoted to Well-Informed Review of Mutual Funds
http://www.fundalarm.com

A noncommercial Web site devoted to the mutual fund industry, with the best commentary and the most accurate reporting of manager changes of any publication I have ever seen, including mainstream magazines.

Type: Web site
First Developed: 1996
Price Range: Connect time
Key Features: The smartest mutual fund writing out there
Ages: Post-high school
Obsolescence: Updated on the 1st of every month

Mutual fund reporting has been a journalistic backwater for so long that our expectations have dropped dramatically. We've gotten so used to reading bland interviews, recycled press releases, and out-of-date performance data that we're surprised when we find something of even mild insightfulness. This is a crying shame, because mutual funds dominate the financial lives of many Americans. With over 5,000 funds out there, and billions of dollars flowing into them in most months, the journalism community should be doing better.

Instead, Roy Weitz, a Los Angeles CPA, mutual fund aficionado, and talented writer, felt compelled to start Fund Alarm. It's a free Web site that contains a wealth of fund data, Weitz's proprietary rankings, and his witty commentary. Most important, it contains a current and historical database of manager changes, accompanied in many instances by Weitz's perspective, gained over many years of tracking the industry and its players. Fund companies have historically been reticent about sharing manager change information, except in rare instances. But Weitz's sleuthing and his near-obsessive knowledge of the industry make up for the industry's shyness and the journalism community's delinquency. If you're invested in mutual funds (or just want to read good financial writing) you owe the site a visit and Weitz your thanks.

—*Ravi Desai*

Vcall

Investors' Presentations and Conference Calls

http://www.vcall.com

Best Calls

Internet Investors' Conference Call Directory

http://www.bestcalls.com

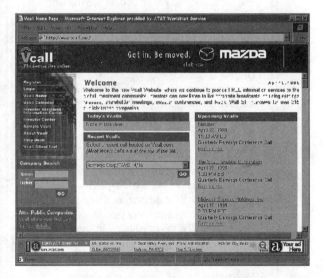

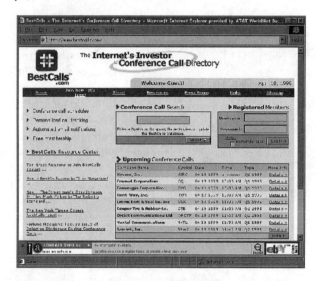

Sites offering individual investors access to the same presentations and conference calls as the big institutional investors, at the same time or only slightly delayed.

For years now, individual investors have watched in frustration as stock prices have gyrated wildly for no apparent reason. In many instances the gyrations were caused by company presentations and quarterly earnings conference calls, typically restricted to large institutional investors—mutual funds, hedge funds, investment banks, and the like. During the presentations, cell phone-toting traders would huddle at the back of the room and react to the information in real time, leaving individuals with no chance to participate until it was too late.

Type: Web sites

First Developed: 1997–1998

Price Range: Connect time

Key Features: Access to the same information as the big guys

Ages: Post-high school

Obsolescence: None. Constantly updated

Vcall and Bestcalls are both on a fundamentally democratic mission, forcing companies to open up these calls and presentations to individuals.

Vcall tends to focus on conference presentations and Web casts using RealAudio; Best Calls lists an enormous calendar of conference calls on its Web site and provides the dial-in numbers (typically toll-free) and the necessary access codes.

Both sites are free, remarkably well organized, and intuitive; the hiccups typically experienced with Web multimedia experiences are almost completely absent here.

—Ravi Desai

The Pencil Pages
Web Site Devoted to Basic Technology
http://www.pencilpages.com

Type: Web site

First Developed: 1996

Price Range: Connect time

Key Features: A narrow but engaging subject, treated thoroughly

Ages: 10 and up

Obsolescence: Medium

Further Information: The Pencil Palace at
✳ *http://www.teleport.com/ ~ bbrace/palace.html*
for more pencil obsession

You simply cannot talk about tools for the management of information without talking about pencils. Most everybody started working their ideas with a pencil. It seems as though everybody has a favorite tool (see WORK, LIFE, TOOLS), and for a lot of people it's a simple pencil.

Some folks like mechanical pencils (the Pentel 205 seems a favorite), some go for the basic Eberhard Faber #3. My Mom used to love the Blackwing, which came with a removable eraser. I can't find them anymore. Pencils have not disappeared, even under the duress of word processing. They are the cockroaches of the world of machinery.

WOOD PENCILS
from www.pencilpages.com

The most common of all pencils are the wood-encased types. A thin rod of a graphite composite or other material is sandwiched between two precisely formed strips of wood. An illustration of the steps involved in making wood pencils can be found here. Wood pencils are usually made with cedar because it can withstand the tortures of sharpening and stresses of writing without cracking or splitting. Recently, some pencils are being made using tropical "rain-forest" woods.

Wood pencils are most commonly hexagonal or rounded in shape, but some types may be triangular, octagonal, or otherwise. Some specialized pencils, such as carpenters pencils, artists' pencils, etc. may be flat or elliptical in shape.

Mechanical Pencils

Mechanical pencils come in many styles. Generally speaking, mechanical pencils consist of an engineered case made from metal, plastic, or a combination of both. The case contains an internal mechanism for advancing a thin, replaceable shaft of lead, which is actuated by twisting, pressing, or clicking some external gadget. Considerable design effort has gone into many of today's precision mechanical pencils.

Other Types

With increased awareness of environmental issues, some manufacturers are now producing pencils made from recycled materials, such as plastics, cloth, and sawdust. These pencils usually resemble wood-encased pencils and are comparable in quality to their wood counterparts. Examples of such pencils include Sanford Berol Eagle brands and Eberhard Faber American Ecowriter.

ColorMarketing

Design Industry Web Site

http://www.colormarketing.org/

Type: Professional group Web site

First Developed: 1962

Price Range: $650 for professionals to join up, including full access to the material on the web site

Key Features: The inside skinny on color

Ages: Post-college

Obsolescence: Medium

Ever since World War II when the U.S. Army studied the psychological impact of color, the use of colors to manipulate people's psyches has been standard practice.

The people who run the Color Marketing Group make a profession of the use of colors in products, media, and services. Though this is a pretty expensive organization to join, the people who belong gather and archive a great deal of the empirical evidence about the impact of color.

They also—in a loosely organized fashion—discuss the trends, and in so doing, reinforce them. If lime green shows up on SUVs, these will be the people to blame.

CMG (Color Marketing Group): FORECASTING THE COLOR OF PROFIT

CMG's Forecast Palettes are color "Directions," not directives. The colors selected for CMG's four Palettes show the course that colors are likely to take. Each Forecast Palette is an invaluable tool that members use and interpret for their specific industries and products.

Consumer and Contract Color Directions® Forecast Palettes Development Process

Step 1: This unique method of color forecasting is an ongoing process and begins well before CMG members convene. Conference registrants develop individual forecasts that encapsulate a wide variety of influences or trends that each color designer identifies within his or her industry.

Step 2: More than 650 CMG members from around the world collaborate during two international conferences each year to analyze color trends.

Step 3: Color Forecast Workshops take place concurrently at which CMG members interpret the direction of color and influences including the economy, the environment, politics, sports, demographics, social issues, technology, and cultural events, worldwide.

Step 4: Following a day and a half discussion of the many influences on colors and the shifts likely to occur in the coming years, a Color Directions Forecast is developed from each of the 45 Workshops.

Step 5: Through a Steering Committee, these Workshop Forecasts are consolidated into a final Palette.

This process is repeated during Colors Current® Workshops, which evaluate colors that are currently identified as "best sellers" in the marketplace. Participants also identify colors that are scheduled to appear in the marketplace within the next 12–18 months.

The Industry Standard

An Internet Newspaper Devoted to the Internet

http://www.thestandard.com/

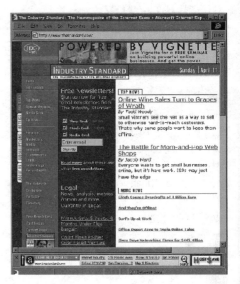

Type: News Web site

First Developed: 1998

Price Range: $0

Key Features: Reverse directory of the Net

Ages: 10 and up

Obsolescence: Medium

Further Information:
❋ *http://www.wired.com/news/* for interesting coverage, not quite so complete, but with real attitude

The Internet creates is own reality distortion field. Into the vortex are sucked people's brains, their money, and industry analysts. It even creates time distortions. Days are weeks, months are years. The Net makes for interesting times, and they are covered to a fare-thee-well in The Industry Standard (including really good statistics).

"The Best Publication Covering the Net"

—ABC News

"Saw the magazine. It looks great. The Internet Economy Index and metrics are killer."
—Rich Lefurgy, Chairman of the Internet Advertising Bureau

"It is the first magazine in a long while that I feel compelled to read cover to cover in one sitting as soon as I get it. Congratulations aplenty."
—Steven Nelson, Principal, ClearInk Corporation

"I really like The Industry Standard, and it has also become a rapid favorite around CitySearch. Here are a few comments:

1.) Everyone loves the statistics section. It always has something surprising in it and is very easy to absorb (kind of like the last page or two in the Economist, which is also excellent).

2.) I like the attitude/voice in the stories. Much more interesting commentary than Interactive Week, but not to the point of arrogance/self-absorption/cynicism of, well, most of the Web and Web focused commentary. We are all tired of the affected, oh-too-cool, oh-too-cynical voice of most of the Web-focused writing fraternity. I hope you keep avoiding it."
—Charles Conn, CEO, CitySearch, Inc.

The information really wants to be free on this site. It is rich with news, gossip, and speculation. Although they seem to threaten to cut off the air supply at any moment, the worst thing that happens is a constant request for your e-mail address and a commitment to a subscription. If you can stand it, this is a great place to get sucked in to the vortex.

Brittanica Web Site

Metasite Including Brittanica's Selection of Best Sites

http://www.britannica.com/

Were you to dash into a college-town Borders bookstore and kidnap all the people tending the information desk and sitting in the adjoining Starbucks, then set them all to work finding the best sites on the Web, the Brittanica site would be the result.

Type: Metasite

First Developed: 1997

Price Range: Connect time.

Key Features: Smart people's judgment as to what is best on the Net

Ages: 10 and up

Obsolescence: Medium

Further Information:
✱ *http://www.eb.com/* for Encyclopedia Brittanica on-line 7-day free trail.

These folks rate and review thousands of Web sites. Inevitably, the selection is somewhat academic, and some of the URLs disappear (there is no way any group of people could keep up with the Web these days).

Also on the site is a search engine leading to a short form of the *Encyclopedia Brittanica*, and that is handy too.

Britannica also publishes a feature called Bookmarks of the Smart & Famous. *So far the contributors seem to be a bit bookish (a dollop of* Washington Post *and a smidge of* Vanity Fair *would help), with a '60s counter-culture twist, but it is very interesting to see what interesting people find interesting on the Net.*

Contributors to Brittanica's Bookmarks of the Smart & Famous

Sven Birkerts	Mary Matalin
Alain de Botton	James McManus
Marisa Bowe	Marvin Minsky
Click & Clack	Phil Patton
Marshall Crenshaw	Henry Petroski
Ana Marie Cox	Howard Rheingold
Aaron Freeman	Douglas Rushkoff
David Gelernter	Aliza Sherman
Danny Hillis	Bruce Sterling
Stacy Horn	Sallie Tisdale
Michael Kinsley	Scott Turow

Dave Middleton's Flight Simulator Site

Metasite for Aircraft, Scenery, and Utilities for Microsoft Flight Simulator

http://www.avnet.co.uk/dmid

Type: Web site

First Developed: 1997

Price Range: Zero; everything here is free, and a work of love and art by folks obsessed with flight simulation

Key Features: An amazing array of airframes, ready to be used with MSFS

Ages: Junior High and beyond

Obsolescence: Low

Further Information:
❊ *http://www.microsoft.com/ games/products.asp?filter = fsim* for Microsoft's tarted up Web page dedicated to MS Fight Simulator

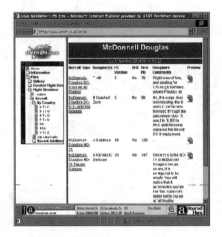

This is an extraordinarily rich place to go, if you have a copy of Microsoft Flight Simulator. Middleton has aggregated what appears to be the most and best of simulated airframes and scenery for use with MSFS.

There are hundreds of planes to download here, most of them less than 100K. I have downloaded several spectacular planes. A P51 that was a thrill to fly, an SR-71 that was very fast. The Space Shuttle had flight characteristics unlike any other craft, and I trust they were close to real. Every one of them comes with a preview, and most of them are desirable. Betcha can't download just one.

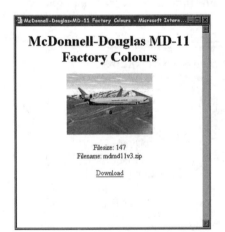

The scenery, although far more difficult to install than the planes (that's the fault of Microsoft and the MSFS originator Bruce Artwick, not Dave Middleton), was equally gratifying. I was able to get West Los Angeles in detail (it's fun to fly over home, and unless you live in downtown Chicago, the off-the-shelf version of MSFS doesn't naturally yield that thrill). I was also able to find a scenery file for Area 51/Groom Lake.

Middleton's site is an exemplar of good organization and rich resources.

The Coca Cola Formula
Web Site Devoted to the Secrets of Soft Drinks
http://www.sodafountain.com/softdrnk/cokercp.htm

Type: Web site

First Developed: 1998

Price Range: Connect time

Key Features: The big secret and lots of insights into the rest of popular foods

Ages: Junior high and beyond

Obsolescence: Low

Further Information:
✻ *http://www.alwayscocacola.com/LINKS.htm*
for a Coca Cola addicts site, and
✻ *http://www.coke.com/home.html*
for the corporate site

A healthy part of the romance of the Internet is finding out things you aren't supposed to know. The government, in particular the military, has cracked down on the proliferation of Web sites revealing classified information (amazingly, there were a lot of them).

After government secrets, the most closely guarded, highly valued secret is likely the Coke formula, and here (maybe) it is.

This site is much richer than that, however. It has recipes for pudding, the history of Campbell's Soup and Eskimo Pies, and a decent explanation of why egg creams don't have eggs.

Tabulatures on the Net
Documentation for Guitar Riffs On-Line
http://www.endprod.com/tab/

When I was growing up, guitar lessons were very popular. Nothing seemed hipper than playing lead guitar in a rock band. The lessons I took erased my enthusiasm fairly quickly, with their emphasis on basic technique.

Type: Source

First Developed: Distant past and revived for the Net

Price Range: Connect time

Key Features: Transcriptions of guitar recordings

Ages: 10 and up

Obsolescence: Low

Further Information:
✻ *http://www.olga.net/*
for the remnants of the legally castrated On Line Guitar Archive and
✻ *http://www.harmony-central.com/Guitar/tab.html*
for an entry to the OLGA database

Other than occasional air guitar shows, I left the instrument well behind until recently. It was then that my fifteen-year-old son Sean took an interest in guitar (I knew he had a taste for the stuff when I found him one day after school using the CD player to listen again and again to the Neil Young guitar intro to "Ohio" by Crosby, Stills, Nash, and Young). While he saved up to get an entry-level Fender Stratocaster, I looked around on the Net for guitar-related stuff. I found that the Net is chock-full of sites devoted to "tabs." ➔

Tabulatures on the Net *continued*

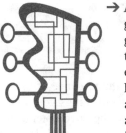

→ A tab is a six-line staff that graphically represents the guitar fingerboard, with the top line indicating the highest sounding string (high E). By placing a number on the appropriate line, the string and fret of any note can be indicated. The number 0 represents an open string.

More often than not, tabs are simply ASCII text files, with loving, attentive transcriptions of recorded music. You can get very precise tabs for "Stairway To Heaven." or all the songs by the Eagles, or the most obscure rock, R&B, and jazz recordings.

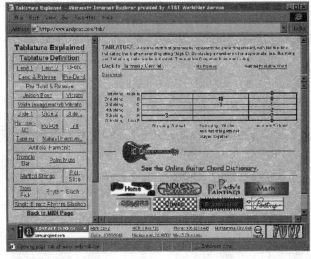

```
[Intro]
                    G                                    D
e:--------------------------3-3----------------------------2-2----|
B:--------------------------3-3-3--------------------------3-3----|
G:o--0h2p0-----0--0--0-0-0----0h2p0----0--4p2p0----2-2-----0|
D:o---------4p0----0--0-0----------4-----------0---0--0---o|
A:-----------------2------2-2------------------------------|
E:--------------------3----------------3------------------|

e:--------------------------3-3----------------------------2-2-----------|
B:--------------------------3-3-3--------------------------3-3-----------|
G:----------------0--0-0-0--0h2p0----0--4p2p0----2-2-----------|
D:----2--0-2-0----0--0-0----------4----------0--0-0---------|
A:0-2---2------2------2-----------------------------------|
E:----------------3--------------------------------------|
```

Above, a Sean Black favorite: the opening notes to Led Zeppelin's "Over the Hills and Far Away". Tabbed by Jimmy Pena.

Sean didn't take lessons, he took to the Net. Within two months, he was knocking off Jimmy Page riffs with gay abandon (he got his Stratocaster and a distortion box as well) and picking up all kinds of additional stuff. We had to tear him away from the guitar, as his grades began to suffer.

Tabs are a great learning tool, and another exemplar of Stewart Brand's assertion that information wants to be free. So free, in fact, that the people who make money by publishing music are trying to kill off the free distribution of tabs over the Net. I suspect they will be as successful as those folks trying to get rid of MP3 (see OLGA sidebar, next page).

All you have to do to find tabs on the Net is go to a search engine and search on tabs and whatever may be the name of the group or the song you are looking for (e.g. +tabs +eagles). The same holds true for MIDI files, but the quality of the transcriptions is not always high.

Tabulatures on the Net *continued*

From the OLGA (On Line Guitar Archive) Web site at www.olga.net:

Apr. 21st

The Polish and Californian sites appear the most reliable at this time.

Feb. 1st Update

Despite the official closure of OLGA, at least six renegade sites (Belgium, California, Poland, Slovakia, New Jersey and South Africa) are still distributing the OLGA collection. After the way that the International Lyrics Server (ILS) was treated recently, it's a surprise anyone is making lyrics/chords available on the Net.

The ILS people are talking about a licensing agreement with the companies that are suing them. That would be a very sad outcome to something that began as a spontaneous outgrowth of cooperation and community spirit on the Net, around 1988. Like OLGA, the ILS, and before it the Lyrics Archive at UWP (University of Wisconsin, Parkside), served as a place where people could share the music they loved and encourage the joy of singing.

OLGA will consider licensing only as a last resort, and we're not quite there yet. So for the meantime, guitar-players across the Net will have to hang on a little longer. In the meantime, chords and tab are still being exchanged in the guitar tab newsgroup.

Newsgroup

On Usenet, guitar players hang out in the group rec.music.makers.guitar.tablature. Check it out! Here's the FAQ file for the newsgroup.

OLGA Inc.

OLGA has incorporated. In order to pursue a legal resolution to the legality of by-ear transcriptions, OLGA needs to raise funds. So if you want to go on freely sharing crd and tab on the Internet, please make a donation to OLGA. We're also running advertisements on the Web pages only (not on files). OLGA is a registered nonprofit organization.

Revealing Things
The Smithsonian's On-line Exposition
http://www.si.edu/revealingthings/

The Smithsonian runs some of the best museums in the world in Washington, D.C. (the Air and Space Museum and the American History museums are great). For years the Smithsonian has toyed with multimedia, first with videodisc, then with CD-ROM, and now on the Net.

Type: Web site

First Developed: 1998

Price Range: Connect time

Key Features: Very fancy technology (watch out for Java applet errors)

Ages: 10 and up

Obsolescence: Medium

Further Information:
✳*http://www.si.edu*
for the main Smithsonian Web site

This is a very artsy-craftsy site, and requires all kinds of plug-ins and other such things that soup up your browser. It has all kinds of fancy animations and a navigation technique that owes a debt of gratitude to the THE BRAIN.

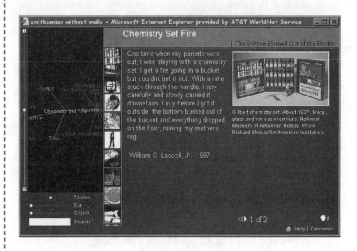

Virtual Hospital

Consumer Health and Medicine Web Site

http://www.vh.org/

Type: Resource and research Web site

First Developed: 1992

Price Range: Connect time

Key Features: Good concise information on common health issues

Ages: 10 and up

Obsolescence: Medium

Further Information:
✳ *http://www.pedinfo.org/*
for a good pediatric metasite

The Virtual Hospital is a digital health sciences library created in 1992 at the University of Iowa. It is the place you want to go before you go to your doctor, if you think your doctor is not the greatest communicator in the world. The searchable resources range from technical papers and morbidity reports to common-sense briefing on the most normal of things. →

from www.vh.org:

TEST CASE: What the Virtual Hospital has to say about tattoos...

You might want to know:

✚ Unsterile tattooing and piercing equipment and needles can spread serious infection, hepatitis, tetanus, or possibly even HIV.

✚ Asking a friend to apply a tattoo may ruin a friendship if the tattoo doesn't look like you thought it would.

✚ Tattoo removal is very expensive. A tattoo that costs $50 to apply may cost over $1000 to remove.

✚ The law in many states prohibits the tattooing of minors.

✚ Tattoos are not easy to remove and in some cases may cause permanent discoloration. Think carefully before getting a tattoo. You can't take it back if you don't like it.

✚ Some people are allergic to the tattoo dye. Their body will work to reject the tattoo.

✚ Blood donations cannot be made for a year after getting a tattoo, body piercing, or permanent makeup.

Questions to ask friends...

First:

✚ Talk to your friends or others who have been tattooed or pierced

✚ Ask them about their experience, the cost, pain, healing time, etc.

✚ Ask them what they would do if they had a chance to do it over again.

Second:

✚ Understand that you do not have to tattoo or pierce your body to belong.

✚ Remember that you are directly involved in decisions that affect your health and body.

✚ You can always change your mind or wait if you are not sure.

Third:

✚ If you decide to have a tattoo or body piercing, never tattoo or pierce your own body or let a friend do it because of potential complications.

Virtual Hospital *continued*

➔ Doctors use this site—it was designed to help keep them current. Patients are the ones who obsess. I'm sure doctors get sick of all the questions and the doubts (they have their own, I trust) and perhaps that was part of the motivation for the obvious care and diligence standing behind this site. Until recently, getting the answers was tough. The Virtual Hospital lowers the barriers.

TESTIMONIALS TO THE CREDIBILITY OF THE VIRTUAL HOSPITAL SITE

■ Professional Journals

1. JAMA—October 2, 1996 (review)

    "The Virtual Hospital is one of the best medical sites and a compelling demonstration of the Internet's potential to impact medical training and practice."

2. JAMA—January 8, 1997

    "Virtual Hospital listed as one of 18 'Sites to See' on the Internet"

3. The Lancet—December 23/30, 1995

    "(The Virtual Hospital) is an example of the potential for the World Wide Web in medical education…".

4. M.D. Computing—March 1995 (review)

    "The approach to medical education in the Virtual Hospital is original and successful. The concentration on clinical material makes this Web site an easy-to-use, enjoyable learning resource for students, clinicians, and medical informaticians."

5. Medicine On the Net—January 1999 (review)

    "The Virtual Hospital and its two subsidiary sites provide an important basic medical library. Many providers and patients will find this a good starting point for searching for information about virtually all kinds of conditions."

6. Advance for Health Information Executives— October 1997 (review)

    "I found the Virtual Hospital to be a user-friendly resource, a vivid example of what can be accomplished when technology leverages medical information."

7. American Medical News—May 11, 1998

    "The Virtual Hospital was listed as one of 4 quality medical gateways to the Web that can help physicians navigate the on-line environment."

8. American Family Physician—February 15, 1996

    "The Virtual Hospital is an excellent place to begin exploring the medical resources of the World Wide Web."

■ News Magazines

1. Time—Fall 1996

    "The Virtual Hospital was listed as one of 10 sites 'that your doctor might even recommend."

2. Time Special Issue on the Frontiers of Medicine— Fall 1996

    "At the University of Iowa, researchers have assembled an online hospital…. The multimedia Web pages are literally saving lives."

3. Newsweek—February 27, 1995

    "Virtual Hospital listed as one of 4 authoritative Internet health resources."

4. IEEE Computer Graphics and Applications—May 1996 (review)

    "Not a bad day's work for an electronic apprentice."

Federal Web Locator

Metasite for Access to U.S. Government Agencies

www.vcilp.org/Fed–Agency/fedwebloc.htmlsearch

Type: Metasite

First Developed: 1994

Price Range: Connect time

Key Features: Lots of links and a targeted search engine for federal agencies

Ages: Junior high and beyond

Obsolescence: Low

Further Information:
❋ *http://www.cilp.org/ newhome/welcomeam.html* for the CILP Web page

Somebody had to do this. The U.S. government is so big and far-flung, the only thing that could handle it all is the Net. Virtually every government agency now has a Web site (even many of the ones that are supposed to be secret, like the National Reconnaissance Office, the National Security Agency, etc.).

However, the URLs are all made of letter-salad, and are nonobvious, to say the least. So a couple of universities got together and created this terrific metapage. They keep it current, and apparently can't seem to stop finding new government agencies. They have a summary called "Latest Links." They didn't call it "What's New" as (I suppose) that would have implied the creation of new government agencies by legislative parthenogenesis. It would have been too depressing.

As it stands, it's hard enough to kill the present batch of the critters. Ask any Reaganite.

---

from www.vcilp.org:

About the Center for Information Law and Policy

The Center for Information Law and Policy (CILP), is dedicated to exploring issues at the intersection of law and technology. CILP is a joint effort between the Villanova University School of Law and the Illinois Institute of Technology's Chicago-Kent College of Law. CILP, a National Center for Automated Information Research–sponsored project, began as a research institute that developed wide-area networking needs for legal information from governmental sources, such as courts and federal agencies. CILP's current emphasis is on technology development and on articulating a vision of the role of the Internet in the National Information Infrastructure (NII). Most recently, CILP has been an active participant in the development of a global domain name policy, and in developing systems for Internet-based public office elections.

Home Energy Saver

Energy Use Analyzer

http://hes.lbl.gov

Type: Web site

First Developed: 1998

Price Range: Connect time

Key Features: Clever, simple analysis of home energy usage

Ages: Old enough to own or manage a household

Obsolescence: Low

Further Information:
❋ *http://www.homeorganizer.com/core/energy%20audit.htm*
for another Net audit of energy use (designed to take 10 minutes) and automated suggestion list of methods of improvement

Energy bills, even in Los Angeles, can get hefty. Many states are now phasing in electricity deregulation (e.g., California, Pennsylvania, Massachusetts) that will eventually impact every homeowner's utility bill. There is much to be done to reduce energy consumption, improve comfort levels, and realize annual savings that can increase and compound over the years.

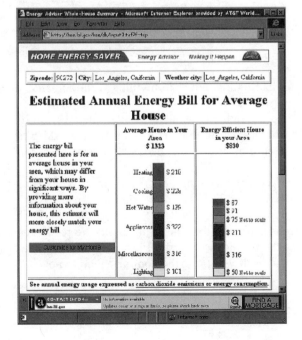

Because there is rarely any rational basis for comparison (other than a neighbor's bill, or the questionable info on your water and power bill), I find it hard to determine whether I'm using too much and/or paying too much. I haven't the vaguest idea what to do to make things more efficient.

A bit of Web searching found this site, carrying the imprimatur of the Department of Energy, the EPA, and the Lawrence Berkeley Labs. It seems to do a serviceable job of identifying relative values and will take the details of my energy life and render an evaluation. Pretty slick.

Corbis

Web-Based Repository for Humongous Image Library

http://www.corbis.com/

Type: Web site

First Developed: 1997

Price Range: From free to expensive, depending upon how you expect to use the image

Key Features: Good digitizing and rich inventory

Ages: Junior high and beyond

Obsolescence: Low

Further Information:
✳ *http://www.nara.gov/*
for the National Archives, which you own if you are a United States citizen, not Bill. Same goes for
✳ *http://lcweb.loc.gov/*
The Library of Congress

Corbis is one of Bill Gates' very big ideas. In the mid-eighties, when everyone thought content was king (largely the result of the appearance of the CD-ROM —when you have a hammer, everything looks like a nail), Gates started on a content acquisition binge.

He hustled almost every publisher in the Western world, trying to buy the digital rights to their properties. Nobody bit. Then he started working on the museums, and some of them rolled over a bit, but not many.

By that time, Gates had figured out that anything with the name Microsoft on it scared the spit out of everybody. So he started another company and focused on acquiring the rights to as many images, pictures, and films as he could. His big win was getting the Bettemann Archive, which held the best photographic record of history for the last 150 years or so.

The result is a spectacular collection, a Microsoft-like "give it away for free" marketing premise, and little or no mention of Gates.

All in all, it's a wonderful resource. The digitizations are really good, the promotions clever, the freebies wonderful. I just have this nagging suspicion that the Big Bad Wolf will be at the door any minute now.

IBM Patent Server

Search Site for Patents

http://www.patents.ibm.com

Type: Metasite

First Developed: 1998

Price Range: Connect time

Key Features: Extraordinary depth

Ages: 10 and up

Obsolescence: Low

Further Information:
❋ *http://ep.dips.org/*
for the European Patent Office; and
❋ *http://colitz.com/site/*
wacky.htm for a selection of weird
patents

Nothing is quite so fascinating as innovation, and IBM has created a database that recollects the sum total of innovation (at least those that someone cared enough about to protect legally).

IBM's collection is worldwide, and vast in its breadth.

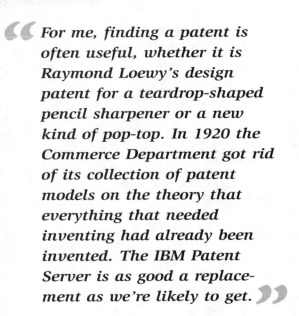

> **" *For me, finding a patent is often useful, whether it is Raymond Loewy's design patent for a teardrop-shaped pencil sharpener or a new kind of pop-top. In 1920 the Commerce Department got rid of its collection of patent models on the theory that everything that needed inventing had already been invented. The IBM Patent Server is as good a replacement as we're likely to get. "***
>
> **—Phil Patton**
> **author of Dreamland**
> **(the novel)**

→

IBM Patent Server *continued*

from www.patents.ibm.com
IBM Patent Server Search Results for *"mouse trap:"*

Patent Number	Issued	Title	Score
US04569149	02/11/1986	Disposable mouse trap	94%
US04127958	12/05/1978	Mouse trap	94%
US04270299	06/02/1981	Mouse trap	93%
US05832656	11/10/1998	Mouse trap	92%
US05005312	04/09/1991	Disposable mouse trap	92%
US05528853	06/25/1996	Magnetic computerized mouse trap	89%
US05107619	04/28/1992	Electric mouse trap	89%
US04468883	09/04/1984	Mouse trap	88%
US03992802	11/23/1976	Jar lid mouse trap	88%
US03769742	11/06/1973	MOUSE TRAP	88%
US04803799	02/14/1989	Mouse and rat trap	87%
US04641456	02/10/1987	Mouse trap	87%
US05471781	12/05/1995	Mouse trap	85%
US03757456	09/11/1973	TRIGGER AND BAIT ARRANGEMENT FOR MOUSE TRAP	85%
US05386663	02/07/1995	Multiple live mouse trap	84%
US05074819	12/24/1991	Toy bank novelty device	84%
USD0386554	11/18/1997	Mouse trap	84%
USD0382039	08/05/1997	Mouse trap with ramp and spinning bait bobbin	84%
USD0360251	07/11/1995	Mouse trap receptacle	84%
USD0335325	05/04/1993	Mouse trap	84%
USD0335325	05/04/1993	Mouse trap	84%
USD0335324	05/04/1993	Mouse trap	84%
USD0320833	10/15/1991	Mouse trap	84%
USD0273605	04/24/1984	Mouse trap	84%
USD0264867	06/08/1982	Mouse trap	84%
USD0261025	09/29/1981	Mouse trap	84%
US05142813	09/01/1992	Mouse trap apparatus	82%
US04154016	05/15/1979	Mouse trap with bait holding tilt tube	82%
US03786591	01/22/1974	MOUSE TRAP	82%
US05706601	01/13/1998	Trap and method for trapping a mouse or other rodent	80%
US05611171	03/18/1997	Multiple-catch mouse trap	80%
US05501031	03/26/1996	Mouse trap	80%
US05337512	08/16/1994	Mouse trap	80%
US05265371	11/30/1993	Box shaped rat trap	80%
US05123200	06/23/1992	Rat and mouse trap	80%
US05009317	04/23/1991	Animal trap with sanitary handling means	80%
US04845887	07/11/1989	Scented mouse trap	80%
US04787170	11/29/1988	Low oxygen scented mouse trap	80%
US04706408	11/17/1987	Marbles counter weighted repeating mouse trap	80%
US04662101	05/05/1987	Rat or mouse trap	80%
US05009317	04/23/1991	Animal trap with sanitary handling means	80%
US04845887	07/11/1989	Scented mouse trap	80%
US04787170	11/29/1988	Low oxygen scented mouse trap	80%

→

IBM Patent Server *continued*

→

Patent Number	Issued	Title	Score
US04706408	11/17/1987	Marbles counter weighted repeating mouse trap	80%
US04662101	05/05/1987	Rat or mouse trap	80%
US04583483	04/22/1986	Mechanical meter tampering indicator	80%
US04557066	12/10/1985	Animal trap	80%
US04508352	04/02/1985	Mouse trap game	80%
US04291486	09/29/1981	Rodent trap	80%
US04245423	01/20/1981	Animal trap	80%
US04241531	12/30/1980	Mouse trap	80%
US04161079	07/17/1979	Instant mouse trap	80%
US04030230	06/21/1977	Animal trap and package therefor	80%
US03992803	11/23/1976	Mouse trap	80%
USD0275511	09/11/1984	Mouse trap	80%
US05588249	12/31/1996	Humane rodent trap	77%
US05001857	03/26/1991	Animal trap	77%
US04413439	11/08/1983	Mousetrap	77%
US03883980	05/20/1975	Mousetrap	77%
US03628792	12/21/1971	GAME APPARATUS INVOLVING MAGNETIZED SELECTION OF GAME PIECES	

U.S. Patent and Trademark Office

http://www.uspto.gov/

The U.S. government's Web site, recently enhanced to cover just about everything; and it includes downloadable artwork. Starts in 1976 and runs though present day (for the U.S. only).

from www.uspto.gov

USPTO Search Results for "*mouse trap*":

	PAT. NO.	Title
1	5,706,601	Trap and method for trapping a mouse or other rodent
2	5,588,249	Humane rodent trap
3	5,528,853	Magnetic computerized mouse trap
4	5,386,663	Multiple live mouse trap
5	5,265,371	Box shaped rat trap
6	5,107,619	Electric mouse trap
7	5,074,819	Toy bank novelty device
8	5,009,317	Animal trap with sanitary handling means
9	5,005,312	Disposable mouse trap
10	4,583,483	Mechanical meter tampering indicator
11	4,574,519	Mouse trap
12	4,569,149	Disposable mouse trap
13	4,270,299	Mouse trap
14	4,245,423	Animal trap
15	4,127,958	Mouse trap
16	4,030,230	Animal trap and package therefor
17	3,992,802	Jar lid mouse trap

BrainMaker

Neural Net Software for Your PC

http://www.calsci.com/

Type: Software

First Developed: 1998

Price Range: $200–$250

Key Features: Figures stuff out; Spooky

Ages: Junior high and later

Obsolescence: Medium

Further Information:

❊ *http://www.ee.ed.ac.uk/ ~ aa/ old/nn.html*
for a good metapage on neural nets, and

❊ *http://www.eeb.ele.tue.nl/ neural/neural.html*
for the Carnagie Mellon metapage on same

BrainMaker, like TRUSTER, is voodoo software. It does things humans can't do. Apparently, all you need is a PC or Mac and sample data to build your own neural network. They have sold 25,000 of these packages, so it must do something beside eat processor cycles. Apparently, with enough raw data and the right organization, wonders can be worked.

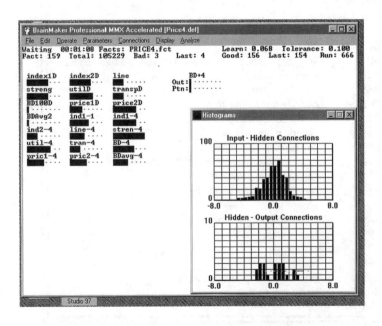

How BrainMaker Neural Networks Work

Neural networks are named after the cells in the human brain that perform intelligent operations. The brain is made up of billions of neuron cells. Each of these cells is like a tiny computer with extremely limited capabilities; however, connected together, these cells form the most intelligent system known. Neural networks are formed from hundreds or thousands of simulated neurons connected together in much the same way as the brain's neurons.

Just like people, neural networks learn from experience, not from programming. Neural networks are good at pattern recognition, generalization, and trend prediction. They are fast, tolerant of imperfect data, and do not need formulas or rules. Neural networks are trained by repeatedly presenting examples to the network. Each example includes both inputs (information you would use to make a decision) and outputs (the resulting decision, prediction, or response).

Your network tries to learn each of your examples in turn, calculating its output based on the inputs you provided. If the network output doesn't match the target output, BrainMaker corrects the network by changing its internal connections. This trial-and-error process continues until the network reaches your specified level of accuracy. Once the network is trained and tested, you can give it new input information, and it will produce a prediction. Designing your neural network is largely a matter of identifying which data are input, and what you want to predict, assess, classify, or recognize.

BrainMaker *continued*

from www.calsci.com

Here's how some of those copies have been put to use (drawn from the Web site, with claims unverified). I was most impressed with the mosquito sex determination—that's a job no human being should have to do.

Stocks, Commodities, and Futures

Standard and Poor's 500 Prediction
Predicts the S&P 500 one day ahead and one week ahead with better accuracy than traditional methods.

Predicting Mutual Funds
A neural network to predict next week's price of ten selected mutual funds with 70 percent accuracy.

Forecasting Stock Prices
Neural networks rate underpriced stock beating the S&P.

Business, Management, and Finance

Cost Prediction
Predicts gas price change with 97 percent accuracy.

Direct Marketing Mail Prediction
Improves response rates from 4.9 percent to 8.2 percent.

Credit Scoring
Predicts loan application success with 75–80 percent accuracy.

Identifing Policemen with Potential for Misconduct
The Chicago Police Department predicts misconduct potential based on employee records.

Finding Gold with Neural Networks
U.S. Mineral Labs uses advanced soil analysis and BrainMaker to find gold deposits.

Medical Applications

Breast Cancer Cell Analysis
Image analysis ignores benign cells and classifies malignant cells.

Hospital Expenses Reduced
Improves the quality of care, reduces death rate, and saved $500,000 in the first 15 months of use.

Diagnosing Heart Attacks
Recognizes Acute Myocardial Infarction from enzyme data.

Classifying Patients for Psychiatric Care
Predicts length of stay for psychiatric patients, saving money.

Sports Applications

Thoroughbred Horse Racing
22 races, 17 winning horses.

Thoroughbred Horse Racing
39 percent of winners picked at odds better than 4.5 to 1.

Dog Racing
94 percent accuracy picking first place.

Science

Solar Flare Prediction
Predicts the next major solar flare; helps prevent problems for power plants.

Mosquito Identification
100 percent accuracy distinguishing between male and female, two species.

Predicting El Nino
A research team at the National Oceanic and Atmospheric Administration in Boulder, Colorado, has trained a neural network to predict El Nino.

Manufacturing

Computer Chip Manufacturing Quality
Analyzes chip failures to help improve yields.

Beer Testing
Identifies the organic content of competitors' beer vapors with 96% accuracy.

Optimizing Enzyme Synthesis
Predicts the outcome of a chemical reaction controlled by molar ratios, temperature, pressure, amount of enzyme, and stirring speed.

Pattern Recognition

Speech Recognition
Voice mail recognition for rotary phone systems.

Classification of Text
Classifies information read in from OCR.

Working with Chaos
Search for strange attractors.

TEN SMART WEB SITES
THE INFORMATICA GUIDE TO BUYING
KNOWLEDGE-BASED PRODUCTS ON-LINE

1. **World Of Science**
   http://www.worldofscience.com/

   A Web-based retailer, with a wide array of science-based products, primarily learning tools for kids. See also *http://letsget-growing.com/pages/lenses.html* for a fine Web site devoted to educational materials associated with the outside, and *http://www.indigo.com/* for more fine educational products.

2. **Discovery/The Nature Store**
   http://shopping.discovery.com/

   The aggregate retail chain run by the Discovery Channel. The bricks and mortar retail storefronts have remained the same, with The Nature Store bearing more of a green, organic feel, and the Discovery stores more in the science/gadget domain. Part of the inventory available via the Web site.

3. **Lakeshore**
   http://www.lakeshorelearning.com/home.htm

   For years, Lakeshore has been a trusted supplier of educational tools, toys, books, and manipulatives via a catalog (7,000,000 mailed every year) and several retail stores. Now some of the 12,000 products in inventory are available via the Web site.

4. **Edmund Scientific**
   http://www.edsci.com

   No kid who grew up in the '50s and '60s recollects the Edmund Scientific catalog with anything less than pure pleasure. Many of us got our first binoculars, telescopes, magnets, radiometers (that neat thing that twirls in the sunlight), and other sundry crud from Edmund. The catalog is still rich and varied, and a revamped Web site brings the catalog into cyberspace.

5. **Bookworm**
   http://www.kidsreads.com/

   Thousands of kids' books, and all of them look pretty good. How to choose? This Web site, created and maintained by a former editor from one of the big publishing houses, does a yeoman's job of keeping up and letting you know what's what.

6. **Explorastore**
   http://www.explorastore.com/

   Inspired by San Francisco's Exploratorium, this site focuses on those products that make a point of demonstrating scientific and technical realities. →

KNOWLEDGE-BASED PRODUCTS

(THE LAST FOUR OF THE INFORMATICA GUIDE TO BUYING KNOWLEDGE-BASED PRODUCTS ON-LINE

7. BookReporter
http://www.bookreporter.com/brc/index.asp

Thoughtful, well-informed Web site, devoted to making sense of the current crop of books.

8. Amazon
www.amazon.com

As big and aggressive as it is, Amazon benefits by its early start in book e-commerce. The database is excellent for research, and many (if not all) of the listed books benefit by Amazon reviews, citations from published reviews, and consumer reviews (which we find so insightful that we have used them liberally throughout *Informatica*).

9. The New York Times
http://archives.nytimes.com/archives/

All the news that's fit to digitize stretching back for decades. It costs a bit for some of the archival stuff, but there is nothing like it in the world. There is precious little hyperlinking from within the articles, but that can be overcome through judicious use of the search facilities.

10. USA Today
http://archives.usatoday.com/plweb-cgi/fast-web?searchform+view1

Almost two decades worth of the peppy, broad-based culturally attuned material from the paper that wouldn't go away, no matter how much stuffy journalists disdained it. Costs are a bit high, but I suspect the free market, and microtransaction technology, will take care of that.

20 WEB SITES
OFF THE BEATEN PATH
THE INFORMATICA GUIDE TO KEEPING IN TOUCH

1. The Scout Report
http://www.scout.cs.wisc.edu/scout/report/index.html

Done up at the University of Wisconsin at Madison, The Scout Report is the flagship publication of the Internet Scout Project. Published every Friday both on the Web and by e-mail, it provides a fast, convenient way to stay informed of valuable resources on the Internet. A team of professional librarians and subject matter experts select, research, and annotate each resource. The "Current Awareness Metapage" they maintain in several categories of information is simply amazing.

2. Popular Science Best of What's New
http://www.popsci.com/bown/

Always the most fun part of the magazine, the Popsci Best of What's New section of their Web site is kept up to date and draws neat new stuff from a variety of territories, not just consumer electronics. Check out Andy Pargh's Gadget Guru Web site at *http://www.gadgetguru.com/* for a slightly more press release-driven summary of what's new.

3. MetaSpy
http://www.metaspy.com/

MetaSpy, operated by Go2Net, is a live report on what queries are being passed through the Metacrawler metasearch engine, as well as the top queries over the past few days (see Culture Wars). A very effective read on what's passing through the popular mind. Like Metaspy, AskJeeves (*http://www.askjeeves.com*) publishes both the current and most popular recent queries. Here the users are less technically sophisticated (makes sense, as they are looking for the help of natural language queries) and probably a bit more representative of noncyberenhanced humanity.

4. Centers for Disease Control
http://www.cdc.gov/od/oc/media/

If you're traveling afar, or just not certain of the meat you bought at the market, this site has the best, most authoritative material on health threats of all kinds. →

5. U.S. Census Population Clock
http://www.census.gov/main/www/
popclock.html

Just a little reminder of how many people are likely to move in next door, no matter where you think your property boundaries exist.

6. It's About Now
http://seaborg.nmu.edu/seaborg/internet/
now.html

Devoted primarily to the current state of the physical universe, this is a terrific metapage for imagery of the solar system, weather, and other kinds of physically sensed conditions. See also Earth Now at *http://metosrv2.umd.edu/~owen/EARTHCAST/BUTTONS1/buttons1.html*, a fine physical sciences metapage run by the University of Maryland's Meteorology Department.

7. U.S. Navy's Fleet Numerical Meteorology and Oceanography Center
http://www.fnmoc.navy.mil/

If you want to see weather the way people who live and die by it (literally) look at it, this is the place to go. No fancy packaging, just the real stuff, right now.

8. Flight Tracker
http://www.thetrip.com/usertools/
flighttracking/

Follow that commercial flight, wherever it is going in North America.

9. GossipCentral
http://www.gossipcentral.com/

BRILL'S CONTENT says, "Inquiring minds ought to know about Gossip Central, a page with links to the Web's whisper circuit. The site collects 17 of the best gossip sheets in the business, including columns from dish legends Liz Smith and Army Archerd and publications such as *People* and *The Hollywood Reporter*." →

KEEPING IN TOUCH

(FIVE MORE OF THE iNFORMATICA GUIDE TO 20 WEB SITES OFF THE BEATEN PATH...)

WEB SITES

10. Computer Emergency Response Team
http://www.cert.org/

CERT is the Net's fire department. When there's an outbreak of something bad (virus, worm, or other attack on the Net, operating systems, and the like), these guys are the first to have reliable reportage on the matter. See *http://www.mids.org/mapsale/world/* for a world map showing the number of Internet servers, and where they are.

11. Society of Amateur Scientists Discussion Forum
http://earth.thesphere.com/SAS/

A multiplex of discussions about all kinds of new topics in the sciences. See also *http://www.eurekalert.org*, a comprehensive Web site about the latest research advances in science, medicine, health, and technology, with 20 news releases posted each day, on the average.

12. Recent Earthquake Reports
http://hoshi.cic.sfu.ca/~hazard/RECENT/recent.quake.html

Good metapage leading to current info on seismic activity around the world. Also, check out the Seismocam in Southern California at *http://www.scecdc.scec.org/seismocam/realtime.cam/realtime.html*, and the USGS Seismic report at *http://quake.wr.usgs.gov/recenteqs/Maps/Los_Angeles.html*, and *http://volcano.und.nodak.edu/vwdocs/current_volcs/current.html* for currently erupting volcanoes.

13. NASA's Real-Time Data
http://38.201.67.72/realdata/tracking/index.html

Shows the present position of the MIR Space Station and any Space Shuttle that might be aloft. Gives time and location for sighting from Earth, as well.

14. The World Right Now
http://www.cam-orl.co.uk/world.html

A metapage of Netcams (live video cameras, hooked up to the Web and constantly broadcasting live), maintained by ATT's Cambridge Research Center. See the world from your desktop. See also *http://www.earthcam.com/*, another metapage for Netcams. →

KEEPING IN TOUCH

(THE LAST FIVE OF THE iNFORMATICA GUIDE TO 20 WEB SITES OFF THE BEATEN PATH...)

WEB SITES

16. The History Channel's This Day in History Report
http://www.historychannel.com/thisday/

A little bit of history, daily, is good for perspective.

17. Maxwell Traffic Report
http://traffic.maxwell.com/

Real-time travel advisories and highway maps for major American cities.

18. Economeister
http://www.economeister.com/

An effective presentation of real-time economic decisions. See also *http://www.vcall.com*, and *http://www.bestcalls.com* for sites offering individual investors access to the same presentations and conference calls that the big institutional investors are getting.

19. The Drudge Report
http://www.drudgereport.com/

Michael Kinsley says Drudge is irresponsible, often inaccurate, and hopelessly biased. But he checks it all the time and says that Slate is a copy of the idea. It's a good idea, and Drudge is always fast and interesting.

20. USA Today's Best-Selling Books
http://www.usatoday.com/life/enter/books/leb.htm

Scott Turow says, "I regard the site as invaluable, since they survey booksellers more widely than any other list. I also appreciate that they report raw numbers, without attempting to weight for factors such as category (that is, they have cookbooks and juvenile fiction running head to head) or what the editors' choices are. I want to hear from Joe Friday—just the facts—and that's what I get there."

CYBERBROWSING

HOW MARY FINDS QUALITY ON THE NET

Here's what Mary Matalin, author and political strategist, has to say about shopping for used, rare books. "Shopping sites are particularly practical for those necessary quality-of-life items I never make time to purchase in person: books and music. Amazon.com is my favorite source for current books, especially for the reader reviews, which are much more helpful than the elitist traditional ones. For secondhand books, Advanced Book Exchange (*http://www.abebooks.com*), Bibliofind (*http://www.bibliofind.com*—now an Amazon subsidiary), and Interloc (*http://www2.alibris.com/cgi-bin/texis/bookstore* ...aka *Alibris*) are better. The one-click service is a godsend."

Amazon.com established a truly fine bookseller standard right out of the box. Giving readers a space to include their own comments on titles not only honors the interactive spirit of the Net but also informs your search for the right reading material like nothing else can.

HOW SUE FOUND *LIVERPOOL JARGE*

My sister Sue Black, the designer of *Informatica*, explains how she found one of my favorite books on the Net: "I was once searching for an old out-of-print novel of classic English humor (*Make Way for Lucia*, by E.F. Benson) and—though Amazon.com didn't have the book in stock—I was able to find the title in their cyberstacks complete with plenty of reader commentary. I chose a particularly insightful reader review and e-mailed the writer to see if she had a clue as to where I might find the book.

Waltraut, a true lover of books, wrote back without delay offering a number of ideas including Bibliofind.com—a literary electronic community and treasure trove of out-of-print and hard-to-find volumes. Not only did I find my *Lucia* there, but also a crisp, beautiful, signed edition of a rare, limited edition, privately printed book that my father used to read to my brother and me when we were kids (*Liverpool Jarge*, by Halliday Witherspoon—a total hoot—Ed.).

I snapped that one up in seconds, and it arrived in time to render Peter utterly speechless on his birthday. A sweet sidenote is that the bookseller was willing to send it to me immediately, trusting me to put a check in the mail. It was a charming combination of computer-age efficiency and old-world community. Not to mention that Waltraut and I continue a wonderful e-mail correspondence to this day. Who says cyberspace is cold and impersonal?"

These are the only known likenesses of Liverpool Jarge, a salty dog of considerable ill-repute. Below, the inside front cover of my cherished volume. Note the author's signature (#119 of 1000 signed copies) across Jarge's elaborately tattooed chest.

Philip Hale, Boston Herald, Hayden Jones & Anonymous Artist—

A Million Thanks!

Copyright 1933

Square Rigger Co.

Philip Hale

writes

The Preface

#119

Slinky Physics
A Web Tutorial on the Complexity of Something Simple
http://www.eecs.umich.edu/mathscience/funexperiments/agesubject/lessons/newton/slink.html

Type: Web site

First Developed: 1995

Price Range: Connect time

Key Features: Very simple, easy to use

Ages: Junior high and later

Obsolescence: Low

Further Information:
❋ *http://users.andara.com/ ~ bpaul/slinky.html*
A Slinky metapage with a boatload of Slinky links

Slinkys are now over 50 years old. When they were first introduced, they cost $1.00. Today they cost $1.99. There have been 250 million sold, and they are still made on the machines designed for their manufacture in 1945.

There's way more to them than that, however. The neatest stuff about Slinkys is their physics. They are pure wave motion. They trade on inertia and friction. They are worth your attention.

from http://www.eecs.umich.edu

SLINKY INSTRUCTIONS

1. TO WALK SLINKY DOWN STAIRS
Place Slinky on top stair. Grip coil at top and flip it over toward middle of the next lower step, releasing hold on Slinky. Now Slinky takes over and walks downstairs all by itself.

2. TO PLAY WITH SLINKY IN HANDS
Hold end coils of Slinky with both hands. Now raise and lower each hand in a rhythmic motion.

3. TO WALK SLINKY DOWN INCLINE OR SLOPE
Any board or table top with a nonslip surface will do. Slope surface so rise equals about 1 foot for every 4 foot length. Place Slinky at top, flip and watch Slinky start down, end over end.

4. TO BOUNCE SLINKY UP AND DOWN
Hold a few coils tightly in one hand, allowing (the) rest of Slinky to hang down. Now in a bouncing motion, move hand slowly up and down.

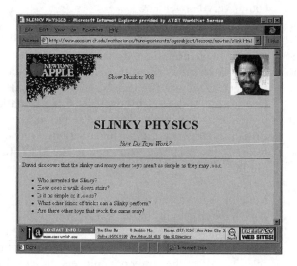

PGP (Pretty Good Privacy)

Software for the Encryption of Digital Messages

http://www.pgpi.com

Type: Web site

First Developed: 1994

Price Range: Connect time

Key Features: Free encryption technology

Ages: 10 and up

Obsolescence: Good question

Further Information:
✳ *http://www.wired.com/wired/archive/7.04/crypto.html*
A Wired Article—an excerpt from Steven Levy's forthcoming book on cryptography—that dramatically revises the history of PGP, and by implication calls into question the surety of PGP

[The PGP story is...conceivably, a brilliant deception carried on for a quarter century to the benefit of the interests of the United States and Britain.]

The PGP story is one of amazing technological achievement, distrust of the government, intellectual arrogance, and, conceivably, a brilliant deception carried on for a quarter century to the benefit of the interests of the United States and Britain.

The generally accepted history of PGP holds that a crackerjack group of M.I.T. students discovered the "Trapdoor Algorithm" in the 1970s, an unexpected mathematical manipulation that made possible the holy grail of international statecraft—an unbreakable cipher.

The unbreakable cipher is an intellectual conceit that occurs every generation or two. During World War I, the "unbreakable" ciphers of the time fell prey to the new science of statistics. Analysis of English showed, for example, that the character *e* was the most common letter to occur. Whatever character occurred most often in the ciphertext was most likely e. Bingo, messages thought secure were easily decrypted.

In World War II, the German Enigma machine was thought to be beyond the reach of cryptanalysis. But the development of the computer in association with advanced traffic analysis techniques led to breaking Enigma, a secret that was kept well after World War II. But why not reveal the triumph, once the war was over?

Because, in the emerging Cold War, Britain found it useful to manufacture Enigma machines and see to it that the diplomats and militaries of a very large number of Third World countries adopted the Enigma for their secure communications. Other countries couldn't crack it, but the U.S. and Britain could. Very convenient.

As Stephen Levy recently revealed in an April 1999 *Wired* Magazine article, a member of Britain's GCHQ (Government Communications Headquarters), the peer agency to the U.S. NSA (see NATIONAL CRYPTOLOGIC MUSEUM), discovered the mathematical principle back in the 1960s, and others in the British intelligence establishment figured out how to apply the principle years before the M.I.T. folks did it.

None of that was revealed when the *Scientific American* article on the M.I.T. discovery ran in July 1977, even after the NSA had requested that the material not be published, in the interest of national security. All of the "trapdoor" players presented themselves as Davids against the Goliath of the NSA and fought the good fight to give everyone secure communication. ➔

PGP Encryption Software *continued*

→ They became cult heroes and were succeeded by Phil Zimmermann. Zimmermann crafted PGP (for Pretty Good Privacy), a practical implementation of the "Public Key System" that was refined from the Trapdoor Algorithm. It worked on the Mac, it worked on the PC, and Zimmermann posted it on the Net. The laws forbade cross-border distribution of high quality encryption systems, but—with a wink and a nod—Zimmermann noted that he couldn't control what people did with his freeware.

Most folks in the computer industry cheered Zimmermann on, lobbied for free exchange of technologies, and fought against government initiatives to control the distribution of PGP. While they were fighting the good fight, PGP made its way to every nook and cranny of the computerized world.

All the while, folks at the FBI, NSA, and Department of Defense warned that putting powerful encryption systems in the hands of terrorists, drug cartels, and rogue nations could harm the U.S. They were largely ignored. So goes the legend.

Legend is an interesting word. It is the term of art used in the →

From the PGP Web site (www.pgpi.com):

Introduction

PGP (short for Pretty Good Privacy) is a public key encryption program originally written by Phil Zimmermann in 1991. Over the past few years, PGP has got thousands of adherent supporters all over the globe and has become a defacto standard for encryption of e-mail on the Internet. If you don't know whether PGP is something for you, please take some time to read Phil Zimmermann's article on why you should use PGP. Adam Back has written this history of PGP.

Platforms

PGP is available for many different platforms, including Unix, MS-DOS, Windows, OS/2, Macintosh, Amiga, and Atari.

Latest versions

The latest international freeware versions of PGP are 6.0.2i (Windows 95/NT and MacOS only) and 5.0i (other platforms). The older 2.6.3i is still available, but you may experience incompatibility problems if you are communicating with users of PGP 5.0 and later. You can download all versions here. However, there are many other versions of PGP, both freeware and commercial.

Documentation

The PGP documentation is a good starting point. If you have a question about PGP, it is probably answered in one of the many FAQs. A number of PGP books are also available.

Language support

PGP and the PGP User's Guide have been translated into many different languages. There are also a number of non-English PGP resources available on the Web.

Legal stuff

Contrary to what many people seem to think, PGP is perfectly legal to use, provided that you choose the right version and don't download the program from a site in the USA if you're somewhere else in the world.

Other PGP products

PGP is primarily used for encrypting e-mail. PGPfone and PGPdisk are two other products that use PGP encryption technology to secure phone calls and encrypt disk partitions, respectively. The PGP message format has now been standardized through RFC 2440, and in the future we will undoubtedly see many new PGP compatible products

PGP resources on the Web

The PGP Directory is a good starting point for PGP exploration on the Web.

PGP Encryption Software *continued*

→ intelligence community for a false cover story constructed to mask the real intentions of players in a covert enterprise.

So comes the question: what if PGP isn't secure? What if the NSA and GCHQ figured out years ago how to crack the system? What if there are other more advanced systems in development in the public sector—systems that are harder to crack, systems that the authorities really doesn't want to see proliferate?

...not a soul can prove that PGP has not been cracked.

What if PGP is an elaborate, stunningly successful ruse, built to trade on the intellectual arrogance and knee-jerk antigovernment leanings of the computer culture? What if the Enigma scenario has been played out again? Nobody has suggested it in public. It would be too damaging for the security agencies. It would be too embarrassing for the techies. It would be a hoot.

And not a soul can prove that PGP has not been cracked.

From Adam Back's History of PGP

(http://www.dcs.ex.ac.uk/ ~ aba/timeline/)

History of crypto as it applies to PGP

1. The year is 1976, a cryptographer and privacy advocate named Whitfield Diffie, together with an electrical engineer named Martin Hellman discovers public key cryptography. (DH key exchange is still a commonly used key exchange protocol—DH = Diffie-Hellman).

2. 1977—Ron Rivest, Adi Shamir, and Len Adleman discover another more general public key system called RSA (after surnames Rivest, Shamir, and Adleman). R, S & A were researchers at MIT (significant later, because MIT has part ownership of patents.)

3. NSA tells MIT and R, S & A that they'd better not publish this or else.

4. Amusingly, Adi Shamir (S from RSA) isn't even a U.S. citizen, he's an Israeli national, and is now back in Israel at the Weitzmann Institute. Who knows what the NSA would have done about him if they had succeeded in supressing RSA—not allowed him out of the U.S.?

5. MIT and R, S & A ignore NSA and publish anyway in *SciAm* July 1977, in an article entitled "New Directions in Cryptography." They later published RSA in *Comms ACM* (Feb 1978, vol 21, no 2, pp 120–126 (an international publication) in case you want to see if it's in your library—it's in Exeter Univ (UK) library).

6. Because the publication was a rush job due to the NSA, R, S & A and the later formed PKP and RSADSI lose patent rights to RSA crypto outside the U.S. This is because most places outside the U.S., you have to obtain a patent *before* publication, whereas in the U.S., you have one year from the publication date to file for patents. This also had implications for PGP later. Another issue is that the patent law in the U.S. is unusual in that it allows the patenting of algorithms (well, algorithms as embodied by a system for a specific purpose—what is being patented is the system). The RSA crypto system would probably not have obtained a patent in many other countries due to it being an algorithm, and hence it would probably have been ruled unpatentable, even if R, S & A had not been rushed by the NSA's interference.

U.S. Census Bureau Web Site

Metasite for Census Data

http://www.census.gov/

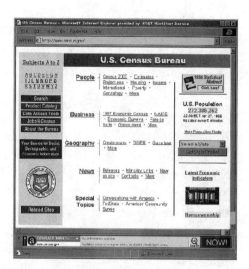

Type: Metasite

First Developed: 1998

Price Range: Connect time

Key Features: Accurate information on who we are

Ages: 18 and up

Obsolescence: Low

Further Information:
✳ *http://www.nwbuildnet.com/ nwbn/mapservice.html*
a fine metapage leading to Web-based resources, including GovSearch, Census Tiger Data, Four11 Email, USPS Zip+4, OSHA Search, US Constitution, Home Finder, SIC Codes, Web site Registration, Trade Shows

"The Congress shall have power to lay and collect taxes on incomes, from whatever source derived, without apportionment among the several states, and without regard to any census or enumeration."

—16th Amendment

Census data are used to allocate seats in the U.S. House of Representatives and to distribute federal funds based on population. That's why the recent dispute over using statistical sampling to determine the national head count was so bitterly fought, and had to be resolved in the U.S. federal courts.

So far, the courts believe that leaving the American census in the hands of computer programmers might not be in keeping with the original intent of the Founding Fathers. When considering the extraordinary breadth of utility of the census data, any mucking with its accuracy would be a very bad idea.

Consider the government's census Web site. The folks who run it seem to be no-nonsense types. Their mission statement is remarkable in its simplicity and clarity: To be the preeminent collector and provider of timely, relevant, and quality data about the people and economy of the United States.

And that it is. This site offers such simple info as birthrates for each year going back for over two centuries. If you want to see what the baby boom actually is, all you need

do is drop that data into a spreadsheet and plot a graph.

The site is rich with more subtle and complex stuff as well. Notable is the Tiger map database, which matches census data with maps. It's fun to enter your ZIP code, and see what census data have to say about where you live and who you are.

Race, income, education—all these statistics and lots more tell us who we are and work as reliable predictors of who we will be.

"No capitation, or other direct, tax shall be laid, unless in proportion to the Census or enumeration herein before directed to be taken."

—U.S. Constitution

Federation of American Scientists Web Site
Web Site Designed to Reveal Government Secrets
http://www.fas.org/irp/offdocs/direct.htm

Type: Web site

First Developed: 1995

Price Range: Connect time

Key Features: Secrets revealed

Ages: 10 and up

Obsolescence: Low.

Further Information:
✷ *http://gopher.nara.gov/*
fedreg/eos/
for executive orders published in
the Federal Registry (not all of them,
as some are immediately classified)

There is a great deal that the U.S. government does that is done quietly. There are a great many policies that are a pure function of the discretion of the president. There are people who think that this stuff should be known and discussed. Some of these people do something about it, and some of them are part of the Federation of American Scientists.

Some of the stuff they put on their Web site probably should not see the light of day, but that's not their fault, rather that is the fault of crappy security within the government and its contractors (and some of it is probably a result of very calculated disinformation initiatives). You figure it out.

"The Federation of American Scientists is engaged in analysis and advocacy on science, technology and public policy for global security. A privately-funded non-profit policy organization whose Board of Sponsors includes over 55 American Nobel Laureates, FAS was founded as the Federation of Atomic Scientists in 1945 by members of the Manhattan Project who produced the first atomic bomb."

—from the FAS Web site

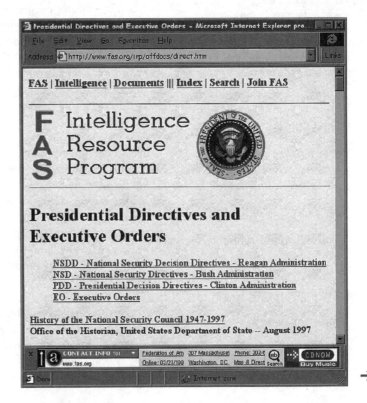

Federation of American Scientists *continued*

→ **From the FAS Web site:**

August 22, 1998

EXECUTIVE ORDER 13099

THE WHITE HOUSE

Office of the Press Secretary
(Martha's Vineyard, Massachusetts)

For Immediate Release August 22, 1998

EXECUTIVE ORDER

PROHIBITING TRANSACTIONS WITH TERRORISTS WHO THREATEN TO DISRUPT THE MIDDLE EAST PEACE PROCESS

By the authority vested in me as President by the Constitution and the laws of the United States of America, including the International Emergency Economic Powers Act (50 U.S.C. 1701 et seq.), the National Emergencies Act (50 U.S.C. 1601 et seq.), and section 301 of title 3, United States Code,

I, WILLIAM J. CLINTON, President of the United States of America, in order to take additional steps with respect to grave acts of violence committed by foreign terrorists that disrupt the Middle East peace process and the national emergency described and declared in Executive Order 12947 of January 23, 1995, hereby order:

Section 1. The title of the Annex to Executive Order 12947 of January 23, 1995, is revised to read "TERRORISTS WHO THREATEN TO DISRUPT THE MIDDLE EAST PEACE PROCESS."

Sec. 2. The Annex to Executive Order 12947 of January 23, 1995, is amended by adding thereto the following persons in appropriate alphabetical order

Usama bin Muhammad bin Awad bin Ladin (a.k.a. Usama bin Ladin)

Islamic Army (a.k.a. Al-Qaida, Islamic Salvation Foundation, The Islamic Army for the Liberation of the Holy Places, The World Islamic Front for Jihad Against Jews and Crusaders, and The Group for the Preservation of the Holy Sites) Abu Hafs al-Masri

Rifa'i Ahmad Taha Musa

Sec. 3. Nothing contained in this order shall create any right or benefit, substantive or procedural, enforceable by any party against the United States, its agencies or instrumentalities, its officers or employees, or any other person.

Sec. 4. (a) This order is effective at 12:01 a.m., eastern daylight time on August 21, 1998.

(b) This order shall be transmitted to the Congress and published in the Federal Register.

WILLIAM J. CLINTON

THE WHITE HOUSE,
August 20, 1998.

NASA
Web Sites for the U.S. Space Program
http://www.nasa.gov/

Type: Web sites

First Developed: 1988

Price Range: Connect time

Key Features: Eyes and ears beyond the Earth's atmosphere

Ages: High school and beyond

Obsolescence: Low

Further Information:
✴ *http://www.cs.umd.edu/ ~dekhtyar/space/*
for a good, simple metasite devoted to the Russian space program

The U.S. space program is one of the most extraordinary achievements in human history. Because it lives by government funding, NASA has become adept at self-promotion. Long before the Web, NASA found ways of distributing great video and pictures, and we at Xiphias benefited by getting free stuff for inclusion in our *Time Table of History* CDs, and more recently, our *Encyclopedia Electronica*.

Others have as well. Were it not for the freely available NASA/JPL satellite imagery of the Earth's surface, such amazing achievements as the Geosphere Project database (*www.geosphere.com*) would never have been possible. NASA has taken to the Web as if it were purpose-built for NASA's use. Here follow some of the best of the NASA Web sites:

Spacelink
http://spacelink.msfc.nasa.gov/.index.html

A fine collection of material for educators. →

→ NASA Web Sites *continued*

From the NASA Spacelink Web Site:

Spacelink (*http://spacelink.nasa.gov*) is one of NASA's electronic resources specifically developed for use by the educational community. Spacelink is a comprehensive electronic library that contains current information related to NASA's aeronautics and space research. Teachers, faculty, and students will find that Spacelink offers not only information about NASA programs and projects, but also teacher guides and pictures that can enhance classroom instruction. While NASA understands that people from a wide variety of backgrounds will use NASA Spacelink, the system is specifi designed for educators and stu dents.

Spacelink also provides links to other NASA resources that are available on the Internet. Educators can access materials chosen specifically for their educational value and relevance including science, mathematics engineering, and technology ec cation lesson plans; informatior NASA educational program services; current status report projects and events; news releases; and television broadcast schedules for NASA Television.

NASA Spacelink's original hardware platform was a Data General Corporation MV7800 minicomputer with eight inbound 2,400 bps modems. In 1991, Spacelink was configured to accept Telnet calls via the Internet, and as the rate of connections soared to more than 1,000 calls

per day, it became evident that a broader platform was required to handle Spacelink's increasing popularity.

The then new and improved system, which was placed in operation on September 2, 1994, included a multiprocessor Sun SPARCServer-1000 with 20 modems and full network connectivity. This system was operated as a true Internet host and served the public through the World Wide Web (WWW), File Transfer Protocol (FTP), Gopher, and Telnet.

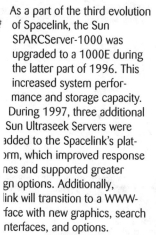

As a part of the third evolution of Spacelink, the Sun SPARCServer-1000 was upgraded to a 1000E during the latter part of 1996. This increased system performance and storage capacity. During 1997, three additional Sun Ultraseek Servers were added to the Spacelink's platform, which improved response times and supported greater gn options. Additionally, link will transition to a WWW-face with new graphics, search nterfaces, and options.

NASA Spacelink is a dynamic system that will change and expand daily. Funding for the program is provided by the Education Division at NASA Headquarters. Spacelink is maintained by the Education Programs Office at the NASA Marshall Space Flight Center in Huntsville, Alabama, and operational support is provided by the Information Systems Services Office at the Marshall Center.

→

→ NASA Web Sites *continued*

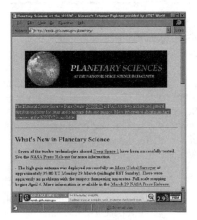

NSSDC

http://nssdc.gsfc.nasa.gov/planetary/

From the NSSDC Web site:

The National Space Science Data Center (NSSDC) provides net-work-based and off-line access to a wide variety of astrophysics, space plasma, solar physics, lunar, and planetary data from NASA space flight missions, in addition to selected other data and some models and software. NSSDC provides access to on-line informa-tion bases about NASA and non-NASA data at the NSSDC and elsewhere and about the spacecraft and experiments that generate NASA space science data. NSSDC also provides information and support relative to data management standards and technologies.

JPL Video Archive

http://www.jpl.nasa.gov/video/

Some of JPL's videos, downloadable in standard file formats for PCs.

→ NASA Web Sites *continued*

JPL Picture Archive

http://www.jpl.nasa.gov/pictures/

JPL's still pictures on the Web.

NASA Realtime Data

http://spaceflight.nasa.gov/realdata/

What an amazing site! Constant graphic updates of the position of MIR and the Shuttle when it's up. Also, great info on how to see both when they pass overhead.

Mars Exploration Web Site

http://www.marsweb.jpl.nasa.gov

The red planet on the Web. Amazing, mind-boggling pictures.

→

→ NASA Web Sites *continued*

The Hubble Telescope Web Site

http://www.stsci.edu/

The Hubble Telescope Web site, and principal resource for the imagery sent earthward by the HST.

From The Hubble Web site:

The Space Telescope Science Institute is the astronomical research center responsible for operating the Hubble Space Telescope as an international observatory. The Steven Muller Building on The Johns Hopkins Homewood campus is the primary site that houses the Institute's staff and support facilities.

The Institute is staffed by astronomers, computer scientists, technicians, and administrative staff from AURA, the European Space Agency (which is a partner with NASA on the Space Telescope Project), and the Computer Sciences Corporation. The Institute has a combined staff of about 500, of whom approximately 100 are Ph.D. astronomers and scientists.

Launched April 24, 1990, the Hubble Space Telescope is the largest and most complex astronomical observatory ever placed in orbit. The telescope studies a wide range of astronomical phenomena. Located outside the distorting effects of Earth's atmosphere, the Space Telescope allows astronomers to see the universe in greater detail than ever before.

The Hubble Space Telescope is expected to return a steady stream of scientific data for an expected lifetime of at least 15 years. Over that period, scientific observations using the telescope's unique capabilities will significantly increase our understanding of the origin, evolution, structure, and dynamics of our universe.

The Space Telescope Project represents the first step in establishing a permanent observational capability for astronomy in space. Following a recommendation by the National Academy of Sciences, NASA established the Space Telescope Science Institute to operate the Hubble Space Telescope as a major observatory for the worldwide astronomical community.

An Atlas of Cyberspace

Metapage for Various Web Maps

http://www.cybergeography.org/atlas/atlas.html

Type: Metapage

First Developed: 1998

Price Range: Connect time

Key Features: Visualizations of the structure of the Net

Ages: 10 and up

Obsolescence: Medium

Further Information: Try and find a copy of John Quarterman's *The Matrix,* a partial history of the technological development of the Net that was so precise and accurate that rumor holds Quarterman was dissuaded from publishing the second volume, as it would have given hackers too much to work with.

Back in the '60s, people tried to map the fluid gyrations of their minds (often artificially distorted and amplified) in art that ranged from rock concert posters, to Day-Glo pop art, to the projected images of colored oils and waters behind rock bands.

There is something of that rambunctious, unexpected stuff in the maps people are trying to draw of the Net. Some of it looks like org charts on acid, some like illustrations of thalidomide-induced defective nervous systems. Some are ugly, some beautiful. Some convey information vividly, some are impenetrable. All are fascinating.

Targeting
Air Force Pamphlet 14-210

http://www.fas.org/irp/doddir/usaf/afpam14-210/index.html

Type: Web site

First Developed: 1998

Price Range: Connect time

Key Features: The real stuff

Ages: Post-high school

Obsolescence: Medium—military doctrine is in flux worldwide

Further Information: Search the web for info on infrastructure, warfare, and terrorism for alternative views. Very good info via: American Federation of Scientists 307 Massachusetts Avenue NE Washington, DC 20002 ☎ (202) 675-1023

There are a lot of people, employed by a lot of governments around the world, who spend their careers figuring out exactly how to put the hurt on somebody else. Targeting is the essence of planning for war, and whether you like it or not, it is useful to know what people are thinking about what makes a good target in your neighborhood.

This pamphlet (published on the Net by the American Federation of Scientists, whose Web site is a mother lode of interesting stuff about the military and intelligence communities) represents the essence of conventional thinking in the world military. It's by the U.S. Air Force, and hence it is formal doctrine. It's on the Web, so everybody can read it. Join the people who have their eyes on us, and see what they are looking at.

Crayon
A Web Site for Designing Your Own Newspaper
http://www.crayon.net/

Type: Web site

First Developed: 1995

Price Range: Free

Key Features: Fast access to news sources, easy to personalize.

Ages: All

Obsolescence: Low

Further Information: Almost every portal (Yahoo, Excite and the rest) has the ability to create a personal page at present

The only problem with producing an early morning TV show out of a converted warehouse in Secaucus, New Jersey, is that the newspapers don't arrive until halfway through the show. (OK, that's not the only problem, but why go there?). At least the newspaper quandary has solutions.

One of these solutions is Crayon.net.

CRAYON stands for **CR**e**A**te **Y**our **O**wn Newspaper, and in an odd, understated way, it's what everyone was talking about when they were imagining the Future of the Internet. With one click, you get the headlines and the links to dozens of top news sources—with a minor amount of personalization, you get a fast layout of the exact sources you need to start your day. (You can add in any URL of your choice.)

I suppose you could do this with Active Desktop or your Favorites List or Pointcast, but I've tried them all and they all seem too slow or too limited or just too much trouble to put together.

Crayon just works. Light on graphics, heavy on content. It's the first thing I hit and in about 30 minutes, I can blast through the headlines and first paragraphs of *The New York Times, The Washington Post,* the gossip columns in *The New York Post,* Matt Drudge, Nationline at *USA Today,* the *LA Times,* and the top wires from UPI and Reuters. If there is time, a quick glance at Slate, the Cloakroom, the leads from ABC, and Politicalinsider. A quick search of the headlines to see if my host has made news, and the day has begun.

—Terry Irving

IRS Web Page

http://www.irs.ustreas.gov/cover.html

Type: Metasite

First Developed: 1998

Price Range: Connect time

Key Features: Friendly, creepily friendly

Ages: 18 and up

Obsolescence: Low

Further Information:
✱ *http://www.el.com/elinks/taxes/*
for a metasite devoted to U. S. taxes.

There is something fundamentally weird about this site. After all, for most folks, these guys are the posse raising a dust cloud on the horizon. The biggest check of the year. Sweaty palms and mass confusion.

But here they are with an obsessively friendly, useful Web site. Yikes.

From the IRS Web site:

The first level of the hierarchy:

Tax Regulations
List of tax regulations issued since August 1, 1995, with references to plain language summaries where available. This list also provides a way to comment on regulations with an open comment period.

The next level of the Hierarchy:

Increase In Cash-Out Limit Under Sections 411(a)(7), 411(a)(11), and 417(e)(1)
In the Rules and Regulations section of this issue of the *Federal Register,* the IRS is issuing temporary regulations providing guidance relating to the increase from $3,500 to $5,000 of the limit on distributions from qualified retirement plans that can be made without participant consent. This increase is contained in the Taxpayer Relief Act of 1997. The text of those temporary regulations also serves as a portion of the text of these proposed regulations. In addition, these proposed regulations propose the elimination, for all distributions, of the "lookback rule"' pursuant to which the qualified plan benefits of certain participants are deemed to exceed this limit on mandatory distributions. These proposed regulations affect sponsors and administrators of qualified retirement plans, and participants in those plans. The text of those temporary regulations also serves as a portion of the text of these proposed regulations.

Download Full Text Filesize: 17.5 Kilobytes

American Demographics

Magazine Web Site

http://www.demographics.com/

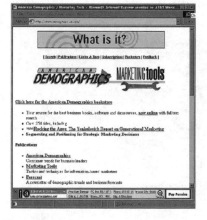

Type: Web site

First Developed: 1998

Price Range: Connect time

Key Features: Archive of key demographic trends and thinking about same

Ages: Post-high school

Obsolescence: Low

Further Information:
❋ *www.rubicon.com/turnpike/demogrph.html* for a fine metapage devoted to Web demographics

It's impossible to understand the game without the stats. In the game of selling stuff to people, whether it is goods, ideas, or politicians, the stats are the demographics.

I first saw *American Demographics* magazine in the early '80s and was fascinated. Somewhere in here was the key to understanding my generation, which has revealed most of its secrets by now. The next set of secrets is in the minds and hearts of the baby boomlet, that immense cascade of kids born to the baby boomers. In the magazine and on the Web site are described the forces they have unleashed—forces that will forge the near future.

The *American Demographics* Web site keeps a healthy archive of past articles and makes for endlessly fascinating browsing.

Intelligence On-Line

Web Site Devoted to Intelligence and Espionage

http://www.indigo-net.com/intel.html

Type: Web site

First Developed: 1995

Price Range: Connect time

Key Features: Broad view, thorough research

Ages: 10 and up

Obsolescence: Low

Further Information:
❋ *http://www.oss.net/*
for an excellent Web site devoted to the exploitation of open sources of intelligence

There is what you read in the papers, and then there is what really is going on. Although an immense amount of what's going on in the world can be gathered from open sources on the Net, the task is time-consuming, and the knowledge of sources has to be thorough.

This digest is pricey, but it is very good and not bound to the point of view of the United States.

A FAILURE OF VISION RETROSPECTIVE

by

Capt. Fred Kennedy, USAF, Capt. Rory Welch, USAF, Capt. Bryon Fessler, USAF

PYONGYANG, KOREA, 2013. "Defeating the United States was a much easier task than we thought possible," Col. Myong Joo Kim said in precise English. Educated at Harvard and CalTech, the haggard 45-year-old North Korean stood at the head of a small table around which sat interested representatives from nine nations. The room was harshly lit, without windows, and electronically screened from the outside world by systems "borrowed" from their prostrate foe. Colonel Kim's speech would never be heard again outside this forum, and the representatives would rapidly disperse after the briefing. However, it was essential for each representative to understand the nature of the successful campaign against the Americans and the implications for his nation. Colonel Kim announced:

> Our plan has succeeded. We have inflicted—to paraphrase the words of an American airpower theorist—a "strategic paralysis" on the United States so that it is incapable of acting. Following our attack on their homeland, the Americans have become defensive, turning decidedly inward. Their influence is rapidly waning around the globe; no longer do they deserve the title "superpower." The remainder of the 21st century is wide open.

Some congratulatory glances were exchanged. Colonel Kim noticed these, then glanced down at his notepad. He spoke louder:

Please do not make the mistake of assuming that this outcome was a foregone conclusion. The United States remains very powerful. There were specific steps that the Americans could have taken that might have prevented us from succeeding, or stopped our efforts in the planning stage. However, to be blunt, they suffer from a rather distressing lack of vision. Their own military strategy documents of the late 1990s anticipated much of the multipolarity and rapid change that have shaped the world of the 21st century—something that we in part helped to precipitate. As the world's last superpower, they acknowledged the dangers posed by aspiring regional powers, the proliferation of advanced weapons, terrorists, and attacks on →

This article was written in the fall of 1997, before the present Iraqi crisis over UN inspections and the recent anthrax scare in Las Vegas. It appears that we are at least beginning to take biological warfare seriously. The authors would like to thank the following individuals for their invaluable assistance in producing this work: Capt. Daniel Dant and Capt. John Shaw, who provided excellent insight into what kind of story to tell; Capt. Kathy "Gus" Viksne, who gave us some useful pointers on air defense; Capt. Bryan Haderlie, who enlightened us on the subject of optical systems for space surveillance; Col. Chris Waln, USAF, Retired, who provided the seeds for the Decapitation scenario; and Col. Michael Mantz.

→ A Failure of Vision Retrospective *continued*

→ *their homeland. However accurate their predictions of the future might have been, they made the mistake of continuing to structure their armed forces for combat between large numbers of conventional forces while paying only lip service to the threat of asymmetric attack. Their arrogance blinded them to the possibility that a potential adversary might actually try to achieve its ends by other than a direct military confrontation. Their folly allowed us to exploit vulnerabilities in their most vital high-technology systems, making the dominance of their conventional forces irrelevant. We should not fault them too much. Events have proceeded apace.*

Without an easily understood and measurable foe, the Americans have floundered for almost 20 years. It is certainly true that they have upgraded their systems along the way, but they never were able to fully realize the true value of their most technologically advanced systems, those that operate in two closely coupled media—space and information. We were able to take maximum advantage of their plodding and uncertainty. Let me start at the beginning.

Like any other nation, the United States is a complex system, and despite its many protests to the contrary, it has systemic weaknesses and leverage points that can be exploited by a knowledgeable adversary.

The Plan

Rangoon, Myanmar, 2009. The first meeting was shrouded in the utmost secrecy. The principals, with a suspicion verging on outright paranoia, shuttled through several unlikely ports of call before finally arriving at their destination. Initial communications were by word of mouth. There would be no "smoking gun" in the form of a document or cellular phone call to betray those involved. All participants prepared decoys who appeared prominently in foreign cities to distract the attention of the American intelligence-collection system. One joked nervously that he was less concerned with potential Central Intelligence Agency (CIA) ferrets than with the ubiquitous representatives of the U.S. media. One reporter might suspect a ruse and inadvertently stumble on a story larger than he or she could easily imagine.

Editor's Note: This is just the beginning of a fine, well-informed scenario published in a military journal called Air Force Chronicles. *Forget Hollywood, forget Clancy, this is the real stuff, as good as* THE COBRA EVENT, *because it is written by people who know the realities. Check out the whole thing at:*

http://www.airpower.maxwell.af.mil/ airchronicles/apj/apj98/sum98/kennedy.html

The Internet Mapping Project
A Metasearch Web Site for the Internet
http://www.cs.bell-labs.com/~ches/map/

Type: Web site

First Developed: 1998

Price Range: Connect time

Key Features: Updated daily

Ages: 10 and up

Obsolescence: Low

Further Information: Go to this site and download the map, or download the text file with all of the routes to all of the nodes on the Internet

One of the great things about big, rich companies is that they spend money on research and development. One of the great things about research and development is that loony ideas are allowed to flourish.

Here is a great, loony idea in full and daily flourish.

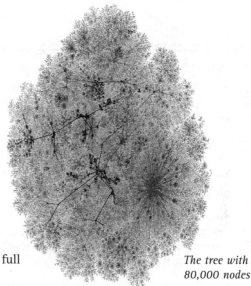

The tree with 80,000 nodes

From the Internet Mapping Project Web Site

We are running a long-term project to collect routing data on the Internet. This mapping consists of frequent trace-route-style path probes, one to each registered Internet entity. From this, we build a tree showing the paths to most of the nets on the Internet.

These paths change over time, as routes reconfigure and the Internet grows. We are preserving this data, and plan to run the scans for a long time. The database should help show how the Internet grows. We think we can even make a movie of this growth.

Maps
This data yields a large tree-like structure. It is not easy to lay out a tree with 80,000 nodes. Standard graph-viewing programs consider 800 nodes a hard task. Our programs jostle the nodes around according to half a dozen simple rules, a process called *annealing*. A typical layout run requires 24 CPU hours on a 400 MHz Pentium.

We have made some maps from this layout. A map helps us visualize things, pick out points of interest, and find things that warrant closer inspection. Once the layout is computed, the map can be colored to show a number of things. We don't try to lay out the Internet according to geography—people like John Quarterman are working on that. Besides, the Internet is its own space. We do plan to color some maps with geographical cues, though ISPs show geography pretty well.

The layout can be colored in many ways: with geographical clues, network capacity, etc. An Internet atlas would be interesting.

These maps are quite smashing, though not altogether useful yet. The December 1998 issue of *Wired* Magazine has the layout generated from data collected in mid-September. Hal generated a color scheme based on the IP address of the nodes. This sick idea ("Excuse me, →

→ may I have a prettier Internet address please?") creates a color scheme that seems to match *Wired*'s traditional typography. But it actually does show communities that share similar network addresses.

Management has given approval for publication of this map as a poster. We expect the top to read "View of the Internet from Bell Labs" and contain a suitable Lucent logo in a corner. We have to find a suitable publisher.

Uses
This data has a number of uses, including collaborations with other Internet mapping projects (see below.) The latest database is available at

http://www.cs.bell-labs.com/ ~ ches/map/db.gz.

It is updated daily around 9 A.M. Eastern Time. The compressed file is running around 5 MB. Uncompressed it is about 100 MB. The format should be fairly self-explanatory, but documentation will follow.

There has been confusion about this database. It is not the picture itself, but the raw data of the traceroute paths. It is a compressed text file, not a Microsoft Excel, or other database file.

We are also scanning Lucent's intranet for a variety of security projects. This information can help us get a better understanding and more control over our large network and its extranet connections.

Mapping Details, or "What are you doing to my Net?"
The Net mapping program sends small UDP packets to random high-numbered ports, while varying the packet's Time-to-Live (TTL) field. The TTL is decremented on each hop out. When it hits zero, the death of the packet is reported back to the sender. We do not expect to reach a working host, much less an active UDP service.

The packets are sent with slowly incrementing TTL fields. When a packet fails to return, perhaps because it was lost or dropped by a firewall, we try a couple more times, then give up, recording any return code.

A few people (about 30 sites, after six months of mapping) have noticed and asked about this activity. If our probes are bothering you, or even are just an annoying presence in your logs, send the network addresses to **ches@bell-labs.com** and we will stop tracing to them.

Future Work
The early results looked like a peacock smashed into a windshield. Though you could pick out the major ISPs and some interesting details around the edges, the map wasn't very useful.

We now run the layout on the minimal spanning tree, and the results on a 36-inch plotter are very close to a nice map, and a terrific poster.

We are working on finding a publisher for this poster. We will let you know when they are available.

This data cries for interactive visualization tools: 3-D might be great. How many paths are served by cable and wireless? Where are the oceans?

One goal is to collect the data over time, and make a time-lapse movie of the growth of the Internet. Time-lapses of the annealing process are already interesting: it writhes and squirms and such.

Lucent Technologies
Bell Labs Innovations

Does the Brand Really Matter?

By David Ellis

President, Vigon/Ellis

Brand Development & Design

It takes a real leap of faith to give your credit card number, phone number, address, and personal data to a company that is composed of bits and bytes. Knowing that the company can rocket your information to anyone anywhere in the world with a click of a mouse makes the decision of which "e-tailers" to choose even more difficult.

Unless you are buying only from big name e-businesses or Web sites that are attached to established brick and mortar companies, you are buying blind. To its credit or its detriment, the Web is the ultimate "level playing field." On the Web, two kids in a garage can have the same presence and power as a Fortune 500 company. And that garage can be in Singapore, Romania, or Rochester. Without doing some research, you won't know the difference.

There is a tendency among many e-commerce companies to get caught up in the hype. Some regard buying products through their sites as a special, almost revolutionary, act—a radically different experience from traditional retailing. Because the Web is cutting edge, the tired fundamentals of great merchandising, pricing, customer service, and follow-through really don't apply.

> **A brand is not the company logo or its advertising, but a set of promises that company makes with its customers.**

Nothing could be further from the truth. In fact, the established foundations of doing business should apply even more stringently to a Web company. Which is why the companies that are thriving on the Web are apostles of branding.

A brand is not the company logo or its advertising, but a set of promises that company makes with its customers. The brand promise mitigates the risk involved in any purchase decision. For example, customers considering Saturn automobiles expect to have access to an organization that will take excellent care of them and their cars. Sony Electronics promises its customers quality technology. Starbucks promises a casual environment of superior coffee and related specialty foods. These companies, along with other leading brands, thrive because they keep their promises. Ask Mac users what it means to be a Mac owner, they will more than likely play back some interpretation of Apple's campaign, "Think Different."

Successful Web companies, like their conventional counterparts, understand that establishing trust is critical to their ongoing success and represents →

213

Does the Brand Really Matter? *continued*

→ their core business challenge. Consider Amazon.com. The purpose of Amazon.com is not just to sell books, but to establish relationships between the company and its customers. The reason buyers come back to Amazon.com isn't its prices (they are usually more expensive), but that customers believe that that Amazon.com delivers quickly and reliably, and that Amazon knows who they are and what products they like. That relationship is the core of the Amazon.com brand and is the primary reason Amazon.com is valued at thousands of times its earnings.

So how do you choose one site from another and have a positive experience on the Web?

- Take your time. Do some homework before you spontaneously download your personal and financial information. When you log-on, read about the company's background.

- Read about the site's security technology and guarantee—most reputable sites will make good any charges that result from the deliberate or inadvertent release of your credit card information. If a site will not make such assurances and back them up in writing, shop elsewhere.

- Pick up the phone and talk to the customer service reps—e-mail is not good enough. See how long it takes for you to actually speak to

a real human being—after all the Web is not some virtual life form, it's a new communications channel ultimately operated by real people. Find out what the procedure might be if you have to return an order or get warranty repair.

One way to be more certain is to let the brand be your guide. Recognizable brands thrive because they have earned consumers' trust, not necessarily because they have spent zillions of dollars on advertising. It is unlikely that a company such as Schwab.com will not follow through on your stock order, or take your money and run. There may be occasional technical glitches, as there are throughout the Web, but the underlying businesses of most of the major brands are rock-solid.

This is not to say that there aren't some fabulous start-up companies that are worthy of your patronage. There are great companies in every product category that are worth a try. The Web and e-commerce are in their infancies and there will be dozens of new brands generated from the Internet that will be as powerful as any that have been established in real space.

With a minimum of research, you can confidently shop the world and locate products that are impossible to find any other way. Just ignore the hype and hold Web companies to the same standards that you would any other business.

The Platypus

A Web Site Devoted to the Cross-Training of Journalists in Digital Photography

http://www.digitaljournalist.org

Type: Web site

First Developed: 1997

Price Range: The Web site is free; training and photo equipment varies in cost

Key Features: A cross breed of artistic technology. Lower cost.

Ages: All

Obsolescence: Reverses the obsolescence of the print photographer

Dirck Halstead is *Time* magazine's senior White House photographer and a veteran of photojournalism from the days of Vietnam. He is also a charming, stubborn romantic with this crazy idea that just won't go away. The idea is that the skills and technique of a photojournalist aren't limited only to the world of still photography—or to the dying world of print magazines.

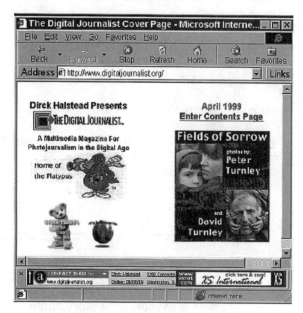

Why not crosstrain still photographers with radio reporters, print journalists, and television cameramen? What would you create and how would it fit in in an on-line world?

After a number of false starts (several of which I have to confess I edited and helped to produce), Dirck's concept found fertile ground. Another company, Video News International (now New York Times Television), began to cross-train journalists and send them out with still cameras, notepads, and the new, small but high-quality 8-millimeter video cameras. The results aired on *Nightline* and The Learning Channel; stories that combined artistic composition with the intimate access that only a single journalist can readily achieve. →

Platypus Digital Photojournalism *continued*

→ The first class of platypi has graduated from a Missouri workshop—still photographers now trained in video and sound technique. Several are reporting from the war-torn Balkans, and a bevy of "reality" TV shows are on cable channels. As the bandwidth increases on the Internet, this type of convergent technology will become more and more visible.

Digitaljournalist.org is the Web site that details all this creative ferment. It features still photo collections, RealVideo clips, equipment reviews, and artistic hints from masters.

—*Terry Irving*

"The 'platypus' is Dirck Halstead's vision that a still photojournalist with a passion for a story could research, report, shoot stills and video, then end up with both a still project for a magazine or newspaper and a good video story for TV. It's a concept that might keep photojournalism alive for years to come."

—*From a review of the first class for Platypi*

"Tom Burton, of *The Orlando Sentinel,* brought up the story of the platypus and how its discovery in Australia in the mid-18th century threw the zoological community into an uproar. Biologists had comfortably placed the animal kingdom into distinct categories—birds, mammals, reptiles, etc.—but once this new beast appeared that crossed the lines between the classifications, it threw all the conventional thinking on the subject out the window. Burton asked, 'Is there anything like a platypus in photojournalism today?'"

—From the Platypus Manifesto

The Hotline: National Journal's Daily Briefing on Politics
A Web Site Devoted to U.S. Political News
http://www.cloakroom.com

Type: Web site

First Developed: 1980's

Price Range: $4,649 a year

Key Features: Overnight summaries of political news and views from virtually all American newspapers, magazines, radio, and television outlets; poll results; archives searchable by keyword and issue

Ages: Adult

Obsolescence: Low… what you pay for is expertise and hard work—the content changes with the times

How do reporters, political consultants, and politicians know what's going on?

And, more important, know that there isn't anything going on that they don't know about.

This is one of the great secrets of the news business.

I remember reading *The Hotline* while I was covering the Carter/Kennedy race in 1980 and bleary-eyed reporters waited at hotel desks across the country for it to arrive by fax. Now it's a Web site and a series of e-mail newsletters but the essence is the same.

Smart, politically savvy people watch and read EVERYTHING and tell you about it: 350 newspapers, national and local magazines, TV talk shows, radio talk shows, network news broadcasts, local editorials, polls, even the jokes on Leno and Letterman. It's the ultimate political horserace handicapper.

Want to know how the President is polling? What's going on in the Philadelphia mayoral contest? Where the money is flowing in the race for the White House? What the pundits are talking about and who they are NOT talking about? It's all there.

And there's more…a special newsletter on issues that affect women, searchable archives that allow you to find a particular event or follow the evolution of a specific issue, "buzz" columns that let you know what the insiders are talking about (odds are, the insiders are talking about what they read in *The Hotline*), and a smart-aleck sense of humor that takes no sides and no prisoners.

It's not really a case of technology as much as hard work and intelligence. What you pay for (or, usually, your company pays for) is the hard work of dozens of really smart young people from politics, television, and newspapers. It's a distillation of the vast sea of information in which we live.

—Terry Irving

The Obscure Store and Reading Room

A Web Site for Obscure and Tangential News

http://www.obscurestore.com

Type: Web site

First Developed: 1990s

Price Range: Web page is free; fanzines range in price

Key Features: A daily quick read of national news, concentrating on gossip and inside media news but offering links to a good deal of what's worth reading on-line

Ages: Adult

Obsolescence: Low

This is for the people who just can't come up with the four grand a year to get the *National Journal Hotline* but still want to be way ahead of everyone else on what's hot across the country. Jim Romenesko claims to have a paying job, but it's hard to see what he could be doing after spending the time he does scanning on-line publications to come up with the tasty tidbits he presents daily in *www.obscurestore.com.*

Ranging from newspaper leads to the traditional "news of the weird" and specializing in the gossip of the world of big media, it's an essential part of my morning. And, if you don't like the news, you can wade into the bizarre world of fanzines—strange little magazines like *Protests Are Your Best Entertainment Value* or *The Hungover Gourmet.*

Jim Romenesko has been publishing *Obscure Publications*—a print newsletter that covers the fanzine subculture—since 1989. He is the author of *Death Log,* a book of coroners' reports he compiled in his final months as a police reporter. He has taught Fanzine Publishing and History at the Milwaukee Institute of Art and Design and newspaper feature writing at the University of Wisconsin in Milwaukee.

As a magazine writer, he chased after albinos, sat about 10 feet from Jeffrey Dahmer at the serial killer's trial, hung around eccentric people, and covered too many murder cases. He now works for a Knight Ridder paper in the land of Gopher.

—Terry Irving

Cyndi's List

Metasite for Genealogy Resources on the Net

http://www.cyndislist.com/

Type: Metasite

First Developed: 1998

Price Range: Connect time

Key Features: Access to tools for genealogical research

Ages: 10 and up

Obsolescence: Medium

Further Information:
✳ *http://www.cyndislist.com/ nettable.htm*
to buy via e-commerce *Netting your Ancestors,* Cyndi's book on the subject ($20.00)

When I last looked, well over nine million people had visited this site since it's inception (current rate is 15,000 a day). Since people looking into their family's history tend to become obsessive, there are undoubtedly a lot of return visitors to this site. And things spiked when *Cyndi's List* was featured in an April 1999 *Time* magazine cover story on genealogical research.

The people at Ancestry.com ran a vote and found cyndislist.com to be the best on the Net (theirs was second best—see sidebar). It says something about the culture of the Net that a company would boost their competitor in such a fashion.

With over 41,750 links, categorized and cross-referenced, in over 100 categories, this site seems to be the mother lode. One netizen (in an e-mail review posted on Cyndi's site) claimed that he had this as the opening page in his browser. A bit much for me, but this site is nonetheless fascinating.

Site links listed for one month included one dedicated to photo restoration, the 21st Missouri Infantry Volunteer Regiment, how to cite death certificates, and Krumwiede: Descendnats of Heinrich Konrad Krumwiede.

Ancient cultures committed their family trees to memory, stretching back for hundreds of generations. The Mormons put all their records in salt mines in Utah (and recently debuted their own site: www.familysearch.org). We seem to have decided that we will store our genealogical record on thousands of distributed hard drives all over the world.

RESEARCHING GENEALOGY

Though Cyndi's List won the vote for best genealogy site, the folks at Ancestry.com posted the runners up:

▪▪ Ancestry.com at
http://www.ancestry.com

"This is the site I keep going to, because I have such a good chance of finding something in all the databases. Also, thanks to their GEDCOM databases, I've found two second cousins I didn't know existed! We've burned up our keyboards catching up on family events."
—K.A.

▪▪ Family Tree Maker at
http://www.familytreemaker.com

"Familytreemaker is great because it give me access to all the people interested in researching the family names I am working on and others I do not know yet. I like the program and the changes over the last 3 years have helped a lot." —A.W.

▪▪ JewishGen at
http://www.jewishgen.org

"This site is spectacular—chock full of searchable and ever-expanding databases such as the JewishGen Family Finder (a database of over 90,000 surnames and towns), the Jewish Records IndexingPoland database, ShtetlSeeker, and other useful databases...." —M.W.D.

→

SOURCES

Cyndi's List *continued*

→ ■ **Tri-County Genealogy Site at**
http://www.rootsweb.com/~srgp/jmtindex.htm

"Joyce M. Tice has developed a site which a MUST for anyone doing research in the Tioga/Bradford County areas of Pennsylvania. What a pleasant surprise to find over 7,000 online obituaries, the entire 1850 census of Tioga County and over 400 cemeteries just waiting to be explored." – C.C. (Editor's comment: This site focuses on only three counties: Bradford County, PA; Tioga County, PA; and Chemung County, NY. Yet it received a lot of votes!)

■ **Luzern Co. (Pennsylvania) Website at**
http://www.rootsweb.com/~paluzer

"This website is the result of the long hours of dedication that Tammy Lamb and the members have devoted to making this a genealogist "Pot of Gold"!! There is only one way to find out what I mean and that is by going to the URL above to see just how much is there. It is just packed with data, copied by members for the benefit of all who are searching for information on their Luzern Co., Pa. ancestors! Unheard of on many of the other County sites in any state. This is a First Class effort and it is not going to stop as there are plans for more great information to be added!! Tammy Lamb and her members deserve Best Genealogy site on the WWW!!" –C.G.F.

■ **RootsWeb at** *http://www.rootsweb.com*

"The Rootsweb Surname List site has been my most fruitful way of finding cousins, information on many great grandparents and books and sources for this data. This site is easy to use and easy to understand. And there are links to other sites: for instance, surname mailing Lists, county mailing Lists, archived queries on mailing Lists, etc." –S.W.

from www.cyndislist.com
NETTING YOUR ANCESTORS
TABLE OF CONTENTS

CTheory
Web Site of Edgy World Views
http://www.ctheory.com

Type: Web site

First Developed: 1998

Price Range: Connect time

Key Features: An unsettled view of the world

Ages: 18 and up

Obsolescence: Paranoia never gets old

Further Information:
❋ *http://www.redacted.com/* for an interesting take on why we don't know what's going on

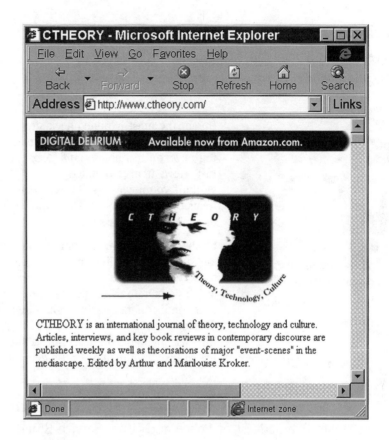

The future isn't what it used to be. This academic journal is the film *The Matrix* on steroids. Original commentary, essays, and multimedia presentations dealing with the darker side of technology. The folks behind *CTheory* haven't decided whether to celebrate the future or fear it as man merges with machine and we face our own humanity square in the eyes.

Brought to you by the same people who brought us the *Panic Encyclopedia: The Definitive Guide to the Postmodern Scene* (*http://www.freedonia.com/panic/*), this site offers a wealth of what I would qualify as "alternative" academic writings regarding society, culture, current events, and technology, all cross-banded together with the personal perspectives of the diverse contributing body.

—Matt Devost

Slashdot

Web Site Town Crier for the Geeks

http://www.slashdot.org

Type: Web site

First Developed: 1998

Price Range: Connect time

Key Features: What's going on at the leading edge

Ages: 10 and up

Obsolescence: Low

Further Information:
✳ *http://www.osnews.com/* for a site devoted to the future of computing

One of the most heralded geek sites on the Internet, Slashdot provides breaking news on technology and geek culture. News items, compiled by a network of volunteer Slashdotters, tend to focus on the Linux operating system and cutting edge technological development like VR eyeglass displays.

Slashdot, unlike conventional news sources, provides just a snippet of data and analysis regarding the feature item with relevant links, but also captures the comments of its visitors in an infospace beneath the article. Some articles generate discussions lasting for weeks, and the average number of user comments ranges in the hundreds per article. Sites featured on Slashdot are known to be exposed to the Slashdot effect, the documented Internet phenomenon describing a site that goes off-line due to the unanticipated heavy volume of traffic generated by the Slashdot troupe (see SURGE).

—Matt Devost

Police Scanner

Over the Net Rebroadcast of Police and Other Service Broadcasts

http://www.policescanner.com

Type: Source

First Developed: 1998

Price Range: Connect time

Key Features: Live radio from around the U.S.

Ages: Junior high and beyond

Obsolescence: Low

Further Information:
✳ *http://www.pursuitwatch.com/* for a very strange service – they will page you when the next police pursuit happens

PoliceScanner.com

Before Broadcast.com got to this, when the site was independent, it was more fun. Now, before you can listen to the streaming audio, you have to listen to an ad. Oh well.

If you are unsure whether you want to spend the money to get a scanner (like the ICOM PCR 1000/100, or the SONY ICF-SC1PC), you might want to spend some time listening to the stuff on this site. It has feeds from several major cities, and includes police, fire, rail, and even a bit of aviation stuff.

Silly for some, addictive for others.

Amazing to radio junkies, who can listen to police action thousands of miles away: they know the radio signals, by themselves, can go only a maximum of 90 miles.

Quickbrowse

Reconfigurable Metapage

http://www.quickbrowse.com

Type: Web site
First Developed: 1998
Price Range: Connect time
Key Features: Flexible news display
Ages: 16 and up
Obsolescence: Low

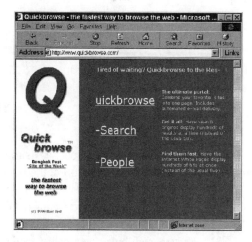

The elegant answer?

I have no time to browse the Web. And even if I start browsing, I feel guilty about wandering aimlessly. My conservative upbringing brings on pangs of guilt within four minutes after I begin following Web whims-of-the-moment.

I'm utilitarian. When I open my browser, I open it for a specific thing. And once I have the information I need, I'm off the Web and back to work.

The problem with my virtuous, parsimonious approach is that it doesn't allow me to make discoveries. I'm like a horse in blinders when it comes to the Web.

Quickbrowse.com permits the user to aggregate a number of URLs he or she'd like to visit (if he or she could take the time to call them up separately) and presents them all on one page.

Quickbrowse enables me to check my traps daily using a one-stop approach. It eliminates the time-consuming call-up of multiple Web addresses. It lets me work smarter, quicker. It's true: the best ideas are the simplest.

—Tom Bradford

Visible Human

Web Site with Cryogenic Cross-Sections of the Human Body

http://www.nlm.nih.gov/research/visible/photos.html

Type: Web site
First Developed: 1994
Price Range: Connect time
Key Features: The whole man
Ages: 10 and up
Obsolescence: Low

This is a very simple story. They froze a guy and sliced him into pieces, like a delicatessen does salami. Then they digitized the results. Then they posted the imagery, and animations derived therefrom on the Net.

It's all waiting there for you to explore. Not right after dinner.

Visible Human *continued*

From www.nlm.nih.gov

THE VISIBLE HUMAN

Background

The Visible Human Project has its roots in a 1986 long-range planning effort of the National Library of Medicine (NLM). It foresaw a coming era where NLM's bibliographic and factual database services would be complemented by libraries of digital images, distributed over high-speed computer networks and by high-capacity physical media. Not surprisingly, it saw an increasing role for electronically represented images in clinical medicine and biomedical research. It encouraged the NLM to consider building and disseminating medical image libraries much the same way it acquires, indexes, and provides access to the biomedical literature. Early in 1989, under the direction of the Board of Regents, an ad hoc planning panel was convened and made the following recommendation: "NLM should undertake a first project building a digital image library of volumetric data representing a complete, normal adult male and female. This Visible Human Project will include digitized photographic images for cryosectioning, digital images derived from computerized tomography, and digital magnetic resonance images of cadavers."

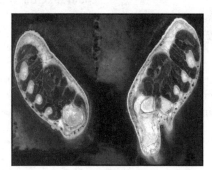

A cross-section of feet!

Initial Aim

The initial aim of the Visible Human Project was to acquire transverse CT, MRI, and cryosection images of a representative male and female cadaver at an average of one-millimeter intervals. The corresponding transverse sections in each of the three modalities were to be registered with one another. A contract for acquisition of these pixel-based data was awarded in August 1991 to the University of Colorado at Denver, with Victor M. Spitzer, Ph.D. and David G. Whitlock, M.D., Ph.D. as the principal investigators.

The Visible Human Male data set consists of MRI, CT, and anatomical images. Axial MRI images of the head and neck and longitudinal sections of the rest of the body were obtained at 4 mm intervals. The MRI images are 256 pixel by 256 pixel resolution. Each pixel has 12 bits of grey-tone resolution. The CT data consist of axial CT scans of the entire body taken at 1 mm intervals at a resolution of 512 pixels by 512 pixels where each pixel is made up of 12 bits of grey tone. The axial anatomical images are 2,048 pixels by 1,216 pixels where each pixel is defined by 24 bits of color, about 7.5 megabytes. →

Visible Human *continued*

→ The anatomical crosssections are also at 1 mm intervals and coincide with the CT axial images. There are 1,871 crosssections for each mode, CT and anatomy. The complete male data set is 15 gigabytes in size.

The Visible Human Female data set has the same characteristics as the male cadaver with one exception. The axial anatomical images were obtained at 0.33 mm intervals instead of 1.0 mm intervals. This resulted in over 5,000 anatomical images. The data set is about 40 gigabytes. The spacing in the "Z" direction was reduced to 0.33 mm in order to match the 0.33 mm pixel spacing in the "XY" plane. This enables developers who are interested in three-dimensional reconstructions to work with cubic voxels.

Internet Access

Sample full-scale images are available via NLM's FTP site (*nlmpubs.nlm.nih.gov*). Eleven full-color anatomical images and an explanatory "color24.txt"

file can be found on the FTP site in (*visible/bitmaps/color24*) as (**.raw*). Please be careful, as each of these images is over 7 megabytes in size. Ten CT scan images and an explanatory "ct.txt" file can be found in (*visible/bitmaps/ct*) as (**.fre*) (5 images captured while the cadaver was fresh) and (**.fro*) (5 images captured after the cadaver was frozen). Six MRI scan images and an explanatory "mri.txt" file can be found in (*visible/bitmaps/mri*) as (**.t1*). Scaled-down versions of all of these image files can be found on NLM's FTP site in (*visible/gifs*) as (**.gif*). On the World Wide Web (*http://www.nlm. nih.gov/research/visible/visible_human.html*), the sample images can be found by linking to "images and animations" under the topic "Further Information." These images are in JPEG format (**.jpg*), thereby requiring a Web browser enabled to read files of this format. A license agreement for use of either of the Visible Human Project data sets is required, and it can be retrieved from NLM's Web site.

Fractals and Wavelets
Two New Ways of Breaking Things Down
http://www.ncsa.uiuc.edu/Edu/Fractal/Fractal_Home.html

Type: Web sites

First Developed: 1998

Price Range: Connect time

Key Features: First introduction to wavelets and fractals

Ages: Junior high and later

Obsolescence: Low

Further Information:
✳ *http://www-groups.dcs. stand.ac.uk/~history/index.html* for a fine history of mathematics on the Web

At the turn of the last century, statistical analysis was a new, magical way of looking at things. Making the probability of something happening into a set of numbers and formulas blew the lid off of an array of important businesses and activities. It cracked unbreakable codes, eked great productivity gains out of crude assembly lines, revealed trends in markets and generally revolutionized stuff all over the place. Fractals and wavelets are two new ways of looking at things that are in the process of blowing a set of new lids off. →

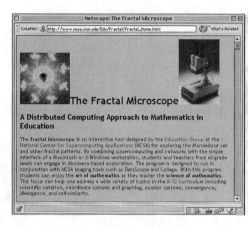

The Fractal Microscope

A Distributed Computing Approach to Mathematics in Education

The Fractal Microscope is an interactive tool designed by the Education Group at the National Center for Supercomputing Applications (NCSA) for exploring the Mandelbrot set and other fractal patterns. By combining supercomputing and networks with the simple interface of a Macintosh or X-Windows workstation, students and teachers from all grade levels can engage in discovery-based exploration. The program is designed to run in conjunction with NCSA imaging tools such as DataScope and Collage. With this program students can enjoy the **art of mathematics** as they master the **science of mathematics**. This focus can help address a wide variety of topics in the K-12 curriculum including scientific notation, coordinate systems and graphing, number systems, convergence, divergence, and self-similarity.

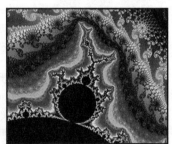

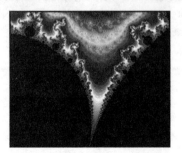

From the Fractal Microscope Web site:

Many people are immediately drawn to the bizarrely beautiful images known as fractals. *Extending beyond the typical perception of mathematics as a body of sterile formulas, fractal geometry mixes art with mathematics to demonstrate that equations are more than just a collection of numbers. With* fractal geometry *we can visually model much of what we witness in nature, the most recognized being coastlines and mountains. Fractals are used to model soil erosion and to analyze seismic patterns as well. But beyond potential applications for describing complex natural patterns, with their visual beauty fractals can help alter students' beliefs that mathematics is dry and inaccessible and may help motivate mathematical discovery in the classroom.*

Fractals and Wavelets *continued*

→ Fractals

Fractals are a method of approximation. If one were to try to measure the length of the coastline of Britain, the more precise one wanted to be, the harder the task would get. Every time the coastline took a turn, the measuring tape would have to be bent. How many bends are necessary to do the job? Fractals provide a method of seeing the bends as a repetitive set of patterns, which duplicate themselves in large and small forms.

Fractals have been put to use in predicting natural events, encoding digital images, creating creepy computer graphics, and handling a vast array of other activities.

Wavelets

http://www.monash.edu.au/cmcm/wavelet/wbasic.htm

Turns out you can break complex waveforms into something like an alphabet of waves—the word is the wave; the characters are the "wavelets." This means that a lot of the things people have done for years with digital information, like encoding and compression (see SILICON DREAMS), can be done with analog information. The breakdown can be used for everything from fiddling with sound, to understanding earthquakes, to encrypting and decrypting messages.

From the Centre for Machine Condition Monitoring Web site:

Before rushing into the applications of wavelet analysis, a brief expose on some of the basic concepts that make wavelet analysis such a useful signal processing tool shall be presented. It is not the purpose of this article to provide a detailed mathematical foundation for wavelets but instead to enable the reader to grasp the underlying features that make wavelets one of the most exciting research areas in signal processing today.

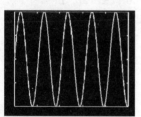

A comparison of the sine wave and Debauchies 5 wavelet.

Wavelet analysis is similar to Fourier analysis in the sense that it breaks a signal down into its constituent parts for analysis. Whereas the Fourier transform breaks the signal into a series of sine waves of different frequencies, the wavelet transform breaks the signal into its "wavelets," scaled and shifted versions of the "mother wavelet." There are, however, some very distinct differences, as is evident [at left], which compares a sine wave to the Debauchies 5 wavelet. In comparison to the sine wave, which is smooth and of infinite length, the wavelet is irregular in shape and compactly supported. It is these properties of being irregular in shape and compactly supported that make wavelets an ideal tool for analyzing signals of a nonstationary nature. Their irregular shape lends them to analyzing signals with discontinuities or sharp changes, while their compactly supported nature enables temporal localization of a signal's features.

Traveling with a Laptop

Traveling with a laptop is simple if you are going from city to city, from business hotel to business hotel. The minute you escape the bounds of the United States, things start to get dicey. A few years ago, when I traveled to London for a week or so, I abandoned AOL, and did all my e-mail via Compuserve—then the dominant supplier of on-line services in the U.K. I had already bought a connection kit that made it possible for me to use the local power (called mains connections) and the local telephone plugs (big, unwieldy things). It worked.

Compuserve is no longer the big force there, or anywhere else. If I had to do it again, I would take advantage of all the research my Mom did right before she went to Portugal in Spring 1999. She finally decided that it would be too complex to take a portable, but some folks don't have the luxury of such a decision.

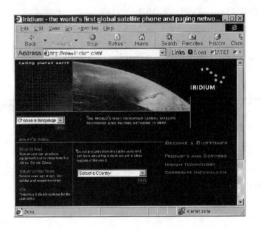

http://www.iridium.com

Phones are a problem all over the world, and Iridium makes a phone that will relieve you of that problem. It operates a system of satellites the world over, and an Iridium phone will connect you virtually anywhere. It ain't cheap, and there are some technical prices you will pay (one of which is privacy—the Iridium system can physically pinpoint you anywhere on the surface of the Earth. Depending upon where you are going and what you are doing, that could be very good, or very bad).

http://www.laptoptravel.com

Here's a good place to spend a bit of money. This site will tell you what you need and then sell it to you.

→

Traveling with a Laptop *continued*

→   **http://www.roadnews.com/**

Nothing sold here—at least directly—but it's got up-to-date, practical info on how to make your way and stay connected.

http://www.ipass.com

Ipass does what ATT Worldnet, Earthlink, Mindspring, and the rest don't. It can get you on the Net in most civilized places in the world.

Thingys on the Net

Metasite for Web Thingys

http://www.oink.com/thingys

Type: Metasite

First Developed: 1998

Price Range: Connect time

Key Features: Loose collection of fascinating thingys

Ages: 10 and up

Obsolescence: Low.

Further Information:
✳ *http://dir.yahoo.com/ Computers_and_Internet/ Internet/Interesting_Devices _Connected_to_the_Net/* is Yahoo's directory of Web thingys

The Web seems to draw the brilliant, the clever, and the weird. Many of the weird devote themselves to hooking peripherals up to the Net. Netcams were one of the first thingys, and Geocities, a spectacularly successful Net company recently acquired by Yahoo, started with a live camera aimed at a street corner in Beverly Hills.

Some of the net-cams look at the sky, some at desks, some at water coolers and Coke machines—alternately fascinating and boring stuff. But there are other thingys too. Several telescopes are hooked up to Web sites and controllable over the Net (in a scaled down imitation of the Hubble Space Telescope). Recently a slew of radios have been hooked up, and their audio digitized and put up for downloading.

Pagers, radar, weather stations, and all kinds of data-gathering devices render every Web-connected PC a beneficiary of a loosely organized, ever-expanding remote sensing system. Ill-organized and spotty now, this system will likely become one of the great technical achievements of the 21st century. Take a look now.

Sky and Telescope
Astronomy and Space Web Site Index

http://www.skypub.com/resources/links/links.html#menu

Type: Web site

First Developed: 1995

Price: Connect time

Key Features: Very simple, easy to use

Ages: Junior high and later

Obsolescence: Low

Further Information: Sky Publishing
(617) 864-7100

Something about the Net syncs with astronomy and space. The number of related Web sites is—forgive me—astronomical. It's very hard to figure out what's good and what's bad, and the Web search engines are entirely useless in this regard. It takes a human, not an algorithm, to sort wheat from chaff. The charter naturally belongs to the editors of *Sky and Telescope* (a magazine I recollect with deep affection from my childhood). They have taken their charter seriously, and passed with it intact into the new world. This Web site is terrific. Check out the links system, but one of the many fine features of the site. The hyperlinked index to related astronomy and space sites (see box on following page) allows you to quickly find the top places selected by the *Sky and Telescope* experts. (How great to be a kid today.)

THE UNIVERSE ON THE WORLD WIDE WEB
A *Sky and Telescope* Web Index

Indexes of Astronomical Web Sites	Ground-Based Telescopes
Events, Conventions & Star Parties	Airborne Astronomy
Professional Research	Space Agencies & Space Centers
Amateur Research	Space Astronomy Missions
Equipment & Telescope Making	Planetary Science Missions
Observing & More!	Piloted Space Flight
Online Star Charts	Online Data & Catalogs
Astronomical Software	Online Astronomy Newsletters
Astronomy Education	Magazines & Journals
Museums & Planetariums	Images
Public & Private Observatories	Astro Education

SETI@home
Web-based Search for Extraterrestrials
http://setiathome.ssl.berkeley.edu/

Type: Web site

First Developed: 1998

Price Range: Connect time

Key Features: Be a part of something big, really big

Ages: Post high school

Obsolescence: Medium

Further Information:
Search on the phrase "massively parallel computing" to find the latest on this subject

We heard about this site from a guy named Craig Hockenberry, designer of a nifty utility to help you pretty up your Mac desktop called IconDropper (*www.iconfactory.com*). Craig (aka The Chief Typist) is very clever and into a lot of different, interesting stuff, which he readily shares with his subscribers. This is what he wrote about SETI in a recent Iconfactory newsletter:

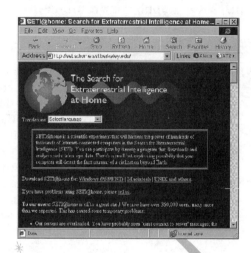

Life Out There...

We invite you to join our quest for alien intelligence. Yes, Team Iconfactory has become a part of the wildly popular SETI@home project.

There are few minutes each day when our pixels don't get pushed around. During these idle times, we use our Macs to comb through mountains of data from radio telescopes pointed at the stars. Our results are then sent back to UC Berkeley for further analysis.

This all sounds much more complicated than it really is. Any computer can do it. You just install the software and connect up to the Internet. The program handles all the rest (and shows you some neat-o graphics while it's working).

One of the Chief Typist's favorite things about this whole project is that you can see how fast computers are at cruching data: (see *http://setiathome.ssl.berkeley.edu/stats/platforms.html*).

The average time it takes a Pentium machine with Windows to crunch through all this data is about 45-1/2 hours. Funny how a Mac with a "slower" processor only takes 26-1/2 hours to do the same amount of work. It's also cool to see a Mac with Rhapsody doing it in 14 hours!

Editor's Note: The really interesting thing about the SETI initiative is that it turns every participating computer into a component of a vast parallel processing computer. This concept, here obviously put to use for good, is equally amenable to bad things—watch this space).

—Susan Black

III. Software

Meade Epoch 2000sk

Astronomical Software

http://www.meade.com/catalog/epoch/epochsk.html

Type: Software

First Developed: 1990s

Price Range: $3000 -$4000

Key Features: Tight integration of telescope and PC

Ages: Post-teen

Obsolescence: Medium

Further Information:
http://www.skyshow.com/
(check this site out for LX200 satellite tracking software and info)

Meade Instruments
☎ (714) 451-1450

This is IT for a serious private astronomer—the software that turns the right telescope (like the Meade LX series) into a robotically controlled device. No eyeball sighting. Target the celestial object on the computer screen and the telescope mechanically responds, targets, and locks in on the object. Then, it manages the digital images of the object, which supercedes the light-gathering powers of your eyes, giving you the ability to look at the object based on a longer exposure, developing a more detailed image than your eyeball could. Here's a bit of promo fluff from the Meade Web site that captures the rush this system can deliver:

> Listen to this! I installed Epoch 2000sk-CD in my computer and set up my 8" LX200... clicked on Betelgeuse with the mouse; when the telescope stopped moving, there was Betelgeuse exactly in the center of the crosshairs. For the next two hours I kept going from a star, to a cluster, to a nebula, etc. When you advertise that the telescope is accurate to one arc-minute, you are conservative, as it is much better than that.
>
> —*L.S., Laguna Hills, California*

This system is very expensive, very advanced, very hip.

NGCView

Celestial Software

http://www.rainman-soft.com/

Type: Downloadable software (30-day trial)

First Developed: 1990s; Rainman Software

Price Range: $40-$50

Key Features: Simple, graphically straightforward

Ages: Junior high and later

Obsolescence: Low

Further Information:
See FOUR BIG ISSUES WITH OPTICS

Rainman Software
☎ (804) 296-6569

Before you head out into the backyard to observe the heavens, it's a good idea to figure out what you are going to be looking at. That changes all through the year for the stars. And the moon and the planets are never in quite the same place. You can't follow the celestial game without a scorecard.

In the '50s and '60s, the best way to know what was going on was to get a monthly issue of *Sky and Telescope* magazine. It had an oval map of the night sky, and if you looked at it in just the right way, you could figure out where most of the obvious objects in the sky could be found.

More recently, with the advent of PCs with enough processing honk to run good graphics and a bunch of math at the same time, an array of celestial display programs have been offered. Some are rich and complex (see RED SHIFT III), and others like NGCview are meant to be simple and quick.

For the backyard astronomer, this program provides a little bit more than enough. It has enough depth, however, so that an occasional hobby can turn into a minor obsession without having to ditch the software.

Atomic Clock

http://search.shareware.com/

The best little utility for getting your PC to agree with the international time standard.

There is something utterly irritating about having your PC's clock drift. Two seconds or two minutes, nothing as smart and precise as a PC should ever get so damned...wrong. Happily, there is a constant river of superaccurate time flowing through cyberspace, and it costs nothing to tap in. Atomic Clock is one of many time utilities that look over the Web to sites that feed atomic clock signals.

This one is particularly good, as it offers a display of local and Greenwich times, can be set to automatically sync up on a regular basis, actually corrects for the milliseconds in lag time as the signal bounces around the Net, and gives you a selection of time sources. I prefer Paris, the international hub of the time standard.

Type: Shareware

First Developed: 1996

Price Range: $20 for full license

Key Features: Highly reconfigurable

Ages: 10 and up

Obsolescence: Low

Further Information: See the US Navy Atomic Clock Web Site
✱ *http://tycho.usno.navy.mil/what.html*

AtGuard

Net Garbage Filter

http://www.atguard.com

Type: Browser enhancement software (downloadable 30-day trial)

First Developed: 1997

Price Range: $30

Key Features: Good first line of defense against bad Web manners

Ages: From first computer use

Obsolescence: Medium.

Further Information: WebWasher and InterMute can be downloaded from the Internet at:
✳ *http://www.siemens.de/servers/ wwash/wwash—us.html*
and
✳ *http://www.intermute.com*

WRQ Inc. makes AtGuard:
☎ (206) 217-7404

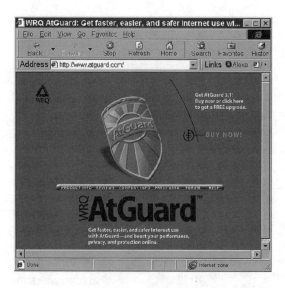

When you browse the Web, you invite a lot of people into your virtual home who you would not care to have for dinner. These are the kind of folks who go through your drawers, steal the silverware, and ask annoyingly personal questions. They obnoxiously interrupt the dinner table conversation and have little sense of good manners.

Their ill-mannered Net counterparts constantly dump banner advertising on you and harvest all kinds of personal info which—if you were to look at it all together—would amount to a terrific invasion of privacy (pilfered from little chunks of data about you stored locally on your computer—called "cookies").

Worse, it's entirely possible for the more larcenous of these Net visitors to burrow into your hard drive, steal files, deposit viruses, and extract info on your personal and intimate interests by perusing the contents of your files.

Yikes.

There are an increasing number of security systems (often referred to as "ad blockers") that you can install on your PC. One of the most highly regarded, AtGuard will block annoying ads, graphics, and animated GIF files, and in so doing bump up the speed at which Web pages come up on your computer.

AtGuard also lets you decide whether to allow Web sites to collect cookie-based data about you and your Web use. Lastly, AtGuard makes for a simple personal firewall, disallowing intrusion by anyone other than you.

Keep in mind that firewalls—ways of keeping the riffraff out of your PC—have varying levels of sturdiness. There is no standard measurement of their effective security, and there are bright new hackers tending to the business of breaking in all the time. Further, the advertisers on the Net are clever, too. Some people think there is a war looming between the ad blockers and the advertisers, just like the war between anti-virus programs and hackers.

MyFonts

Super Font Manager for Windows

http://www.mytools.com

Type: Software (downloadable 30-day trial version)

First Developed: 1998

Price Range: $35

Key Features: Good, if slightly goofy, user interface. Very practical

Ages: 10 and up

Obsolescence: Medium

Further Information:
✽ *http://www.alsoft.com/ MJPinfo.html*
for Masterjuggler Pro font manager for the Mac OS 8.5. MyFonts comes from UniTech:
✽ *www.MyTools.com*
☎ (314) 770-2770

In the mid-'80s my company actually made digital type-fonts (you can still find a few of the ones we made in Windows 98). We always had a problem managing fonts. With the 256 character slots in fonts, the varying character set standards, Postscript vs. Truetype, and a hundred other tiny issues, digital type-fonts are a study in complexity.

It used to be a *whole* lot simpler. But ever since the advent of the Mac in 1984 (and the demise of hot lead typography), font utilities have blown through the cyberworld, with few of them sticking, while the number of digital typefonts has multiplied constantly.

MyFonts seems to be the best of the current crop of type management software for Windows. It previews TrueType and PostScript Type 1 fonts in any size and treatment up to 99 points. MyFonts produces some very good-looking specimen sheets and manages the installation and removal of fonts individually or in "Font-Packs." It even scrounges your system for duplicates.

A SMATTERING OF FONT FOUNDRIES

There are zillions of places to find fonts on the Net—some funky, some free, some corporate. Here are just a few of them...

http://cuiwww.unige.ch:80/OSG/Fonts
http://graphicdesign.miningco.com/
http://idt.net/~sini4me2/
http://soup.swankarmy.net/index2.html
http://tjup.truman.edu/dtr/home.html
www.3st.com/
www.adobe.com/Type/browser/
www.atypi.org/
www.bitstream.com

www.Chank.com/
www.devicefonts.co.uk/
www.dol.com:80/TypeLab/
www.emigre.com/
www.esselte.com/itc/index.html
www.eyesaw.com
www.fontbureau.com/cgi-bin/index.cgi
www.fontdiner.com
www.FontFabrik.com/index.html

www.fontfont.com/
www.fonthead.com/main.html
www.fontshop.de
www.fontworld.com/
www.fountain.nu/index2.html
www.fuse98.com
www.garagefonts.com
www.girlswhowearglasses.com
www.graphic-design.com/ →

Font Reserve 2.0
Super Font Manager for the Mac
http://www.fontreserve.com

Type: Software (downloadable demo)

First Developed: 1996

Price Range: $100

Key Features: Nimbly manages and protects huge numbers of fonts

Ages: 10 and up

Obsolescence: Medium

Further Information:
☎ (415) 381-3303

I wasn't especially looking for a new font manager when my Mac guru Ken Love at Machanics told me about Font Reserve... after years, I was habituated to using Suitcase and a little wary of change. But I found the transition painless, and well worth the short amout of time it took to reconfigure my font sets.

Font Reserve is a truly professional font management tool that takes advantage of the Mac's drag-and-drop technology to help you organize your library. It provides flexible font storage options, isolates corrupt fonts, repairs fonts that are repairable, removes duplicate fonts, and organizes your fonts in its "Font Vault" for added protection. At the same time, it compiles the information into a powerful database, driven by a very user-friendly browser.

"Font Reserve's strong organizational concepts are the future of font management programs," says Publish Magazine *(1998).*

Best of all, you can preview any font you've got with a mere *command-click*, and easily print a variety of font sample templates and character maps right from the browser.

—Susan Black

→ MORE FONTS...

www.houseind.com/
www.imageclub.com
www.itcfonts.com/
www.letterror.com/
www.microsoft.com/typography/
www.mindcandy.com/
www.monotype.com/
www.omnibus.se
www.originalab.se
www.p22.com/

www.philsfonts.com/
www.prototype-typeo.com/
www.quixote.com/serif/
www.ragnarokpress.com/scriptorium/
www.rotodesign.com
www.shiftype.com/
www.slip.net/~graphion/
www.soib.com/ef/links.html
www.subnetwork.com/typo/
www.surface-type.com
www.synfonts.com/

www.t26font.com/
www.tau.it/lightsoft/
www.treacyfaces.com/
www.typ.nl/TYP08/typ08-index.html
www.type.co.uk/
www.typeart.com
www.typeindex.com
www.typeright.org/
www.typography.com/
www.virus.net/
www.will-harris.com/type.htm

Red Shift III
Digital Planetarium
http://www.maris.com

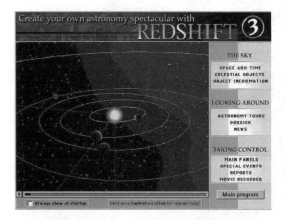

Type: CD-ROM

First Developed: 1995

Price Range: $50-$60

Key Features: Great detailed digital planetarium, with lots of little videos

Ages: 10 and up

Obsolescence factor: Re-released about every two years

Further Information: Good (but much simpler) freeware orreries and planetariums available on the Net (see NGC VIEW, WINTRACK).

A digital planetarium, crafted by the cream of Russia's space scientists. Stunning, with great depth.

One day in the summer of 1963, I got to go to the Cincinnati Planetarium and have the controls to their Zeiss celestial projector all to myself. I turned the dials and the stars sped through the sky, eons of celestial development passing by in seconds, planets flashing by like meteors.

I get the same rush from Red Shift, but in some ways even better. The people at Maris in London pillaged the Russian space program for astrophysicists after the Soviet economy collapsed in the early '90s, and set them to creating a virtual planetarium. They made Red Shift, and continue to add to it year by year. It is a truly wonderful CD-ROM that will appeal to more than just astronomy buffs.

If you've got a backyard, an occasional clear night, and maybe a kid, you ought to have Red Shift. It's like having the playbook to read before you go out to watch a game of celestial football.

Astronomica
http://www.astronomica.com

Type: Shareware

First Developed: 1998

Price Range: $25

Key Features: Simple, very well written

Ages: Junior high and beyond

Obsolescence: Medium

Further Information: North American download site: * *http://www.tsnsoftware.com/entries/00000d03.sml*

Unlike RED SHIFT, which is so rich in assets it requires a CD-ROM for playback, or NGCView, which is largely designed to be a space mapping program, Astronomica is a planetarium designed to both reveal the night sky and animate its motion. This night sky software hails from somewhere deep inside Poland. Given the post-Soviet origins of Red Shift, one must wonder how many marginally employed space physicists and rocket scientists there are running around Eastern Europe. Imagine what would happen if they turned themselves to games. Or cyberterrorism. Yikes.

European contact address:
element 5 AG
Habsburgerring 3
D-50674 Koeln, Germany

Astronomica *continued*

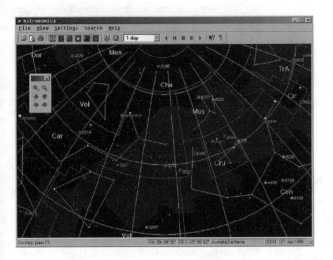

**Specs from
the Astronomica Web site**

➤ 9096 stars to 6.5 magnitude in colors based on their spectral types

➤ Constellation boundaries and constellation lines

➤ 110 deep sky objects from Messier Catalog and 100 of the most popular from New General Catalogue

➤ Milky Way and Magellanic Clouds

➤ All planets, Sun, and Moon with its phase

➤ Equatorial coordinate grids, ecliptic, horizon, and compass horizon points

➤ Labels for stars, constellations, planets, and deep sky objects

Claris Emailer

http://www.claris.com/

Type: Software for the Mac
First Developed: 1996
Price Range: $50-$60
Key Features: Gathers AOL e-mail
Ages: 10 and up
Obsolescence: Medium
Further Information: Lots of add-ons and utilities through the Fog City Web site:
✳ *http://www.fogcity.com/em_software.html*

One of the very best e-mail managers for the Mac. Before the iMac, this was one of the last, resilient reasons to own a Mac.

Claris Emailer makes the assembly of e-mail from multiple accounts a breeze, gives terrific control over the organization and archiving of your incoming missives, and best of all, will download AOL mail. Almost nothing else can do that—not Microsoft's Outlook (e-mail and personal organizer), not Goldmine (e-mail and contact manager)—none of the others. I have no idea how Claris (now Filemaker) penetrated the secrets of AOL's utterly non-standard mail POP (=Post Office Protocol), but in so

doing they have freed the world from the cheesy, exploitive junk merchandising that you have to pass through every time you pick up your AOL e-mail (unless you by-pass the site by using AOL's automatic session that will go retrieve your new mail and sign off before the stream of merchandising can assault you.)

Today, at our company Xiphias, we use Claris Emailer to suck in AOL mail, archive it, and then forward it to the Internet e-mail accounts we can get to from Outlook. Such a pleasure to escape AOL's bad manners. Unfortunately, Apple seems to have assimilated Emailer and made it disappear. Too bad.

The Brain

http://www.thebrain.com/

Type: Shareware

First Developed: 1998

Price Range: $50 for full-use license

Key Features: Win95 compatible

Ages: 10 and up

Obsolescence: Medium (constant downloadable revisions)

Further Information: Check it out on the disk enclosed with this book

The best idea organizer the industry has yet served up.

Sometimes you get so habituated to doing things a particular way that it never dawns on you that there has got to be something better. Flat lists and computers seem inextricably tied together. Drop down menu: long list of stuff. More stuff, longer lists. Yup. Yup.

Then along comes something like The Brain, which blows the hair out of your eyes. This may not be the final, definitive innovation in this area (the area being: organizing your stuff), but it'll probably be a while before something quite so interesting and good comes along. It got all the heavies at the recent Esther Dyson Agenda 98 conference worked up, and for good reason. It'll likely become a permanent part of your desktop.

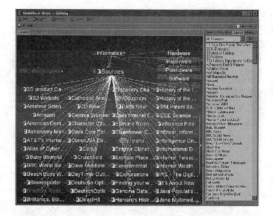

The premise is simple: you can link anything to anything else via an elastic line on the screen. You can link Web sites (URLs), all kinds of files —even e-mail messages—and establish a large number of relationships between them. The whole complex is then presented in an animated web on the screen.

FROM VANNEVAR BUSH'S "AS WE MAY THINK"

Wholly new forms of encyclopedia will appear, ready made with a mesh of associative trails running through them. Ready to be dropped into the memex and there amplified. The lawyer has at his touch the associated opinions and decisions of his whole experience, and of the experience of friends and authorities. The patent attorney has on call the millions of issued patents, with familiar trails to every point of his client's interest. The physician, puzzled by his patient's reactions, strikes the trail established in studying an earlier similar case, and runs rapidly through analogous case histories, with side references to the classics for the pertinent anatomy and histology. The chemist, struggling with the synthesis of an organic compound, has all the chemical literature before him in his laboratory, with trails following the analogies of compounds, and side trails to their physical and chemical behavior.

The historian, with a vast chronological account of a people, parallels it with a skip trail which stops only on the salient items, and can follow at any time contemporary trails which lead him all over civilization at a particular epoch. There is a new profession of trailblazers, those who find delight in the task of establishing useful trails through the enormous mass of the common record. The inheritance from the master becomes, not only his additions to the world's record, but for his disciples the entire scaffolding by which they were erected. Thus science may implement the ways in which man produces, stores and consults the record of the race.

TEN RULES TO BUY BY
THE INFORMATICA GUIDE TO SOFTWARE

1. Never buy version 1.0.

Version 1.0 of every piece of software ever written, throughout history, without exception, stinks up the room. The best publishers release version 2.0 as quickly as they can with more new features than bugs, and with most or all of the first generation bugs gone (there aren't many best publishers, but v. 2.0 is almost always better). If you must get version 1.0, make sure there is a clear and inexpensive upgrade path.

2. Buy what you friends have.

At two o'clock in the morning, when the thing has crashed and you need to know how to resurrect the data, you want to depend on people who know and love (or at least tolerate) you. You do not want to talk to some geek on a support line. (The exception to this rule is when your friends have a penchant for version 1.0.)

3. If it handles data, it must have good, industry-standard import and export facilities.

You probably already have done what you are doing with the new program with another program, or your friends have. Hence you want to be able to suck in the data from the old to the new. You probably will want to switch to a better program sometime in the future, hence you want to blow your present data out in a compatible form.

4. It should be Internet savvy (the meaning of that varies from program to program).

By now, any program that does take advantage of the Internet is being maintained by people who are hopelessly out of touch with technical and marketing realities. If they screw up on that, they'll have hosed other issues as well.

5. Get it free first (if you can), then buy it later when you know it works.

Loss leader downloads (see VIRAL MARKETING) are more and more common. Anybody who is not willing to let you test drive an expensive program has something to hide (either a bad program, or marketing myopia—see rule 4 above).

6. Make sure there is a good strategy for downloading upgrades over the Internet.

You should not have to wait for a new disk in order to get bug fixes. Good software publishers have figured out that it pays to make it easy for their customers to get the latest and greatest over the Net, via their Web site. Check out the product's Web site before you buy. →

→ **(THE LAST FOUR OF THE INFORMATICA TEN RULES TO BUY SOFTWARE BY...)**

7. If the software depends on any other software, make sure that software is included in the package.

"Batteries not included" is the fulcrum of anguish in consumer electronics. If your software requires a certain video driver, multi-media playback capability, browser or plug-in, make sure it is included in the box. It is NOT a safe bet that a compatible version of the required software will be available over the Net.

8. Check the quality of the soft documentation (on the disk or available on-line).

Nobody reads the printed manual. Not you, not me. Hence, the integrated software documentation (the stuff you get to through the Help menu) should be clear and complete. If it makes constant reference to the printed docs, you have a problem – the developer was too lazy to make a good integrated help system. In that case, you have to consider where else they cut corners in the creation of the software.

9. Get software that has an auto-update capability.

Good examples of this are the Norton Utilities from Symantec, which remind you to check for updates regularly and then with the click of a button automatically take care of the download and installation. Intuit's Quickbooks is also good at this, and elements of the Microsoft Office Suite (2000 version) are very good. They have an 'Office on the Web' file menu option, and a 'Detect and Repair' option in the same menu to find and replace damaged and/or corrupted files. When it comes to Microsoft code, this is a necessity because of the vast number of files it installs, and the B+ nature of the code (see MICROSOFT OUTLOOK).

10. Buy more RAM (random access memory).

You think this sounds like filler, drawn from the ten hardware rules just to make an even ten here? Wrong! Nothing will improve the responsiveness of your software more than added RAM installed in your machine.

Microsoft Outlook 98/2000

http://www.microsoft.com

Type: Software

First Developed: 1998

Price Range: Nothing. If you play your cards right. Incalculable, if the right hacker gets at you and the rest of us

Key Features: Deep integration with the rest of the Microsoft world. It's their world, we just live in it. For now

Ages: Junior high and later

Obsolescence: Medium

Further Information: The Microsoft Outlook Updates/Downloads Web page

✴ *http://officeupdate.microsoft.com*
If you are involved in sales, you should consider GoldMine

✴ *http://www.goldminesw.com/*

First things first: I dislike Microsoft as much as the next guy. It's despicable the way they use their Windows/OS profits to underwrite giving away their applications for free, hence stifling and killing off competitors. That's the software publisher in me talking.

But here's the consumer talking. Outlook is a great deal: it's pretty much free. You can download it from Microsoft, or get it on a CD-ROM with one of the Microsoft Press books on Outlook. It gets a solid B+ as a personal information manager (PIM). Others are better (GoldMine has a spectacular reputation), but they aren't free.

More importantly, because of the wide proliferation of Outlook over the last few years, a lot of people use it. That means that every Palmtop has to sync with it in order to be competitive. There are a bazillion add-on shareware and freeware enhancements for it on the Net.

Further, it is deeply integrated with the rest of the Microsoft Office family of products. In particular, it works well with Word (you can set it up to use Word as the e-mail editor, and you can send e-mails in

Web-compatible HTML), and Microsoft Project. It's about 95% stable (that means it crashes now and then, but not enough to really bother me, and so far no crashes have lost any of my data), and though it suffers from a bad case of featuritis (sometimes it seems a bit Rube Goldberg-ish), the features are very rich.

The downside of that feature bloat was brought into relief in late March 1999, when a virus called Melissa (see MELISSA'S LESSONS) exploited one of the features of Outlook to blather the net with millions of bogus e-mails, choking mail servers all over the world. Microsoft's response was that their ciustomers insisted upon such features. I doubt any customer insisted that Microsoft leave a backdoor open for clever hackers to make life miserable for the rest of us.

I use it for managing e-mail, with everything else (address book, calendar, tasks, etc.) playing a secondary, supporting role. Outlook's biggest weakness is this: it will not pick up your AOL e-mail.

If you are highly motivated, you can work around that shortcoming by running CLARIS EMAILER on a Mac (the only known e-mail management program that breaks into the AOL mail pick-up system), and having CLARIS E-MAILER route your AOL mail to another account. Then Outlook can pick it up.

Enigma Cipher Simulator

http://www.blueangel.demon.co.uk

Type: Freeware

First Developed: 1998

Price Range: Free

Key Features: Works as advertised

Ages: Post-teen

Obsolescence: A classic implementation of a key 20th-century technology

Further Information: This site also has simulators for other classic cipher devices.

Software emulating the German encryption system.

The Enigma machine was at the core of what Churchill called the "wizard war" of competing technologies during World War II. The Germans used the machine (somewhat sloppily), and as a result the Poles and subsequently the English cracked its secrets. Thereafter, the Allies proceeded to have an insight into the thinking and plans of Hitler throughout the war.

Front: in the wooden box, an Enigma machine; Rear: Colossus, the early electronic device designed to decode the Enigma

The ability to crack the Enigma code was kept secret for decades after the war. In a move of clever calculation, the English arranged to have Enigma machines endorsed and used throughout the third world in the post-war years, thus guaranteeing their ability to read the message traffic of those countries for years to come.

Here is a piece of free, downloadable software that demonstrates how the device worked. That is to say, it emulates the Enigma machine, and will actually encode your messages. The NSA will be able to crack it, but many third world countries and most of your friends won't.

Cardscan

Software to Read Business Cards

http://www.cardscan.com/

Type: Software

First Developed: 1994

Price Range: Nothing, if it comes bundled with a scanner. A free trial version can be downloaded from the Web site. Approximately $50 for the upgrade that makes it fully functional.

Key Features: Deep integration with the rest of the Microsoft world, both scanners and personal information managers (PIMs)

Ages: Junior high and up

Obsolescence: Medium

Further Information: See Hewlett Packard CAPSHARE 910 for a new take on scanning things.

Business cards collect like grime in the kitchen floor corner. I wish I could get rid of the thousands I have collected over the years. Somewhere in the stacks are some historic ones; for example, a pristine Bill Gates in the early Microsoft green color scheme. The rest of them are largely useless, given the speed at which people jump from job to job.

The new ones, though, are important. I need to get them into my copy of MICROSOFT OUTLOOK as soon as possible. Keying them in by hand makes me feels like a keypunch operator. My mind begins to empty out, and my sense of self-worth takes a power dive.

The only corrective I have ever found to this is Cardscan. I don't use it all the time, but when I end up with batches of new cards—after trade shows, for example—I crank up the scanner and start slamming the cards through.

I inherited Cardscan; it came bundled with an inexpensive Visioneer scanner. The version that came with the scanner worked fine. It is very clever at fig-

uring out what's a name, what's an address, what's an e-mail address, and what's a phone number. This free version made a point of reminding me that, were I to invest in an upgrade, I could directly scan cards into OUTLOOK.

I couldn't resist. In one of those rare, thrilling consumer experiences, I paid my money, and when the CD with the full-featured version showed up, IT WORKED. In went the cards, and with a couple of mouse clicks, the new contact info was plopped in Outlook.

Mind you, you have to watch the thing, like a child you have assigned to a household task. It doesn't scan everything well, especially cards with weird type and dark backgrounds. Every now and then, it gets confused about a character, and you have to intervene and correct its work. But it is much faster than keying in the data yourself. This is a very worthy product, as long as you are prepared for it not to be perfect.

VisualRoute 4.0

http://visualroute.com/

Type: Software (downloadable 30-day trial version)

First Developed: 1997

Price Range: $29

Key Features: Wonderful way to learn how the Internet works

Ages: 10 and up

Obsolescence: Low

Further Information: A white paper called "The Hitchhiker's Guide to the Internet":
✳ *http://www.cis.ohio-state.edu/htbin/rfc/rfc1118.html*
GeoBoy, another tracer program out of Australia, with a spectacular 3D earth map:
✳ *http://www.ndg.com.au/products/gb/*

> *I was having lots of problems getting to our Web sites until I ran VisualRoute and was able to narrow where the problems were. I called my ISP and gave them the names of the problem nodes and voila, my connections are now a LOT faster.*
>
> —JIM STARKE

One of the more impressive scenes in the crypto-movie *Sneakers* was when the heroes set up shop, called the NSA, and watched a computer screen as the NSA return-traced a phone call.

There isn't any easily available program to trace phone calls, but there's a dandy down-loadable piece of code called VisualRoute™.

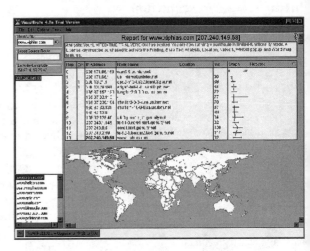

The undisputed king of route tracing programs.

—*Bill Machrone, PC WEEK*

VisualRoute, by the assertion of the folks who make it, is a visual, fast, and integrated ping, whois, and traceroute program that automatically analyzes connectivity problems, displaying the results on a world map.

Aside from being really neat to look at (and that counts for a lot), VisualRoute—once you get handy with it—is quite a weapon.

Once you put a DSL, cable modem, or ISDN line into your home and find the speed of the line isn't what you expected (don't be surprised), you can check it out with this program and document the lousy performance. The geeks in tech support will be deeply impressed.

You can trace back seemingly blind junk e-mail (*spam* to the digerati) and make misery for the authors. Further, you can see which of the big networks (MCI, Sprint, UUNET, MSN, etc.), lie in the path your bits and bytes take.

This is a really great piece of code and quite a bit of fun.

Accuset

Software Utility for PCs

http://www.retsik-software.com/

Type: Shareware

First Developed: 1994

Price: $10 registration fee

Key Features: Presently at version 5.0b

Ages: 10 and up

Obsolescence: Medium, seems to be keeping pace with OS changes

Further Information: Retsik Software (717) 732-7636, and ❊ *http://www.boulder.nist.gov/ timefreq/javaclck.htm* for the National Institute of Standards and Technology clock.

Your computer drifts. It's probably off a couple of seconds every day. If that bugs you, here's the way to fix the mistake. This is a terrific piece of software that uses your modem or any other Internet connection to connect to sources to sync up your machine's clock to the international time standard (see GUARDING THE SOFT EMPIRE—SYSTEMS).

There are others—to find them go to www.shareware.com and search on *atomic clock*—but this is the one I prefer.

It is complete with a world map showing where the shadow of night is falling, sunrise and sunset, and even Big Ben chimes on the half hour if you want them. Further, it will keep a log of the inaccuracies of the clock on your computer.

MELISSA'S LESSON

(as first printed in the *LA Times,* March 1999)

In March 1999, the virus Melissa landed like a ton of bricks on North American businesses and then proceeded to get worse. It doesn't damage files on your PC; rather, it clogs the e-mail system. Its effect is to crash e-mail servers and as a result deny e-mail service. The speed with which Melissa has proliferated has left even the most seasoned computer experts breathless.

Melissa might not be a clever cracker's stunt. She might not be a terrorist attack. She might be an effective tactical move in a new style of warfare—**infrastructure warfare.**

The point of infrastructure warfare is to use any and all means, whether a cyber attack or the destruction of bricks and mortar facilities, to crash critical systems in the United States infrastructure. Those systems can be things like e-mail, but they can also be things like natural gas pipelines, transportation systems, and power grids. Are we prepared for such attacks? Hardly.

In the coming century, war-making will undergo a fundamental change, and the military planners in Washington call it "asymmetric." The change comes when the bad guys represent an entity far smaller than the U.S., with far more limited resources. It could be a nation-state, but it could just as easily be a fundamentalist religious group or a drug cartel. It doesn't take much money, nor does it require sophisticated weapons systems. The requirements are know-how and the ability to move quickly. →

Melissa's Lesson *continued*

→ Two years ago, the Department of Defense discovered just how vulnerable the United States has become to this form of attack when it ran an exercise called Eligible Receiver (for the official congressional testimony on this exercise see *http://www.senate.gov/ ~ gov_affairs/62498dci.htm)*. A team of sophisticated information warfare specialists from the Air Force, National Security Agency, and other government agencies undertook a 20-day exercise, with the goal of crashing the military command, control, and communications systems in the Pacific. Within the first four days, they had gotten so far that the exercise had to be stopped early. During the course of the exercise the "Red Team"—the government's hackers—discovered an effective way to attack the U.S. power grid as well.

The disconcerting reality of Eligible Receiver is this: the Red Team used information and techniques drawn from open, easily accessible sources. It could have been done by a team in Belgrade or Baghdad or Beijing.

The fundamental idea is ageless: remove an adversary from the contest with the least risk of loss to your own side. In the 21st century, the technique will be an attack on infrastructure. Fifty years ago, infrastructure-based war, or I-War, wasn't really possible. Infrastructure was not tightly integrated by communications and computation technology as it is today. Because the linkages were haphazard and weak, the destruction of a core component—like the ball-bearing factory—had a limited "ripple effect."

Today, with almost every detail of modern life controlled or influenced by computers and communications-driven systems, our infrastructure has an exposed underbelly: software. Try to imagine something important that doesn't run on a software system

of some kind. The threat doesn't end there. Water systems, power grids, and oil and gas pipelines can be physically attacked with great ease and in ways that would take months and in some cases, years to repair.

Choose the right systems, damage them in the right way and at the right time, and the ripple effect can be massive.

Several years ago, President Clinton established a commission dedicated to the protection of critical infrastructure (*www.pccip.gov*), and this year the White House announced that a healthy part of the multi-billion-dollar counterterrorism budget would be devoted to that end. In a perfect example of big talk and lousy execution, the elements of the budget earmarked for infrastructure protection were red-penciled last week by the Office of Management and Budget. Because no government agency is legally chartered to address this transborder threat, the funds cannot be allocated.

Today, the U.S. has tiny digital fire departments like CERT, the Computer Emergency Response Team at Carnegie Mellon University (*www.cert.org*), that tracked Melissa. There is no grand strategy for defense or offense. We are not prepared.

Most of the men and women who create policy in government are not of the computer generation. They don't understand software, or the fundamental value of data, or the inherently "soft" way the world works. No one is planning for the grand-scale attack. No one is planning for the grand-scale defense. No one is planning for the "soft kill."

That attack will come. That defense will be necessary.

TOP TEN U.S. WAR TARGETS
(updated from the original list in
Wired Magazine, Issue 1.3)

🔥 **Funds Transfer Systems**—In Culpepper, Virginia, several electronic switches handle federal and commercial funds transfers and transactions.

🔥 **Internet**—Subject to both cyber and "bricks and mortar" attacks.

🔥 **Phone Systems**—Electronic Switching Systems (ESS) subject to hackers with techniques well documented at an array of sites in the Internet, and in such magazines as *2600*.

🔥 **Alaska Pipeline**—Carries 10 percent of domestic oil for the US.

🔥 **Time Distribution System**—All major systems depend upon accurate time.

🔥 **Panama Canal**—Still immensely important in the transport of raw materials and goods.

🔥 **Worldwide Military Command and Control System (WWMCCS)**—Particularly susceptible to soft attack, as demonstrated by Eligible Receiver.

🔥 **Natural Gas Pipeline system**—Once crashed would take months to restore.

🔥 **Power Grid**—Highly interdependent, as demonstrated when the 1994 L.A. earthquake crashed systems all the way up to Idaho.

🔥 **National Photographic Interpretation Center (NPIC)**—a ten-minute walk from the U.S. capitol, this is the repository and processing facility for all of the government's photographic intelligence.

IT'S TOUGH TO TRACK A CRACKER

On March 28, 1994, the computer systems administrators at Rome Labs, Griffiss Air Force Base, New York, discovered their network had been penetrated and compromised. Rome Labs, among other things, is where the U.S. Military Command, Control, and Communications systems are researched and designed—a place worth protecting. This was done with a "sniffer"—a program designed to penetrate computer systems by sniffing out weaknesses. Once detected, the system administrators notified the Defense Information Systems Agency. The cybercops immediately went to Rome Labs to investigate what happened.

They found that sniffer programs had penetrated a total of 30 of the lab's systems, and gone undiscovered for five days. The crackers used the penetration to gain access to over 100 other systems in the military and related networks. It got big and scary very fast.

One of the crackers was foolish enough to use a name he had used before, and he was hunted down fairly quickly. His chat room traffic indicated he was a 16-year-old English kid, and what sites he liked to hack, and even his home phone number. Painstaking analysis showed that every time Rome Labs was attacked, this boy was phone phreaking the telephone lines to make free calls. On May 12th, the New Scotland Yard arrested "DataStream." Even though DataStream was the one who broke into Rome Labs, he was working with the guidance of another cracker, Kuji. Kuji very cleverly masked his identity and whereabouts, and the Cybercops think he may be a real spook, using Datastream as a "cutout"—an unwitting pawn.

Read the real story drawn from chief Cybercop Jim Christy's congressional testimony at the following URL:

✱ *http://www.cs.virginia.edu/~survive/PAPERS/Christy.html*

THE U.S. ARMY'S CYBER SECURITY RULES

The following message was sent out by the network security manager at Fort Bragg in the early stages of the NATO attack on Yugoslavia. It offers a sophisticated guide to the principles behind protecting yourself from attack over the Net.

From: *(deleted)*

Sent: Wednesday, April 21, 1999 2:12 P.M.

Subject: Information Assurance Message

THIS MESSAGE IS BEING SENT TO ALL E-MAIL USERS ON FT BRAGG SO THERE IS NO NEED TO FORWARD THIS MESSAGE.

DO NOT REPLY TO THE SENDER. IF YOU HAVE RECEIVED PRO-SERB SPAM AS DISCUSSED BELOW, NOTIFY THE SECURITY MANAGER AT THE E-MAIL ADDRESS PROVIDED AT THE END OF THIS MESSAGE.

[Ed.—If you think you have been attacked, call the local office of the FBI.]

Due to the increasing evidence of pro-Serb Internet attacks on e-mail users in NATO countries, e-mail users should exercise defensive measures to guard against unsolicited e-mail and potential computer virus infection.

Key indicators to watch for based on previous e-mail spam attacks from pro-Serb/anti-NATO sources:

1. Messages from unknown senders relating to Kosovo or NATO bombing of Serbia

2. Unsolicited MS Word attachments with a political content

3. Very poor English language usage

4. Cartoon graphics with an anti-NATO message

5. Extensive routing of the message through various senders

→

U.S. Army Cyber Security Rules *continued*

→ 6. Return e-mail addresses that originate or are routed through Europe (may be determined by a routing address ending in a two letter country code such as .yu)

7. Invitation to visit web sites that provide more information or the "truth" about the NATO bombing of Serbia/Kosovo.

Defensive measures for military e-mail users:

1. Update antivirus software signature files at least once a week by going to (an Army Net) at (An Army URL, details deleted by the Editor) and selecting the appropriate virus signature update.

[Ed.—The virus protection people live and breathe to update your virus definitions (that's part of their marketing effort). Take advantage.]

2. Do not open attachments from unknown senders fitting the above profile.

[Ed.—Attachments from people you don't know are dangerous. Attachments from people you do know can be dangerous too, especially if they are Microsoft Word or Excel documents. Never OK enabling macros on a document you don't already know is safe.]

3. Do not visit pro-Serb/anti-NATO Web sites either by invitation through e-mail or while surfing the net (visiting a potentially threatening site may allow them to capture your address, allowing for future attacks)

[Ed.—People who sleep with dogs get fleas. Be careful where you surf.]

Military members may also be targets for pro-Serb/anti-NATO propaganda or attack through personal accounts on commercial e-mail providers. In addition to the above defensive measures, the following measures can be taken to prevent unsolicited e-mail on civilian e-mail accounts.

→

U.S. Army Cyber Security Rules *continued*

→ **Defensive measures for civilian e-mail account users:**

1. Some commercial e-mail accounts (AOL, Bigfoot, Netscape, etc.) allow users to build a descriptive profile of themselves. Recommend you remove all references to being a military member. Keyword searches of account profiles can reveal those members who are military members and make them vulnerable to unsolicited e-mail and potential virus attack.

[Ed.—Revealing too much (where you live, what you do, how many children, etc.) can be an open invitation to bad folk.]

2. Military members with commercial screen names that may indicate a military affiliation should be wary of unsolicited e-mail with pro-Serb/anti-NATO connotations. If you should experience e-mail that fits this profile, you should consider changing your screen name to one without a military theme.

[Ed.—Same goes if you work for a rich, high-profile, or politically controversial organization.]

In all cases, report all incidents (military and civilian) of unsolicited e-mail or virus infection relating to this profile to your immediate supervisor. Supervisors should report incidents to the Network Security Manager.

[Ed.—For the rest of us, it's the FBI.]

---

*See **www.army.mil/webmasters/checklist.htm** for the Army's guide to protecting Web sites.*

Intruder Alert

Software Prophylactic for Your PC

http://www.bonzi.com/intruderalert/ia99.htm

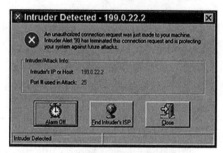

Type: Software

First Developed: 1994

Price Range: $30

Key Features: A guy with a digital shotgun standing at your front door

Ages: Junior high and later

Obsolescence: Medium

Further Information: For a fancier, far more technically sophisticated solution, look into the SonicWall/10 (P/N: 01-SSC-2550) firewall from SonicSolutions at

✱ *http://ww.sonicwall.com*

I found out about this utility when I was reviewing one of Ravi Desai's recommended sites (VCALL.COM). The minute the site came up, up popped a window with a message indicating that my computer could be under attack and that Intruder Alert could help me fend off attackers and track them down thereafter. What really got my attention was this: the box had my gateway address.

I figured if they were clever enough to merchandise that way, somebody else might be clever enough to get at me that way, too. I am, in effect always online and always vulnerable now, because I am using a DSL, rather than a dial-up connection.

I bought it and installed it and then began to wonder whether it was some terribly clever scam. No way of knowing whether it works or not, unless you have a hacker friend who will attack your computer for fun. I have some friends like that, but I'm not sure I would be wise to let those particular dogs of war loose.

So it was moot until I came in one morning and found Intruder Alert had trapped an attempt to get in to my computer, logged the source, and given me

A sample attack report.

enough to track the responsible party down. It was benign, but next time it may not be. I'm glad I bought it, and I now have it running on the other machines hooked up to the DSL at home. Is it thorough? Is it impenetrable? Who knows? But it seems to be a good first line of defense.

From www.bonzi.com:

Every time you browse the Internet, send e-mail, or submit any private information to a Web site, you broadcast your computer's unique IP address over the Internet. With this IP address, someone can immediately begin trying to break into your computer without you even knowing it. Until now, there has been no way of telling if this has happened or any way of stopping it. Well not anymore!

Intruder ALERT '99 is a one-of-a-kind Internet utility that can notify you if someone is trying to break in to your computer, stop them dead in their tracks, and even build a visual map showing you the intruder's ISP (Internet Service Provider), allowing you to see where the intruder is located and report it.

Truster

Software for Determining the Truth

http://www.truster.com/

Type: Software

First Developed: 1998

Price Range: $150

Key Features: The ability to discern who is naughty and who is nice

Ages: All

Obsolescence: Low

Further Information:
❋ *http://www.polygraph.com/* for an interesting site on how to beat a polygraph

I would have a difficult time determining whether this product works or not. If I am surrounded by liars, I haven't discovered it yet. I imagine I could hook it up to the phone and call people who owe me money, but I'm not sure I could handle the truth.

Voice-stress analyzers, including Truster, measure changes in voice frequency. The trick is picking up stress that occurs when the mind and the mouth are not in sync.

Still, the concept behind this product is so simple, yet so far-reaching as to make it impossible to ignore. Truster was created for the military to use in stopping terrorists at Israeli border checkpoints. That would seem to define the concept of a mission-critical application.

Don Weinstein of the American Polygraph Association, quoted in *The New York Times,* said he had yet to see reliability studies for any voice-based stress evaluators, the general category of this technology. The polygraph people say that voice-based truth tests aren't proven. Polygraph machines, which cost thousands and require skilled operators, measure respiration, blood pressure, and pulse.

"When people lie, their mind is not happy with what their mouth is saying," say the marketeers. "This conflict is shown in very specific frequencies. This is where we hunt the deception." Some experts say that voice-stress analyzers need trained personnel, just like conventional lie detectors. What if the answer is, "Yes, we have no bananas"? What if you ask someone if they have stopped beating their wife? What have you learned? Further, in many states it is illegal to tape a conversation without a person's knowledge. The guys who market Truster recommend getting legal advice before using the product.

Apparently, it's necessary to establish a baseline of truthfulness in a conversation. That allows the software to calibrate the person's stress level when he or she lies.

With all that said, it seems to me that if this thing works without the intervention of an expert, the best possible use would be to hook it up to the audio feed of your TV and tune in to C-SPAN. What a revelation that would be. ➔

→ Truster *continued*

An Evaluation from www.truster.com
By Dr. Guy Van Damme, Criminologist
July 1998

An evaluation of Truster was made by myself and colleagues from our Academic Computer Sciences Department.

1. PROCEDURE FOLLOWED
1.1 Stimulation tests
Fifty subjects were tested with the use of the figure stimtest. Each subject was asked to choose a number between one and ten. After the calibration period, the subject was asked to say "No, definitely not" towards each question ("Did you choose number X"?) Forty one subjects were found deceptive towards the number they chose, three subjects were deceptive towards three numbers, four subjects were deceptive towards a wrong number.

Statistically: *82% success rate*
10% inconclusive
8% false

1.2 Field Test
Twenty five subjects were asked to tell us briefly what they did during the past day. This interview was used as the calibration period. We asked ten subjects to tell us a few definite lies when asked again to tell us the same story, fifteen subjects were asked to tell the absolute truth. From

the ten subjects asked to lie, eight were found deceptive. From the fifteen asked to tell the truth, four were found deceptive.

Statistically: *76% success rate*

1.3 Truster used during polygraph pre-test interview
Seventeen subjects who came for polygraph tests were subjected to Truster during their pre-test interview (we used a Screen Ware amplified microphone). Six people showed an indication of deception using Truster during their pre-test interview. The eleven subjects showing an indication of no-deception went also clean using Truster.

Statistically: *100%*

2. SUMMARY
All tests, apart from 1.3, were so-called laboratory tests, meaning that the subjects were fully aware of being tested and had nothing to lose. The subjects tested during the pre-test interview were obviously stressed, knowing they were to undergo a polygraph examination. The 100% scoring rate should therefore be regarded as abnormally high. It is however interesting to see the same indications from the polygraph (we used Lafayette LX3000-SW) and

from Truster. More extensive tests should be required to formulate an acceptable comparison.

3. NEGATIVE POINTS
As an academic exercise, Truster proved to be reasonably accurate. However, the following negative points (let us call it positive criticisms) were raised:

3.1 Reports
The reports given by Truster are very vague and do not include a statistic (percentage of deception etc.). It is understood that TrusterPro will include this facility.

3.2 Calibration Period
The calibration period is rather long. If the program is used on a subject over the telephone, the average period of twenty seconds needed for calibration will create a certain suspicion from the part of the subject.

4. SUMMARY
Truster is a very user-friendly, affordable truth verification program.
Truster should only be used as a certain form of an indication with doubt towards its results. However, as said above, it is extremely user friendly, easy to learn, affordable, and reasonably accurate.

WinTrak

Software for Tracking Satellites

http://www.hsv.tis.net/~wintrak/index.html

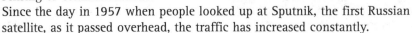

Type: Software

First Developed: For DOS, in the late '80s

Price Range: Less than $100, order by phone or e-mail

Key Features: Beautiful graphics, rich database

Ages: Post-teen

Obsolescence: Low, constantly updated with data from the Net

Further Information:
✳ *http://www.skyshow.com/* (check this site out for Meade LX200 satellite tracking software and info); see also NASA shuttle/MIR tracking Web site at:
✳ *http://38.201.67.72/realdata/ tracking/index.html*

There are thousands of thingies—human designed thingies—orbiting the Earth. Not space junk, but devices designed for remote sensing or communications.

Since the day in 1957 when people looked up at Sputnik, the first Russian satellite, as it passed overhead, the traffic has increased constantly.

Lots of it can be seen as it passes overhead, if you know where to look. And this program shows you where to look. Further, it does beautifully rendered projections of the Earth and the evening sky—planets, stars, and all.

The real value here is in the story it tells about what is circling the Earth, and why it's there. The program is designed to go to the Net and download updated information about new launches and new satellites. It'll track the Space Shuttle and space stations as well. Fascinating. And so fancy-looking that it was used in the James Bond film *Goldeneye*.

It's worth noting that the home for this program is Alabama, near the Redstone arsenal, where Werner Von Braun and his engineers started the U.S. space program. Software from Star City.

From the WinTrak Web Site...

✳ Quick, simple, clean operation; fast, accurate results
✳ Next pass, next mode displayed and updated with a simple mouse click
✳ Nearly unlimited number of satellites
✳ User-configured, multiple-tracking stations, over 2,100 cities included
✳ Multiple satellite tracking
✳ Predict upcoming satellite passes

✳ Fast tabular satellite rise/set options
✳ Real-time or simulated-time satellite tracking modes
✳ GPS interface for position data
✳ 3D fully rendered Earth views—these will take your breath away!
✳ Fully rendered Mercator map Earth views
✳ Multiple station/satellite modes
✳ Edit satellite elements on-line
✳ Simple easy installation program included
✳ Supports any video mode used by Win95/98/NT 4.0

→ WinTrack *continued*

---

* Satellite database of over 850 satellites included
* Constellation views for pass planning
* Doppler shift calculations, both uplink and downlink
* Squint angle calculations for the OSCAR satellites
* Phase-to-mode tables for OSCAR operations
* Interface to the Auto Tracker for automatic antenna pointing and radio tuning
* Logging radio contacts option included

* Predict upcoming satellite passes
* Track the sun and moon
* Satellite tracks across a star background
* Stars to magnitude 6.0 included
* Optical tracking options with range limits
* Sun terminator plotting options
* Print high resolution maps
* Free technical support via Internet

Alexa

Web Site Identifier

http://www.alexa.com/

Alexa is a freeware add-on for Internet Explorer (4.0 and later) and Netscape Navigator that reports exactly who operates the Web site you are visiting, where they are found in the physical world (address, phone numbers, and the like), how much traffic they actually get, along with a list of other sites which might interest you.

Web sites are lousy about betraying anything that might result in non-digital human contact. Alexa does a decent job of parting the curtain to reveal the people behind the scenes operating most Web sites. I run Alexa in a window at the bottom of my browser. As often as not, I find that the Great Oz is, as might be expected, less than what the smoke and mirrors of the site would indicate.

Alexa gives a measure of how much traffic the site actually gets, and encourages folks to vote their approval and/or disdain for the site in question (though it appears that few people care to waste their time voting—instead, "Hello, I must be going" seems to be the height of social grace on the Net).

There's a guilty pleasure in every newsroom in America—the reverse directory, where you can look up a phone number and get the name and address. Alexa brings that guilty pleasure to the Net.

Type: Browser enhancement software

First Developed: 1998

Price Range: $0

Key Features: Reverse directory of the Net

Ages: 10 and up

Obsolescence: Medium

Further Information: Good, but not exhaustive way to find sites related by use or subject matter to the site you are visiting. Look at INTERNIC:
* *http://www.internic.net/*
for more info on who owns and operates Websites.
Contact Alexa Internet at:
Presidio Bldg 37
POBox 29141
San Francisco, CA
☎ (415) 561-6900

Omiga

PC-Based Genetic Explorer Software

http://www.oxmol.com

Type: Software

First Developed: 1998

Price Range: $1,995.00

Key Features: Speadsheet for genes

Ages: Post-graduate

Obsolescence: Medium

Further Information: See the
HUMAN GENOME PROJECT

I certainly don't understand this stuff. When I noticed an ad for Omiga in *Science* magazine, it caught my attention. Gene-splicing on a desktop. Laptop recombinant DNA engineering. E coli on the fly.

It gives me the willies, but it is somehow breathtaking and beautiful as well. I hope the people who know how to use this know how to be responsible grownups. →

FROM THE OXMOL WEB SITE:

In its review, *Biotechnology Software & Internet Journal (BSIJ* Sept/Oct 1998) noted that "OMIGA 1.1 is an extremely powerful and versatile sequence analysis program that brings a welcome addition to the Windows 95 platform. Given the complexity of this software and its relatively early stage of evolution, it is remarkably free from bugs or failures."

OMIGA 1.1 features PCR prediction, built-in multiple sequence alignment, desktop protein analysis, and support for the latest 32-bit graphics standard, EMF. The Project View window organizes sequences and analysis results on a project-by-project basis, and edits to a sequence are instantly reflected across the entire program. OMIGA is compatible with sequence files from MacVector™, the GCG Wisconsin Package®, and other programs, facilitating collaboration with colleagues using other computer platforms. The current shipping version, OMIGA 1.1.3, is Year 2000 compliant and includes the Project Packager, which enables OMIGA projects and their associated files to be moved easily between computers. Also, the new Extensions menu allows users to conveniently access other Windows programs, shortcuts, text files, and Web sites from within OMIGA.

Omiga Genetic Explorer *continued*

→ When searching for similarity and/or mutations between multiple sequences, OMIGA uses the powerful Clustal W algorithm, which is rapidly becoming the standard for desktop computing. Once alignments are found, users have the option of a variety of text and graphic displays for presentation and publication. For ease in editing alignments and locating regions of interest, OMIGA uses the color display to group similar residues by color.

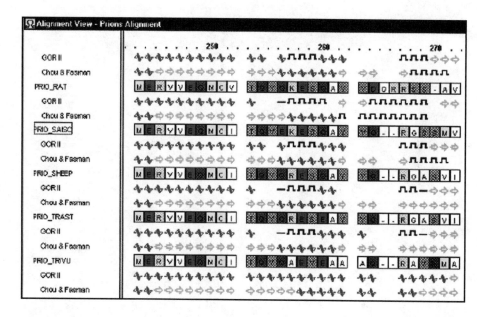

This is an example of OMIGA's sequence alignment editor. Each color is used to designate a group of chemically similar residues. In addition to a range of residue-based coloring schemes, residues may be colored to reflect the degree of consensus within the alignment. The example also shows secondary structure predictions that can be used to assist in alignment interpretation.

iv. Plastic *ware*

Powers of Ten (VHS)

Filmed by Charles and Ray Eames

http://www.powersoften.com/

Type: VHS tape

First Developed: 1968

Price Range: $40 (personal use); $80 (institutional)

Key Features: Striking visuals

Ages: 10 and up

Obsolescence: Never

Further Information:
❋ *http://www.pyramidmedia .com/home3.shtml*

Eames Office:
P.O. Box 268,
Venice, CA 90294, U.S.A.
☎ Phone: (310) 396-5991

Charles and Ray Eames did some remarkable stuff. The Eames chair is still a triumph of design (still sold by Herman Miller). The Mathematica exhibit (elements of which are still on display at the California Museum of Science and Industry in downtown Los Angeles) is still one of the best hands-on exhibits ever put together (for others, see EXPLORATORIUM OF SAN FRANCISCO). But the thing they did that may just last forever is the *Powers of Ten*.

Originally, it was an experimental film done in black-and-white, underwritten by IBM. They called it. "A Rough Sketch for a Proposed Film Dealing with the Powers of Ten and the Relative Size of Things in the Universe." Catchy.

The notion was to give a visual sense of scale in the known universe. The first image is of a guy sleeping on a picnic blanket on Soldier's Field in Chicago.

Every second, the camera zooms ten times farther away, and in a little over a minute there's no farther to go. Then the camera zooms back in to the guy's hand, and reverses the process, traveling ten time slower every second until the subatomic level is revealed.

The effect is so powerful that it has been knocked off constantly. Recently in the opening sequence of a Star Trek movie (marginal), and in the opening sequence of *Contact* (pretty good, especially the conceit of playing the audio tracks of TV and radio programs at roughly the distances they might have traveled since first broadcast, traveling back in time the farther away from Earth).

But nothing matches the original, which strives to be scientifically correct, and when finished was done in color. Both are on a video tape called *The Films of Charles & Ray Eames—Volume 1.*

Earthlight (DVD)

http://www.earthdvd.com/

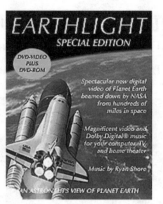

Type: DVD-ROM

First Developed: 1998

Price Range: $25-$30

Key Features: High quality digital imagery and MPEG II video

Ages: All

Obsolescence: Low

Further Information: Much of the source video material available from NASA and JPL
✼ *http://spaceflight.nasa.gov/shuttle/index.html*

The best video of the Earth, from the vantage point of the Space Shuttle, delivered on DVD.

This is a ridiculously simple product. It's a PC screen saver with a bunch of high resolution images and over an hour of video—all shot from the space shuttle. A bunch of people my age remember the first time they ever saw a picture of the Earth—the whole Earth—shot from space. It was a show-stopper. Arguably, there never would have been a powerful ecology movement without those pictures that made it possible to comprehend that the Earth was one living thing. But those images seem to have lost their power by now, over-merchandised.

This disk throws you back in your seat, and grabs you by the neck, or the soul, or whatever got grabbed by those first images 30 years ago. This one will actually make your jaw drop and the fire in your spirit burn a tad brighter. It is the definition of perspective.

Great Speeches of the 20th Century (Audio CD)

http://www.rhino.com/Catalog/Cat14/Cat14_index.html

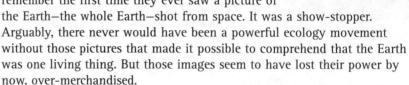

Type: Audio CD (4 disks)

First Developed: 1994

Price Range: $40-$50

Key Features: Multiple samples of many varied historical figures

Ages: All

Obsolescence: Low

Further Information:
Another fine entry in the series,
The Library Of Congress Presents: Historic Presidential Speeches (1908-1993)
☎ Rhino Records: (310) 474-4778

From Edison and Teddy Roosevelt, to Reagan and Clinton, the best oratory of the century. Somebody at Rhino—the people who republish all the great old rock 'n' roll and R&B recordings—disappeared into the maw of the National Archives, and likely into several other dusty old places, to pull out all these fine old recordings. Some are immediately recognizable—Kennedy, Johnson, Reagan. Some are yanked out of the far mists of history—Woodrow Wilson, Hoover, and the like.

I was particularly thrilled to hear the scratchy old recording of Teddy Roosevelt. There's something comforting in knowing that you can be that great and still have a reedy voice. I suppose TV has led us to believe that you've got to sound like James Earl Jones to cut the mustard. In all, there is no substitute for the tone and timbre of the human voice, and these four audio CDs are a feast.

World War I (VHS)

Type: VHS (5 cassettes)

First Developed: 1965

Price Range: $79.95

Key Features: Fine CBS-style production

Ages: High school and up

Obsolescence: Low

Further Information: Much of the source video material still available in the National Archives in Washington, D.C

The classic mid-'50s CBS News documentary has Robert Ryan's voice as narrator and Burt Benjamin's production savvy. Unlike the recent PBS documentary series on World War I, this one gets it. Maybe it's because it was made by people who had living memories of this horror. Maybe it's because it was made at CBS, when people like Ed Murrow were looking over the creators' shoulders.

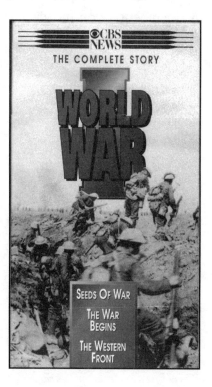

In preparing the video for the *Encyclopedia Electronica,* I found myself lingering over the World War I materials in the National Archives. There were photographs and films of all those people trying to grasp what industrialized warfare was going to mean. There were 19th-century European politicians eyeing Woodrow Wilson and his Fourteen Points like so much easy prey. There was Churchill drawing the boundaries of the Middle East on a map over breakfast. There was Ho Chi Minh in a morning suit, trying to make a place for his Viet Nam as the world was divvied up at the Paris Peace conference.

And I could never get Robert Ryan's rasping, knowing, world-weary voice out of my head as I looked at the raw stock. Most of the good footage in the National Archives can be found in this exceptional work.

There is no one in statecraft, government, or the professional study of history who will tell you any different: You can't grasp what has happened in this century without wrapping your brain around what led up to, and occurred during and immediately after World War I. And it's all here in these five video cassettes.

Visions of Light: The Art of Cinematography (VHS)
A Documentary on the History of Cinematography

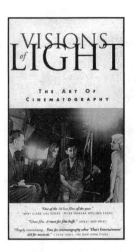

Type: VHS tape (no DVD yet)

First Developed: Original documentary,1993; VHS, 1998

Price Range: $20–$30

Key Features: Beautiful

Ages: 10 and up

Obsolescence: Low

Further Information: The American Society of Cinematographers Web site
❋ *http://www.cinematographer.com/*
For those who love to see the world as if through the eyes of a director, there are directors viewfinders, a fundamental tool of cinema
❋ *http://www.birnsandsawyer.com/s1-4.htm*

I grew up in a Beverly Hills home. My first step-father (very L.A., huh) was a television director, and then later a film director. Hence, I grew up around cameras, and had a deep appreciation for the composition of a frame. It's something of a learned taste, and it leaves you with the habit of composing camera shots in your head when you look at things and people.

When I heard of *Visions of Light*, I really wanted to see it. Great cinematography is utterly thrilling. It was playing in a small theater on Sunset Boulevard in Hollywood (in a minimall built on the land that used to have a set of bungalows called the "Garden of Allah"—the place carries a bit of the waft of old Hollywood).

I spent the whole ninety minutes spellbound. This documentary may not have all of the best (how could it, given its length and the legal rights clearance nightmares the producers must have waded through?). But what it does have is totally wonderful.

This isn't pop culture, with stars and the like. This is art, beautifully composed moving images. This is the distilled essence of everything that is visually good about movies. Some of it is in standard 4:3 aspect ratio (like a TV screen); some of it is in widescreen. None of it has been cropped, clipped, or presented in anything other than a loving respect for the original artistry.

👁 VIEWER COMMENTARIES

Comments from the Net:

A viewer from Los Angeles , March 4, 1999
reader, October 10, 1996
The most brilliant chronicle of movie-making ever ★★★★★
This film is regarded by all as THE movie about movie making. Legendary filmmakers from around the world are interviewed, lending opinions, advice, and behind-the-scenes stories that are heard nowhere else. A must-see for any aspiring filmmaker or film fan.

Tupperware

The Original Plasticware

http://www.tupperware.com

Type: Plasticware

First Developed: 1946

Price Range: $3.99 and up, plus the patience to sit through a Tupperware demo

Key Features: Simple, clean, efficient, easily maintained

Ages: Pre-school and up

Obsolescence: Low

Further Information:
✽ *http://www.rubbermaid.com* for a competitor's approach to plasticware (as we don't have a category for *rubberware* in this edition)

(Editor's Note: One of Informatica *book designer Sue Black's best friends is Dan Kempler, a very clever fellow and expert in linguistics. When he heard about* Informatica, *and its classifications—hardware, software, paperware, plasticware, and sources—he came back with the following...)*

A chapter about plastic without mention of Tupperware is unthinkable.

Tupperware may be best known for its quintessentially suburban American sales "parties," at which a Tupperware representative demonstrates and peddles plastic containers. However, in addition to its signature marketing approach, this plasticware empire is innovative in manufacturing and design—all in the service of keeping food fresh.

Of all the plasticware included in this book, Tupperware food storage containers are arguably:

☐ **The oldest:** born in 1946.

☐ **The cheapest:** some items are even free: these are called "gifts" and can be very useful; my favorites include the Beater-Cheater, Save-A-Nail, the Butter Up, and the much sought-after baby Tupperware bowl keychain, complete with tiny, snap-on lid.

☐ **The most beautiful:** always a leader in design, T-ware is represented in the Museum of Modern Art Design Collection by its classic pastel tumblers.

☐ **The most practical:** what's more efficient than a storage bowl that burps its excess air?

☐ **The only one with a lifetime guarantee:** they really will replace your Tupperware if it cracks, peels, or breaks during the →

TUPPERWARE Facts at a Glance: In 1998...

✓ ...a Tupperware demonstration started every 2.2 seconds somewhere in the world

✓ ...around the world, more than 105 million people attended a Tupperware demonstration

✓ ...Tupperware® brand products were sold in over 100 markets around the world by approximately 950,000 independent salespeople

✓ ...worldwide net sales were $1.1 billion

Tupperware *continued*

→ normal course of use; this guarantee generally excludes damage by melting or canine bite.

❑ **The most widely used:** T-ware is found in a large percentage of American homes, and in over 100 countries.

❑ **The most innovative in its sales technology:** you could buy it from your own home long before e-commerce or the cable shopping network.

❑ **The most maligned:** why do people make fun of Tupperware?

❑ **The most imitated:** note the vast Rubbermaid and no-name sections of plastic storage containers in your local drug, grocery, and 99-cent stores.

❑ **The most airtight:** they really keep food fresh for days!

❑ **The most versatile:** some of the newer models can be used in both the microwave *and* the oven. Don't try that with a video tape!

❑ **The best example of "re-tooling":** Earl Tupper invented a method of purifying a by-product of the oil refining process into a material that was durable, flexible, odorless, nontoxic, and lightweight and used it for manufacturing plastic gas mask parts during World War II; after the war, the technology was reharnessed (and could be said to fuel the great post-war domestic boom in the U.S.) to produce food storage containers.

❑ **Virtually indestructible.**

—*Daniel Kempler, Ph.D.*

This is the time-saving, money-saving Tupperware seal. It makes life easier by making Tupperware plastic bowls, canisters and tumblers airtight. Locks in freshness and flavor. Keeps moist foods moist, crisp foods crisp. Tupperware is fun to use and fun to buy. Tupperware's versatile housewares are demonstrated at a leisurely home party, yours or a friend's. Put that meal-saving seal to work for *you!* Call the local Tupperware distributor for your nearest dealer's name, or write to Dept. LM-1, Tupperware, Orlando, Florida.

A Tupperware ad in 1954

Video Essentials (DVD)

DVD for Testing DVD Systems

http://www.videoessentials.com/

Type: DVD

First Developed: 1997

Price Range: $35

Key Features: Sophisticated tests for a home theater system

Ages: All

Obsolescence: Low

Further Information:
✳ *http://www.imagingscience.com/* for an explanation of display standards and a downloadable utility for adjusting your PC monitor

DVD is so good that proving its quality is fun. Same as when CD audio appeared—it was fun to get a test disk and simply listen to the purity of the test tones, from low end to dog whistles.

In effect, this disk from Joe Kane (a recognized expert in video systems and standards) is just such a test disk, but for DVD video and the associated audio formats. Video Essentials offers both audio and video test signals, with easy-to-understand instructions for tune-up of a home theater system.

DVD does require a bit of tweaking. Improper adjustment of the sharpness control, for example, will add noise to the picture that is not on the DVD. The interactive material on the disk assists in adjusting the main front panel controls on your set, including brightness, contrast, color, tint, and sharpness. →

LISTING OF VIDEO ESSENTIALS DISK CONTENTS

- Title 1: A/V System Tour
- Title 2: Audio System Connections
- Title 3: Left Channel
- Title 4: Center Channel
- Title 5: Right Channel
- Title 6: Surround Channels
- Title 7: Subwoofer Channel
- Title 8: Center Channel Polarity Check
- Title 9: Video System Calibration
- Title 10: Brightness

- Title 11: Contrast
- Title 12: Overview of Color & Tint
- Title 13: Adjusting Color & Tint
- Title 14: Sharpness
- Title 15: Video Test Material
- Title 16: Acknowledgments
- Title 17: Monitor Evaluation Test Patterns
- Title 18: Monitor Evaluation Test Patterns continued
- Title 19: Montage of Images
- Title 20: Anamorphic Test Patterns

Video Essentials *continued*

→ In the video there are test patterns for the enhanced 1.78:1 wide-screen format, otherwise known as anamorphic video. Also full Dolby Digital® 5.1 channel and separate Dolby Surround® mixes in each of three languages: English, Spanish, and Japanese. A geek's dream.

Video Connections to Avoid

The composite video output should be used only when the component and S-Video connections are not available. In the composite signal, the Y and C of the S-Video signal are added together. As much as going from component to S-Video loses color resolution and adds noise, going from S-Video to composite video adds all sorts of artifacts to the picture that are difficult, if not impossible, to remove. Two artifacts in particular are dot crawl and color moire. You will obviously lose a lot of the quality capability of the DVD format if you use the composite video to route the DVD player to the display device. Look at the Snell & Wilcox Zone Plate test pattern near the beginning of Chapter 15 for a clear demonstration of the difference in any of the connections.

Some DVD players also provide an RF output. In this case the video and audio are modulated to a TV channel and routed to the tuner input of your TV set. This type of connection will further reduce picture detail and add more noise to the video.

Short Cinema Journal (DVD)
Fine Compendium of Rare Film and Video Work
http://www.videoessentials.com/

Type: DVD
First Developed: 1997
Price Range: $25
Key Features: DVD magazine with rarely seen short films
Ages: Grown-ups
Obsolescence: Low
Further Information:
✳ *http://www.broadcastdvd.com* for more on Film-Fest

The idea behind the Short Cinema Journal series is to use DVD as a medium of distribution for fine short film and video material that you would never otherwise see. It also serves as a showcase for new talent.

Some of the material is Academy Award stuff. Some of it is weird, out there, fringy work. Often there is stuff that is not for kids. But the presentation is elegant, the use of DVD sophisticated.

For example, the first in the series was the first broadly distributed disk to exhibit the multiple camera angle feature of DVD. Since then, most of the disks to exploit this feature have been pornographic, so Short Cinema Journal One is worth stowing in your DVD collection.

This first one also features other interesting material, including the predecessor to Billy Bob Thornton's *Sling Blade,* called *Some Folks Call It A Sling Blade.* A short film with Henry Rollins entitled *Henry Rollins—Easter Sunday In NYC* uses four soundtracks →

Short Cinema Journal *continued*

→ and demonstrates Rollins's strange lifestyle and public persona. *The Big Story* is an animation piece that uses multiple camera angles, and it offers a complete pencil test of the finished product running with the finished audio.

The video transitions are handled in a very elegant manner, and the subsequent issues of SCJ are just as interesting. Recently, a spin-off has surfaced by some of the same people. It's called Film-Fest: a Virtual Ticket to the Best Films and Film Festivals in the World.

Trinity and Beyond (VHS)

A Documentary Of Classified Film of the American Nuclear Weapons Test Program

http://www.vce.com/trinity.html

Type: VHS (NTSC)

First Developed: 1996

Price Range: $20–$25

Key Features: Stunning, well restored historic color film

Ages: 15 and up

Obsolescence: Low

Further Information:
✳ *http://www.atomicarchive.com/ AAInternet.shtml*
for more on the bomb and it effects, known and hypothesized.

I bought this video after seeing a late night cable TV offer for it. In spite of the overblown sales rhetoric, the pitch was enticing. The tape had digitally restored color film of virtually all of the big U.S. nuclear blasts, most of which had heretofore been classified. I'm an utter sucker for this sort of thing, and I ordered it pronto.

When I got *Trinity and Beyond,* I waited until after the kids were in bed, and flaked out on the couch to watch. What I saw was very unsettling, yet spectacular. I grew up under the threat of nuclear war. We had civil defense drills when I was a kid, and the sirens went off every Friday morning. We saw all the grainy black-and-white newsreels. We saw the *Life* magazine color spread on a hydrogen bomb test out in the Pacific.

Movies like *On The Beach, Fail Safe,* and *Dr. Strangelove* purported to show the full horror of nuclear war. None of it came close. None of it. →

Trinity and Beyond *continued*

→ This film begins to capture the power, the horrifying destruction, and the pure majesty of the bomb. It has film of atmospheric tests from 1945 until 1963. The narration by William Shatner is understated and spooky, and the original score, performed by the Moscow Symphony Orchestra, augments the unnerving visual impact of the film.

This is something I am going to make sure my children see, when they are old enough not to think of it as special effects.

◉ VIEWER COMMENTARIES

Comments from the Net:

A viewer from New York, NY, USA, January 29, 1999
The most powerful anti-nuclear documentary I've ever seen! ★★★★★
Almost every nuclear explosion on Earth has been captured. From the awesome soundtrack (which I'm desperate to own) to the breathtaking shots of the nukes themselves, this documentary speaks strongly about how far we've come and how low we've gone in order to wield ultimate power, regardless of what we do to ourselves and the world around us.

A viewer from Toronto, Canada, January 16, 1999
Wagnerian Music Enhances A-Bomb Footage ★★★★★
This is a film which works on many levels. The degree to which the testers of nuclear weapons, French, English, Chinese, Soviet, and American, flagrantly detonated their weapons into the biosphere is astounding and appalling. The damage that these tests have done to the planet is incalculable.

Yet, the restored footage reveals what a beautiful sight those detonations were. The immense power which was unleashed by these weapons must have made their builders feel like gods. I am sure there was the arrogance of the gods present as well.

For me, apart from Bill Shatner's above-average narration, the music is what pulls all the words and imagery together. Composed especially for the film, it is as stunning a score as I have ever heard on film. Communicating awe, dread, and majesty, the music counterpoints the film and narration in a unique, three-way ballet.

This should be required viewing for every high school student in North America. Remember: we still have lots of the damn things.

V. PAPER*ware*

→

V. PAPERWARE*continued*

→

V. PAPERWARE *continued*

→

V. PAPERWARE *continued*

Breaking Up America:
Advertisers and the New Media World
Written by Joseph Turow

Type: Book (248 pages)

First Developed: 1997; The University of Chicago Press

Price Range: $16 in paperback; $22 in hardcover

Key Features: Pointed analysis of the social impact of modern marketing

Ages: Post-high school

Obsolescence: Low.

Further Information:
✳ *http://www.press.uchicago.edu/ Misc/Chicago/817490.html*

"Divide and conquer" is an age-old technique for overwhelming an opponent. It is also, apparently, the primary strategy of late 20th-century marketers (see SRI VALS). Some people say that the mass market is a goner (see THE ONE TO ONE FUTURE), replaced by targeted marketing.

Systems like SRI VALS and Claritas Prizm combine computer-driven data harvesting with a divisive notion of who we all are. The result is not only a bazillion cable channels, but also political campaigns that spend most of their resources upon very narrow audiences—the swing vote.

This targeted marketing obsession is probably not safe. Breaking Up America does a very good job of lifting up the rock and seeing what crawls out from beneath. Turow shows how advertisers exploit differences between consumers based on income, age, gender, race, marital status, ethnicity, and lifestyles.

The really interesting question is this: If targeted marketing can reinforce social divisions, will "one-to-one" marketing be a good thing (attenuating those divisions) or a very bad thing (heightening the divisions between individuals, creating families and businesses full of loners).

Yet to a number of highly competitive cable network executives during the mid-1990s the subtlety of signature shows such as Double Dare and Biography was out of touch with the competitive environment. To them, standing out with an attitude meant creating a series with such a fix on separating its audience from the rest of the population that it sparked controversy among people who were clearly removed from the "in" crowd. The resulting publicity across a wide spectrum of media would, they argued, virtually guarantee sampling by the target audience. E!'s marketing director pointed out that executives chose radio star Howard Stern for a network signature program because on radio he reached the age demographics that E! coveted and because his outrageous jokes about politics, race, and celebrity would undoubtedly place the network in the spotlight and draw →

> *Provocative, sweeping and well made... Turow draws an efficient portrait of a marketing complex determined to replace the "society-making media" that had dominated for most of this century with "segment-making media" that could zero in on the demographic and psychodemographic corners of our 260-million-person consumer marketplace.*
>
> —Randall Rothenberg
> THE ATLANTIC MONTHLY

Breaking Up America *continued*

> "Say what you will about the moronic duo [Beavis and Butthead], they've helped to cement MTV's identity with viewers and advertisers."
>
> —*Los Angeles Times*

→ viewers with lifestyle interests that resonated with E!

The classic example of this "in your face" approach was MTV's animated Beavis and Butthead. Centering on two social misfits who spent their time commenting grossly on rock videos and getting into trouble, the series was a nonstop parade of violence and aggressively stupid sexuality—what most parents and other authority figures considered highly objectionable in adolescent behavior. Far from hiding the program, though,

MTV showcased it, using it at the beginning and end of its evening schedule. In this role as the network's prime-time bookends, the series tagged its channel with a hard-edged anti-authority personality that MTV's programmers associated with adolescents and young adults who did not watch much TV and whom the network's advertisers were seeking to embrace. Pressure-group anger at the show, far from endangering it and its image, probably served to reinforce it in the eyes of its target audience.

The One to One Future:
Building Relationships One Customer at a Time
Written by Don Peppers and Martha Rogers, Ph.D.

Type: Book (paperback, 429 pages)

First Developed: 1993; Doubleday Currency

Price Range: $16.95 in paperback; $24.95 in hardback

Key Features: Undersize, well designed, inside and out

Ages: College and later

Obsolescence: Low

Further Information:
✳ *http://www.1to1.com/*
(The One to One Web site)

Theses folks understood the implications on the Internet, before the Internet *was* the Internet. They figured out that it would be possible for modern communications to make selling people deeply personal. With all the assaults on personal privacy, the blatant exploitation of children, and the array of ways that Net entrepreneurs figure out how to steal your silverware, this is precisely the way that selling things is going. It has come full circle from the neighborhood butcher who knew what cut of meat your mom liked for Thursday dinner, to the e-commerce bookseller who today knows what kind of book you'd probably like the next time you visit their site. The Net means the end of mass marketing.

> "Most businesses follow time-honored mass-marketing rules of pitching their products to the greatest number of people. But selling more goods to fewer people is more efficient—more profitable. Welcome to a radically different business paradigm of 1-to-1 production, marketing, and communication."

One To One Future *continued*

→ *The One to One Future* gives a good description of life after mass marketing. In the authors view, a "1to1" competitor focuses on share of customer —one customer at a time—rather than just share of market. Their little handbook has a sense of foreboding to it. The rumble of bricks-and-mortal retailing, shaken and ready to fall. And amazingly enough, only the later editions mention the Internet by name at all. The authors' most recent book is the follow-up, *Enterprise One to One: Tools for Competing in the Interactive Age* (1997, Doubleday Currency).

Value Migration: How to Think Several Moves ahead of the Competition
Written by Adrian Slywotzky

Type: Book (hardcover, 327 pages)
First Developed: 1996; Harvard Business School Press
Price Range: $23.95
Key Features: Thick, businessy, highly worthwhile
Ages: MBA and later
Obsolescence: Low
Further Information:
Get a copy of *"Marketing Myopia"* at
✳ *http://www.hbsp.harvard. eduhbsp/prod_detail.asp ?75507.html*

"One of the most influential marketing articles ever written was Theodore Levitt's 'Marketing Myopia'"
—(Harvard Business Review, July-August 1960, pp. 45-56).

At the Harvard Business School they ram this article down the throats of MBA students. It's thesis, simply stated, is this: If you don't know what business you're in, you are liable to end up as somebody else's lunch.

The stories are many. The railroads thought they were railroad companies, when they should have known they were in the transportation business. Slide rule companies cratered when Texas Instruments introduced electronic calculators. They didn't see it coming. IBM makes mainframes. In come PCs, and they gave away the operating system business to Bill Gates. It wasn't that IBM didn't or couldn't understand software; they just didn't see that as the soul of their business. As Ted Nelson noted about IBM, "Obsolete power corrupts obsoletely." →

> **"Obsolete power corrupts obsoletely."**

Value Migration *continued*

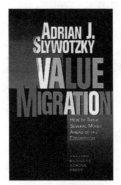

→ The question is this: How do you move your stuff into the future? Everybody's got a story to sell you, and there are consultants galore that claim that they know the secret.

The guys who wrote this book have a pretty good concept of how it ought to be done. They've built their notion around the concept of a business design—some sort of mobile, aerodynamic, "do it like an engineer would do it" approach. Business as architecture. Business as wing design, with fluid dynamics and reduced drag as the goal. Value Migration is written in standard business terminology, but heavy with real-world anecdotes (that's the part that I like).

Offbeat Museums: The Collections and Curators of America's Most Unusual Museums

Written by Saul Rubin

Type: Book (240 pages; hundreds of photographs and illustrations)
First Developed: 1997
Price Range: $17.95 in paperback
Key Features: Short, well written
Ages: Post teen
Obsolescence: Low
Further Information: Random search for museums on the Net.

Across the street from our office in Los Angeles is a strange little place called the Museum of Jurassic Technology.

Our friend Dan Kempler has been a member for five years or so, and extolls its virtues. "The collection shows range from the serious to the absurd, and often it is hard to tell which it is. And that's the point. The shows are both serious and absurd. They poke fun at museumisms and at the same time hone and exult the essence of museumness. A recent lecture series featured a range of experts on sound with lectures on, among other things, the auditory experience of numinous objects and birdsong."

All that notwithstanding, I have never felt compelled to enter the Jurassic. And had I not found *Offbeat Museums*, I would never have known of its peculiar wonders: an exhibit with a petrified ant climbing a tree trunk; a miniature Goofy mounted on a pinhead; two mice on toast.

This book is full of great and strange museums, most of which appear to be safe to visit and utterly fascinating. Two I can vouch for are the NATIONAL CRYPTOLOGIC MUSEUM, and the Nikola Tesla Museum of Science and Industry. The rest, partially listed at right, speak for themselves.

Included among the places you will visit are:

☺ Cockroach Hall of Fame

☺ The Museum of Questionable Medical Devices

☺ Mister Ed's Elephant Museum

☺ The Museum of Jurassic Technology

☺ The Mütter Museum

☺ Houdini Historical Center

☺ UFO Enigma Museum

☺ The Museum of Menstruation

☺ Nut Museum

☺ The Time Museum

☺ *50 museums in all!*

Net.gain: Expanding Markets through Virtual Communities
Written by John Hagel III and Arthur G. Armstrong

Type: Book (240 pages)

First Developed: 1997; Harvard Business School Press

Price Range: $24.95 in hardback

Key Features: Business-schoolish, but heavily admired in the cyber-community

Ages: High school and later

Obsolescence: Medium

Further Information:
✳ *http://www.mckinsey.com/ books/netgain.htm* (The official McKinsey site)

"Stickiness" is the present watchword in the Internet business. The speed at which folks click through Web sites is beginning to give advertisers a sense of wasted money. Who actually looks at those banner ads? So the advertisers are beginning to look for stickiness—some way of getting cybersurfers to hang around long enough to actually see the ad and absorb some of its message.

As usual, an old reality is being dressed up in new clothing. The old reality is the necessity of building customer loyalty. Building such relationships with customers has been a buzz phrase in many business circles for years. Lots of lip service. John Hagel is one of those folks who makes a living by being brilliant. He's an analyst at McKinsey, one of those consulting shops business people regard with reverence. He thinks that business success in the very near future will depend on using the Internet to build not just relationships, but communities. A lot of people also seem to believe that is true, given the high prices paid for the likes of community-oriented Web sites like Geocities. →

CATASTROPHE THEORY
http://www.ideatree.com/articles/change.html

Back in the '60s, the editors of the Whole Earth Catalogue promoted a pet set of ideas and thinkers. One of the most notable was Gregory Bateson, who came up with a terrific definition for information as "the difference that makes a difference." In many ways, the same definition can be applied to the concept of change.

Recently, in the computer/Internet business, change has been so rapid as to induce psychic convulsions. Everyone has ceased to measure speed, and thinks in terms of acceleration. It's important to get a grapple on how change works, and one of the finest concepts to apply to all this is catastrophe theory. Advanced a generation ago by French mathematician Rene

Thom, the fundamental premise is easily imagined as a wave. The smooth surface of the ocean rises, and tension on the surface of the ocean mounts until there is a catastrophic change, induced by an apparently small trigger effect. The stability of ships at sea, prison riots, Black Friday, pandemics—all can be explained mathematically with catastrophe theory (some even think prediction is possible). In many ways, chaos theory helps explain change from a different standpoint. Equally interesting is the concept of friction, not as it is normally used in physics, but as it was used by Clausewitz in his military treatises (see ON WAR).

Also check out:

✳ *http://www.exploratorium.edu/complexity/ CompLexicon.html*

Net.Gain *continued*

→ The payoff will be phenomenal customer loyalty and high profits, for folks who act fast. Nobody knows for sure. It's worth noting that Hagel's analysis has held up for two years, and that's a decade in Internet time.

The appearance of the global computer network has set in motion an unprecedented shift in power from the producers of goods and services to the customers who buy them.

Skunk Works: A Personal Memoir of My Years at Lockheed
Written by Ben Rich and Leo Janos (contributor)

Type: Book (paperback, 400 pages)

First Developed: 1994; Little Brown

Price Range: $13.95 in paperback; $24.95 in hardback

Key Features: A great read

Ages: High school and later

Obsolescence: Low

Further Information:
✳ *http://www.skunkworks.net/lmsw/docs/index.html*
(The official Lockheed Martin Skunk Works site)

There is something wonderful, even romantic, about secret stuff. This book is about Lockheed's Skunk Works, and it's role in designing and producing the supersecret SR-71, U-2, and the F117 Stealth fighter. If you have any interest at all in these planes (arguably very much a "boy thing"), the first read of this book produces high levels of serotonin. It tells the whole story, from the pitch to the Pentagon, to the CIA-driven designs, to the brilliance of the famed Kelly Johnson, to little manufacturing details that are the soul of this sort of enterprise.

Skunk Works Rules

The heart of the book is a small set of rules, originally written decades ago, by Kelly Johnson. Some examples:

Rule 3: The number of people having any connection with the project must be restricted in an almost vicious manner. Use a small number of good people.

Rule 5: There must be a minimum number of reports required, but important work must be recorded thoroughly.

Rule 11: Funding a program must be timely so that the contractor doesn't have to keep running to the bank to support government projects.

The rest of the book is the story of how these rules were applied. It is the soul of a success story.

Historical note: The term 'Skunk Works' is named after the Skonk Works, an illicit distillery in Al Capp's comic strip, Li'l Abner.

Underneath the shrouds, however, is a real, abiding secret. This is a business book, and as such worth a second and third read. These people designed some of the most successful, sophisticated things ever made. They did it under extraordinary pressure, and often delivered on time and under budget. Rich even tells a story (hard to believe) about offering a refund to the government when he didn't spend all of the allotted funds.

The American Black Chamber
Written by Herbert Yardley

Type: Book (out of print in original), Paperback reprint from Aegean Park Press

First Developed: 1931

Price Range: $8-$28 in reprint

Key Features: Short, very well written

Ages: Post-teen

Obsolescence: The scholarship has held up for 68 years

Further Information: Yardley also wrote a terrific book on poker playing, *The Education of a Poker Player*

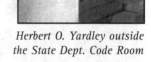

Herbert O. Yardley outside the State Dept. Code Room

After American Secretary of State Stimson closed down the American Black Chamber in the late 1920s, as the State Department codebreaking operation came to be known, it's head guy was out on the street. Stimson thought it was ungentlemanly for nations to "read other nations' mail."

Herbert Yardley was both angry and resourceful (a bad combo for a cashiered government bureaucrat). He set about writing the history of his codebreakers, and it's publication caused a sensation. It also let the Japanese in on the fact that the U.S. had read their diplomatic traffic during a critical naval disarmament conference, and snookered them into a bad deal.

A whole generation of Japanese militarists, the ones who would conduct World War II, developed a very bad attitude over that one. And that is just one of the amazing stories built into this book. It is the natural successor to *The Zimmermann Telegram* by Barbara Tuchman.

Interestingly, that same Stimson saw the light about "reading other gentlemen's mail" during World War II. He was Roosevelt's Secretary of War, and one of the beneficiaries of intercepts of cracked German and Japanese messages, and he encouraged vast investment in and dependence upon the decrypted traffic.

Detail: Improvised Cipher Disk of Mexican Army, from The American Black Chamber

---

➤ READER COMMENTARIES FROM THE NET

A reader from Canada, July 1, 1998 ★★★★★
A great inside look at the earliest days of cryptography.
Anyone interested in the inner workings of ANY cryptoanalyst needs to read this book. Told in the first person Yardley reveals the amazing amount of genius and hard work cryptography required before the days of calculators and computers. It really is a great read.

The Puzzle Palace
Written by James Bamford

THE NATIONAL BESTSELLER

THE PUZZLE PALACE

INSIDE THE NATIONAL SECURITY AGENCY, AMERICA'S MOST SECRET INTELLIGENCE ORGANIZATION

JAMES BAMFORD

This book picks up where *The American Black Chamber* leaves off. It covers the development of the cryptanalysis/signals intelligence community from just before World War II, when each of the armed service had their own groups for this purpose.

After the war, President Harry Truman decided 1) that gathering radio messages and cracking the codes that hid the messages was extraordinarily important, and 2) that it was really stupid to have different services—Air Force, Navy, Army, and State Department—overlapping. So, in a very secret presidential order, he created the precursor to the National Security Agency.

The NSA, though it ate up billions, underwrote the development of the transistor and the supercomputer. It was not formally acknowledged to exist (they used to say NSA stands for No Such Agency) until Bamford published this book. Then the shroud was sufficiently removed that the NSA went public. Today it has a Web site, and a public museum!

Type: Book (655 pages)

First Developed: 1973, reprinted in 1983 by Viking Press (paperback)

Price: $8–$12 in paperback

Key Features: Amazing revelations

Ages: Post teen

Obsolescence: Slightly out of date, given the digital revolution since first publication. As history, however, it is absolutely first rate. For more recent information on the NSA, browse the Federation of American Scientists Web site at
✳ *http://www.fas.org.*

Further Information:
The NSA Web site at:
✳ *http://www.nsa.gov*

•⟶ READER COMMENTARIES FROM THE NET

A reader , August 3, 1998 ★★★★★
A little paranoid...
I don't know if this is true, but I heard that if you purchase this book ANYWHERE, your name and everything about you goes into some kind of NSA list.

The Cobra Event
Written by Richard Preston

Type: Book (432 pages)

First Developed: 1998; Ballantine Books.

Price Range: $7–$9 in mass market paperback.

Key Features: Excellent story, founded in little known fact.

Ages: Post-high school

Obsolescence: Low.

Further Information:

✳ *http://www.pbs.org/wgbh /pages/frontline/shows/plague /etc/synopsis.html*
PBS Frontline Web pages for the documentary "Plague War"

✳ *http://www.fas.org/bwc /index.html*
Federation of American Scientists site on Biowar/terrorism

The story goes that President Clinton read this book and was so spooked that—policy wonk that he is—he immediately undertook to establish additional funding and better policy to combat bioterror (Presidential Decision Directive 62, issued in May 1998).

Preston's book would be nothing more than a first-rate thriller, were it not seasoned with whole chapters devoted to the history and present-day reality of biowarfare. When I first read it, I discounted the reality stuff, as so little had appeared elsewhere.

> ## "This book scared me to death."
> —Hudson, a reader

Mind you, it sounded real, but the best policy on the sort of thing is the one the network news departments used to use, when they actually did news: don't stand behind a fact until you have two independent and unbiased sources.

That fell into place when I saw a PBS documentary called "Plague War," which, in large part, confirmed just about everything Preston wrote. In particular, it featured Dr. Kanatjan Alibekov, former first deputy chief for the Soviet biological weapons program Biopreparat. He revealed that tens of thousands of people worked in over forty facilities scattered throughout the Soviet Union, stockpiling smallpox, plague, and anthrax. All these deadly agents, said Alibekov, were readily convertible to biological weapons that could be mounted in special ICBM warheads targeted at major American cities. ➔

∞ READER COMMENTARIES FROM THE NET

A reader, January 21, 1999 ★★★★★
The best.
This book scared me to death.

A reader from Annapolis, Maryland, February 25, 1999 ★★★★☆
Great fiction begins with facts and history.
That's why this book will scare you to death. It could happen here. My wife is a hospital microbiologist and epidemiologist. The book is being passed rapidly among the staff. The "peer review" so far has been excellent.

The Cobra Event *continued*

→ Preston also wrote *The Hot Zone*, a best-selling book on the Ebola virus, and appears to have proven his bona fides. All this comes down to one thing. This is the single scariest book you will ever read. Honest.

"While researching The Cobra Event, *I spent much time interviewing FBI sources and top goverment officials. What they probably fear the most is 'invisible bioterror,' a biological Unabomber with scientific training who releases an unidentifiable bioweapon into the human population."*

—*Richard Preston*

The Influence of Sea Power upon History, 1660-1783
Written by Alfred Thayer Mahan
http://www.visitnewport.com/buspages/navy/index.htm

Type: Book (557 pages)

First Developed: 1890, reprinted recently (1987) by Dover Books, among others

Price Range: $30–$50 in used hardback, $12–$15 in Dover paperback

Key Features: The real stuff

Ages: Post-high school

Obsolescence: Low—this book has held up for over a century

Further Information: Generally available in any bookstore with a good military history section

When the *U.S. Naval Proceedings* magazine recently did a survey of senior officers in the U.S. Navy, asking what books they kept on their shelf, this one was in the top 10.

It is 110 years old, but still that important. Virtually every potentate, president, despot, and ruler of a land anywhere near an ocean has read it avidly. Required reading through the turn of the century, this, in essence, is the *Hoyle's Rules* of modern power-mongering.

Captain Alfred Thayer Mahan was the second president of the U.S. Navy's War College. He added immeasurably to the stature of the new school through his published writings on sea power. The first of these, based on his college lectures and entitled *The Influence of Sea Power upon History, 1660-1783*, won international acclaim shortly after its first appearance in 1890, and firmly established the reputation of Mahan as a naval historian and of the college as a seat of higher learning.

This book is a rough read, but it is one of the conceptual building blocks of the 20th century.

THE
INFLUENCE
OF
SEA POWER
UPON
HISTORY
1660–1783
BY
ALFRED THAYER MAHAN

Guarding The Information Empire:

THE INFLUENCE OF SYSTEMS ON WORLD HISTORY

It was computers that modeled nuclear fission and designed the devices that could make it happen. It was numerically controlled machine tools—computers—that crafted the nose cones of the offensive and defensive missiles to counter the early Soviet threat, and computers that coordinated the massive Defense Early Warning (DEW) system which did electronic picket duty for over three decades. The very same technologies for which the U.S. defense establishment paid the design bill were put to work throughout Western businesses, and were ultimately brought into people's homes in the form of advanced telephone systems, computers, and a host of other rewarding consumer technologies.

In many ways the military created a world which today it is ill-prepared to defend: the soft empire. At the heart of the soft empire ticks a clock.

Every minute of every hour of every day. The distilled intelligence of a whole civilization, resolved into a pneumatic drone. Boring at the threshold of pain, but strangely comforting. Like the appearance of the same Christmas tree decorations every year, it's the guarantee that someone's looking after things.

Were that system of coordinated, super-accurate universal time stilled (see wwvh), one could assume the end of things. No longer would the regulation of civic life matter. No reason to make it to work on time. Nor would navigation be necessary. No particular place to go. Nor would secure communica-tions be necessary. Not much left to protect, nor much in the way of worthy adversaries. No one would be interested in the regularity of TV and radio broadcasts. Catching a plane or a train on time of no further use. A second could be two or three. A nanosecond or a millisecond, no great matter. No harm done.

But that will not happen. The demands of civilization are too stringent, too persistent, to allow even a moment to be lost. Time is a fundamental system, the department of water and power of modern civilization. The system for the manufacture and distribution of time is simply too important to destroy. But there exists a web of interrelated systems built on top of that, a matrix of soft infrastructure, which is open and exposed to attack (see MELISSA's LESSON). Poke here and the transporta-tion system falters; push there and the communications sys-tem goes down. Give it a good whack, and the electrical grid fails. Tactical moves, designed to give six hours or six days of opportunity to an aggressor.

Deliver blows in the right sequence, and an economy stum-bles. An industry fails. A government falls. Perhaps a new nation takes the leading role in the world.

In the 19th century, the salient was the sea, the territory of influence the sea lanes (see THE INFLUENCE OF SEA POWER ON WORLD HISTORY). Today, as the 21st century nears, the salient is the soft empire, the territories of influence are the digital systems and networks within.

The 48 Laws of Power

Designed by Joost Elffers, written by Robert Greene

Type: Book (452 pages)

First Developed: 1998; Viking Press

Price Range: $18–$25

Key Features: Extraordinary design, amazing content

Ages: Post-high school

Obsolescence: Low

First things first. The contents of this package are dangerous. In the wrong hands, the knowledge herein could cause great harm. Really. You are forewarned.

Set all that aside. This is one of the most beautifully rendered books I have ever seen. The use of typography is both beautiful and precisely aligned with the material. Typography, at its best (see WORDS INTO TYPE), is a part of the information communicated, throwing emphasis where needed, indicating contrast when required, and visually reinforcing recurring patterns.

Joost Elffers, the designer, has an exceptional grasp of how to package a book.

Robert Greene, the author, in part dedicates his book to "those people in my life who have so skillfully used the game of power to manipulate, torture, and cause me pain over the years, I bear you no grudges, and I thank you for supplying me with the inspiration for *The 48 Laws of Power.*"

Clearly, they got him good. He has written a truly inspired book. Apparently Elffers and Greene started musing about putting this book together when both were going to art school in Italy, home of Machiavelli.

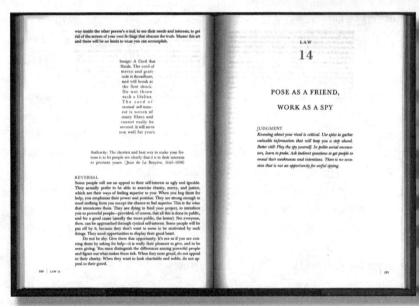

A page spread from 48 Laws of Power: *Pose As A Friend, Work As A Spy. Note how designer Joost Elffers enjoys shaping type into geometric forms.*

Machiavelli, however, is only a departure point for this work—to reduce it to a retread of *The Prince* would be to do a great disservice to an extraordinary work. Each one of the laws is presented as an ➔

48 Laws of Power *continued*

→ aphorism. Then, in a strictly formalized fashion, the law
is presented in an array of stories. The first story is the transgression—a story
about someone in history who foolishly broke the law and suffered for it. Then comes the
story of a success through the observance of the law.

Then comes a segment called the "Keys to Power," an extended restatement of the law in an applied and practical
form. Lastly, a counterintuitive section called "Reversal," where Greene presents the value of turning the law on its
head from time to time.

All throughout, the marginalia present quotes, anecdotes, memoires, and the like, chosen for emphasis—a fugue
on each and every one of the laws. This is a work or art and insight, breathtaking in its scope and depth,
scary when one contemplates the practical reality of its subject matter.

•❖ READER COMMENTARIES FROM THE NET

A reader from Darlington, Maryland, February 10, 1999
★★★★★
Great book...wonderful reading and learning experience
After 44 years in the corp world of DuPont, General
Electric, Black & Decker, Sunbeam, and Steelcase, I
relate to all of the laws one way or another. Many of my
mistakes in my career could have been avoided if I had
this book at my desk side. I was a naive, honest, ethical
engineer, manager, V.P., and President... and was blind-
sided by my inability to see the manipulations, dishon-
esty, political, manipulations of my trusted leaders. My
wisdom came too late. Business ethics be damned... the
game is winning and gaining power forgetting the customer, company, the employees and pleasing the share-
holders and Wall Street above all to gain personal reputation and be hailed by *Fortune, Forbes, Business Week,*
etc. feeding the ego trips of top management, taking
credit for all that is good and shedding the blame on
others when things go bad. This should be preferred
reading in the Business Schools. A great job done by
the Authors. —Al Lehnerd

A reader from San Francisco, January 13, 1999 ★
Excellent if you're selling swampland to suckers
This book is pure evil...

A reader from North Carolina, March 11, 1999
★★★★★
**A brilliant, useful, insightful, amoral piece of litera-
ture**
...reading this book as a manual of discovering ways to
manipulate others ignores the real power of the work....
From a completely historical perspective, it gives a great
history lesson, and one that is both easy and fun to
read.

A reader from Moreno Valley, CA, March 23, 1999
★★★★★
**As the book cover says, "For those who want power,
watch power, or want to arm themselves against
power..."**
...It take you straight where you want to go, baby.

Scientific American

http://www.sciam.com/Scientific American

Type: Web site magazine

First Developed: 1997

Price Range: Connect time

Key Features: The best stuff, with illustrations

Ages: 10 and up

Obsolescence factor: Medium

Further Information:

❋ *http://www.spectrum.ieee.org/* IEEE Spectrum, the engineers' magazine does the same loony thing.

❋ *http://www.pbs.org/saf* Scientific American's Frontiers program on PBS

Stewart Brand, the guy who in the '60s started *The Whole Earth Catalog: Access To Tools* (after which *Informatica* is loosely patterned), wrote a book called *The Media Lab* a few years ago. It was a take on MIT's Media Lab and all the amazing things they were working on at the time. Everything he covered was neat, and seemed like it could never really find it's way into the real world. Most of it has, in just a few years.

He articulated a slew of rules about high technology in this book. The one that stayed with me asserts that "Information wants to be free." That rule is the only way I can explain the amazing Scientific American Web site. For some reason, they seem to have put EVERYTHING and more on the site. Why buy the magazine? Sure they sell stuff on the site. Maybe even they keep some of the current issue for use only on paper. But you can search the site, and find all kinds of great material from past issues. They must be following the Xoom principles (see XOOM).

I hope they are making money, as I really don't want them to stop this. It's too good.

Sample articles from the April 1999 section of the Scientific American Web site:

The Promise of Tissue Engineering

"Bioartificial" pancreases, livers and kidneys. Freshly grown skin that can be bought by the yard. Honeycombs of collagen for breast reconstruction after mastectomy. Plastic-coated pellets of cells implanted in the spine to treat chronic pain. No, this isn't science fiction: it's tissue engineering, and as these pioneers in the field explain, it's already changing people's lives.

Growing New Organs

David J. Mooney and Antonios G. Mikos

Is Space Finite?

Jean-Pierre Luminet, Glenn D. Starkman and Jeffrey R. Weeks

The universe may look infinitely large, but that could be an illusion. If space folds back on itself like the braids of a pretzel, it might be boundless, and light could spool around the cosmos endlessly. Astronomers are looking for patterns in the star field that could signal a finite volume for space.

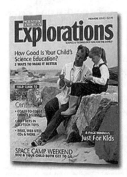

As robust as the Web site appears to be, Scientific American is forging ahead in the world of paper. Explorations (http://www.explorations.org/), a magazine aimed at families and young adults, is doing well. Further, they seem to sell loads of their special issues (under the Scientific American Presents *banner).*

Mathematics: From the Birth of Numbers

Written by Jan Gullberg with Peter Hilton

Type: Book (1120 pages)

First Developed: 1997; W.W. Norton & Company

Price Range: $35–$50 in hardcover

Key Features: Encyclopedic, well illustrated with everything from cartoons to scans of century-old documents.

Ages: Post-high school

Obsolescence: Low.

Further Information:
✳ *http://galaxy.einet.net/galaxy/Science/Mathematics.html*
a very good metasite for sources on mathematics
✳ *http://www.mathsoft.com/asolve/constant/constant.html*
a site dedicated to mathematical constants

"The book is an enthusiastic and utterly amazing popularization that promises to be in print for decades... It is an important reference and a book that is plain fun to dip into. If a family is to have only one mathematics book on the reference shelf, then this is the one."

—*Donald J. Albers,*
Scientific American

Gullberg spent ten years writing this book, and promptly died upon its publication. That comes pretty close to the definition of a culminating life's work.

Gullberg treated the exercise of numbers the way Ansel Adams treated mountains and deserts. The book is a labor of deep love and admiration. And he looks all around the world, treating the mathematics of China and India with as much respect (though not as much depth) as the Western stuff. In his intro, he jots a telling footnote:

> *"Regrettably, statistical evidence is accumulating to indicate that students, offered training rather than education, and fascinated by the potential of modern technology, are increasingly unable to use their language to properly convey their ideas."*

Mathematics is a language to Gullberg, and this is a profusely illustrated guide on how to speak and understand the language. He explains numbers, and their symbols, and every kind of math in which you might have even a passing interest.

One of the Amazon.com reviews indicated the reviewer had read the whole thing straight through. Utterly unimaginable to me. This is one of those books you keep around and sample, like a very rich candy.

⟶ READER COMMENTARIES FROM THE NET

A reader from USA , December 17, 1998 ★★★★★
This book is the all-in-one reference book for math history
I have been a tutor for many years, and this book has proved indispensable to me since I purchased it last year. It has the answers to simple questions (How did Algebra begin?) as well as the complex. I highly recommend it as a reference book and an interesting book just to read and enjoy.

Silicon Dreams: Information, Man, and Machine

Written by Robert Lucky

Type: Book (411 pages)

First Developed: 1989; St Martin's Press

Price Range: $22–$32 used hardcover

Key Features: Very abstruse, with an unexpectedly broad array of charts and illustrations

Ages: Post-high school

Obsolescence: Low

Further Information:
❉ *http://spot.colorado.edu/~craigr/Info-Cyber.htm* for information theory and cybernetics
❉ *http://cm.bell-labs.com/cm/ms/ what/shannonday/paper.html* for the full text of Shannon's paper, "A Mathematical Theory of Communication"

For all the romance and possibility there is in the world of computing (as seen by Vannevar Bush and Ted Nelson), there is also a cold, steely beauty (as seen by Claude Shannon and Robert Lucky).

Shannon was interested in packing as much info over a phone line as possible. In his information theory he tended to the notion of signal and noise (see NOISE), how redundant information could be dropped (by encoding) to reduce the volume of information necessary for transmission, without the disorder caused by entropy.

All this was translated into mathematic formulae, and the practical results are everything from the modems we use to the file compression techniques we use over the Net (GIF files, ZIP files, etc.). The undocumented results involved a revolution in techniques for making and breaking codes and ciphers, which Shannon would see as a simple manipulation of the relationships between signal and noise.

Robert Lucky was the head of research at the Bell Labs long after Shannon was gone. He's a faithful acolyte, and his book *Silicon Dreams* is a word fugue on information theory. It is a very hard book to find now, and once you've got it, it is a very tough read. I can make it through a page or two at a time.

But it is extraordinarily yeasty, and as you peer into its convoluted chambers, you can glimpse some of the mystery and beauty of the pure thought that has underwritten the creation of the digital age.

ENTROPY: *(in data transmission and information theory) a measure of the loss of information in a transmitted signal or message.*

A definition from the Random House Unabridged Dictionary

Black Dog Music Library

Written and Performed by Various Artists and Writers

Type: Hardback (50–100 pages)

First Developed: 1996-1999; Black Dog/Leventhal

Price Range: Budget priced: $10–$20

Key Features: CD-equipped little books.

Ages: Post-high school

Obsolescence: Low

Further Information: Search the on-line book retailers for Black Dog and Leventhal to find new releases.

Music: Mmmmmmmmmm.
Music appreciation: Echhh.
Opera: Mmmmmmmmmm.
Libretto: Echhhhhhhhh.

I remember little from high school music appreciation classes (other than the unusual sound of a French horn. That stuck). When CD-ROMs came along, everyone got fired up by a set of products produced by a professor from UCLA by the name of Robert Winter. Lots of interactivity while you played the music on your CD-equipped PC. Awards (especially for the one on Beethoven, Winter's specialty). Articles in *The Wall Street Journal.* Computer trade show keynotes.

These groundbreaking CD-ROMs, however, missed one fundamental fact: Most of us want to flake out on the couch when we listen to beautiful music. In an apparently nonobvious point of dissonance, most of us find it impossible to flake out with a computer. Thus the idea for these wonderful musical CD-ROMs did not take off and have been consigned to recent history.

In an amazing coincidence, only recently recognized by media moguls, most of us want to flake out on the couch when we read a book while listening to music. Ahah.

This brings us to the Black Dog Music Library. These tiny little books, joint works of Black Dog/Leventhal publishers and EMI Music, each have an audio CD (scrap the computer) with beautiful music (ballet, opera, symphony in dandy, well recorded performances), and with text and photos laid out to coincide with the progress of the music itself.

The copy is written in a light, *Life Magazine* style, helped along with lots of pictures and illustrations. Once the musical descriptions start, the text is indexed to the tracks on the audio CD, with hour:minute references. The CDs are easy to stop, start, and reindex with a remote control. This is an ever-expanding group of books, each one generally containing from 50 to 100 pages each. Very pleasant Sunday afternoon programming.

➥ READER COMMENTARIES FROM THE NET

A reader, June 15, 1997 ★★★★★

Fantastic package for opera beginners and aficionados

The Black Dog Opera Library series are beautifully packaged and way underpriced. They each contain 2 CDs of the complete opera in the inside covers of a compact hardcover book which contains photos and commentary, as well as an annotated libretto in the original language and English translation, referenced to the CD, and notes and photos of the main performers and conductor. The performances are usually classic ones and though not necessarily recorded in the digital age they all sound gorgeous. I have only been able to find 4 (Magic Flute, Aida, La Boheme, and Carmen) and wish there were more. The only flaws in my opinion are that there is no information regarding the date or location of the performances nor is there a complete cast listing. *[Fixed since then. —Ed.]*

Language, Thought and Reality
Written by Benjamin Whorf

The Power of Aleph Beth
Written by Phillip S. Berg

Garland of Letters
Written by Sir John Woodroffe

Type: Books	
First Developed: Years ago	
Price Range: $22–$32 used	
Key Features: Off the beaten path, mystical, sometimes way out there	
Ages: Post high school	
Obsolescence: Low	
Further Information: Literature on Tantric Yoga, mantras, and related stuff	

A long time ago, in places far away (this is for real—places like ancient India, Israel, and North America) the human voice and spoken language were thought to have great power. A great many cultures held that the letters of the alphabet were the work of the gods—in fact were the physical expression of the divine on earth.

If you put the right sounds together in the right words, it could influence the world. In the present day, we pay a thin-blooded homage to this notion with such assertions as "the pen is mightier than the sword."

> "[Our minds] dissect nature along lines laid down by our native languages."
>
> —Benjamin Whorf

Just a few linguistic scholars have ever paid any attention to this at all. One is Benjamin Whorf, who wrote about this stuff, even coining a term "oliogosynthesis" to describe the belief in the power of phonemes. His thoughts, although now many decades old, are still in print in a fine series of essays compiled into a book called *Language, Thought and Reality*.

Equally interesting is the insider's view of this notion. *The Power of Aleph Beth* has become something of a cult item in Hollywood recently, with the likes of Madonna and Roseanne singing its praises. The overheated publisher's synopsis gives some idea:

> Hebrew letters according to Kabbalah are the formulas for 22 energy forces that were active in the creation process prior to the appearance of our universe as we know it today. The letters of the Hebrew Aleph Beth are the DNA code of the cosmos. Understanding the individual and combined powers of the Aleph Beth helps us to connect to the primordial energy of creation, which can then help us remove the chaos and disorder that permeate our lives. →

Books on Language *continued*

→ There are other places to look, as well. Sir John Woodroffe was a prolific Sanskritist of the 19th century (Sanskrit was the language of most ancient India), and he documented a variety of Hindu mystical beliefs. The oliogosynthetic (whew!) stuff was covered in a book called *The Garland of Letters*. You won't find it at Amazon, as it is published by an obscure Indian house called Garland.

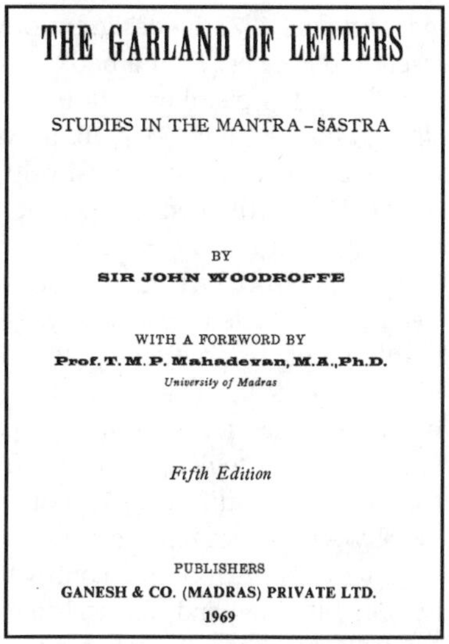
THE GARLAND OF LETTERS

STUDIES IN THE MANTRA - ŚĀSTRA

BY

SIR JOHN WOODROFFE

WITH A FOREWORD BY

Prof. T. M. P. Mahadevan, M.A., Ph.D.

University of Madras

Fifth Edition

PUBLISHERS

GANESH & CO. (MADRAS) PRIVATE LTD.

1969

However, that book and its like can be found at such stores as The Bodhi Tree in Los Angeles and Books from India Ltd. in London (see GREAT SOURCES sidebar).

When the digital-empirical-humanist fervor that so absorbs the West grows tiring, exposure to these entirely different ways of thinking can be very refreshing.

Informatica's Great Sources for Books on Ancient India/Mysticism/Spirituality

D. K. Agencies (P) Ltd.
A/15-17 Mohan Garden
Najafgarh Road
New Delhi - 110 059 (India)
Phones: (+91-11) 559-8897; 559-8899
Fax: (+91-11) 559-8898; 555-8898
E-mail: custserv@dkagencies.com
❋ ***http://www.dkagencies.com***
❋ ***http://www.indianbooksearch.com***
–Amazon-like search engine for Indian books

Motilal Benarasidas Publishers (P) Ltd.
Indological Book Services 7 Exporters
41 UA Bunglow Road
Delhi 110 007 (India)
Phones: (+91-11) 291-1985; 291-8335; 252-4826
Fax: (+91-11) 293-0689; GRAM: GLORYINDIA
–The definitive source for many excellent books on Hinduism and Vedic thought

Books from India Ltd.
45 Museum Street,
London WC1A, (UK)
Phones: (+44-171) 405-7226
–The scholar's resource, right next to the British Museum

Twenty First Century Bookstore
401 N. 4th St.
Fairfield, IA 52556 (USA)
Phones: (800) 593-2665 [(800) 593-book]
Fax: (515) 472-5105
E-mail: books21st@aol.com
–General source for Vedic/Hindu material. They claim (justly) that theirs is the largest selection in the Midwest. If they don't have the book in stock, they will order it for you (even from India, where they appear to have good connections). They have a small catalog you can ask for and they ship anywhere in the world. In the same city as Maharishi International University.
❋ ***http://ww.21stbooks.com*** →

→ ## More of Informatica's Great Sources for Books on Ancient India/Mysticism/Spirituality

Vedanta Society Bookstore
1946 Vedanta Place
Hollywood, CA 90068-3996 (USA)
Phones: (800) 816-2242; (213) 856-0322
Fax: (213) 465-9568
E-mail: info@vedanta.com
❊ http://www.vedanta.com
—Dates back to the days when Hollywood was interested in this stuff, and the likes of Christopher Isherwood and Aldous Huxley were patrons.

East West Bookstore
Phone: (800) 909-6161
❊ http://www.eastwest.com
—They carry around 20,000 books. Emphasis on New Age books. They are an excellent general source for books on spiritual matters. They ship to all countries, with a catalog available through the toll-free number

Bodhi Tree Bookstore, Inc.
8585 Melrose Avenue
West Hollywood, CA 90069-5199 (USA)
Phones: (310) 659-1733; (800) 825-9798 except from 213, 310, or 818 area codes
Fax. (310) 659-0178
❊ http://www.bodhitree.com/
—This place has been around since the '60s. It is a regular haunt of Hollywood types who have recently discovered God.

Navrang Inc.
507 Seminole Drive
Blacksburg, VA 24060 (USA)
Phone: (540) 961-2003 (If you are lucky, a person might answer.)
Fax: (540) 961-4007 (Anytime is good.)
E-mail: navrang@bev.net (Anytime is good.)
❊ http://www.navrang.com/navrang
—Very large on-line collection.

A DEFINITION OF "TOOL"
from Random House Webster's Dictionary

tool (to͞ol), *n.* **1.** an implement, esp. one held in the hand, as a hammer, saw, or file, for performing or facilitating mechanical operations. **2.** any instrument of manual operation. **3.** the cutting or machining part of a lathe, planer, drill, or similar machine. **4.** the machine itself; a machine tool. **5.** anything used as a means of accomplishing a task or purpose: *Education is a tool for success.* **6.** a person manipulated by another for the latter's own ends; cat's-paw. **7.** the design or ornament impressed upon the cover of a book. **8.** *Underworld Slang.* a. a pistol or gun. b. a pickpocket. **9.** *Slang (vulgar).* penis. –*v.t.* **10.** to work or shape with a tool. **11.** to work decoratively with a hand tool. **12.** to ornament (the cover of a book) with a bookbinder's tool. **13.** to drive (a vehicle): *He tooled the car along the treacherous path.* **14.** to equip with tools or machinery. –*v.i.* **15.** to work with a tool. **16.** to drive or ride in a vehicle: *tooling along the freeway.* **17.** tool up, to install machinery designed for performing a particular job: *manufacturers tooling up for production.* **tool′er,** *n.* —**tool′less,** *adj.* —**Syn.** 1. TOOL, IMPLEMENT, INSTRUMENT, UTENSIL refer to contrivances for doing work. A TOOL is a contrivance held in and worked by the hand, for assisting the work of (especially) mechanics or laborers: *a carpenter's tools.* An IMPLEMENT is any tool or contrivance designed or used for a particular purpose: *agricultural implements.* An INSTRUMENT is anything used in doing a certain work or producing a certain result, especially such as requires delicacy, accuracy, or precision: *surgical or musical instruments.* A UTENSIL is especially an article for domestic use: *kitchen utensils.* When used figuratively of human agency, TOOL is generally used in a contemptuous sense; INSTRUMENT, in a neutral or good sense: *a tool of unscrupulous men; an instrument of Providence.*

Work, Life, Tools: The Things We Use to Do the Things We Do

by Milton Glaser (Editor), Matthew Klein (Photographer), Stanley Abercrombie (Introduction), George Beylerian

WORK, LIFE, TOOLS.
The things we use to do the things we do

Type: Paperback (240 pages)

First Developed: 1997; Monacelli Press

Price Range: $28–$35

Key Features: A book with a finely honed point of view

Ages: Post-high school

Obsolescence: Low

Further Information: The Steelcase Web page associated with *Work, Life, Tools:*

❋ *http://www.steelcase.com/ corporatehtml/ftoolwrk_center.html*

When I first started to develop the idea of what *Informatica* would be, I looked everywhere to see what might function as a competitor. I was fully aware that the standard for this kind of book had been set 30 years ago by Stewart Brand's spectacular *Whole Earth Catalog.* In its time *WEC* literally changed the way people looked at the world.

From the color picture of the Earth on its cover (an innovation, at the time), to the "green" ethos of the content (the first Earth Day took place soon after the publication of the first edition), *The Whole Earth Catalog* was designed to reorient the way people thought about things.

Happily, I couldn't find anything that approached that kind of focus and power in the present array of books (the Random House folks, being highly rational, didn't see much value in duplicating someone else's work).

I did find one book that was a beautifully rendered guide to some of what *Informatica* could and should be. *Work, Life, Tools* is a beautifully designed study of what things people use to do their work. It is broad in its scope, equally admiring of everything from a good mechanical pencil to laptop computers, from pianos to calipers. Glaser's book is drawn from an exposition underwritten by Steelcase (the office furniture people), and the choice of elements redefines the word "tool."

➥ READER COMMENTARIES FROM THE NET

A reader from Chicago, Illinois, January 3, 1999 ★★★★★
An elegant visual book for/about people who love tools
My favorite Christmas gift—the cover is red, the stock feels great to the touch, and there's plenty of white space. It's a book and an exhibition in one. It's filled with people who love their work. *Work, Life, Tools* qualifies as great design. (Hats off Milton Glaser and to Steelcase for being enlightened enough to fund the exhibition.) This book cum exhibition guide ranks high on the visual, aesthetic, and conceptual pleasure scale. My favorite aspect: the way the bios portray the multiple talents and the "I don't just do one thing" truth about their subjects. It's filled with lots of practical ah-has. You get to peek into people's work spaces. It represents a fascinating spectrum of thinking about work. And, it's amazing to me how loyal people are to their fountain pens (as one who's committed to Deluxe Uni-balls). I loved it!

The Zimmermann Telegram
Written by Barbara Tuchman

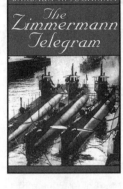

Type: Book (244 pages)

First Developed: Originally published in 1960's, Ballantine reprint 1986

Price: $8–$12 in paperback

Key Features: Short, very well written

Ages: Post teen

Obsolescence: The scholarship has held up for 30 years

Further Information:
Barbara Tuchman's *Guns of August*

The most enduring secret of the 20th century is just how much of its history has been determined by gentlemen reading each other's mail. The National Security Agency is rumored to be the government agency with the biggest budget—bar none. What they do is trap and decrypt other countries' communications. When one of their folks turns and gives up their secrets to anyone, friend or foe, they throw 'em in the clink for a VERY long time. That's how important this stuff is.

One of the few books where you can get one of the stories of this black world in full measure is *The Zimmermann Telegram*. It tells of duplicitous Germany trying to compel Mexico into opening a second front with the U.S. at the outset of World War I, with promises of lots of cash and territory (including Texas!). It tells of an encrypted telegram from Berlin to the German ambassador to Mexico being intercepted by Britain (signals intelligence), and cracked by the group at the infamous Room 40 in the British Admiralty (cryptanalysis).

Then comes the tale of how the British arranged to use their proof of Germany's duplicity to manipulate the U.S. into entering the war (statecraft), and how they shielded the secret of their ability to read the German diplomatic traffic (deception). There are only a few other places where such stories have been told reliably (THE AMERICAN BLACK CHAMBER by Herbert Yardley, THE PUZZLE PALACE by James Bamford), and most of the published material is about events that predate the Cold War (though it's worth taking a look at the Venona transcripts at the NATIONAL CRYPTOLOGIC MUSEUM Web site).

Guarding The Information Empire:

SIGNALS INTELLIGENCE

In 1913 came the watershed for radio in the U.S. Navy. A fleet maneuvering in Chesapeake Bay had been experimenting with radio for centralized command. The trial would have been logged as a minor success, were it not for the unexpected occurrence of a squall. Visibility was reduced to zero, and the storm lasted for half an hour. When it cleared, all the ships could be seen in formation, exactly as they had been ordered over the radio. Tactical signaling by radio became standard practice in all the navies of the world soon thereafter.

As did the interception of signals. The exploitation of an adversary's radio signals came as an unexpected and extremely welcome surprise to British commanders on the ground. The German high command had resorted to radio to coordinate the attacks through Belgium and into France. In the chaos of battle, transmissions were made "en clair." Amazed British radio operators listened to Germans conveying detailed instructions. Little by little, their commanders pieced together the order of battle and began to halt the German advance.

The British were so enamored of the interceptions that they successfully sought to cut all of the key undersea telegraph and telephone cables running in and out of Germany. Thus, the Germans were forced to resort to the extensive use of radio for military and diplomatic communications. Much of the material was intercepted and broken, often by the British Admiralty's legendary Room 40.

The Germans discovered the same tricks and used them to advantage. Both sides quickly realized the advantages of encrypting their radio messages, cloaking them in a mathematically predictable jumble. Both sides developed advanced Black Chambers (see THE AMERICAN BLACK

CHAMBER)—intelligence organizations dedicated to the cracking of codes and ciphers.

This is how the arts and sciences of signals intelligence evolved. Useful insights were gained—not just from intercepting and cracking encrypted radio signals—but also from simply watching the volume of radio signaling in what came to be called traffic analysis (see PGP). Increased volume often foreshadowed military moves, as it did in the case of the Battle of Jutland (see WORLD WAR I).

The research and analysis of call signs, radio direction finding, and a host of other disciplines evolved during World War I, only to be left to atrophy in the years following the war. The quiet enterprise of signals intelligence was rebuilt in the years leading up to World War II. Much of it was inherited from small countries like Poland which, in the shadow of Hitler's growing empire, could not afford to miss reading some of his mail. A small group of brilliant Polish cryptanalysts, using an amalgam of traffic analysis, mathematical theory, and common sense, reconstructed the German ENIGMA encryption device used by both military and diplomatic interests. Ultimately they built a device they are said to have called the "Bombe." It was, in fact, a protocomputer dedicated to the task of cracking the ENIGMA.

In the weeks before Poland fell, they passed along their secrets to the French and the British. Just outside of London, the British refined the devices and insights they had gained from the Poles. Eventually they built over 800 advanced versions of the Bombe. The men who did the work invented the fundamental concepts of computing. In many ways, our modern "soft empire" was built in Black Chambers and fired in the crucible of war.

The Rough Guide to the Internet 1999

Written by Angus J. Kennedy

http://www-2.roughguides.com/net/

Type: Paperback (512 pages)

First Developed: 1999; Rough Guides

Price Range: $8–$12

Key Features: Tiny, versatile, practical

Ages: High school and later

Obsolescence: Medium (for which Rough Guides compensates with a Web site with much of the same material, updated)

Further Information:
✱ *http://www2.roughguides.com/rock/*

These folks maintain a very interesting on-line guide to rock music, as well.

Little books are far more convenient than big ones (see CYCLOPEDIA). Truly pocket-sized books, if jammed with basic, straightforward facts are a treasure. This one fits the bill.

This guide is anything but bland, and is often highly opinionated: on *Suck*, an on-line magazine, it says, "In a smug class all by itself and arguably the only e-zine that ever mattered." On Underwire, MSN's channel for "women's issues," it comments, "You might wonder if you really need to go on-line to read this sort of stuff."

If I were to get a relative started on the Net—one who was new to the whole process—I would equip them with this book. It has all the basics of browsing and fiddling with the computer side of things, plus a reasonably current categorized summary of the better and more important sites (and some of the weird, outré sites as well).

➤ CRITIC & READER COMMENTARIES

Newsweek, 2/2/98

"Smarter than *Dummies*... This pocket-size guide packs plenty of informative how-tos... Now even 'Idiots' can become Internet savants."

A reader from Houston, Texas, USA , March 2, 1999 ★★★★★

Top Stuff Mate!
This book by Kennedy is unbelievably good for learning about the Net and how to use it. I'm a big Net head so I get lots of people asking me questions about the Net. I just tell them to get Kennedy's book, and they have big smiles for me the next time I see them! Buy it, you won't be sorry.

Cigars, Whiskey & Winning:
Leadership Lessons from Ulysses S. Grant

Written by Al Kaltman

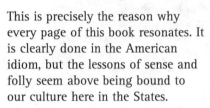

Type: Book (336 pages)

First Developed: 1998; Prentice Hall Trade

Price Range: $15–$18

Key Features: A book with a finely honed point of view

Ages: Post-high school

Obsolescence: Low

Further Information:
http://www.cigarswhiskeywinning.com/
for a fine Web site dedicated to promoting this book, but featuring a terrific metapage dedicated to Grant and leadership Web sites

The blather of business books, with their top ten rules, seven secrets, and hidden mysteries, is irritating. There cannot be that many ways to manage a business and handle people. I hope there aren't because I'm nearing fifty, and I haven't mastered many of them.

So much unsubstantiated stuff turns into noise (see NOISE), and I hunt for signal. I glean quality information, as often as not, from good histories. The lessons I trust are the ones other folks have learned, often as not through some measure of suffering, loss, and pain. No lessons are more severe, or sound, as those learned in war. The determining factor is the stakes. Profit and loss is one thing. Men's lives and nations' futures are quite another.

This is precisely the reason why every page of this book resonates. It is clearly done in the American idiom, but the lessons of sense and folly seem above being bound to our culture here in the States.

The book is written chunk-style, as a series of vignettes, with quotes from Grant and his contemporaries, and the lesson is driven home by Kaltman. Yeasty, irregular reading.

"The great thing about Grant... is his perfect correctness and persistency of purpose."

—*Abraham Lincoln*

"I doubt his superior can be found in all history."

—*Robert E. Lee,*
Commander of the Army
of Northern Virginia

⚫➤ READER COMMENTARIES FROM THE NET

A reader from Connecticut, February 24, 1999 ★★★★★
Best book on leadership that I ever read.
This book is a must read for anyone in a leadership position or one who aspires to be a leader. It is also a great book for students that will enable them to set the correct moral tone for the rest of their lives. As a Naval Academy graduate and former Marine officer I wish that I had read this book when I was younger. The insight into the proper ways of handling difficult and everyday situations are not matched by any book on leadership that I have ever read. I checked the book out of our local library and before I finished it I ordered seven copies from Amazon to give to my friends and colleagues. Today, I just ordered ten more. I tip my hat to Mr. Kaltman for an outstanding job. I have also come to appreciate General Grant as a man of honor and outstanding leadership.

The Cartoon Guide to Statistics
Written by Larry Gonick, with Woollcott Smith (Contributor)

Type: Book (240 pages)

First Developed: 1993; HarperCollins

Price Range: $12–$15 in paper-back

Key Features: Funny, loose and substantial

Ages: Post-high school

Obsolescence: Low

Further Information:
✳ *http://www.minitab.com/*
the Website for the dedicated statistics package used by the authors of the book. It costs about $1000. Be happy you have Excel.

A quick review of the Amazon reader's reviews of this book demonstrates that some folks like this approach, and some folks don't. I do.

All I ever knew of statistics was 1) they were useful, 2) they were abused, 3) I wanted to understand them properly, and 4) statistics book were written to be some sort of rite of passage rather than a way to understand the matter at hand (see the excerpt from the help system of Microsoft Excel as proof that you do not want to go there).

Stats are particularly interesting because they are a part of the hidden power in every decent spreadsheet program. Excel is chock-full of statistical functions, and terrible at explaining them.

Put this book next to your computer, and try comparing the functions in Excel with the explanations in the book. It works. Honest.

SUPPLEMENTAL INFORMATION About Statistical Methods And Algorithms

Here's what Microsoft Excel 2000 recommends for statistics reading. Take two and call me when you wake up:

For detailed information about the algorithms used to create the Microsoft Excel analysis tools and functions, see the following book:

- Strum, Robert D., and Donald E. Kirk. *First Principles of Discrete Systems and Digital Signal Processing.* Reading, Mass.: Addison-Wesley Publishing Company, 1988.

For detailed information about statistical methods or the algorithms used to create the Microsoft Excel statistical tools and functions, see the following books:

- Abramowitz, Milton, and Irene A. Stegun, eds. *Handbook of Mathematical Functions, with Formulas, Graphs, and Mathematical Tables.* Washington, D.C.: U.S. Government Printing Office, 1972. →

Statistics *continued*

→ ■ Box, George E.P., William G.
Hunter, and J. Stuart Hunter.
*Statistics for Experimenters:
An Introduction to Design,
Data Analysis, and Model
Building.* New York: John
Wiley and Sons, 1978.

■ Devore, Jay L. *Probability and
Statistics for Engineering and
the Sciences.* 4th ed.
Wadsworth Publishing, 1995.

■ McCall, Robert B.
*Fundamental Statistics for the
Behavioral Sciences.* 5th ed.
New York: Harcourt Brace
Jovanovich, 1990.

■ Press, William H., Saul A.
Teukolsky, William T.
Vetterling, and Brian P.
Flannery. *Numerical Recipes in
C: The Art of Scientific
Computing.* 2nd ed. New
York: Cambridge University
Press, 1992.

The Number Devil:
A Mathematical Adventure
Written by Hans Magnus Enzensberger, and illustrated by Rotraut Susanne Berner

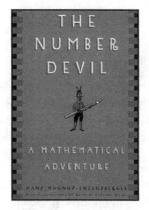

I never had a good math teacher when I was a kid. What a shame! Having now—after years of computer graphics, statistics, and spreadsheets—come to value the exercise of numbers, I disdain lousy math teachers. The world is filled with them.

But here and there, there are brilliant ones. One of them is Hans Magnus Enzensberger, who has written a book of fancy, a bit like *Alice in Wonderland* in its whimsy and charm. It first was written in German, then translated, but it still works just fine.

In twelve dreams, the number devil introduces a twelve-year-old boy who hates math to the world of numbers: infinite numbers, prime numbers, Fibonacci numbers, numbers that magically appear in triangles, and numbers that expand without end. The tools are giant furry calculators, piles of coconuts, and endlessly scrolling paper to introduce basic concepts of numeracy, from interesting number sequences to exponents to matrices.

As the dreams progress, the boy flies further and further into mathematical theory, until numbers are nothing more than what they are—a marvel.

Type: Book (260 pages)

First Developed: 1998; Metropolitan Books

Price Range: $16–$20 in hardcover

Key Features: Charming prose, perfect for bedtime

Ages: 2–12

Obsolescence: Low

Further Information: See THE CARTOON GUIDE TO STATISTICS, also
✳ *http://www.csun.edu/
~ vcact00g/math1.html*
for home tutoring of math.

❧ CRITIC COMMENTARIES

The Los Angeles Times Sunday Book Review

"No book about mathematics written for young children could less resemble a textbook than *The Number Devil*... [T]his is just the book to give to an intelligent child who falls asleep in mathematics classes."

—Martin Gardner

McGuffey's Eclectic Readers
Written by William Holmes McGuffey

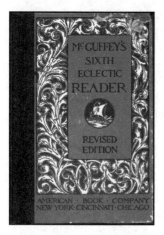

More than a million Americans are estimated to be homeschooling their kids today. They do it to escape school violence, weak curriculums, thin values, and a bunch of other reasons. In 1992, there were an estimated 300,000 folks doing it, and they were seen as backwoods loons. Things are different now.

The tradition of homeschooling stretches back to a time when it was the only alternative for many Americans. Between 1836 and the turn of the century, many Americans taught their kids to read with McGuffey's Readers. Over 120 million sets of the books were sold. ➔

Type: Boxed set of books with six volumes, plus Primer and Spelling Book

First Developed: 1836; reprinted in 1989 by Van Nostrand Reinhold

Price Range: $40–$60

Key Features: Classic

Ages: Post-high school tutors of early readers

Obsolescence: Low

Further Information:
❋ *http://www.howtotutor.com/index.html* (a good homeschooling source); also search the Net with the keyword "homeschool."

BREAKIN' DOWN McGUFFEY

The First (96 pgs.) and **Second** (160 pgs.) **Readers** picture children in their relationship with family, teacher, friends, and animals. Articulation and punctuation are introduced.

The Third Reader (208 pgs.) expands this world of language, introducing the "Art of Emphasis" and dictionary definitions (which are continued in the Fourth Reader).

The Fourth Reader (256 pgs.) begins with sections on: 1. Punctuation Marks, 2. Articulation, 3. Accent and Inflection. Next come 90 selections written by a wide variety of authors, from Daniel DeFoe to Louisa May Alcott.

The Fifth Reader (352 pgs.) begins with sections on: 1. Articulation, 2. Inflection, 3. Accent, 4. Emphasis, 5. Modulation, 6. Poetic Pauses. Next come 117 writings also by a wide range of sources, from The Bible, to Charles Dickens, James Russell Lowell, and James Fenimore Cooper.

The Sixth Reader (463 pgs.) begins with sections on: 1. Articulation, 2. Inflection, 3. Accent and Emphasis, 4. Instructions for Reading Verse, 5. The Voice, 6. Gesture. This is followed by 138 selections from such authors as Longfellow, Tennyson, William Blackstone, Poe, Byron, Shakespeare, Jefferson, Bacon, Scott, Disraeli, plus samplings of great literature. McGuffey's Spelling Book (144 pgs.) is divided into 248 lessons, and showcases very good, largely non-archaic word lists.

McGuffey's Eclectic Readers *continued*

→ The material in the readers was taken from writings which extol, explain, and illustrate such virtues as honesty, charity, thrift, hard work, courage, patriotism, reverence toward God, and respect for parents.

Way old-fashioned. Very hip. No other books, religious texts aside, ever had so much influence over so many children over such a long period.

McGuffey begins, in the Primer, by presenting the letters of the alphabet to be memorized, in sequence. Stories in the Readers picture children in their relationships with family, teacher, friends, and animals. In the Third Reader, in a story entitled *"The Widow and the Merchant,"* a merchant befriends a widow in need. Later, when the widow proves herself to be honest, the merchant gives her a handsome gift.

LEADING PUBLISHERS/SUPPLIERS OF CHILDREN'S SOFTWARE

❋ Broderbund: *http://www.broderbund.com/*
❋ Creative Wonders/ABC Interactive: *http://www.ea.com/Creative_Wonders/CWmain.html*
❋ Davidson: *http://www.davd.com/*
❋ Edmark: *http://www.edmark.com/*
❋ Headbone Interactive: *http://www.headbone.com/*
❋ Houghton Mifflin Interactive: *http://www.hminet.com/*
❋ Humongous Entertainment: *http://www.humongous.com/*
❋ Living Books: *http://www.livingbooks.com/*
❋ Maxis: *http://www.maxis.com/index.html*
❋ MECC: *http://www.mecc.com/*
❋ Soleil: *http://www.soleil.com/*
❋ Theatrix: *http://www.theatrix.com/*
❋ Voyager: *http://www.voyagerco.com/*
❋ Zenda: *http://www.zenda.com/*

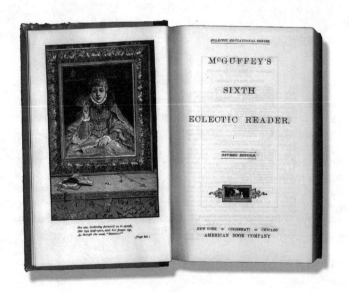

Title page from the author's copy of McGuffey's Sixth Eclectic Reader

INFORMATICA'S
TOP 10
HOMESCHOOLING SITES

❶ Ask Me About Homeschooling

✣ *http://www.geocities.com/*
EnchantedForest/Dell/3719/index2.html
Lycos rates this in the top five percent of sites. Here's what you see first:

> Before you even start... ask yourself if you are prepared and willing to put in the time, effort, and commitment needed. My husband and I have made this commitment twice, once with our oldest daughter and now with our son who is in 9th grade. Our daughter was homeschooled from 7th grade through 12th grade and went on to graduate from Seattle Pacific University.

❷ Welcome to Homeschooling (The Mining Company)

✣ *http://homeschooling.miningco.com/*
This is a typical "about.com" treatment of a subject—not particularly exhaustive but not particularly biased. A good place to nose around if you're just interested in getting an idea of what homeschooling is about.

❸ Homeschooling Information

✣ *http://www.dimensional.com/ ~ janf/home-*
schoolinfo.html
Provides a good set of links. Here's what you see first:

> We are always looking for Web-based information to help us in the homeschooling process. Below are a few links to valuable resources. If you have a Macintosh, be sure to first check out our own *Homeschool Planner,* which will assist you in planning and logging your homeschool day.

❹ Biblical Foundations for Christian Homeschooling

✣ *http://pages.prodigy.com/christianhmsc/home.htm*
Point makes this one of the top five percent of sites on the Web. This is an excellent departure point for those who want to dose homeschooling with a good measure of Christian values and teachings. Here's what you see first:

> THANK YOU FOR VISITING OUR HOMESCHOOLING CENTER. We are the Moore family from Ponca City, Oklahoma. My name is Robert. My wife, Christina, and I homeschool our three children—Susanna (12), Elizabeth (10), and David (8). We teach our children in response to God's instruction in Deuteronomy 6:5–7: "And thou shalt love the LORD thy God with all thine heart, and with all thy soul, and with all thy might. And these words, which I command thee this day, shall be in thine heart: And thou shalt teach them diligently unto thy children, and shalt talk of them when thou sittest in thine house, and when thou walkest by the way, and when thou liest down, and when thou risest up."

❺ Homeschooling—Who Me?

✣ *http://www.concentric.net/ ~ haynes2/homeskl.html*
Includes a radical article entitled "School Is Dead—Learn in Freedom" Here are the first few sentences from that article:

> This site is all about learning in freedom, taking responsibility for your own learning. It's about using your initiative to seek out learning, and using schools and teachers only if they are helpful to you, and voluntarily *chosen* by you. There are countless resources on and off the Web to help you find the freedom to learn independently, and this site gives you the courage to use them. ➔

Homeschooling Sites *continued*

MORE OF INFORMATICA'S TOP 10 HOMESCHOOLING SITES

⑥ Homeschooling Resources

✳ *http://www.amasci.com/home.html*
Heavy emphasis on science here—a part of the Science Hobbyist Web site. Lots of excellent links.

⑦ Homeschooling FAQs

✳ *http://millennium.fortunecity.com/ quarrybank/334/school.html*
A fairly personal page, getting inside the heads of people who chose this route for their children. Here's what you first see:

> We homeschooled Megaera, who is now attending the University of Guam. This page is for people who are interested in the hows and whys of homeschooling.
> Why did you homeschool Megaera?
> 1) Megaera wanted to do it. 2) Megaera was willing to cooperate. 3) The schools on Guam aren't very good, and Megaera had bad experiences with both teachers and kids there. 4) We, the parents, enjoy spending time with Megaera. 5) We felt that we could give her a better education than she could receive at school and meet her needs better. 6) We didn't want her subjected to bullying, sexual harassment, and drugs. 7) The schools here aren't set up to meet the needs of exceptionally bright children.

⑧ Homeschooling

✳ *http://www.life.ca/hs/*
A practical guide to homeschooling in Canada, with lots of emphasis placed on "unschooling." Here's what you first see:

> Here are articles, resources, contact names, and more, all designed to help you learn everything you need to know about homeschooling (sometimes called deschooling, unschooling, or child-directed home-based learning).

⑨ Heather's Homeschooling Page

✳ *http://www.madrone.com/home-ed.htm*
Another very personal Web site. Here's what you first see:

> Welcome.
> Our wonderful adventure in homeschooling began four years ago when our oldest daughter was not quite five. At the beginning, I was unsure of the process of homeschooling and of my ability to handle my children's education. I read extensively about learning, about formal education, and about the business of raising happy, healthy, productive human beings. I talked to homeschooling parents and children, both on-line and in real life. Slowly, bit by bit, I constructed a homeschooling philosophy of my own.

⑩ LDS Homeschooling Page

✳ *http://home1.gte.net/shannon2/*
Though this is not the official Morman take on homeschooling, it certainly carries the flavor of the Church of the Latter Day Saints. From a note on the site:

> A few years ago I started getting e-mail from LDS homeschoolers around the world. I discovered that I was listed as the LDS homeschooling contact on several Web sites. Imagine my surprise! This site is a collection of the information I usually share with those considering the option of homeschooling. I have attempted to address all the issues that are usually raised. I hope you will find it a valuable resource. Please feel free to e-mail me with additional concerns or questions. A big THANK YOU to my son Andrew, who at age twelve, worked patiently with me to create this site. It was his knowledge of HTML that made its creation possible.

The Computer Museum Guide to the Best Software for Kids

Written by Alison Elliott and Cathy Miranker

http://www.tcm.org/html/info/exhibits/kidsware.html

Type: Book (300 pages)

First Developed: 1996; IDG Books

Price Range: $20–$25 in paperback

Key Features: Good, but somewhat out of date as a book

Ages: Kids ages 2-12 and Parents

Obsolescence: Medium. Book is out of print though available from The Boston Computer Museum and Amazon Web site keeps up-to-date links to kids software publishers.

Further Information:
❋ *http://www.softwareforkids.com*
❋ *http://www.childbright.com*

In a demonstration of modern economics, this used to be a book, and now it's a place—real and virtual. It probably didn't make sense to keep republishing the book. Software packages multiply like ticks, and every time this book was published, it was immediately out of date.

However, The Computer Museum in Boston still sells the book. Far more importantly, they maintain a gallery with the best of the current software on display. All software is grouped by age as well as skill group and type of experience, so you can browse lists of software by numerous categories: best math titles, for instance, or best software for parents and kids to use together. Or you can search for titles based on criteria you select, such as age, publisher, price, platform, and more.

Though The Computer Museum does not keep a current set of reviews on its Web site (I can't imagine why not), they do keep a good list of links to the Websites of most of the major suppliers of children's software.

⊶ READER COMMENTARIES FROM THE NET:

A reader , January 25, 1997 ★★★★★
Finally a "one stop" source for software for your kids
If you're a parent and you have kids and a computer this is the essential text. It's filled with lots of specific recommendations to help you find the best software programs by age or subject. Plus it gives you lots of tips to help you and your kids get the most educational value from these programs. Worth the price when you think how much you can save from not buying one bad piece of "so-called" educational software. A real public service.

Running Press Cyclopedia: The Portable Visual Encyclopedia

Compiled by the Diagram Group

Type: Book (638 pages)

First Developed: 1995; Running Press

Price Range: $8-$10 in paperback

Key Features: Handy little books

Ages: High school and later

Obsolescence: Low

Reference works often equate quantity with quality. Encyclopedias have to be big and cumbersome, else they will seem... well, lightweight. However, when a kid has to look something up for homework, or a term paper due TOMORROW, weight doesn't count. The *Cyclopedia* is a handy little volume, designed to make quick work of simple, common questions. It boasts 20,000 facts, and more than 800 full-color maps, diagrams, and illustrations. It is structured in six parts: The World, Countries of the World, History, Science, The Arts, and The United States. The top of each page hold titles on the left side of the folio, section titles on the right. The outside of each page is color-coded for reference. The *Cyclopedia* is simplicity and concision incarnate. If everyone who made dictionaries, encyclopedias, thesaures, and sundry reference works followed the model of the *Cyclopedia* (created by the inspired and eccentric English Diagram Group), kids would likely learn more. At the price, it's silly not to buy this tiny, useful book.

Little-Known Museums in and Around London

Written by Rachel Kaplan

Type: Book (216 pages)

First Developed: 1997; Harry Abrams

Price Range: $16-$18

Key Features: A walking tour with fine pictures and annotation

Ages: Post-high school

Obsolescence: Low

Further Information:
❋ *http://www.citygardentours.co.uk/* for a Web site devoted to London's secret gardens

I discovered this book hidden away in the book section of a J. Peterman store. It sat right next to a similar volume dedicated to the little-known museums of Paris. The publisher is normally known for big, beautifully printed art books, and though small, this book is consistent with the rest of the Abrams product.

From the Bank of England Museum to the Bramah Tea & Coffee Museum to the Cabaret Mechanical Theatre and the Museum of Garden History, this well-illustrated tome sneaks you into the cultural nooks and crannies that make London a wonderful place.

Military Enterprise and Technological Change: Perspectives on the American Experience

Edited by Merritt Roe Smith

Type: Book (408 pages)

First Developed: 1985; MIT Press

Price Range: $50 in hardcover

Key Features: Great articles; no uniform point of view; good history

Ages: Post-high school

Obsolescence: Low

Further Information:
❋ *http://www.fas.org/index.html*
The Web site of the American Federation of Scientists, a great compendium of information on current military technology and policy.

Though great technological things have been accomplished all over the world during wars, the lion's share in the past 120 years has been done in the U.S. This book is a collection of essays and articles detailing some of the greatest of these technological achievements and their relation to military uses.

Wars have invariably started when the smart folks fail or give up, and the stupid, cruel people prevail. Wars end when the stupid, cruel people are exhausted, and the smart people can take over again.

War destroys old stuff, which inevitably must be replaced by new stuff. The story of how the smart people have taken over, and in particular, the development of war-making technology in this century is largely ignored in most coverage of science and technology. War is so devastating and awful that any technology that comes of it is inevitably tainted by this connection. Remarkably, after reading each one of the articles in this book, one comes away with no greater admiration or disgust with war. Rather, one is left with a kind of wonder that people can accomplish what they do, and a sense that it is often duress that pulls the best out of mankind.

The book covers the development of railway systems; radio; the transistor; numerically controlled manufacturing; and complex, centralized computing systems. All of these were products of war, and all of these came to deliver great benefit to mankind after the wars were over.

Sadly, the date of this compilation forbids it's covering some of the great recent achievements, such as stealth technology (see SKUNK WORKS), advanced computing (see NATIONAL CRYPTOLOGIC MUSEUM), the Global Positioning System (see LOWRANCE GLOBALMAP 100), and the Internet (see HISTORY OF THE INTERNET AND WWW).

Eyewitness to History

Edited by John Carey

Type: Book (752 pages)

First Developed: 1997; Avon

Price Range: $11–$14

Key Features: A book with the real stuff, unembellished

Ages: Post–high school

Obsolescence: Low

Further Information:
✱ *http://startingpage.com/html/ quotations.html*
a metapage for quotes and quotations

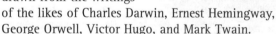

Everything seems different when you get back to sources. This book is nothing more and nothing less than a well-chosen assembly of first-person reportage on some of the great events in Western history (it runs light on the Near and Far East, and is silent on Africa and South America).

quotes to as many stories as we could. Battles, atrocities, disasters, coronations, assassinations, and discoveries that shaped the course of Western history are drawn from the writings of the likes of Charles Darwin, Ernest Hemingway, George Orwell, Victor Hugo, and Mark Twain.

It was perfect for our purposes, and it seemed to constantly be floating around the office. It is that interesting. All the entries are short; hence it can be sampled constantly, not requiring a sustained read.

When we were writing "The Time Table of History" (part of our *Encyclopedia Electronica*), this book figured heavily into our project to attach first-person

This book should be on every decently read, English-speaking person's shelf, as a constant reminder not to trust historians.

**⚡ READER COMMENTARIES
FROM THE NET**

A reader from Manhattan, August 22, 1998 ★★★★★
The single most interesting book I've read.
I love this book! If there was one book I could take to the proverbial desert island, this would be it. I've read it so many times, and always find something new to delight in. The publisher should reissue it; I'm tired of lending it to friends.

A reader, August 7, 1997 ★★★★★
Reading it for the fourth time!
Today I ordered my fourth copy of Eyewitness to History (Carey, John) since it first was published. Why? When

my guests have seen it in my home, some have borrowed it and become addicted to it, and I end up telling them to keep it. It makes a good gift and great reading. I enjoy reading both history and short stories: Eyewitness to History is the best of both in one volume! The authenticity is appealing, but the spontaneity of the eyewitness accounts is without equal. The simple, forthright eyewitness accounts are devoid of the verbose, protracted, and often biased interpretations that one frequently encounters in most historical texts. Mr. Carey, when are you going to write an updated edition with more accounts? I want to be the first to know.

Path Between the Seas: The Creation of the Panama Canal, 1870–1914

Written by David McCullough

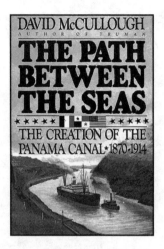

Type: Book (600+ pages)

First Developed: 1978; Simon and Schuster

Price Range: $13–$15

Key Features: Fine history from a popular historian

Ages: Post-high school

Obsolescence: Low

Further Information:
✽ *http://panamacanalmuseum.org/*
for the Panama Canal museum Web site;
✽ *http://www.pancanal.com/cnews/*
for a chatty Web site devoted to the canal

I had the great good fortune a decade ago to have this book on my lap as I sat on a cruise ship bound for a Pacific-Atlantic transit of the Panama Canal. For three days out of Acapulco, I plowed through McCullough's detailed history, and it was all fresh in my mind as we spent the day making the passage eastward.

driving energy behind the work was Teddy Roosevelt, but the intellectual soul was Alfred Thayer Mahan (see INFLUENCE OF SEA POWER ON WORLD HISTORY) and his belief that control of sea lanes meant military pre-eminence.

The remarkable technical achievements, from the defeat of malaria and other jungle diseases by great leaps forward in sanitary sciences, to the maintenance of a rail line through an ever encroaching jungle, to the fabrication of the massive steel doors and their installation in delicately balanced hinges —stuff that probably could not easily be fabricated today—are testimony to the sophistication of American technology at the turn of the century.

Since then, I have never lost sight of the extraordinary investment the U.S. made in this great work of infrastructure (see TOP TEN I-WAR TARGETS). The

Moreover, it is all a record of what can be done when a nation with strong leadership sets its mind and spirit to a task.

➥ READER COMMENTARIES FROM THE NET

A reader from Boston, July 16, 1998 ★★★★★
Epic!
Perhaps I am biased, having grown up in the Panama Canal Zone. All prejudices apart, though, this is the single best "history" book I have ever read. With a cast of characters worthy of a Tolstoy novel, McCullough gives the reader a thorough understand-

ing of the magnitude and impact the little Isthmus of Panama has had on the history of the world. This is much more than history. Indeed, the common claim that it reads like a novel is not an exaggeration. The 600+ pages overflow with unrelenting drama, vividly painted larger-than-life characters, exotic vistas, bustling courtrooms, etc. This is more a story about the people who struggled to realize a dream than it is about the little canal that captured their imaginations for centuries. This book moved me to tears.

A Spy's London: A Walk Book of 136 Sites in Central London Relating to Spies, Spycatchers & Subversives

Written by Roy Berkeley

Type: Book (384 pages)

First Developed: 1997; Combined Books

Price Range: $14–$18

Key Features: Well illustrated walking tour

Ages: All

Obsolescence: Low

Further Information:
✻ *http://www.cc.umist.ac.uk/sk/index.html*
for a terrific unofficial index to secret governement agencies in the UK.

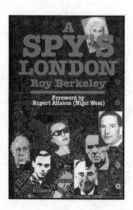

Once familiar with the history of espionage (see THE SPY BOOK), nothing is quite as much fun as finding the places you are not supposed to know about and having a look.

Until the appearance of this fine book, and UNDERCOVER WASHINGTON, the only technique was to scrounge the literature and ask the cabbie to take you there. The secrets well known to every military attaché, in every embassy, were hidden from the interested tourist.

London is a walking town, and the misery of long days on one's feet is well attenuated by the easy availability of one of the finest undergrounds in the world. *A Spy's London* was made for walking, and I have done it. Because the majority of the entries have decent street level photographs, there is rarely doubt as to what you are looking at.

Part of the fun is that there is always doubt as to whether the secret facilities from World War II and the Cold War dead drops might not still be in use.

Great fun.

⚫➤ READER COMMENTARIES FROM THE NET

A reader, January 19, 1997 ★★★★☆

A captivating tour guide and history of the best known and lesser known spies of London.
Not your everyday tour guide to London, that's for sure. Roy Berkeley's meticulously researched book reads like a spy novel. But this is no work of fiction. The author takes you on a tour of more than 130 places where some of the more notorious spies plied their craft. Nondescript flats were home to the likes of double agents Kim Philby and Donald Maclean, who betrayed their country. And while Baker Street will always be known as the home to Sherlock Holmes and Dr. Watson, a whole stretch of Baker Street during World War 2 was home to the British espionage and sabotage organization known as SOE (Special Operations Executive). Berkeley even touches on the home and workplace of the most famous spy writer in history, Ian Fleming. Complete with photos and diagrams to get you around the espionage haunts of the city. A real gem!

The Pinball Effect: How Renaissance Water Gardens Made the Carburetor Possible and Other Journeys Through Knowledge

Written by James Burke

Type: Book (320 pages)

First Developed: 1997; Little, Brown & Co.

Price Range: $12–$15

Key Features: A deeply inter-twingled book

Ages: Post high school

Obsolescence: Low

Further Information:
✻ *http://www.mcrel.org/ resources/plus/timeline.asp*
A fine Web page dedicated to connections in history.
Also, Burke's latest book: *The Knowledge Web: From Electronic Agents to Stonehenge and Back, And Other Journeys Through Knowledge (1999)*

In one of his early tomes, Burke linked underwear to literacy. It went something like this: books had been transcribed on crude paper for a thousand years when Europeans started to wear linen underwear. As time went on, used linen rags piled up, and clever paper-makers found a way to use them to create papers of uncommon smoothness and ink absorption characteristics. With such paper, and only with such paper, Gutenberg was able to create a press with movable type, which could create a predictable image as the type was stamped onto the smooth paper. Following Gutenberg (and the recent plague, which winnowed down the population of Europe and made the fast and inexpensive dissemination of knowledge a primary requirement for getting things back up and running) came a rebirth of knowledge through the distribution of relatively cheap books to the masses.

With his PBS *Connections* series, Burke made an entertainment of history, through the demonstration that (in Ted Nelson's words) everything is deeply intertwingled. In fact, in the structure of this particular book, Burke borrows liberally from Ted Nelson's storehouse of ideas about hypermedia. ("Everything is deeply intertwingled.")

Exposure to Burke yields a healthy reminder that man's works are a deep and continuing matrix of interactions, plans, and serendipities. No bit of knowledge is forever lost, and its relevancy is never fully understood.

> "*It would be hard to find a more whimsical history of science and technology than* THE PINBALL EFFECT *by James Burke, host of the popular* CONNECTIONS *television programs. Through his show, Burke has been doing for technology what Joseph Campbell once did for myth, making it a new branch of popular culture. In Burke's view, the factors that lead to discoveries and inventions are so interconnected, unpredictable, and often accidental that their history is more like the path of a "pinball caroming about its table than a linear chain of events." And he invites us to read this history with a "Look at that!" attitude, jumping from page to page, chapter to chapter, as our interest is caught, following marginal notes that indicate where to pick up the many threads with which each story is woven. There are, Burke notes, at least 447 ways to read this book.*"
>
> —THE SMITHSONIAN, *August 1997*

The Pinball Effect *continued*

A reader from St. Helens, Oregon,
February 19, 1999 ★★★★☆
Interconnectedness of history.

Since chaos burst upon the intellectual consciousness of the 20th century, examples of the butterfly effect have inundated our lives. Chaotic systems exhibit a type of behavior where vanishingly small perturbations in initial conditions result in wild and unpredictable alterations in a system's final state. The butterfly in China, flapping its wings, results in a hurricane off the coast of Florida 100 years later.

James Burke takes us on an intersected voyage through the web of history, and in the process shows the intricately connected nature of our lives in a chaotic mishmash of intersecting events. The mental imagery I concocted while reading his book was one of a small worm making its way through a biscuit of shredded wheat. With thousands of intersecting strands, and billions of route possibilities open at each juncture, my biscuit gives a feel for the intricate connection that every event in history shares with everything else. In fact, Burke has written his book from the worm's perspective, with branch points identified in the margins so you can follow a thread (instead of the book) as it weaves its way through history. You do not need to read this book sequentially, and quite possibly might choose to read it worm style rather than cover to cover.

When I first began Burke's book, I looked for the obvious connections but soon learned that was not his objective. Though he illustrates obvious connections, much of the interrelatedness in Burke's book deals with subtle effects that changed people's lives and resulted in dramatic changes in history. Sometimes the stories become so intricate I found myself taking notes so I could mentally trace back through the web of events.

Most of the historical events he covers relate in some way to scientific or technical achievements and discoveries. In some of these, I found myself confused about the terminology used. Burke is not always clear when he comments about a particular discovery whether he is making a statement about the way things are viewed today, or how they were viewed by the original discoverers. Because of this, I found myself sometimes irritated by technically incorrect descriptions. For example, on page 198 Burke says:

> "There was only one thing that would reflect radio waves besides metal reflectors like the ones Hertz had used: ionized atoms, which had lost one or more of their electrons. These atoms became positively charged and would reflect electronic signals (which were negative)."

While it is true that ions are positively charged, radio waves are not negative. In another place, he describes voltage as charge (see page 186). He also mentions, offhandedly, that collimated laser beams spread by only "a few feet" over the distance between the Earth and moon (see page 75). [A collimated beam, with a wavelength of 600 nm, will have a half-beam divergence of about 48 feet over the distance between the Earth and moon when →

The Pinball Effect *continued*

→ collimated with a telescope having a 10-meter-diameter primary mirror. See, for example, Saleh, Teich, *Fundamentals of Photonics*, Wiley Series in Pure and Applied Optics, equation 3.1–20.]

These examples left me with a sometimes uneasy feeling about the book's technical accuracy, yet I cannot discount the possibility that Burke was simply explaining these phenomena in the context of the way they were understood when first discovered.

The book has an excellent index. The figures, however, are of generally poor quality and hard to see. Another irritant was the frequent and often detailed descriptions Burke gives of ingenious and complex machinery and gadgets. These descriptions are often very hard to follow and would benefit greatly from drawings that support the textual descriptions.

Aside from these few criticisms, however, I found Burke's book most enjoyable. It will broaden your horizons and make you appreciate history from a new perspective. An ideal book for just before bedtime. I highly recommend it.

Spy Book:
The Encyclopedia of Espionage
Written by Norman Polmar and Thomas B. Allen

Type: Book (656 pages)

First Developed: 1997, Random House

Price Range: $15–$20

Key Features: First-rate summary of the world of Spooks

Ages: All

Obsolescence: Low

Matters of espionage tend to be rendered in sensational terms. The choice in fiction is often between the romantic (James Bond) and the despondent (John LeCarre and Somerset Maugham). Sadly, fiction is where the greatest measure of material on espionage lives, because spies are expected to be quiet, and their stories to be untold.

It is, by and large, an unpleasant profession, as it trades in lies and deceits. I spent an afternoon with a very famous spook one time. He had run a healthy chunk of South America for the CIA through the late '50s and into the '60s and '70s. He was haggard, substantially depleted, and apparently in his cups. The CIA was not in favor at the time, and this man in particular had been bound to a conspiracy to kill JFK in the popular radical press. Much of the romance was lost for me by the end of that afternoon.

However, espionage does not seem as dark and grim to me as LeCarre and Maugham might have it. The gathering of intelligence and the means man has constructed to do so represent one of the abiding intellectual investments throughout history. Nothing is thrown out. Today's tradecraft is →

> **"He was haggard, substantially depleted, and apparently in his cups."**

Spy Book *continued*

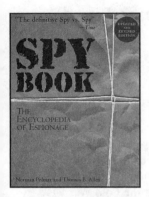

→ bound to a legacy that stretches back 4,000 years and finds its roots in each of the ancient cultures, China and India in particular.

Polmar and Allen have given honorable and thorough treatment to the subject. They pay proper attention to both Indian Artha Shastra and modern satellite-based signals intelligence (Sigint). Particularly well covered is the history of American intelligence activities, which began with Washington, crested during the Civil War, and became world class in the U.S. Army's Military Intelligence Division (MID) during World War I.

This book is the best foundation document for a study of the spy trade. It is well prepared to correct errors and disinformation and to give the present era a finely detailed contextual history.

"This work by two military historians has some 2,000 entries on people, places, institutions, code words, operations, and other aspects of spying. The wide variety of sources used by the authors includes previously unavailable archival sources (e.g., the CIA and the KGB) as well as interviews with individuals involved in espionage/intelligence activities, court documents, private correspondence, and presentations at intelligence conferences. Many entries include information as recent as 1995 or 1996."
—*Booklist*, April 15, 1997

⊷ READER COMMENTARIES FROM THE NET

A reader, January 13, 1997 ★★★★★
Most readable, most complete spy compendium ever!

Few books on spycraft or actual spy cases capture a reader as well as a spy novel [does]. This book, however, does that and more—it grabs you.

With numerous discussions of famous and not so famous spy cases, spy rings, and spies, you will find yourself flipping through the book, tying the pieces together. Written much like a Web site, the first time an encyclopedia entry appears within another entry, it appears in a special font. This allows the reader to flip from one story to another.

Much of the appeal of the book comes from its currency. Events as recent as the second half of 1996 made it into the book, yet there is in-depth coverage of every major exposed spyring throughout the 1900s. Additionally, any spy master of repute throughout history (such as Moses and George Washington) receives an entry.

In addition to [the discussion of] the spies and their work, detailed information is provided about their agencies, such as the KGB, MI6, and the CIA, and the locales in which they operated (e.g., Cambridge, Berlin, and Vienna). I can't give a stronger endorsement to any work. This beats Clancy, LeCarre, Fleming, and →

Spy Book *continued*

> Deighton—hands down. The saying "Fact is stranger than fiction" is never truer than in the story in which a CIA operative created added distrust and confusion between two factions by having his agents kill people in such a way that it appeared one faction was composed of vampires.
>
> Don't miss the Literary Spies section, which includes information not only on your favorite fictional spies, but also on famous authors (such as Somerset Maugham) who actually spied themselves.

Undercover Washington: Touring the Sites Where Infamous Spies Lived, Worked, and Loved

Written by Pamela Kessler

Type: Book (159 pages)

First Developed: 1992; EPM Publications

Price Range: $10

Key Features: Well informed guide to a spy's Washington

Ages: All

Obsolescence: Low

Further Information:
✳ *http://www.fas.com*
for greater detail on some of Washington's present-day secret facilities

Whereas *A SPY'S LONDON* betrays a boatload of that city's secrets, it is necessarily bound by the fact that the hubs of espionage during the Cold War were Washington and Moscow, and today is Washington alone, now that the U.S. is—for a while—the only world power.

That means that Washington is filled with spooks, ours and theirs. One need only walk down

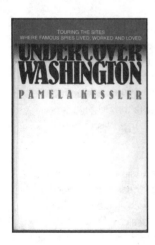

Massachusetts Avenue pondering the fields of antennas atop the embassies, and the security systems wrapped around each building, to guess that there is a lot of interesting stuff going on in Washington today.

I have no idea who Pamela Kessler is, and a search of Amazon reveals no other published work. The flyleaf leaves the impression she is some sort of suburban housewife in the D.C. area. She must have some really interesting late afternoon teatime discussions, as she seems to have the goods on spy stuff in D.C.

From Civil War intelligence operatives, to the whereabouts of the now long-gone German embassy, from Nazi and Soviet dead drops, to secret U.S. intelligence offices right in the heart of downtown Washington (some of them cannot be more than a few miles distant from the White House by law), Ms. Kessler (a nom de plume?) seems to know precisely what's going on.

When you have finished with the Smithsonian, and the other standard fare of Washington, take a copy of Ms. Kessler's book and start walking.

The First Casualty: From the Crimea to Vietnam: The War Correspondent As Hero, Propagandist, and Myth Maker

Written by Phillip Knightley

Type: Book (465 pages)

First Developed: 1976; Harcourt Brace

Price Range: $15–$20

Key Features: History with many direct quotes from published news accounts and private correspondence and diaries

Ages: All

Obsolescence: Low

Further Information: BBC's World Service news broadcast is often, but not always, a reliable source of information on conflicts throughout the world

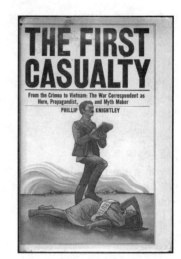

This, like *MIND OF THE SOUTH*, is another gem from the bookshelf of my stepfather, Bill Stout. He had been to war in Viet Nam and had his career trashed after he testified before a congressional committee about the fabrication of news by the major TV network news organization for which he worked.

Beginning with dispatches from the Crimean War, the personalities and politics of war reportage are tracked through the Civil War, on to the amazing fiddling Hearst did to incite the Spanish-American War.

This is not a simple read and some of the details—especially those in the citations from private, unpublished dispatches—are rough stuff, but the book is rich and well put together. The healthy after-effect of this read is a permanent skepticism of everything called news delivered from the front.

➺ READER COMMENTARIES FROM THE NET

A reader from North Carolina, December 19, 1998 ★★★★☆
A fascinating history of news coverage and war,
An excellent, well-written book dealing with many complex issues of news coverage and war. Includes real-life examples of objective coverage…expropriation by the military, propaganda, and many other aspects of truth as the first casualty in wartime. Especially relevant today with media/military merging in high technology presentations.

Selling the Invisible: A Field Guide to Modern Marketing

Written by Harry Beckwith

Type: Book (252 pages)

First Developed: 1997; Warner Books

Price Range: $12–$15

Key Features: A book with a finely honed point of view

Ages: Post-high school

Obsolescence: Low

Further Information:
✳ *http://www.janal.com/id6.htm*
for more business bestsellers

Here's the hustle. By the beginning of the next century well over three-quarters of Americans will be working in service businesses. If you buy that vapor (who's going to be making the computers and cars?), then this book will hold a great deal of value for you.

Beckwith argues that what consumers are primarily interested in today are not features but relationships. One of Beckwith's examples: when a customer buys a Saturn automobile, he or she isn't buying the car but the way that Saturn does business. This is a bit of a stretch; however, there is a kernel of truth in it, and more important, it reflects the way a lot of marketers are conducting their business.

The book is written chunk-style, like good ad copy, and hence makes for a staccato read. Like candy, reading too much of it at one time may not be good for you.

> "In the first major book on service marketing, Harry Beckwith, a pioneer in this area, provides quick, practical strategies to improve the bottom line in any business by perceiving and fulfilling a client's every need."
>
> —HARVEY MACKAY

◆◦ CRITIC COMMENTARIES

From Booklist, March 1, 1997:

Advertising professional Beckwith startles and disarms all potential doubting Thomases with one fact—that by the year 2005, eight out of ten Americans will be working in a service business. Chapters here are remarkably short; they are intended to convey one point (summarized in one sentence in boldface italics) and are blessedly free of jargon.... Forget questionnaires and focus groups; instead, ask individuals what improvements are needed—not the dreaded "What don't you like?"

Syntopicon
The Greatest Ideas in Human History

Written by Mortimer Adler

http://www.thegreatideas.org/term.html#A

Type: Book (two volumes)

First Developed: 1960s

Price Range: $100

Key Features: Long view of human history

Ages: All

Obsolescence: Low

Further Information:
✳ *http://www.mcs.net/~jorn/html/ ai/prehistory.html*
How Adler's Syntopicon figures into the prehistory of the development of artificial intelligence—see sidebar, "The Prehistory of AI"

When Mortimer Adler, the celebrated editor of the *Encyclopedia Brittanica*, restructured the encyclopedia, he caused great controversy and anticipated the future, hierarchical nature of digital publications (where one level leads to another level). Ted Nelson recognized this in his *COMPUTER LIB, DREAM MACHINES* and paid the work its necessary due.

The structure, breaking the work into the Propedia (a kind of organizational chart of human knowledge), the Micropedia (short articles on everything), and the Macropedia (longer articles on selected subjects, often improved, and substituted with newer information) was a wonderful →

ADLER'S FUNDAMENTAL CONCEPTS FROM *SYNTOPICON*

Angel	Custom and Convention	Fate	Infinity
Animal	Definition	Form	Judgment
Aristocracy	Democracy	God	Justice
Art	Desire	Good and Evil	Knowledge
Astronomy	Dialectic	Government	Labor
Beauty	Duty	Habit	Language
Being	Education	Happiness	Law
Cause	Element	History	Liberty
Chance	Emotion	Honor	Life and Death
Change	Eternity	Hypothesis	Logic
Citizen	Evolution	Idea	Love
Constitution	Experience	Immortality	Man
Courage	Family	Induction	Mathematics →

Syntopicon *continued*

→ attempt to make the material more accessible, and at the same time accommodate the volatility of human knowledge.

Adler created something else of great value as well: the Syntopicon. The idea was to take the great abstractions of the human experience and link them (as if in a filing or classification sys-

tem) to great literary works. He imagined that every great thought was composed of one or more great fundamental concepts, as words are crafted from alphabets. He wasn't the first to attempt to classify human thought—the examples in Indian and Chinese philosophy through the millennia abound. But he was able to grasp a healthy chunk of Western thought—a remarkable achievement.

GREAT BOOKS OF THE WESTERN WORLD

Introductory Volumes:

1. The Great Conversation
2. The Great Ideas I
3. The Great Ideas II

4. HOMER
5. AESCHYLUS
   SOPHOCLES
   EURIPIDES
   ARISTOPHANES
6. HERODOTUS
   THUCYDIDES
7. PLATO
8. ARISTOTLE I
9. ARISTOTLE II
10. HIPPOCRATES
    GALEN
11. EUCLID
    ARCHIMEDES
    APOLLONIUS
    NICOMACHUS

12. LUCRETIUS
    EPICTETUS
    MARCUS AURELIUS
13. VIRGIL
14. PLUTARCH
15. TACITUS
16. PTOLEMY
    COPERNICUS
    KEPLER
17. PLOTINUS
18. AUGUSTINE
19. THOMAS AQUINAS I
20. THOMAS AQUINAS II
21. DANTE
22. CHAUCER
23. MACHIAVELLI
    HOBBES
24. RABELAIS
25. MONTAIGNE
26. SHAKESPEARE I
27. SHAKESPEARE II

GREAT BOOKS OF THE WESTERN WORLD

28. GILBERT
    GALILEO
    HARVEY
29. CERVANTES
30. FRANCIS BACON
31. DESCARTES
    SPINOZA
32. MILTON
33. PASCAL
34. NEWTON
    HUYGENS
35. LOCKE
    BERKELEY
    HUME
36. SWIFT
    STERNE
37. FIELDING
38. MONTESQUIEU
    ROUSSEAU
39. ADAM SMITH
40. GIBBON I

41. GIBBON II
42. KANT
43. AMERICAN STATE
    PAPERS
    THE FEDERALIST
    J. S. MILL
44. BOSWELL
45. LAVOISIER
    FOURIER
    FARADAY
46. HEGEL
47. GOETHE
48. MELVILLE
49. DARWIN
50. MARX
    ENGELS
51. TOLSTOY
52. DOSTOEVSKY
53. WILLIAM JAMES
54. FREUD

→ **MORE OF ADLER'S FUNDAMENTAL CONCEPTS FROM *SYNTOPICON***

Matter	Philosophy	Religion	Theology
Mechanics	Physics	Revolution	Time
Medicine	Pleasure and Pain	Rhetoric	Truth
Memory and Imagination	Poetry	Same and Other	Tyranny
Metaphysics	Principle	Science	Universal and Particular
Mind	Progress	Sense	Virtue and Vice
Monarchy	Prophecy	Sign and Symbol	War and Peace
Nature	Prudence	Sin	Wealth
Necessity and Contingency	Punishment	Slavery	Will
Oligarchy	Quality	Soul	Wisdom
One and Many	Quantity	Space	World
Opinion	Reasoning	State	
Opposition	Relation	Temperance	

Syntopicon *continued*

THE PREHISTORY OF ARTIFICIAL INTELLIGENCE

Strangely enough, the first recorded human attack on the problems of AI came from the fortune tellers. If their systems for generating predictions had overlooked certain classes of human events, then obviously those systems could never even accidentally predict them!

Beginning before 1,000 B.C., astrologers were already exploring an especially rich (though arbitrary) system of planetary relationships with three orthogonal dimensions (planet, sign, and house), trying to map them onto human experiences. The *I Ching,* slightly later, explored the 64 precise permutations of a six-bit binary system, as well as the eight three-bit half-words they contained. *The Kabalah* and *Tarot* offered simpler systems around 1,000 A.D., tied more directly to particular human meanings like virtue and vice.

Orthogonality is a critical concept in software design. The name implies a set of *dimensions* that are at "right angles" to each other, so that any "point" can be defined in terms of one-value-for-each-dimension. A vivid example of this arrived with the 1984 debut of MacPaint, where one could easily vary the following orthogonal dimensions for each graphic "object": shape, size, position, fill-pattern, border-thickness, and border-pattern.

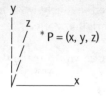

The beauty of orthogonality in software design is that it allows an extremely broad range of objects to be defined with a minimal set of parameters. Consequently, one need only remember these few commands to master all the objects so created. ("An ounce of orthogonality is worth a ton of 'added-features' tinsel.") And the programming code required to implement them is also minimized! So the dream of an orthogonal analysis of all natural and social phenomena is an enticing one…

Aristotle made a much more *grounded* assault on the range of human meanings around 300 B.C. Aquinas later extended Aristotle's analysis to include Christian ethics. The Middle Ages brought Raymond Lull playing mystical combinatorial games, leading eventually to Leibnitz's (1646–1716) dream of a purely rational culture, where all concepts will have been encoded as mathematical formulae, and philosophical disputes will be met with the cry, *Calculemus*… "Let us calculate!"

In modern times, the most disciplined attempt to codify philosophy is probably the *Syntopicon* from Mortimer Adler's Great Books series. Here's a brief glance at Adler's scheme, in light of AI and modern science.

Giovanni Battista in his *New Science* (1725, pars 161–162) was likely the first to anticipate a universal dictionary of *concepts,* realized in 1852 with the thousand categories of Peter Mark Roget's *Thesaurus.* The Dewey Decimal System (1876) and Library of Congress Classification are two later evolutions, but all of these are plagued by redundancies and ambiguities. Two net-specific proposals are "Joel's Hierarchical Subject Index" (JHSI, which appears to be a top-down analysis) and the Usenet hierarchy itself (here, just the groups that have FAQs). (The Usenet hierarchy can usually be examined on UNIX systems via: */usr/lib/news/active or /usr/lib/news/newsgroups.*)

Fritz Lehmann (fritz@rodin.wustl.edu) is collecting a master-list of indexing schemes, or "concept systems," that currently numbers over 150 entries, many extremely obscure.

AI views **hierarchies** as networks of "nodes" connected by "IsA links." In computer memory, any clump of data can be a node, and any pointer to such a clump can be a link. "IsA" is the particular relationship between a more-specialized and a less-specialized form of the same thing: "hunger IsA motive" translates as: "Motive is a general class that includes hunger as one specialized form." (Another common sort of link is "part Of.")

While hierarchical thinking comes naturally to most people, the implementing of hierarchies in computer memory allows one to extend the hierarchy-structure in ways that are less intuitively obvious. It's cheap and easy, for example, to allow a single element to be "multiply indexed" at more than one location in the hierarchy… but even this minor tweak comes only slowly to human thinking-habits.

Pacific Destiny: Inside Asia Today
Written by Robert Elegant

Type: Book (523 pages)

First Developed: 1990

Price Range: $6–$15

Key Features: Clear view of the East

Ages: All

Obsolescence: Low

Further Information:
currently out of print, so try
✳ *http://www.bibliofind.com*
also
✳ *http://www.learner.org/*
collections/multimedia/
worldcultures/pcseries/
for *Pacific Century* documentary

Now almost ten years old, this book would seem increasingly dated. It lacks the transition of Hong Kong back into the grasp of China, the crash of the several Asian economies, and the rise of China as a threatening world power.

All of these, however, are brief blips on the radar of Asian history. So much has come before, so much of today is a legacy of the far distant past, and so much of the future is bound to that past that this book, designed to be an omnibus review of Asia's powers, is still extraordinarily valuable.

Just as the Middle East demands to be honored for its history, and considered for its relevance to the present day (see THE PEACE TO END ALL PEACES and FROM BEIRUT TO JERUSALEM), Asia demands attention. This book is a terrific place to start.

Brill's Content
A Magazine about the Media
http://www.brillscontent.com

Type: Magazine

First Developed: 1998

Price Range: $12–$15 per annum

Key Features: Utterly refreshing

Ages: Post high school

Obsolescence: Low

Further Information:
✳ *http://www.newswatch.org/*
for a consumer's guide to the news
✳ *http://www.slipup.com/*
for a running record of media slip-ups

This is, bar none, the best new American magazine. There are several reasons why:

1) Its charter is to take on, and subject to critical public review, a bunch of lazy, arrogant, powerful people who have always reserved the right to conduct critical, public review for themselves.

2) It has taken pains to subject itself to critical public review. When it is caught doing something dumb, it corrects itself, publicly, with material that is as prominent in the magazine as the original gaffe.

Virtually everything I have ever found in it has been worth reading. The stuff they write about advanced technology is normally very good and well-informed. As is just about everything else. →

Brill's Content *continued*

➔ The editors are very clever. One stand-out example is the Charlie Rose meter, with which they measure exactly how long Charlie Rose talks on his show, compared to his guests (lately, Rose is averaging around 25 percent).

The most satisfying sound in the world is the deflation of puffed egos. Every page in Brill's Content goes whoosh.

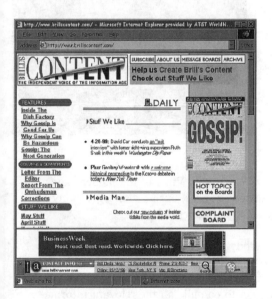

A NOTE FROM MR. BRILL

Q: Name the industry that, when it comes to power, lack of accountability, arrogance, and the making of money in the name of sacred constitutional rights, actually makes lawyers look good....

A: Media.

It would be hilarious if it weren't so true....

The fact is, it's time we told the media, "Enough!"

It's time to hold journalists accountable; it's time we embarrass them into doing their jobs the way they're supposed to—with integrity, honesty, fairness, and accuracy.

I'm Steve Brill and that's why I've launched *Brill's Content*, the new consumer guide for the information age.

Six years ago I started *Court TV* to "expose" the inner workings of the legal system. The good parts and the bad. What resulted was a renewed appreciation and respect for a system of justice which is the model for the world—and a healthy, informed understanding of what needs to be fixed.

I want *Brill's Content* to do the same for journalism. By exposing the bias, the imbalance, the inaccuracies, the untruths—while praising those who get it right—I hope to hold the media to strict new standards we can all benefit from.

I want to tip the balance of power away from the increasingly arrogant and defensive media and put it back with those who use information, not those who manufacture it.

If we fail—if the media goes unchecked, unquestioned, and unscrutinized—our very freedoms are at risk.

Brill's Content is not about left vs. right, big vs. little, ins vs. outs. *Brill's Content* is about right vs. wrong, truth vs. lies, facts vs. fiction.

I hope you'll take a look at our Premiere Issue and see if you'd like to be a part of what I'm sure will be a fascinating ride.

Can a magazine make a difference? *Brill's Content* can with your help.

Sincerely,
Steven Brill
Founder, Chairman, and Editor In Chief

Bucky Works: Buckminster Fuller's Ideas for Today

Written by James T. Baldwin

Type: Book (256 pages)

First Developed: 1996; John Wiley and Sons

Price Range: $15–$20

Key Features: A guide to one of the most unusual minds of the 20th century

Ages: Post high school

Obsolescence: Low

Further Information:
✳ *http://www.netaxs.com/ people/cjf/fuller-faq.html* for a great FAQ (frequently asked questions) on Buckminster Fuller

Long before clever people talked about "thinking out of the box," long before Apple was clever enough to run the "think different" campaign, Buckminster Fuller was well out of bounds. In the late sixties, when radical politicos and Whole Earthers were convincing themselves that they had found a whole new way of looking at things—*alternate* and *radical* were the key words; alternate realities, alternative health programs, radical politics, and alternate media—Fuller was running a quasi academic community of revolutionary doers and thinkers at the University of Illinois at Carbondale.

R. Buckminster Fuller (1895–1983) was not a da Vinci of the modern age. Da Vinci had folios and brilliant, advanced ideas, but he didn't get many of them turned into reality during his lifetime. Fuller did.

His cars never caught on, but the aerodynamics and efficiencies influenced automobile design for decades afterward. His geodesic domes did catch on, not only as alternative housing, but as the archetypal covering for satellite dishes. He even set in motion a project to compile all the relevant information about the globe into a vast computer database.

He was an architect, inventor, engineer, writer, mathematician, and educator; built a very loyal following throughout the '60s and '70s; and is largely forgotten today. A mistake easily and well-corrected with this book.

Monitoring Times

Magazine Devoted to Radio Monitoring

http://www.grove-ent.com/hmpgmt.html

Type: Magazine

First Developed: 1979

Price Range: $24 for a year's sub-
scription by 2nd class mail

Key Features: Very informed survey
of what's going on in radio

Ages: 10 and up

Obsolescence: Low

Further Information:
http://www.popcomm.com/
for *Monitoring Times'* competitor
Popular Communications

Bob Grove has been
publishing this maga-
zine for years, and I
have been buying it. I
keep it around, because
the back issues are a
treasure trove of fre-
quencies. This rag isn't
for hams, the people
who like to talk to
other folks. This is for
listeners.

From the Monitoring Times Web site:

Here's what you'll get every month with a subscription to *MT:*

- International broadcasting program schedules
- Shortwave and longwave DXing
- Satellite broadcasting
- Pirate and clandestine stations
- Two-way communications monitoring
- Listening tips and insights from the experts
- Frequency lists
- News-breaking articles
- Exclusive interviews
- New product tests and book reviews
- Feature articles and much, much more

Over the years, I've listened to Army, Air Force,
and Navy transmissions, news broadcasts from
around the world, police and fire communications in L.A. and elsewhere, and all kinds of
sundry stuff. More often than not, I've picked up
the frequencies from an issue of *Monitoring
Times.*

Each issue has a complete schedule for the next
month's worth of international shortwave broadcasts (BBC, Moscow, and the rest) and a rich
array of departments. My two favorites are the
Federal File, which often breaks stories about
military and intelligence black programs before
anyone else, and the Computer Corner, which
tracks the fast-paced integration of consumer
computers and radios (see ICOM PCR-1000, and
SONY ICFSC1-PC).

The amount of raw experience with radio both
the writers and the readers display is staggering. →

Monitoring Times *continued*

Kosovo frequencies recently cited in MT:

3178	USAF EC-130 ABCCC Bookshelf Net Push Unknown (Moonbeam Ops)
3900	NATO E-3 AWACS Net (ITU Region 1 only) Magic/Cyrano callsign
4519	USAF EC-130 ABCCC Bookshelf Net Push 78A (Moonbeam Ops)
4724	USAF Global HF System Primary
4742	RAF STCICS "Architect"
5218	USAF EC-130 ABCCC Bookshelf Net Push 79B (Moonbeam Ops)
5763.5	USAF EC-130 ABCCC Bookshelf Net Push 80V (Moonbeam Ops)
6693	USN Adriatic Task Force Voice Coordination Net
6712	USAF Global HF System Primary
6728	NATO E-3 AWACS Coordination Net
6739	USAF Global HF System Primary/RAF STCICS "Architect"
6761	USAF Worldwide Air Refueling Primary
6865	USAF EC-130 ABCCC Bookshelf Net Push 81A (Moonbeam Ops)
6932.5	USAF EC-130 ABCCC Bookshelf Net Push 81B (Moonbeam Ops)
8046	USAF EC-130 ABCCC Bookshelf Net Push 81V (Moonbeam Ops)
8087	USAF EC-130 ABCCC Bookshelf Net Push Unknown (Moonbeam Ops)
8982	USN Adriatic Task Force Voice Coordination Net
8992	USAF Global HF System Primary
9118.5	USAF EC-130 ABCCC Bookshelf Net Push 82A (Moonbeam Ops)
9260	USAF EC-130 ABCCC Bookshelf Net Push 82B (Moonbeam Ops)
10315	NATO Naval Voice Coordination Net
10915	NATO/SFOR Airlift Interplane "JG" callsigns
11173	USAF EC-130 ABCCC Bookshelf Net Push 83A (Moonbeam Ops)
11175	USAF Global HF System Primary
13200	USAF Global HF System Primary
13458	Raven Operations (Frankfurt/Rhein-Main) working various tanker aircraft
15016	USAF Global HF System Primary
15048	USAF EC-130 ABCCC Bookshelf Net Push Unknown (Moonbeam Ops)
16442.4	Naval Voice Coordination Hotel Tracking Net

2600 Magazine

Magazine Devoted to Hacking

http://www.2600.com/info.html

Type: Magazine

First Developed: Magazine, 1987; Web site, 1995

Price Range: $21 for a year's subscription

Key Features: Very informed survey of what's going on in hacking

Ages: 10 and up

Obsolescence: Low

Further Information:
Usenet's alt.2600 and alt.hackers play host to constant flame wars about just who is and who isn't a hacker, what's worth hacking, and what's been hacked

This mag is the brainchild of Emmanuel Goldstein, who isn't really Emmanuel Goldstein. He's somebody else; he just didn't want you, or more importantly an array of state and federal agencies, to know who he was a couple of years ago, when there weren't very many hackers.

Now, he's got a radio show, everybody knows his real name and his nom d'ordinateur, and he doesn't slink about so much anymore.

Now there are boatloads, their ranks swollen by the proliferation of easy-to-use tools, freely available on the Web and through an array of chat groups, FTP sites, and other Web-based means of communicating software and expertise.

In the past days, early and mid-nineties, Goldstein and his peers hacked computer and phone systems largely for the bragging rights: 2600 was an impressive digest of their exploits and summary of all those ridiculously ill-protected systems everybody depends upon.

Now that weapons-grade hacking and cyberterror are present-day realities, Goldstein and his friends don't look as nasty as they did some years ago. In fact, their rant about doing good by demonstrating where the weaknesses lie, which seemed self-serving at the time, seems more and more on the money.

The magazine is still a hoot, and the back issues are still rich in hacker arcana that doesn't go bad as fast as it should, largely because the people who run the systems don't pay enough attention. The Web site is even better. A recent instance features a sample of what a good hack of the Microsoft.com site might look like. Classic.

We Interrupt This Broadcast: Relive the Events That Stopped Our Lives...from the Hindenburg to the Death of Princess Diana

by Joe Garner, Walter Cronkite, Bill Kurtis (Narrator on CD)

Type: Book/CD audio (154 pages)

First Developed: 1998; Source-books Trade

Price Range: $32–$40

Key Features: History on paper and plastic

Ages: All

Obsolescence: Low

Further Information: Much follow-on material can be found in the national archives at
✳ *http://www.nara.gov/*

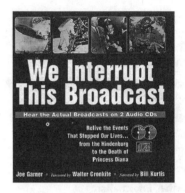

There is nothing in modern life quite so unnerving as the words, "we interrupt this broadcast." Every time I hear them, or see the slide the networks put up when they have a news flash ready to go, my heart stops. For baby boomers, the signature moments are the announcement that JFK had been shot. For their parents, it was Pearl Harbor. For the grandchildren, perhaps it was the death of Diana.

Just hearing the first news flash cannot be enough to resurrect the full impact of these 47 events. No one can understand the emotional impact of →

⤙ READER COMMENTARIES FROM THE NET

A reader from Columbia, S.C., U.S.A., March 23, 1999 ★★★★★

This book is a must for everyone.
Naturally, I was not alive or much too young when events happened during the first half of the century, and unfortunately, I never had an outstanding professor of history either in high school or in college. I, personally, did not care for any of the events pertaining to space because I do not feel that we belong in space.

It seemed as though I were living through the bombing of Pearl Harbor because I could remember my mother telling me how she was feeling so sorry for herself because no family member had remembered her birthday and then she heard on the radio that Pearl Harbor had been bombed. Suddenly, all thoughts of a forgotten birthday disappeared, and she thought how lucky she was to be alive. It seems so real for the first time. The assassination of the two Kennedy brothers and of Martin Luther King—I was, as I am sure many others were, watching television when Lee Harvey Oswald and Robert Kennedy were shot. Everything seemed as though it were just happening. Who can forget the death of Diana, Princess of Wales, and the insincere remarks made by Queen Elizabeth II!!

In the forward Walter Cronkite states, "When the events that change the world occur, we journalists must step up with all the instant thoughtfulness and knowledge we can muster in the face of triumph or tragedy."—page ix.

I highly recommend this book. I purchased mine and read it for the first time just after Thanksgiving. I was so impressed by this book that I purchased three additional books for Christmas gifts.

We Interrupt This Broadcast *continued*

→ Pearl Harbor without having experienced the multi-layered media impressions that followed through the course of World War II: William Shirer reporting from Berlin, Edward R. Murrow from London, and the rest.

No one who lived through the '60s can separate the JFK assassination from the images of his funeral, the increasing doubts caused by the Warren Report, the first time they saw the Zapruder film, the first time they doubted the goodwill and honesty of the government.

This book and the recordings that come with it simply cannot grasp the wholeness of each one of the mainly terrible events covered. Without these recordings, however, one cannot even begin to understand the 20th century.

The Genius of the System: Hollywood Filmmaking in the Studio Era
Written by Thomas Schatz, foreward by Steven Bach

Type: Book (528 pages)

First Developed: 1996; Henry Holt

Price Range: $13–$16

Key Features: Brilliant insight into a mysterious business

Ages: All

Obsolescence: Low

Further Information:
✳ *http://ww.theo.com*
for a take on how the system works today.

I grew up in and around the movie business, and it holds a permanent fascination for me. Not that I'd want to be in it—the people are tough. *Hello, He Lied* is the title of a book about the business, and it captures some of the essence of the industry.

It's hard to imagine it otherwise. After all, the whole business is built around selling people illusions, so why wouldn't the participants constantly be practising.

But there is another facet to the business, which really intrigues me. How do you create intangibles? When the assets of your business drive home at night, how do you sustain an abiding value? What constitutes quality when there are no measurements? In effect, the very same questions apply to the software business. →

Genius of the System *continued*

➜ Everything that a scriptwriter does happens somewhere between his brain and his fingers. Same is true with programmers. How do you manage that (other than heaving people into dark rooms, tossing in pizza, and not letting them out until the project is done)?

This book captures how it was done in the heyday of MGM. It follows some of the most brilliant people ever to work in the business and gets into sufficient detail to cite long sections from transcripts of story meetings. Irving Thalberg, a legendary MGM executive, is a major presence in the book, and it is fascinating to watch him work.

From what I know, if you set aside the changes in technology, the movie business does not work much differently today. This book is one of the secrets of Hollywood.

∞ READER COMMENTARIES FROM THE NET

A reader from Cincinnati, Ohio, June 8, 1998 ★★★★★

Excellent explanation of why the Golden Age was golden.

Schatz's examination of Hollywood's inner workings during its Golden Age (from just before the rise of talkies to about 1960) is enlightening, informative, and entertaining. It's authoritative in its presentation of how studios worked-backing up Schatz's viewpoint that the studio system was as much responsible for the overall quality of that era's films as any other factor (including the stars and directors)-yet it doesn't forget to entertain with intriguing and (dare I say it?) gossipy tidbits about many landmark films and legendary filmmakers. A solid read and, as Steven Bach says in the foreword, an important book.

Churchill and the Secret Service
Written by David Stafford

Type: Book (432 pages)

First Developed: 1998, Overlook Press

Price Range: $25–$30

Key Features: Secret history, authoritative and well-told

Ages: Post–high school

Obsolescence: Low

Further Information: You'll have to wait til the World War II spooks die, because most of the good stories haven't been told publicly yet

In many ways, Winston Churchill founded the modern intelligence business. He drew on his own experience from the Boer War through the 1950s. He understood the value of deception (he will always be remembered by statesmen for his assertion that, in wartime, the truth must be protected by a "bodyguard of lies") and, even more so, the value of knowing what is going on.

All great statesman value intelligence. Lincoln spent the better part of the Civil War across the street from the White House, studying the traffic coming over the telegraph lines. Churchill spent a good part of his tenure as the head of the British Admiralty during World War I in Room 40, the legendary signals intelligence (Sigint) operation he founded. ➜

Churchill and the Secret Service *continued*

→ Churchill early on recognized the windfall of intelligence that could be enjoyed by listening in on radio transmissions and tapping undersea cables (see THE ZIMMERMAN TELEGRAM). This book proposes that the interest began during a visit to Cuba in 1895, when Churchill reported the rebellion against Spain for a British newspaper. Churchill noted the effects of a popular insurrection fought by guerrillas and the value of the good intelligence they had on Spanish locations and operations.

His experience in the Irish troubles and with the rise of the Bolsheviks refined his command of the use of intelligence. When World War II came, with the spectacular opportunity to crack the German Enigma system, Churchill was fully prepared to handle it.

Until World War II, the British were the most sophisticated in the world at the game of intelligence. The mantle was then passed to the Americans, as they had the economic strength to take on the Soviets, in what became a multitrillion-dollar game over the course of the Cold War.

This book holds the kind of history that puts the warp and woof of the 20th century in order.

The Codebreakers: The Comprehensive History of Secret Communication from Ancient Times to the Internet

Written by David Kahn

Type: Book (1,181 pages)

First Developed: 1967, updated 1996; Scribners (reissue)

Price Range: $45–$60

Key Features: The whole story up to the age of computing

Ages: All

Obsolescence: Low

Further Information:
✳ *http://www.aegeanparkpress.com/* for an array of fascinating, rare books about crypto and
✳ *http://www.unimannheim.de/studorg/gahg/PGP/cryptolog1.html* for a very thorough metapage devoted to cryptography

Possibly the strangest outcome of computing is the romanticization of cryptography. Until the last two decades of the 20th century, crypto was the tool of powerful men, the by-product of extraordinary intellects, and an arcane science known and understood by few. It was at the heart of elaborately constructed lies—some spanning several generations—built to guard truths of great consequence.

The Codebreakers may seem tame, even academic today, but when it first appeared—like THE AMERICAN BLACK CHAMBER and THE PUZZLE PALACE—*The Codebreakers* laid out a part of secret history few knew. There was little or nothing romantic about it, however. The tales of deceit, murder, and nervous collapse (codebreaking is very tough on the folks who do it—occasionally driving them mad) abound.

People who follow this stuff keep a copy in their library and always recommend this as the right book to start with. Same here.

Codebreakers *continued*

⊸ READER COMMENTARIES FROM THE NET

A reader from Dallas, Texas,
August 27, 1998 ★★★★★
The definitive book on Cryptography.
David Kahn's newest book updates his previous work, which sits on every cryptographer's, cryptanalyst's, and government Special Intelligence officer's bookshelf in the entire world. If you REALLY want to (know) how ciphers, codes, and systems are broken, Kahn is the author who tells you. Any person knowledgeable in the field of cryptology or intelligence will tell you that Kahn's book has never been equaled. It is known as "The Bible of Cryptology" within the field.

From early Sparta and Rome to the present day, the strengths and weaknesses of systems and devices are presented in clear, concise terms–occasionally with a bit of levity, where appropriate. Novices in the field will find much useful–and highly interesting–information. Professionals always find reminders of the fallibility of "unbreakable" systems.

Kahn's writing style is clear, concise, and analytical. It is never boring.

I was employed by a maker of Cryptographic equipment, and was authorized to discuss key generator and cipher system issues with the heads of national governments. A copy of *Codebreakers* was our most requested–and welcomed–gift. That speaks more eloquently than any words I might craft.

Aviation Week and Space Technology

Web Site for Trade Magazine

http://www.awgnet.com/aviation/index.htm

Type: Magazine (with promotional Web site)

First Developed: 1995

Price Range: Connect time

Key Features: Broad view, thorough research

Ages: 10 and up

Obsolescence: Low

Further Information:
❊ *http://www.oss.net/*
for an excellent Web site devoted to the exploitation of open sources of intelligence

I have subscribed to *Aviation Week* for some years. It is a guilty pleasure, because I have no business doing so. The magazine is devoted exclusively to things that have to do with military and civil aviation, but I always find interesting stuff in *AW&ST*.

Between *AW&ST* and *Monitoring Times*, I have found just about everything worth knowing about black (quiet) aircraft programs like the B-2, F-117 (stealth fighter), and an array of others that aren't yet really public.

There is also consistently great coverage of satellite technology and advanced techniques of warfare, including cyber techniques and infrastructure warfare techniques. The *Aviation Week* folks have access and sources like nobody else.

Inevitably that means that really quiet programs are masked with disinformation, often very subtly rendered. But the *AW&ST* reporters are very sophisticated, and they often signal what's bogus and what's not.

The Web site, although fun, is a pale shadow of the printed magazine. It's meant to be a tease. Get the magazine.

→

Aviation Week *continued*

From an article in *Aviation Week* on the Y2K:

Jan. 1, 2000. The day the dreaded "Millennium Bug" strikes. By now harrowing predictions for the Year 2000 story are a staple of the nightly news. But the aerospace industry has been working on Year 2000 for years. In the following stories, we report on how manufacturers, airlines, the FAA, and Defense Dept. assess the situation eight months before the big event. Aerospace's compliance effort should be placed in the wider context of the industry's immersion in information technology. No manufacturing sector is more complex nor faces as much government oversight. As the industry has moved from software-guided milling machines to software-guided resource planning, some have opted to develop in-house expertise while others

have chosen to contract out. In that regard, Y2K is only one computing issue to be dealt with.

Airlines report that most of them are on schedule to ensure that no New Year's traveler will be stranded when the new decade begins. At the FAA, the main concern is that people keep their hands off systems from June to December to ensure that last-minute monkeying doesn't foul its Y2K fixes.

The Defense Dept. says there are no doomsday nuclear scenarios likely on the big day. Its worry is that small snafus, or cyber attacks, will be the big headache.

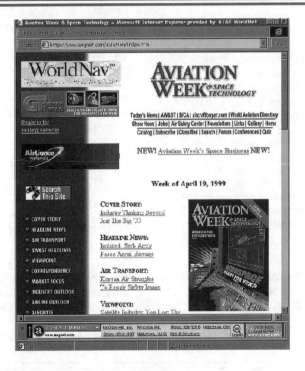

A Peace to End All Peace: Creating the Modern Middle East, 1914–1922
Written by David Fromkin

Type: Book (635 pages)

First Developed: 1990; Avon Books

Price Range: $10–$15

Key Features: Excellent current history

Ages: All

Obsolescence: Low

The Middle East didn't matter a whit to Western people until their navies switched from coal-burning engines to petroleum. Then all hell broke loose. During World War I, it dawned on the British, in particular, that the Middle East was going to become a strategic nexus.

The people, places, and things described in this book are in large measure the major players on the world stage in the first half of the 20th century. If I were to plan a trifecta of great historical reading, I would start with Yergin's THE PRIZE, segue to A PEACE TO END ALL PEACE, and then conclude with the updated version of FROM BEIRUT TO JERUSALEM. Then, perhaps, CRUSADE as a chaser. The arc of power and statecraft in the 20th century is well described in these books.

↝ READER COMMENTARIES
FROM THE NET

A reader from United States, January 8, 1999 ★★★★★
Wonderful book!
The very image of British delegates clustered around outdated maps of Mesopotamia and the Holy Land, muffling curses as they try to pinpoint elusive rivers—with Semitic names they can't even pronounce but which they intend to use as arbitrary borders of the new nations they're delineating—is just one of the many poignant details Fromkin inserts in this marvelous history of the early-20th-century Middle East.

The scope of the work is incredible. Fromkin opens with Churchill as First Lord of the Admiralty, then follows the course of events that led to the dramatic showdown with the Ottoman Empire that erupted into the disastrous and devastating Eastern campaign of World War I.

Kitchener, T. E. Lawrence, Gertrude Belle, Abd al-Azziz, Sykes, Ben-Gurion, Attaturk, Woodrow Wilson, Emir Feisal, and Lloyd George are all participants in this dynamic history and are adroitly described at their best and worst moments. The starry-eyed hopes of the Romantic Arabists opposing the Protestant M.P.s who

envisioned the revival of Israel "from Dan to Beersheba"; Hashemite potentates installed as the ruling monarchs of predominantly Shi'ite territories; British officials in India questioning the motives of their counterparts in Cairo, who hoped to revive a "Moslem Caliphate" to serve as a "Mohammedan" buffer zone stretching from the Levant to Afghanistan, all as an elaborate chess move in the perpetual Great Game, waged between Her Majesty's Government and the uncertain forces—"undoubtedly Jewish"—influencing the Russian Czar.

The fall of the House of Osman and the rise of the C.U.P.; the End of Imperial Russia and the ascendancy of Lenin; the Maronite Christians in Lebanon and Reza Khan in Iran; French colonialism and Italian belligerency; the shocking slaughter of the Armenians and the Greek catastrophe in Smyrna are also discussed in this synoptic overview.

David Fromkin helps elucidate the circumstances that led to the bewildering patchwork of cultures, religions, and ideologies that constitute the modern Middle East. The book would be easier to follow with a few more detailed maps, but it is a beautifully composed and skillfully executed work and well worth the money.

Empire of the Air: The Men Who Made Radio

Written by Tom Lewis and David Ossman, Otherworld Media

Type: Book (402 Pages)

First Developed: 1991; Burlingame/HarperCollins

Price Range: $10–$15

Key Features: Excellent history

Ages: All

Obsolescence: Low

Further Information: This book is out of print and hard to find, but David Ossman of the Firesign Theater (Forward! Into the Past!) has crafted an audio cassette from this work that people say is terrific. It is readily available.

Great advances in technology are always made on the backs of engineers. Rarely do the engineers get their proper historical due. This book tells the stories of three critical figures in the history of the development of radio. Armstrong, who actually made the critical discoveries, DeForest, who took the credit, and Sarnoff, who built the business of radio and hosed the first two guys in the process.

There are similar stories in the history of computing, but they are not yet properly told, because the rich guys are currently writing their own histories.

Some folks think this is the best book ever written on the history of radio, and it is very good indeed—it even makes the arcana of how superheterodyne circuits work comprehensible. But it doesn't get it all. Marconi and Tesla are glossed, and the role the U.S. Navy played in the development of radio broadcasting is trivialized. Those stories can be found elsewhere, in *Tesla: Man Out of Time*, and MILITARY ENTERPRISE AND TECHNOLOGICAL CHANGE.

Extraordinary Popular Delusions & the Madness of Crowds
Written by Charles MacKay

Type: Book (740 pages)

First Developed: 1841; republished by Crown Books

Price Range: $12

Key Features: Introduction by Andrew Tobias

Ages: 18 and up

Obsolescence: Low, too low

Further Information:
✳ *http://isnt.autistics.org/* for further study of human behavior.

Fundamentally, there is no way to properly explain the recent market frenzy over Internet stocks. Anybody with an eye for history can find an array of bubbles like this and tell the tale of how they popped.

The last one like this was built around railroad stocks at the end of the 19th century. When it burst, it scared the bejesus out of everybody, and →

Extraordinary Popular Delusions *continued*

→ only through the attentive ministrations of J. P. Morgan were the panic, and the resultant failure of banks and financial institutions, brought to a halt.

Don't begrudge Bill Gates his spectacular wealth. We may need him, and Warren Buffett—and Michael Jordan for that matter—to bail us out when this bubble bursts.

In the meantime, get a load of this book. It was written in 1841, but it is not dated in the slightest. When human nature changes, then this book will go out of print. No time soon.

↜ READER COMMENTARIES FROM THE NET

A reader from Upper Saddle River, NJ , November 25, 1998 ★★★★★

This is the classic in the field and a must for your library
Just check the stock price of the site you are on or some of the other Internet-based firms, then read about the South Seas bubble and tulip bulb mania and you will understand the relevance of a book written in the 1840s to now.

A reader from Mission Viejo, California, December 22, 1997 ★★★★★

A fascinating journey into the mind of humanity
"Evian" is "naive" spelled backwards. I pay $0.88 per 1,000 liters for water at my house tap. (And I love the taste!) ($3.33/1,000 gallons, in case you are not yet metrified.) Many pay 1,000 times this price for Evian. This just proves that naming, packaging, and imaging are everything when selling to the "general public."

Given this, the book *Extraordinary Popular Delusions and the Madness of Crowds,* by Charles

MacKay, describes the major historical crowd delusions up to 1841, when the book was first published. The forward by Bernard Baruch, written in 1932, is alone worth the price of the book. MacKay does not analyze crowd psychology nor attempt to explain why these events occurred—so don't look here for predictions of the next stock market crash. The events are revealed from a purely historical perspective and in great detail. Overall the book is a fascinating journey into the mind of humanity.

A reader, April 20, 1997 ★★★★★

People never change.
Remember when you were in 8th grade and a cool saying was making its way around? Knowing the saying made you feel cool. How cool do you feel when you hear that in 18th century London for four months the word *Coz!* would reduce bystanders to giggling lumps of jello? Why? Coz! Feeling good about the stock market? Can't suffer more than a 20 percent correction, right? Because all the experts say so. You'll feel so much better after learning of the 17th century tulip market. This book teaches you, in hilariously engaging fashion, with a voice speaking across the centuries, that fads are part of the human condition, not a 20th century phenomenon. Read it and learn.

From Beirut to Jerusalem
Written by Thomas L. Friedman

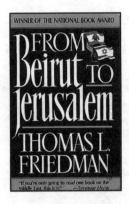

Type:	Book (541 pages)
First Developed:	1990; Anchor
Price Range:	$12–$15
Key Features:	The proper context
Ages:	All
Obsolescence:	Low

Sy Hersh, the famous and controversial investigative journalist, says, "If you're only going to read one book on the Middle East, this is it." Col. David Hackworth, who writes for *Newsweek* and appears on TV constantly as a military analyst, recommends this book to senior grade officers on his Web site. *The New York Times Book Review* says, "*From Beirut to Jerusalem* is the most intelligent and comprehensive account one is likely to read."

The author has a terrific reputation and has been the foreign affairs columnist for the Op-Ed page of *The New York Times*. Comments found on Amazon.com indicate that not everybody agrees. Inevitably, covering a region when people have been ruthlessly murdering each other for half a century is going to lead to charges of bias, and Friedman gets his share, mostly for being pro-Arab.

But a comprehensive take on such a volatile, important area is very rare. There is none I have found for Africa, or South America. Asia has *PACIFIC CENTURY*. The Middle East is richly endowed with both this book and *A PEACE TO END ALL PEACE*.

This book is well worth your time, but make a point of reading *A PEACE TO END ALL PEACE* first, to get historical context. Then, if you are really dedicated, read Yergin's *THE PRIZE*, the story of the oil business, which portrays the realpolitik context within which the world operates when it comes to the Middle East.

**⟿ READER COMMENTARIES
FROM THE NET**

A reader from Portland, OR, February 10, 1999 ★★★★★
For once, a bias in the other direction.
As a Middle Easterner, I can confidently say that this book is an excellent and thought-provoking account of a time and place usually dismissed as inscrutable or treated with facile generalizations. Friedman tells the truth. While he may display a bias to the Arab side, I cannot begin to enumerate the countless books that display a much more significant Zionist bias and escape uncriticized...this book is refreshing, entertaining, and brutally honest. Read it.

A reader from USA, November 24, 1998 ★★★★★
The best book I have ever seen on the Arab-Israeli conflict.
I lived in Israel for seven years, from 1971 to 1978, went to an Israeli high school, and served in the army. I studied Israeli history (through the eyes of the Israel public school system) and have lived among both secular and religious Israelis. I think I can safely say that I had a healthy amount of exposure to both liberal and conservative viewpoints on the Israeli-Palestinian conflict. I consider Thomas Friedman's book an island of sanity in the sea of literature on this subject. I saw no evidence of pro-Arab or anti-Israel bias; he's simply telling it like it is.

The Prize: The Epic Quest for Oil, Money, and Power
by Daniel Yergin, Joseph Stanislaw

Type: Book (928 pages)

First Developed: 1993; Touchstone (reissue)

Price Range: $12–$15

Key Features: Well-illustrated walking tour

Ages: All

Obsolescence: Low

Further Information:
Another excellent book on the subject, now hard to find, is *Seven Sisters* by Anthony Sampson, a writer who published an array of books in the '70s and '80s, most of them quite critical of big business, but all very well researched

The 20th century was made of three things—wings, bytes, and petroleum. The history of aviation can be found on the Discovery and History cable channels Their documentaries, when taken in aggregate, do a spectacular job of telling the story (though you shouldn't ignore SKUNK WORKS by Ben Rich). Computing, in its modern form, is well recollected in the HISTORY OF THE INTERNET Web site, and in the chronological entries devoted to computing in Xiphias' *Encyclopedia Electronica*.

There is only one place to go for the history of oil and that is *The Prize*. This is a companion book to a PBS series (the series itself was terrific, but in comparison to this book, it seems like a gloss on the subject). There is no way you can understand modern statecraft, modern warfare, and modern business without knowing the history of oil.

If you have read this book, the next time someone tells you about the service-based economy of the 21st century, the triumph of cyberspace, or the over-riding strategic significance of information flow, you will know how full of crap they are. Or you can ask a Serb what all that stuff counts for when the lights go out and there is no gas for the car.

The Victorian Internet: The Remarkable Story of the Telegraph and the Nineteenth Century's On-Line Pioneers

Written by Tom Standage

Type: Book (298 pages)

First Developed: 1998; Walker & Co.

Price Range: $15

Key Features: Excellent parallel history

Ages: All

Obsolescence: Low

In the summer of 1996, when I was in London hunting down an encyclopedia database to license for *Encyclopedia Electronica,* I was having breakfast at The East India Club, an 18th-century club for members of the British Raj. Thick with history.

Breakfast is the best meal in the U.K., and it is a delight to read London's papers while enjoying same. Amidst the stack I had on my table was a supplement to *The London Daily Telegraph,* bearing the title, *The Victorian Internet.* Inside was a centerpiece article by Tom Standage, devoted to the parallels between the present day Internet culture and the culture that developed around the telegraph.

It's the same story played out twice, one hundred years apart. 19th-century geeks, altered economies, great stock speculations, and immensely rich men of dubious character. I saved the paper and hauled it out when I started work on *Informatica,* with the intent of finding some way to get the rights to reprint the whole article.

By happenstance, I discovered that Standage had expanded the all too brief article into a full book. History is the best scorecard, and you can't really recognize the players without one.

⟶ READER COMMENTARIES FROM THE NET

A Reader from Waltham, Massachusetts, November 5, 1998 ★★★★★

Great lesson on the introduction of new technology.

This book is a must read for people interested in the introduction of new technology. As the inventor of new technology (including VisiCalc, the PC spreadsheet) I marveled at the parallels with the adoption of the "old" technology of the telegraph. This story really puts the march of new things in perspective.

As an avid reader of the books by Henry Petroski (whose recommendation of this book appears on the back cover), I love anecdotes that help us learn how new technology advances and is assimilated by the general public. This book is full of such insights. Retelling these stories helps us in R&D explain to others how what they may think at first is a seemingly useless invention can actually change the world once its benefits are understood.

This book also shows the opposite, when people expect too much, reminding us to help restrain those that think there is more than is really there. (As Bill Gates reminded people, I believe, at the launch of Windows 95, it doesn't cure diseases, though you'd think so from the hoopla.) This book lets us give direct examples from the 1800s that seem obvious in hindsight.

Star Ware

Written by Philip S. Harrington

http://ourworld.compuserve.com/homepages/pharrington/

Type: Book (paperback, 384 pages)

First Developed: Second edition 1998; John Wiley & Sons

Price Range: $19.95

Key Features: Chunk style writing, very thorough

Ages: Teen and later

Obsolescence: Medium. Book is updated about every two years.

Further Information:
✳ *http://ourworld.compuserve*
.com/homepages/pharrington/
Sw2.htm

Every obsession has its gear, and the best of those obsessions have great books that lay out the gestalt of the gear. If you were into backpacking in the late '60s, nothing came close to *The Complete Walker* by Colin Fletcher. It made the choice of the right drinking cup a key life decision.

This book does the same thing for astronomy. You might find fault in the analysis, and the recommendations Harrington makes, but he is awfully thorough in his coverage of the different gizmos and gadgets. He has suppliers I never heard of, and they have really neat stuff.

His love for astronomy is palpable, even if he is a bit of a gadget freak. *Star Ware* is well worth leaning on, if you are going to spend the kind of money you are likely to spend for good optics and their accoutrements. →

An Excerpt from *Star Ware*

Solar Filters. Monitoring the ever-changing surface of the Sun is an aspect of the hobby that is enjoyed by many. Before an amateur dares look at the Sun, however, he or she must be aware of the extreme danger of gazing at our star. **Viewing the Sun without proper precautions, even for the briefest moment, may result in permanent vision impairment or even blindness.** This damage is caused primarily by the Sun's ultraviolet rays, the same rays that cause sunburn. While it may take many minutes before the effect of sunburn is felt on the skin, the Sun's intense radiation will burn the eye's retina in a fraction of a second.

There are two ways to view the Sun safely: either by projecting it through a telescope or binoculars onto a white screen or piece of paper, or by using a special filter. Sun filters come in a couple of different varieties. Some fit in front of the telescope, while others attach to the eyepiece. **NEVER** use the latter...that is, the eyepiece variety. They can easily crack under the intense heat of the Sun (focused by the telescope as is the Sun's image), leading tragically to blindness. Happily, I know of no new telescope that is supplied with an eyepiece solar filter, but many were in the past.

"If the pure and elevated pleasure to be derived from the possession and use of a good telescope... were generally known, I am certain that no instrument of science would be more commonly found in the homes of intelligent people."

—Garrett Serviss,
Pleasures of the Telescope
(a 19th-century book
quoted in *Star Ware*)

→

Star Ware *continued*

From the Star Ware Web Site:
THREE BROAD TYPES OF TELESCOPES

Today's amateur astronomers have a wide and varied selection of equipment from which to choose. To the novice stargaz-er, it all appears very enticing but very complicated. One of the most confusing aspects of amateur astronomy is "tele-scope vernacular"—terms whose meanings are shrouded in mystery for many novice stargazers. "Do astronomers speak a language all their own?" is the cry frequently echoed by newcomers to the hobby. The answer is "yes," but it is a language that, unlike some foreign tongues, is easy to learn. Here is your first lesson.

Many different kinds of telescopes have been developed over the years. Even though their variations in design are great, all fall into one of three broad categories according to how they gather and focus light. Refractors have a large lens (the objective) mounted in the front of the tube to perform this task, while reflectors use a large mirror (the primary mirror) at the tube's bottom. The third class of telescope, called catadioptrics, places a lens (here called a corrector plate) in front of the primary mirror. In each instance, the telescope's prime optic (objective lens or primary mirror) brings the incoming light to a focus, then directs that light through an eyepiece to the observer's waiting eye.

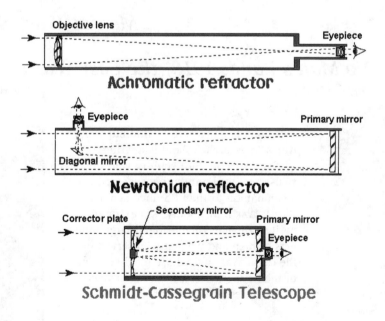

Achromatic refractor

Newtonian reflector

Schmidt-Cassegrain Telescope

Smart Weapons! Smart War?

T*he grinding, awful nature of 20th-century war has remained substantially the same for over 80 years. It has been characterized by masses of men and armored vehicles, tearing at one another with increasingly powerful and destructive weapons.*

The addition of conventional air power and the threat of nuclear weapons have not fundamentally altered the equation. The lives of men traded for territory. It would be wise to ponder the real experience and cost of this kind of warfare before we do it again.

Unfortunately, most of the people who are making such decisions in the U.S. government have never directly suffered such experiences. They would do well to read the following books and ponder the painful sameness of the experience of these men, in these four wars.

Men at War: No Man's Land
Also published as
No Man's Land: 1918, the Last Year of the Great War
Written by John Toland

Type: Book (650 pages)

First Developed: 1994

Price Range: $20–$30

Key Features: First-rate history of the last days of World War I

Ages: High school and beyond

Obsolescence: Low

Further Information:
✳ *http://www.worldwar1.com* for a first class Web site devoted to the Great War. See also Barbara Tuchman's fine history, *The Guns of August,* for insight into how nations stumble into wars

This book is quite hard to find but well worth the search. Toland is a writer whose books on 20th century warfare are well-researched and highly regarded. As a companion to the CBS documentary WORLD WAR I, MEN AT WAR is extraordinarily valuable. Toland found large numbers of men and women who served in the Great War, and whose lucid accounts of their experiences capture the essence of the experience of war.

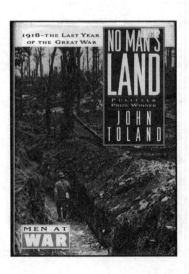

Smart Weapons! *continued*

Band of Brothers: E Company, 506th Regiment, 101st Airborne from Normandy to Hitler's Eagle's Nest
Written by Stephen E. Ambrose

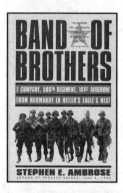

Stephen Ambrose has endeared himself to readers in North America by gathering oral histories of significant campaigns in World War II into coherent history. This book is likely the best of the many he has done. In it, he tells the story of Easy Company and their trip from basic training to Utah Beach on D-day, and on to the Battle of the Bulge, and finally the liberation of part of the Dachau concentration camp. This book gives meaning to the word attrition.

Type: Book (336 pages)

First Developed: 1993

Price Range: $11–$15

Key Features: Quintessential European World War II on the ground history

Ages: High school and beyond

Obsolescence: Low

Further Information:
http://www.uno.edu/%7Eeice/ for the Eisenhower Center, to which Ambrose contributes substantial time and material

➤ READER COMMENTARIES FROM THE NET

A reader from the United States, April 6, 1999 ★★★★★

Window into the souls of the survivors.

As a grandchild of one of the men who fought in E Company and survived, I must say this is the most fascinating account of my grandfather's experiences that I have ever read. Also I was glad that the author reflected the respect shown to Lt. Winters and the scorn shown to Capt. Sobel by both my grandfather and most of the other members of the company. I loved this book because it explains things to generations who have never experienced war, yet still has the opinions of the men who fought the war. Of all the books on the soldier's experience in World War II that I've read, I think this one is the best.

A reader from Provo, Utah, March 6, 1999 ★★★★★

I came to understand my heritage!

I have always tried to understand what my grandfathers went through. World War II seems so distant for our younger generation. I bought the book for my dad but ended up reading it before I gave it to him. I could not put it down. I have never seen history painted so vividly in my entire life. It brought a personal touch that made me feel very emotional as the men of Easy Co. died or were injured in combat. This is a great opportunity to understand what our ancestors went through. Stephen Ambrose writes history smooth as fiction. I loved it!!

A reader from Ledyard, CT, U.S., January 3, 1999 ★★★★★

An Excellant, Exciting, Accurate account of the 506th PIR.

Thank you Stephen Ambrose! My father, George L Potter, was in the 101st Airborne, 506th Parachute Infantry Regiment, E Company World War II. Band of Brothers, is a true story about what my father and his buddies went through during the war. I have learned so much about the war, the men, the battles, and my father.

What a great book about brave young parachute infantry soldiers of World War II. They are all heroes. God bless them.

Smart Weapons! *continued*

The Other Side of Time: A Combat Surgeon in World War II

Written by Brendan Phibbs

Type: Book (341 pages)

First Developed: 1987

Price Range: $11–$15

Key Features: Quintessential European World War 2 on the ground history

Ages: High school and beyond

Obsolescence: Low

Further Information:
❊ ***http://members.aol.com/rhrongstad/hfmed/milmed.htm***
Metapage devoted to military medicine sites

My father sent me this book a decade ago, with a note suggesting that I and my brothers and sisters needed to know how rough the European theater of operations was and what kind of horrors and sacrifices the men who fought in that theater suffered. This book is as difficult to track down as the Toland book on World War I, and just as worth the effort.

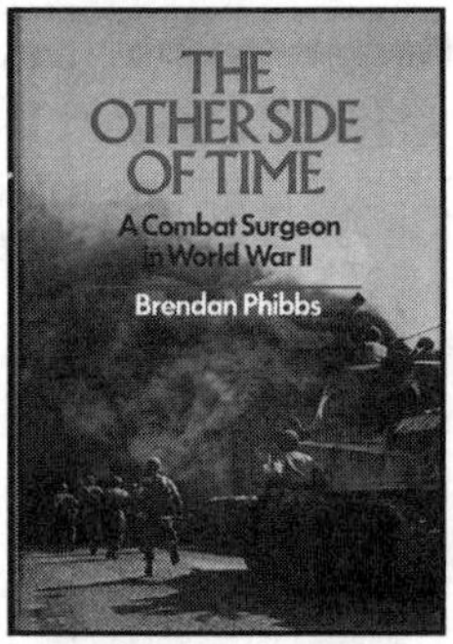

READER COMMENTARIES FROM THE NET

A reader from Washington, DC, October 29, 1998 ★★★★★

My favorite book!

I have an old paperback copy of this book that I have passed from friend to friend. Mr. Phibbs is one of those rare writers who can paint pictures with words. The book should be added to college reading lists. The author writes about his life as a combat surgeon during World War II. It is a classic.

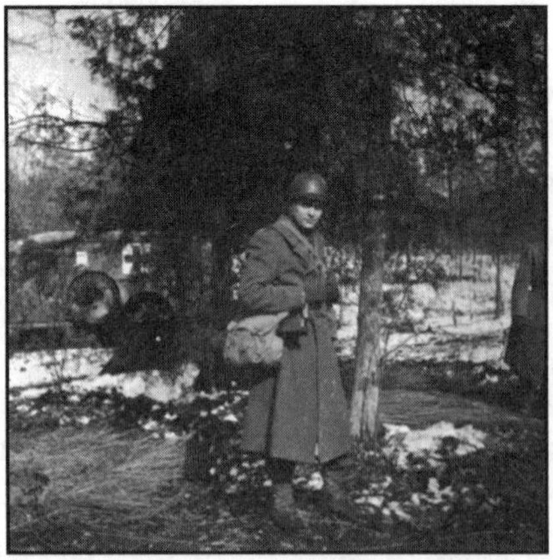

Brendan Phibbs, soldier

Smart Weapons! *continued*

Iwo Jima: Legacy of Valor
Written by Bill D. Ross

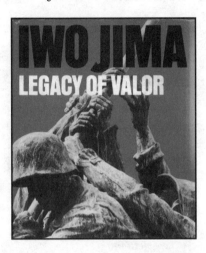

The Japanese were a very brutal and intransigent enemy, as people who are defending their homelands often tend to be. Every time such a campaign against such an enemy is pondered, the planners should reread this book.

Type: Book (380 pages)

First Developed: 1986; Random House

Price Range: $25–$30

Key Features: Quintessential account of the Pacific theater in World War II

Ages: High school and beyond

Obsolescence: Low

Further Information:
❊ *http://www.edu.cn/history/ www.arts.cuhk.hk/NanjingMass acre/NMchron.html*
for a short chronology of Japanese militarism leading up to and through World War II

➥ READER COMMENTARIES FROM THE NET

A reader from Pahrump, NV, December 15, 1998 ★★★★★
Vivid example of doing what it takes to succeed
This book provides a vivid example of the requirements for achieving victory under conditions that are unimaginable. If there was ever a hell on earth it had to be Iwo Jima. It also provides a keen insight into the politics of war.

A reader from Lake City, Florida, October 18, 1998 ★★★★★
Valor, Sacrifice, Suffering, and Savagery
Over the past few months I have read many accounts of the war in the Pacific. E. B. Sledge's *With the Old Breed* told of valor, sacrifice, suffering, and savagery through the eyes of one man. Iwo Jima gives a vast panorama of those things. We see the battle in all its horror, but we also see the good accomplished from the terrible sacrifice of so many men. The book gives a balanced, comprehensive account of a bloody page of American history.

A reader from Maui, Hawaii, April 22, 1998 ★★★★★
Feel what the battle for Iwo Jima was really like.
Iwo Jima was for a month in the course of history a living hell and Bill Ross has been able to capture what it was like to be a Marine fighting and dying for a desolate yet strategic chunk of volcanic rock in the Pacific. This is a book that will put you on the front lines of the battle and leave you in awe at the sacrifice of so many lives to secure Iwo Jima.

Smart Weapons! *continued*

We Were Soldiers Once...and Young:
Ia Drang: The Battle That Changed the War in Vietnam
Written by Harold G. Moore and Joseph Galloway

An account of the 34-day battle that led to the vast expansion of the American commitment to South Vietnam. Grinding, awful, intimate, and inhuman; this battle and its miseries are indistinguishable from the miseries described in Toland's book on World War I.

Type: Book (448 psges)

First Developed: 1993; Harper Perennial

Price Range: $12

Key Features: Quintessential account of the ground war in Vietnam

Ages: High school and later

Obsolescence: Low

Further Information:
✳ *http://students.vassar.edu/ ~ vietnam/*
a fine Metasite devoted to the Vietnam War, rich in hyperlinks.

☛ READER COMMENTARIES FROM THE NET

A reader from New Orleans, LA, July 9, 1998 ★★★★★

David and Goliath—Fear and learning in the Ia Drang

As an Infantry Lieutenant who flew helicopters in Vietnam and a student of military history for the past 40 years I found *We Were Soldiers Once and Young* to be a fascinating read. It is really two books that run concurrently. The first is about the leadership of a small, outgunned army of citizen soldiers who were trying to figure out a way to win against the big guy. This they learned in the Ia Drang and, given that there would be no change in U.S. strategy to negate the knowledge the NVA acquired from this battle, the Vietnam War was effectively lost at that point for the U.S.

The second is as close as you can get to that dirt in the face, taste of terror in your mouth, please God let me live through this feeling that all soldiers experience in battle without having to endure the actual thing. So engrossing was this part of the book that, although I already knew the outcome, I found myself trying to will some of the individual participants in this battle to a different conclusion than the one that was already written for them.

This book is an engrossing piece of living history, and I highly recommend it. Yes, war is hell and a tragedy almost beyond comprehension. Commanders make mistakes that lose them. All men are not heroes and not everybody remembers things the same way, but for those who of you who know a Vietnam era grunt who humped the boonies and you have wondered why he is different from everybody else, this book will help you understand. For those who want some insight into what happened in Vietnam and why we lost that war, this book will answer some of those questions. For those interested in only a gut-wrenching account of ground combat this book will give it to you with nothing held back. I think we all should read it, and maybe again.

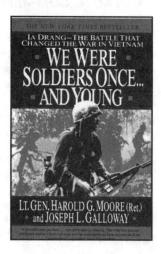

Smart Weapons! *continued*

Crusade: The Untold Story of the Persian Gulf War

by Rick Atkinson

Type: Book (520 pages)

First Developed: 1994; Houghton Mifflin

Price Range: $11–$15

Key Features: Quintessential Gulf War history

Ages: All

Obsolescence: Low

Further Information:
❋ *http://www.pbs.org/wgbh/pages/frontline/gulf/*
PBS's Frontline Web site devoted to the Gulf War

Behind the brilliant slaughter (Atkinson's phrase) of the land campaign are hidden the seeds of a new kind of warfare–war on infrastructure–which may characterize the other means by which the U.S. will conduct its policies in the coming century. The air war aimed at degrading the command and control infrastructure of Saddam Hussein, enhanced by the brilliant new technology weapons without explosives, designed to crash power and communications systems–these are the hidden secrets of this account.

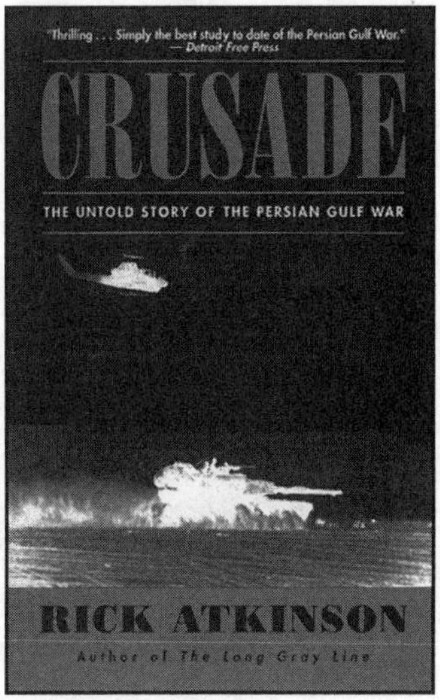

READER COMMENTARIES FROM THE NET

A reader from USA, April 27, 1999 ★★★★★

For military history buffs, this is a real page-turner.

The straight poop on behind the scenes politics and decisions for Desert Storm.

A reader from Mesa, AZ , August 23, 1998 ★★★★★

The single best account of the Gulf War to date

For anybody even remotely interested in what happened on the ground during the course of Desert Storm, this book is a must read! Atkinson keeps his text informative, yet entertaining. His exhaustive research and easy-to-digest prose makes this book a surefire way for the layman with no previous military or historical background to fully comprehend and appreciate the actions of our armed forces in this conflict.

Smart Weapons! Smart War? Part II

As I write this, NATO forces have escaped the long march into a meatgrinder. Kosovo does not have the billiard table terrain of Iraq, with an enemy arrayed in fixed, entrenched positions (see CRUSADE). The enemy would be mobile, clever, resourceful and fighting a defense of their home ground (see IWO JIMA), very much like the NVA in Viet Nam (see WE WERE SOLDIERS ONCE). Even so, largely because of the recent horrific news video of Kosovans executed and displaced, the necessary prerequisites for a U.S. commitment to a ground war were brought into place. Polls showed popular support for ground action, and many members of Congress spoke of a ground war as the only effective alternative.

There was no denying the utter evil of Milosevic, nor the necessity of acting to put an end to it. Equally certain, however, was the stupidity of an armed incursion into the hilly, forested terrain of Kosovo. There was an alternative, and the allies successfully exercised it.

That alternative did not naturally occur to America's middle-aged circle of power. The aging soldiers, politicians, and journalists often chased the demons of their respective pasts. Some of the soldiers wanted to show they could win a land-based war, many politicians (in particular, those in the liberal camps of congress) wanted to demonstrate that it was their constitutional prerogative to authorize war, and the journalists wanted to show that they will not stand in the way of a "righteous" war against an evil adversary. An armed invasion with popular support, undertaken to rid the world of evil, was a lovely dream.

That dream could easily have become a nightmare if U.S. soldiers traipsed into the Balkan quagmire. Every NATO soldier who crossed the border into Yugoslavia would have been perceived as a clear and present danger by the Russians, who have spent two centuries in fearful paranoia of land-based threats—often with good reason. A frightened, skittish Russia, still equipped with a nuclear arsenal and in unsteady hands, is a very bad thing.

Smart Weapons! Part II *continued*

On War

by Carl Von Clausewitz, Michael Howard (Editor), Peter Paret (Editor)

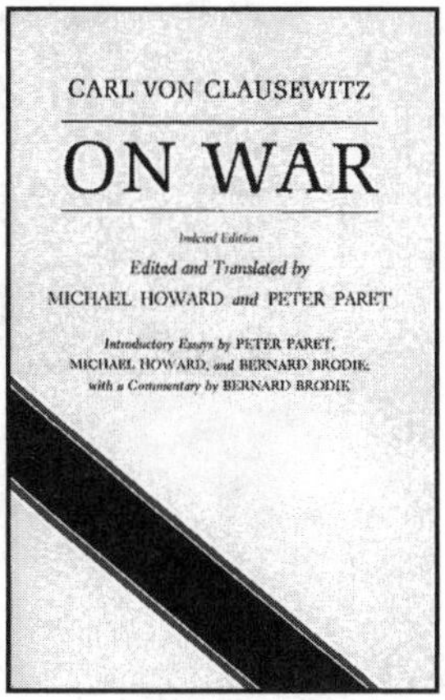

Since the work's first appearance in 1832, *On War* has been read throughout the world, and has stimulated generations of soldiers, statesmen, and intellectuals. It promotes war as the execution of political policy by others means, and introduces the critical concept of friction, the aggregate wearing effect of the unexpected–a particularly familiar effect to those who have fought ground wars.

Type: Book (461 pages)

First Developed: 1989; Princeton Unversity Press

Price Range: $18

Key Features: Fundamental western treatise on the conduct of war

Ages: All

Obsolescence: Low

Further Information:
✻ *http://www.mnsinc.com/cbassfrd/CWZHOME/CWZBASE.htm*
for a Web site devoted to Clausewitz

READER COMMENTARIES FROM THE NET

A reader from White Deer, PA,
August 24, 1998 ★★★★★

teaches you how to think

A fine book that teaches how to think and reason properly. His attitude of taking nothing for granted, and a few exceptionally applicable chapters make up for it's age, and so called out-dated material

Von Clausewitz is read by officers and investors alike. It is a building block in logic. A fine work that must be slowly digested and enjoyed.

Von Clausewitz was a genius.

Every American who might have crossed that border into hostile, non-permissive territory was a potential hostage, worth more to Milosevic alive than dead. He or she could be paraded before cameras, and physically chained to every decent target the NATO forces might designate for destruction from the air. An America paralyzed into inaction by fearful images on the evening news was the certain outcome.

Smart Weapons! Part II *continued*

On Strategy: A Critical Analysis of the Vietnam War

Written by Harry G. Summers

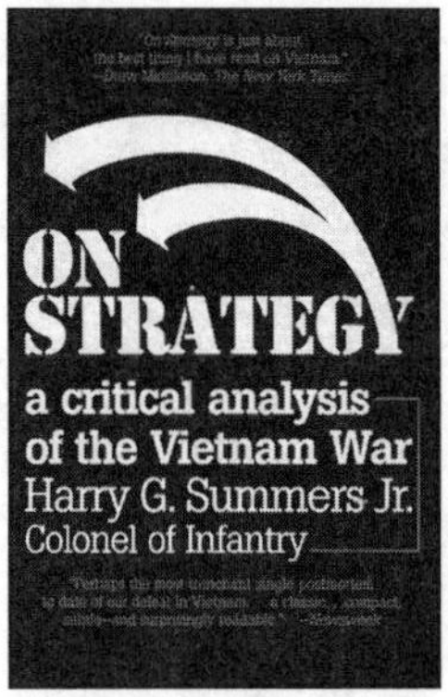

Type: Book (224 pages)

First Developed: 1982; Presidio Press (Reissue)

Price Range: $12

Key Features: Fundamental western treatise on the conduct of war in the age of mass media

Ages: All

Obsolescence: Low

Further Information:
❇ *http://www.vietvet.org*
for the vet's point of view on the matter

Summers made no friends with this book. Rather, he made a point that is as broadly applicable as any of Von Clausewitz' principlas–a point that most of Summer's detractors grudgingly acknowledge. In America, war cannot be conducted without clearly stated aims and popular, politically legitimized support.

The underlying truth of Summers analysis is this: in modern times of mass media, no industrialized society can conduct war without abiding popular support–otherwise, who will make the weapons, ammunition and supplies necessary for technology-driven war?

And the same goes for the adversaries.

READER COMMENTARIES FROM THE NET

A reader from Anchorage, Alaska,
October 28, 1998 ★★★★★

Classic Book about Necessity of Political Support for War

This book should be required reading for all field grade colonels on up. In meticulous detail it details the failing of military strategy in Vietnam because clear goals were not identified and political support obtained for same. It correctly identifies the limitations of military power, which cannot "win hearts and minds" but only bury them. The best tribute to this book is that every American military leader fighting a war after this book was published has followed the letter and tenor of the recommendations set forth in the book. Summers should have received numerous decorations for the contributions to military strategy this book contains. Instead he was shunned by the military establishment (which) nevertheless reads and follows his book, because he had the audacity in his book to name names and criticize those in power who failed to follow even the most basic military tenets in conducting the Vietnam War. However, long after those leaders are forgotten, this book will still be required reading for American military leaders who do not wish to repeat the mistakes made in the Vietnam War.

A reader from North Palm Beach, FL,
January 5, 1998 ★★★★★

A Deep, Insightful Discussion of What Went Wrong in Vietnam

With careful documentation and crystal prose, Summers tells us how and why the Vietnam War went so terribly wrong. Playing Von Clauswitz against Westmoreland and LBJ, we see with shocking clarity how our imprecise political goals gave birth to the crippled military plan, and how we literally won every battle yet lost the war. This is a must-read for all thinking Vietnam Veterans, and belongs alongside Sheehan's *A Bright and Shining Lie*, and Herr's *Dispatches* as library essentials. Buy it, read it, then mail it to your Congressman!

Smart Weapons! Part II *continued*

The alternative, well executed, was war on the Yugoslav infrastructure, conducted with the best of our smart weapons, and designed to deny the Yugoslavian people the services of the modern world. Using the same technology the NATO forces employed to degrade and destroy Milosevic's military, NATO also degraded and destroyed the in-country systems of water, power, communication, and transportation. Little by little, 20th century life came to an end, industry failed, the lights went out.

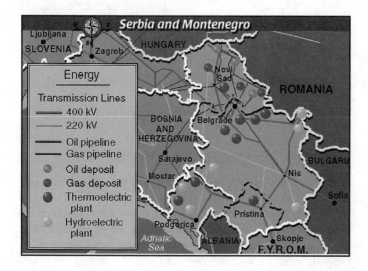

An Image from the CIA World Factbook on the Web (http://www.odci.gov/cia/publications/balkan/serbia4.html), with good insight into the infrastructure targets which drew NATO's attention in the Yugoslavian conflict. In early May 1999, the U.S. Government revealed the use of a remarkable new smart weapon, designed to take out the electrical systems, and used to great effect in Belgrade.

The munition, reportedly designated the BLU-114/B, detonates above an electrical transformer and sprays carbon fiber filaments into the transformers, shorting them out. The targeted transformers were at nodes that covered electrical power in Belgrade. Although NATO sought to target only the "inner spokes of the hub," the ripple effect on the Yugoslavian power grid was widespread. The bomb has been until recently a "black program", meaning its development has been conducted in the utmost secrecy. It does not show up in Pentagon budget documents. The bomb is guided by GPS satellites, and seeks to accomplish what was done by cruise missles in the Gulf War, as described in CRUSADE.

Smart Weapons! Part II *continued*

The Art of War

by Sun Tzu, James Clavell (Editor and Translator)

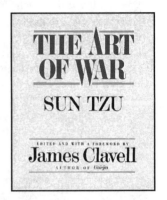

Type: Book (222 pages)

First Developed: 1989; Delacorte Press

Price Range: $12–$14

Key Features: Translation by writer with understanding of the language and reality

Ages: High school and beyond

Obsolescence: Low

Further Information:
http://www.tscm.com/SunTzuGi lestxt.html
over-the-Net translation of Sun Tzu, with classic commentary

The art of military strategy, presented in classic Asian aphoristic form. Well translated by Clavell, who is far better known for such engrossing novels as *Tai-Pan* and *Sho-Gun*. Understanding war at this level of abstraction can provide sufficient distance to think differently.

> "...to fight and conquer in all your battles is not supreme excellence; supreme excellence consists in breaking the enemy's resistance without fighting."
>
> —Sun Tzu

➥ READER COMMENTARIES FROM THE NET

A reader from Florida,
February 23, 1999 ★★★★★
The single best translation of Sun Tzu's The Art of War
I bought this book out of curiosity, as I have read several translations. This one took the cake. It is easy to read and more complete than any of the other translations I have read. And the section on the life and times of Sun Tzu is excellent. I put this book on my shelf as a handy reference.

1n effect, we put the neighborhood bully of Middle Europe in isolation, and took away his privileges. Nothing went in, nothing went out, the goal was complete quarantine. In effect, NATO offered an ultimatum to the Yugoslavian people: stay with Milosevic and return to the 19th century, or leave him and join the rest of the world in the 21st century.

The offer was made by Web site, by TV and leaflet. We conducted psychological warfare by high-tech, and aimed it at the cosmopolitans of Belgrade and the other cities, the urban core of Milosevic's support. All the while, the Allies supplied food and logistical expertise to handle the refugees. We began to arm and train them in preparation for repatriation.

There was no reason to set foot in the land Milosevic controled. There was no reason for the U.S. and NATO to meet any smaller adversary on their ground and their terms.

Smart Weapons! Smart War? Part III

There was no reason to go to battle. There were other means to break the enemy's resistance. Tomahawk Land-Attack Missiles and Joint Direct Attack Munitions, trading on the superaccurate stand-off targeting made possible by GPS (see GPS) can be replaced by mass production, young men and women cannot.

This is minimal risk war-making for the 21st century, with slow and steady impact. Infrastructure Warfare designed with the understanding that modern tyrants have no power without popular support and a working civil infrastructure.

Laser and GPS guided weapons did not amplify Russian paranoia, as ground troops would have. In fact, Russia stood to enjoy a windfall, taking hard Yugoslav currency for the engineering and reconstruction of the bridges, dams, pipelines, power grids, telephone switches, and aqueducts.

Milosevic won the first battle. Kosovo was effectively cleansed. He could have won the war by murderous attrition of our forces on his own ground.

A ground war would have been as silly and pitiful as was the French defense by mounted horseman and infantry in red and blue machine-gunner friendly uniforms at the outset of World War I. It would have been stupid for the U.S. to sacrifice young men and women to fight other people's civil wars, for other people's liberties, with 50-year-old military doctrine.

We took another path. NATO turned Yugoslavia into an isolation ward with the barest of services. We waited for the Yugoslav people to come to their senses. We denied them the comforts of modern life. It didn't take long. They caved.

And in so doing, set the terms for armed conflict in the 21st century. Now the U.S. must look to its own defenses, as it is woefully ill-prepared to handle an Infrastructure attack at home.

Sacred Origins of Profound Things

Written by Charles Panati

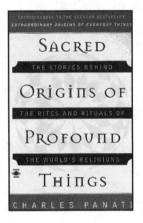

Type: Book (240 pages)

First Developed: 1996; Penguin

Price Range: $12

Key Features: A book with a strange point of view

Ages: Post-high school

Obsolescence: Low

Further Information: Read *Why Christianity Must Change or Die* by John Shelby Spong for a rational approach to resolving faith and history (recommended by my father. When he gave it to my sister, Dorothy to read, she wrote, "This book has had a profound effect on me. For years I've thought that my persistant doubts about common interpreatations of the Bible were indicative of some great moral deficiency on my part. How liberating to find that an Episcopal Bishop feels the same way!")

Charles Panati has been publishing books of peculiar scholarship for years, with great success. The others were devoted to the origin of everyday stuff like safety pins. Here he looks at the arcana of the church, and to a great extent, the Catholic church.

Interesting stuff; however, folks who prefer the spirit of things rather than the secular, material explanation may not be terribly happy. Panati seems to have had a good time—of the research for the book he said, "I never knew religion could be so much fun."

☛ READER COMMENTARIES FROM THE NET

A reader from Cambridge, MA, November 25, 1998 ★★★★☆

An excellent first-stop resource to further study.

I am a Catholic seminarian who spends a lot of time wondering "how it all connects"—which I believe it does. This little handbook helps to initiate further study into the religious customs of Catholic Christianity and the fundamental links they might have to other religions. The book is biased to Catholic ritual and spirituality, but one need simply to jump off that starting point to examine deeper roots that reveal a wider human experience.

A reader from Metro Detroit, MI, March 3, 1998 ★★★★☆

Profound.

An extraordinary read. Though I didn't see eye-to-eye with all the author believes, he does raise significant issues, nearly always backed with historical fact. Sure to shake your religious belief to its very foundations (as it often really needs to be). Personally, I was appreciative of such a book as I was brought up Catholic as a child, fell away, and returned as an adult only to find that what was being preached by the Catholic church (to my adult ears) was NOT in sync with what my adult eyes were reading in the Bible.

Devout Catholics will find this book sacrilege, whereas open-minded Christians of any denomination may benefit from the historical facts and origins to search their souls for truth and enlightenment, instead of blindly being led by religious leaders.

I'll read other books by Panati (with an open mind but not blindly).

The Mind of the South
Written by Wilbur Joseph Cash

Type: Book (464 pages)

First Developed: 1941; (1991 Vintage Books)

Price Range: $12

Key Features: Deep insight

Ages: Post high school

Obsolescence: Low

Further Information:
❋ *http://www.virginia.edu/ ~ history/courses/courses.old/ hius323/cash.html*
for more on the author, Cash

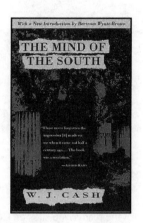

My stepfather, Bill Stout, was a CBS newsman for the better part of his life. He covered the civil rights movement, the Apollo program, and Vietnam. From the time he met my recently divorced mother in 1971 to the day he died in 1989, he had a dramatic effect on my view of the world.

His bookshelf was not vast, though he was a voracious reader. In the latter days of his life, he read good popular fiction. I don't believe he found much joy in reading modern history and commentary. His memories were too fresh, and his views framed and set by his experience.

It was the older books on his shelf that seemed to mean a great deal. This is one that he pulled off the shelf one time and said, "If you want to grasp what goes on down there, you ought to read this."

It's old, and hard to find now, but it describes the forces that made the South and struggled so mightily to keep it that way. There is much in this book that still lives down there, so my step-father said. I don't know by my own lights, but I'll take his word for it and pass his recommendation along.

"No one, among the multitudes who have written about the South, has been more penetrating or more persuasive than Mr. Cash."

—*The New York Times*

"Sometimes insightful, sometimes infuriating, The Mind of the South is mandatory reading for anyone who would understand the region. Wyatt-Brown's brilliant introduction reveals the relevance of Cash and his book to our own times."

-- Charles Joyner,
Burroughs Distinguished Professor of
Southern History and Culture, University of South Carolina

Lincoln on Democracy
Edited by Mario Cuomo

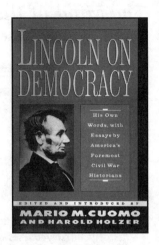

Type: Book (416 pages)

First Developed: 199?

Price Range: $25-$30

Key Features: The essential thoughts of an essential man

Ages: All

Obsolescence: Low

Further Information:
http://members.aol.com/RVSNor ton/Lincoln2.html
of the many Web sites on Lincoln this one stands out; it's maintained by a dedicated history teacher, and he takes e-mail questions.

Perhaps it was the civil rights movement, or the centennial of the Civil War, but baby boomers were given a far greater appreciation of Abraham Lincoln than are children in today's schools.

Perhaps it has become unfashionable to present heroes without caveats, biography without blemish, history without its dark side. In so doing, though, kids are denied something awfully important.

Lincoln was human, but he did extraordinary things. He was a politician, but he made governance something of the highest honor. He gave speeches, but some of them were simply sublime. And he spent the better part of his life pondering American democracy, from when it was hardly in its fourth decade, until it was put to the extreme test of the Civil War. Perhaps our version of Modern Times will no longer tolerate making Lincoln, or anyone for that matter, a hero. But his thoughts and ideas are still pure and heroic. This book is a worthy modern assembly of them.

"I desire to so conduct the affairs of this administration that if at the end, when I come to lay down the reins of power, if I have lost every other friend on earth, I shall at least have one friend left, and that friend shall be down inside me."

—Abraham Lincoln, 1864
(suggested by George Bell,
CEO of Excite@Home)

"...Never give in, never give in, never, never, never, never—in nothing, great or small, large or petty—never give in except to convictions of honour and good sense. Never yield to force; never yield to the apparently overwhelming might of the enemy."

—Winston Churchill, October 29, 1941, Harrow School
(Suggested by my neighbor, Russell Hunziger, who also recommends
http://www.winstonchurchill.org/never.htm)

⊸ READER COMMENTARIES FROM THE NET

A reader, April 23, 1997 ★★★★★

Mario Cuomo Does Lincoln

Mr. Cuomo has put together a rewarding synopsis of several of A. Lincoln's speeches and writings. He added his own editorial content to make us better understand Mr. Lincoln's thoughts. This volume is easy to read and the themes are current for the times. Highly Recommended.

Turn of the Century

There is a great deal of the past turn of the century in the forthcoming turn of the century. Times are good and some businessmen boast extraordinary wealth, Europe is seething, Asia is an uncertainty, the government is filled with backroom dealings and a yen to fix things far from our shores. Science is exploring x-rays, and technology is mass manufacturing cars. It is more than instructive to read about the time, 100 years ago, when the American Century was just about to begin. It is even more compelling to see these times, and the picture books noted here are stunning. Then as now, the forces that will mold the future are at play. If you look hard enough at the pictures, you can read some of it in the people's eyes.

America 1900: The Turning Point
Written by Judy Crichton

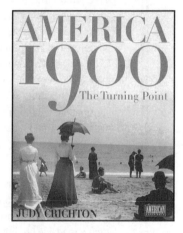

Type: Book (288 pages)

First Developed: 1998; Henry Holt & Company

Price Range: $20–$30

Key Features: Bound to a fine PBS documentary, available on VHS tape

Ages: All

Obsolescence: Low

Further Information:
✳ *http://www.pbs.org/wgbh/pages/amex/1900/*
for the PBS Web site devoted to the three-hour series from which the book was drawn

Built as a companion volume to a three-hour PBS documentary, this book in many ways parallels the video, dealing in vignettes and characters. Employing a month-by-month structure, it reads well and gives a *Ragtime*-like sense of dramatic foreshadowing to the time.

The pictures in the book are not of stiffly posed politicians and luminaries but of normal folk for the most part, conducting the normal business of their lives. There are pictures every couple of pages, on the average.

Every chapter features a sidebar called "Other Stories of Interest" with excerpts from selected newspaper articles of the month (primarily New York papers and *The Washington Post,* with an occasional appearance from the outlying territories, like Indianapolis and San Francisco).

Everything is normal here, but everything suggests the amazing things to come, good and bad, in the 20th century.

∽ READER COMMENTARIES FROM THE NET

A reader from Upstate New York, December 7, 1998 ★★★★★

You'll definitely want America: 1900 in your library!

America 1900: The Turning Point by Judy Crichton is a fascinating read!! This is NOT "just another history book," for Crichton is a master of detail and research. As she writes about the events and characters that define the year 1900, even the most avid history buff will be amazed by hitherto unknown facts and tidbits. Ms. Crichton writes about the terrible labor strikes of 1900—among them the chilling story of the underpaid Italian immigrants who, when trying to get minimum wage raised from $1.35 to $1.50, found themselves facing the N.Y. State militia at Croton Dam. "There are enough soldiers here now to make a lunch out of all the Italians within two miles of the dam," said one Sergeant. The description of this and other events is so vivid that I felt I was part of the scene. This was in America??? At Croton Dam??

Ms Crichton writes: "On Fifth Avenue, men and women of what was called the leisure class were studying the shops and studying each other. The success of the walk could be measured by the briefest encounter, a meeting of the eyes, the slightest bow of the head." You read of "great and ostentatious wealth"; of life in the South where 90 percent of black Americans were in some ways "more limited than it had been in the days of slavery." In 1900, Private Carl Sandburg returned from the Spanish-American War, and the reader learns that although less than 2,000 Americans were killed during the actual fighting, 8,000 died of terrible tropical diseases! I found myself wondering, "Where did she find THAT out?" and enjoyed turning to the many footnotes for additional information. I got to know President and Mrs. McKinley, Jack London, and Theordore Roosevelt much more intimately than when I met them in college, and until this book, I had no idea how remarkable Lou Hoover (Herbert's wife) was. An amazing woman.

The book makes familiar and not-so-familiar names and obscure little facts and observations make events come alive. The writing paints as vivid a picture as the rare photographs that accompany the text. I wondered why I hadn't picked up on some of these events over the years in other books, but I have come to realize that Judy Crichton has an uncanny knack for unearthing the unknown or forgotten. Thank goodness—it's what makes this such a readable book!!

America 1900 is insightful and thoughtful. It doesn't draw conclusions but it does make the reader think, and come to his or her own conclusions. It also makes one realize that the problems of 1900 are very much the problems that exist as we approach the year 2000…I found out quickly that Judy Crichton is the proverbial "fly on the wall," and the book has made the year 1900 come alive.

An added bonus is that I have now discovered a great new book that is reasonably priced to give for presents. Definitely put this one on your list.

Turn of the Century *continued*

1898: The Birth of the American Century

Written by David Traxel

Type: Book (365 pages)

First Developed: 1998

Price Range: $25–$30

Key Features: Good setup to understand the turn of the century, then and now

Ages: All

Obsolescence: Low

Further Information:
❋ *http://www.liberty.edu/resources/library/public/as/history/american/20th/dec0/00.htm*
for a nice chaser, a Web site devoted to historical materials covering the rest of the 20th Century, and
❋ *http://www.studyweb.com/culture/amer/gildage.htm*
for an aggregation of material and links covering the Gilded Age through the World War I

Taking the Spanish-American War as the crux of events in 1898, the author follows the U.S. as it flexes its muscles: the U.S. trade in foreign markets, the arrival of Ford and Westinghouse, the first million-dollar advertising campaign, the electrification of the U.S., the move from a farm-based rural culture to big cities, big ideas, big goals, and, occasionally, big hubris.

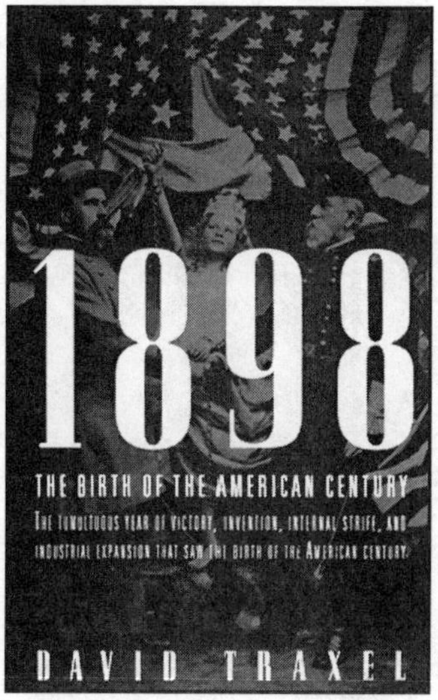

CRITIC COMMENTARIES

Collin Keefe, ***Philadelphia Weekly***

Unlike the usual presentation – stressing names, dates and dry rhetoric – that kept you comatose through semesters of required history courses, Traxel breathes life into the text and evokes visions, sounds and feelings of this time through colorful anecdotes and quotes from dynamic figures like Thomas Edison, Henry Ford, William McKinley and Teddy Roosevelt.

Robert Taylor, ***The Boston Globe***

David Traxel's 1898 is popular history composed with zest and care and an eye for the anecdote. It stakes no claim to original research, though it is conversant with primary source materials, and it clarifies for the general reader the state of mind of Americans who seem both very much like us and as different as the Ostrogoths.

Turn of the Century *continued*

Dreamland: America at the Dawn of the Twentieth Century
Edited by Michael Lesy

Type: Book (207 pages)

First Developed: 1998, New Press

Price Range: $25-$30

Key Features: Great stuff drawn from the Detroit Publishing Company

Ages: All

Obsolescence: Low

Further Information:
✳ *http://www.lcweb.loc.gov/rr/ print/coll/202_detr.html* for the Library of Congress collection from the Detroit Publishing Company.

There is no real theme here, other than the year and the selection of crisp detailed photographs. That is more than enough to give a wonderful sense of the time and the people. The photos—208 of them— are drawn from the archives of the Detroit Publishing Company and filled with skyscrapers going up, urban streets, and country roads; cowboys, steelworkers, farmers, and miners; normal folk; and lovely architecture.

Michael Lesy is the author/compiler of a very peculiar preceding volume, *Wisconsin Death Trip,* which was a photo study of open coffins from the late 19th century.

Creepy stuff that, and there is just a hint of creepiness to his collection here. His visual point seems to be that everybody at the time was clueless as to forces leading into the 20th century. Look beyond that, and you can sense some of the dreams and visions that gave force and direction to the U.S. at the time.

"Eloquent... A strange thing that photos of so much blight should possess so much beauty."

—*The Los Angeles Times*

"Poignantly contrasting with the serenity of the photos are thumbnail histories of the time's roiling social, political, and cultural changes..."

—The New Yorker →

Turn of the Century *continued*

◦➤ READER COMMENTARIES FROM THE NET

A reader from California, March 29, 1998 ★★★★☆

Beautiful, haunting volume of America at the cusp of change

Dreamland is a wonderful, wistful volume of photographs produced just after the turn of the century by William Henry Jackson and the Detroit Publishing Company and collected recently by editor Michael Lesy. The book, with its spare design and reverse-type pages, is beautifully constructed; pairing photographs with summaries of carefully chosen events from the first decade of this century, it slowly builds a clear and compelling portrayal of both the similarities (politicians and scandals seem to be a constant) and differences (crushing loss of life and wilderness) between the America it pictures and that of today.

From its cover image of children rushing into the surf near the Cliff House in San Francisco through its ever-contrasting procession of burgeoning cities, pristine scenery, alternately solemn and carefree faces, and towns sprouting on the edge of the not-quite-tamed wilderness, *Dreamland* continually surprises with its ability to communicate strong emotions of a time long past yet often resonant with today. In my mind, one of the most important aspects of the book is buried at the end: its coda, "The Enterprise and the Undertaking," which provides a history of Mr. Jackson and the making of the photographs, as well as a personal statement by the editor, Michael Lesy, providing insight into his personal obsession with the collection. This would have made an equally enjoyable preface, anchoring the tone for both photos and text. My complaints are few; the book suffers from less than perfect printing, showing unfortunate flaws in the black ink on many of the pages. Also, the decision to relegate the captions of the photographs to an appendix leaves the pages clear and unadorned, but also leads to a great deal of page-shuffling; I found this an inconvenience, as every photo leads you to wonder "where and when was this; who were these people?"

In balance, I very much enjoyed *Dreamland*—for the overall quality of its presentation, for the emotional impact of its subject matter, and especially for its striking evocation of America on the cusp of its irrevocable transition to the modern age. Recommended.

Detail:
Band Concert,
Lincoln Park,
Chicago, 1907

Turn of the Century *continued*

The Man Who Photographed the World: Burton Holmes: Travelogues, 1886–1938

by Burton Holmes

Type: Book (319 pages)

First Developed: 1977; Abrams Publishing

Price Range: $25–$30 used

Key Features: Photos from one of the great travelogue photographers of all time

Ages: All

Obsolescence: Low

Further Information:
✳ *http://www.hidden-knowledge .com/siberia/*
for a Web site on a Holmes tour of the Trans-Siberian Railway and

✳ *http://www.nleditions.com/ PHOTO.html*
for a way to order *The Man Who Photographed The World*

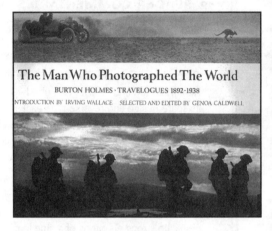

Elias Burton Holmes (1870–1958) traveled to Japan in 1892 and there met (and became a junior associate of) John L. Stoddard, the foremost traveler/lecturer of the late 19th century. Shortly after his return, a stereopticon lecture of his pictures from Japan made good money. Holmes struggled along these lines for four years, until Stoddard retired and arranged for Holmes to fill his engagements for the 1897–98 season. Holmes was spectacularly successful thereafter.

Holmes started using motion pictures as early as 1897, but the early stuff was mainly hand-colored lantern slides. He visited hovels and hotels all over the globe, attended the coronation of Haile Selassie in Ethopia, filmed the construction of the Panama Canal, and toured the Trans-Siberain Railway line. He traveled six times around the world, at a time when it was done by boat, rail, and, occasionally, beast.

The Burton Holmes Lectures were originally published in ten volumes, in 1901. In following years he added several more volumes, and they remained in print under the name *The Burton Holmes Travelogues*. More than 40,000 copies of these sets were sold...one reason why they can still be found in used-book stores across the nation.

This book of Holmes's photographs was published by Abrams in 1977. The *Man Who Photographed the World* is a wonderful book, evocative of the time. My favorite picture is taken from the shore of Port Arthur, where the Japanese have just sunk the better part of the Russian Fleet in harbor. It is colorized, but that does not detract from the utter reality of it.

Turn of the Century *continued*

The Birth of a Century: Early Color Photographs of America
by Jim Hughes, William H. Jackson (Photographer)

Type: Book (223 pages)

First Developed: 1994; St. Martin's Press

Price Range: $28

Key Features: Color images from a time that didn't have many of same

Ages: All

Obsolescence: Low

Further Information:
❈ *http://www.webcom.com/ ~ cityg/earlyphoto/reference/review/index.html*
for a terrific bibliography of turn of the century photography
❈ *http://www.bway.net/ ~ jscruggs/notice2.html*
for a fine history of the technology of color photography.
❈ *http://www.harappa.com/ whj3.html*
for a review of the Photochrom process used by William Henry Jackson.

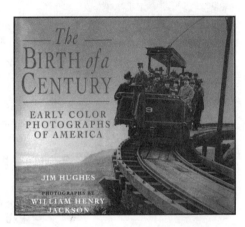

William Henry Jackson took an early color photo process called Photochrom around the world, financed by the Detroit Publishing Company. At the turn of the century, their postcards sold in the millions, and evoked a world of romance, distant and alien nature that we can hardly imagine now, when all cities and products look pretty much the same, and our worldview is defined by just how far into the country a CNN crew with a satellite uplink is willing to hump.

Black and white pictures, for example the great stuff from Matthew Brady's work during the Civil War (which includes 3-D stuff (see 3-D ENTERPRISES), never completely reveal the reality of things to me. Color gives it life and breath. Thus is *The Birth of a Century* all the more startling, as it provides color in a time when I'm not used to seeing color.

This book is a necessary companion to any attempt to grasp what things were like at the time.

Other books on William Henry Jackson

Time Exposure: The Autobiography of William Henry Jackson by William Henry Jackson

William Henry Jackson and the Transformation of the American Landscape by Peter B. Hales

William Henry Jackson: Framing the Frontier by Douglas Waitley

Hayden and His Men: A Selection of 108 Photographs by William Henry Jackson of the United States Geological and Geographical Survey of the Territories by Frank Chambers

William Henry Jackson: An Annotated Bibliography {1862 to 1995} by Thomas H. Harrell, Ph.d. (Compiler)

William Henry Jackson's Colorado by William C. Jones

Explorabook

Written by John Cassidy and the Exploratorium

http://pathfinder.com/travel/klutz/cat/cat2.html#explora

Type: Book; (100 pages)

First Developed: 1992; Klutz

Price Range: $16 in hardcover

Key Features: Neat stuff to futz with

Ages: All

Obsolescence: Low

Further Information: Check out *Zap Science: A Scientific Playground in a Book*

If you haven't gotten one of these books and given it to a son, daughter, niece, nephew, or friend's kid, you have missed out. The Explorabook is a compendium of experiments and demonstrations of physical realities, dealing with light, magnetism, bacteria, and the like.

It is bound together, loosely, with a spiral. Unavoidable, because the stuff they attached, bound, glued, and otherwise joined to the pages of this book make it something that would never work with a stiff spine. It comes equipped with a magnetic wand, mirror, moire spinner, diffraction grating, Fresnel lens, and agar.

The people at Klutz Press say that they were inspired by San Francisco's Exploratorium, and they certainly have captured the flavor of same. Give it to the child, be patient, and after a half an hour or so they will put it down (children's attention spans being what they are). Then you can start to futz with it, with the result being a great long stretch of fun.

Made for kids? Hah! A convenient excuse to sell neat stuff to adults.

Also from John Cassidy and The People at Klutz:

Earthsearch: A Kids' Geography Museum in a Book
by John Cassidy

Comes With: Eight foreign coins

Description: One of our pride-and-joy Museum Books. Our version of a book on geography (defined here as "everything from the tip of your nose going out"). More than 50 educators helped develop 21 different "exhibits" (things besides paper and ink) and "signs" (the words and pictures accompanying them). The whole package is, in our humble opinion, a higher form of multi-media instruction. Wire-bound. 110 pages. Full color.

The Complete Walker III:
The Joys and Techniques of Hiking and Backpacking
Written by Colin Fletcher

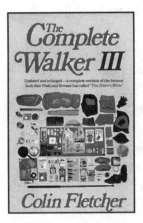

Type: Book (668 pages)

First Developed: 1984; Random House

Price Range: $16

Key Features: Gadgets for the electronically impaired and fresh air

Ages: Post-high school

Obsolescence: Low

Further Information:
✳ *http://www.thriveonline.com/ outdoors/hike/hikingindex.html* for a nice Web site devoted to hiking

I stumbled across this book when I was in college at the University of Wisconsin in the late '60s. I read it hungrily, and developed an obsession with fine hiking gear. For a while I was conversant in welding techniques as they related to backpacks and different types of down fill for cold weather garments. Heavy with experience-driven details, Fletcher suggests which socks to wear in what kind of boots. There's rich detail on the suppliers and what's good and bad.

I've forgotten the arcane stuff, but Fletcher's lessons in paring equipage down to the bare minimum have stuck with me. His thesis was that every ounce counted, in particular after you had carried it ten or twenty miles.

I find these lessons particularly relevant to software design, where the additional weight of features often smothers the real value of the software itself.

Fletcher elevated a hike to art, whether it be into the wilds or out to town. There is a great deal to be learned here, about lots of stuff.

Dutton's Navigation and Piloting
Written by Benjamin Dutton and Elbert S. Maloney

GPS can fail (in fact, early in the year 2000 there are worries that heavy electro-magnetic storms on the surface of the sun will degrade the GPS substantially). Loran can go away. Sometimes it just comes down to Maps, the stars, and a good watch.

When you don't have batteries, solar panels, or an electrical outlet, you want to have a copy of Dutton's. It is full of 2,000 years of assembled human experience and applied intelligence. Worth your time.

Type: Book

First Developed: 1926

Price Range: $50–$60

Key Features: The basic guide to making your way across the surface of the ocean

Ages: All

Obsolescence: Low

Further Information:
✳ *http://www.cs.brown.edu/ people/jfh/boats/postscript.html* for an interesting Web page devoted to postscript-enhanced navigation forms

Dreadnought: Britain, Germany, and the Coming of the Great War
Written by Robert K. Massie

Type: Book (635 pages)

First Developed: 1990, Avon Books

Price Range: $10–$15

Key Features: Excellent history

Ages: All

Obsolescence: Low

Further Information:
❋ *http://www.battleship.org/*
for a web-site devoted to American
battleships

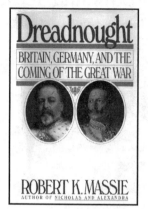

Massie starts this excellent book with an explanation of how pervasive was the impact of Alfred Thayer Mahan's THE INFLUENCE OF SEA POWER UPON HISTORY. Every king, president, and potentate at the beginning of the century was familiar with Mahan's thesis that control of the world meant control of the sea lanes.

From that departure point, Massie paints a series of interlocking character portraits of the men who used steel and steam to prepare for a conflict, the far-reaching effects of which none of them imagined. They focused instead on a contest of technology and logistics. The centerpiece was the battleship, to which they gave the revealing name "dread-nought." If you had enough of them, you had nothing to fear. How silly history made that seem.

The value in this story of the beginning of the 20th century is in the parallels that can be drawn to the beginning of the 21st. Battleships never proved to have any decisive effect during the 20th century, other than to give the countries that owned them a false metric for power comparisons. Could it be that nuclear technologies, and the theories of the stalling effect of mutually assured destruction (MAD) are equally false?

☛ READER COMMENTARIES FROM THE NET

A reader from Monrovia, California, May 13, 1998
★★★★★
Once again Robert K. Massie has brought history to life.
He has accomplished this by describing how personalities and popular views of an era as opposed to primarily describing events and leaving personalities and popular views in a supporting role.

A reader from Lexington, MA, December 5, 1997
★★★★★
The great battleship race and the coming of World War I
This is a well structured history of the competition of Britain and Germany to build Dreadnought battleships—the nuclear weapons of the age. It has good personality analyses of Kaiser Wilhelm II and Edward VII and superb biographical material on Jacky Fisher, the father of the modern British navy. It has the best analysis of the blunders that led to World War that I have read. (For a good biography of Jacky Fisher, see *Fisher's Face* by Jan Morris.)

Making the Corps
Written by Thomas E. Ricks

Type: Book (320 pages)

First Developed: 1998, Touchstone

Price Range: $11

Key Features: *Semper fi* explained

Ages: Post-high school

Obsolescence: Low

Further Information:
✱ *http://www.usmc.mil/*
for the U.S. Marines on the Web

There is something very mysterious about the transformation effected upon young Marine recruits—often lazy, ill-motivated, and apathetic. They become solid, dedicated, and capable men. Every culture, secular and religious, seems to have these rites of transformation. In religion, the results are hard to pin down and subject to a lot of questions.

In the secular world, the results are rarely impressive. In contrast, the Marine transformation is thorough and predictable, and the process has been going on for a century. Amazingly enough, the ethical foundations for the Marine regimens are religious, almost spiritual in character.

If you have ever had a sibling or a child who was spinning out of control, then you have longed to understand better what it takes to whip them into shape. The essence of what's necessary is documented here.

PARRIS ISLAND RULES:

DO YOUR BEST NO MATTER HOW TRIVIAL THE TASK

CHOOSE THE DIFFICULT RIGHT OVER THE EASY WRONG

LOOK OUT FOR THE GROUP BEFORE YOU LOOK OUT FOR YOURSELF

DON'T WHINE OR MAKE EXCUSES

➛ CRITIC & READER COMMENTARIES

From Kirkus Reviews, October 1, 1997

Wall Street Journal Pentagon correspondent Ricks effectively combines a vivid account of the rigorous basic training received by U.S. Marine recruits with commentary on what separates the demanding, disciplined culture of America's military elite from the more permissive culture of its civilian society. The author tracks the 60-odd volunteers who comprised Platoon 3086 at Parris Island in 1995 through the challenging 11-week course known as boot camp. Unlike their counterparts in other branches of the U.S. military, aspiring Marines do not train alongside women; nor do they have access to alcohol, automobiles, candy, cigarettes, drugs, or various other diversions dear to the hearts of young American males. The author argues that it behooves America's largely oblivious middle and upper classes to take a more direct interest in their military. A revelatory briefing on what sets the USMC apart and the consequences of its superiority during a post-Cold War era when, for all the talk of peace →

Making the Corps *continued*

READER COMMENTARIES (cont.)

→ dividends, the wider world remains an armed and dangerous place.

A reader from Virginia, April 1, 1999 ★★★★★
Today's USMC boot camp and civil-military relationships.
If you want a great read about today's USMC recruit training at Parris Island, S.C., and a great insight into the USMC vs. American society "culture war," then don't miss this OUTSTANDING book!

Ricks does a superb job of capturing the challenges and triumphs of a real platoon undergoing boot camp at the Corps' legendary Parris Island Recruit 2 Depot. He explores the recruits' backgrounds and responses to the transforming boot camp experience.

Unlike some other works that seem to exaggerate certain perspectives, this book is an honest, realistic, and well-written collection of astute, in-depth observations. You will understand how the Corps continues to thrive while keeping its numbers small, standards high, and traditions strong.

This book also analyzes the growing cultural gap between the USMC and the very society from which it comes. Ricks did extensive research into this gap and carefully weaves it in throughout the book. He accurately describes the USMC cultural experience and compares it to what you see and don't see in today's society. If you have never given this gap much thought, you will find yourself wondering why you never noticed it before.

Being a Marine, I loved this book. Being a part of American society, I was intrigued and entertained by this book. I recommend this book to any Marine and all citizens who ever considered becoming a Marine, or running for public office, or know others who have done either one. I guarantee you won't be disappointed.

A reader from Tampa, Florida, March 24, 1999
★★★★★
Semper Fi **is for real!**
I am a former Marine. As such, I feel quite qualified to proclaim this book 100% on the mark. It describes boot camp the way it is—intense and, at times, brutal, but for good reason.

However, while I found Mr. Ricks' discussion of the widening gulf between mainstream America and the Corps interesting, I do not share his concern. The civilian and Marine Corps cultures have always been worlds apart. At no time was this proposition ever more apparent than during the '60s and '70s. That is the way it should be. However, this fact shouldn't cause concern.

America has nothing to fear from her Marines. To Marines, *Semper Fidelis* (Always Faithful) is more than just a motto. It is a way of life. No matter how sloppy and undisciplined the world around us becomes, the Marine Corps will always remain faithful. America shouldn't feel threatened by her Marines, her enemies should.

Balkan Ghosts: A Journey Through History

Written by Robert D. Kaplan

Type: Book (307 pages)

First Developed: 1994; Vintage Books

Price Range: $10

Key Features: Deeply unsettling view of the region

Ages: Post-high school

Obsolescence: Low.

I knew something weird was going on in the Balkans when, during the recent troubles, the Battle of Kosovo was constantly cited as a motive behind the animosity between the factions. First, the battle took place many centuries ago. Second, after I looked the battle up in *Brassey's Battles* (a first-rate compendium of the historical record of military conflict), on a ten-point meter of importance, it seemed to rate about a two.

It's easy for people in North America, most of whose history does not extend more than three centuries, to be boggled by the white-hot emotion-

al tendrils that stretch through the history of the Balkans. There is no questioning the reality of it. It was here in the Balkans that World War I started. It was here that the Hapsburgs rose and fell. It was here that the Vatican and the Eastern Orthodox Church fought. It was here that Soviet Communism caught hold, and here where its removal was most violent. It is as if Rome, Istanbul, Athens, Vienna, and Moscow have torn at the belly of this region throughout history, with scabs never ceasing to fester. →

⊷ CRITIC COMMENTARIES

The New Yorker
Combines up-to-the-minute political reporting and literary travel writing...[Kaplan's prose] is vivid, controlled, and sensitive.

San Francisco Examiner
Kaplan is a striking and evocative writer, and the Balkans offer him all the richness of a Garcia Marquez world, where the fantastic is everyday life.

Balkan Ghosts *continued*

→ The unimaginable cruelties we have seen recently become more imaginable with a thorough reading of this book. Not everyone seems to certify Kaplan's freedom from bias, but this is the region, up close and personal. Hard to have everybody like what you say about a place where people torture and murder one another with such abandon.

➝ READER COMMENTARIES

A reader from The Netherlands, May 15, 1999
★★★★★
Brilliant.
Kaplan writes with the finely honed skill of the very best journalism can offer. His talent for description and story-telling cannot be questioned. He is clearly a scholar willing to dig for more. A writer can give only perceptions. I believe history is, as Mark Twain called it, fluid prejudice. History as told, as studied, has the limitation of being from a singular viewpoint. This author has done his homework and braved the terrain to give the reader his own firsthand account. He has told his story with a compelling alacrity and grace, in spite of the tragedy and horror and complexity that is woven throughout this attempt to illuminate the history of the people of the Balkans. I am recommending it to everyone I know. Bravo, Mr. Kaplan.

A reader from San Francisco, CA , March 26, 1999 ★★★★☆
A subjective but valid view.
This book is both a travelogue and history lesson. Kaplan's observations can sometimes be as subjective as his travel plans, but I've read this book twice (the second time after the NATO action in Serbia/ Kosovo) and it holds up as a good primer (albeit subjective and incomplete) of Balkan history. If you want to start learning about the Balkans, you could do a lot worse than to start here. Recommended.

Visual Explanations
Written By Edward Tufte

Type: Book (157 pages)

First Developed: 1998

Price Range: $40–$48, depending upon which book

Key Features: Utter command of the tactics of visual display

Ages: Old enough to have to make a point

Obsolescence: Medium

Further Information: Sadly, Tufte has no Web site. He's apparently too picky to do it in a fashion that is anything less than perfect

This book, like 48 LAWS OF POWER, is beautifully laid out and printed, as it must be. Tufte makes his living by doing things on paper the right way. His first book, *The Visual Display of Quantitative Information*, is considered by just about everybody to be a classic treatise on how to make numbers make sense when presented as graphics in print.

He has published two additional books over the years, and they form a system. The first is dedicated to pictures of numbers and enforcing statistical honesty.

The second, *Envisioning Information*, is about pictures of nouns (Tufte's conceit is that maps and aerial photographs are graphic representations of nouns lying on the ground).

The last, *Visual Explanations*, is devoted to pictures of verbs. Here he deals with truthful, understandable representations of mechanism and motion, processes and dynamics, cause and effect.

The graphic designs presented in the books are largely self-explanatory. I like picture books, and this is a set of very challenging picture books. Often, I can only view (you don't read a Tufte book so much as view it) a few pages at a time and then have to spend a bit of time absorbing. This is prime steak, and it requires a bit of chewing.

His first book has made one particular graphic very familiar to many people. It is a graph of the attrition suffered by Napoleon's armies on the way to (and back from) Moscow one terrible winter. Hitler should have had this graphic plastered on his forehead. Lucky he didn't. →

Visual Explanations *continued*

→ *Visual Explanations* has two striking case histories. One follows the cholera epidemic, and its termination, in London in 1854. The conclusions from the correct and incorrect presentation of the data are strikingly in contrast. Another is devoted to the *Challenger* disaster.

The life and death implications of poorly presented data, produced and consumed at the last moment, in an environment noisy with bureaucratic agendas are both chilling and instructive. This is a righteous book and worth the money and the time invested.

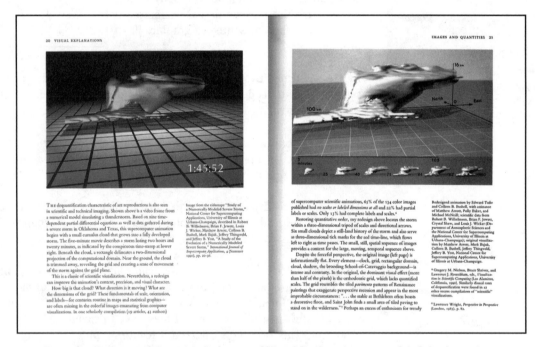

From the "Images and Quantities" chapter of Visual Explanations, *a study of the formation of a storm. On page left, an image from the videotape, "Study of a Numerically Modeled Severe Storm" from the National Center for Supercomputing Applications; on page right, the redesigned animation by Tufte and Colleen B. Bushell.*

→

Visual Explanations *continued*

⚓ READER COMMENTARIES FROM THE NET

As I drove into the parking lot to attend a one-day course taught by Edward Tufte, it occurred to me that all I really knew about Tufte, I learned from Ray Duncan's book review in the June 1997 issue of Dr. Dobb's Journal. I quickly learned something else about him as I unsuccessfully tried to find a parking spot—Tufte is a very popular guy.

Over 375 people payed $300 to attend Tufte's course on information design and receive copies of his three self-published books: *The Visual Display of Quantitative Information, Envisioning Information,* and *Visual Explanations: Images and Quantities, Evidence and Narrative.* The books alone could have made the fee worthwhile; the opportunity to hear Tufte passionately preach his design principles (peppered with not-so-occasional one-liners) made the fee a steal.

INFORMATION DESIGN
The problem with presenting information, as explained by Tufte, is simple—the world is high-dimensional, but our displays are not. To address this basic problem, Tufte offered five principles of information design:

1. Quantitative thinking comes down to one question: Compared to what?

2. Try very hard to show cause and effect.

3. Don't break up evidence by accidents of means of production.

4. The world is multivariant, so the display should be high-dimensional.

5. The presentation stands and falls on the quality, relevance, and integrity of the content.

(For the rest of the review, check out *http://www.ercb.com/feature/feature.0008.html*)

Endless Frontier: Vannevar Bush, Engineer of the American Century

Written by G. Pascal Zachary

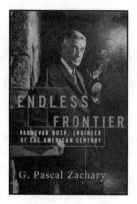

Type: Book (512 pages)

First Developed: 1997; The Free Press

Price Range: $22- $32 in hardcover

Key Features: Fundamental personality of the 20th century; a story well told.

Ages: Post-high school

Obsolescence: Low

Further Information:
❋ *http://www.theatlantic.com/unbound/flashbks/computer/bushf.htm*
(link to the original Atlantic Monthly essay by Vannevar Bush, *"As We May Think"*)

The founders of the computer industry owe an abiding debt of gratitude to Vannevar Bush. Not only because of the eternally valuable and seminal article he wrote at the end of World War II, predicting the present-day world of cyberspace, but because of the things he made happen throughout his life.

First, while at MIT, he crafted one of the first real computers in the 1930s, called the differential analyzer, which inspired a whole generation of computer engineers.

During World War II, while he was running the U.S.'s "wizard war" (as Churchill called the contest of high technologies), he funded the development of an array of calculating machines enabling the development of the atomic bomb, proximity fuses, radar, and the means to decrypt secret codes.

Then, as the war drew to a close, on the eve of the first use of the bomb, he penned an article for *The Atlantic Monthly,* designed to show up in August 1945 on the verandas and doorsteps of all the nation's movers and shakers.

The essay, called *"As We May Think,"* imagined thinking machines that would handle and store all of human knowledge. That article inspired most of the people who made the computer a personally relevant device for us today.

This book, written by Greg Zachary, a well-known and competent tech industry journalist for *The Wall Street Journal,* is a first-rate way to track the beginning of the computer age.

A Book Review Excerpt

Vannevar Bush is best known for his 1945 essay *As We May Think,* which described an imaginary, automated system to link together all of humanity's knowledge. It was a system, in short, that prefigured hypertext and the Web by almost 50 years. But this visionary essay was really just a footnote to the life of a man...

Endless Frontier... describes how Bush stamped his indelible imprint on our times. But, the ironic coda to this story is that after having helped create the military-industrial complex that defined the postwar era, Bush was deeply unhappy with what he had wrought. Here, Zachary becomes most eloquent, almost elegiacal.

—Steve G. Steinberg, *Wired*

Computer Lib/Dream Machines

Written by Ted Nelson

http://www.sfc.keio.ac.jp/~ted/

The central folio of the da Vinci of the Computer Age. This guy, and this book, are the reason a lot of us got into computing to begin with. In 1973, seeing anything wonderful in a computer took an extraordinary act of imagination. Ted Nelson saw EVERYTHING wonderful in computing.

He saw it, and then he described it, and then he drew little pictures and diagrams of it. Computer Lib/Dream Machines is a book as imaginative, as prescient, as noble as any da Vinci folio. Everything great about computers today was imagined by Ted Nelson before Jimmy Carter was elected, before Steve Jobs took drugs, before Bill Gates went to Harvard. Get a copy (even if it's the bastardized, shrunken version put out by Microsoft Press), and discover where personal computing is going, as described by Ted Nelson before the trip began.

Cover (above) and detail (right) from Ted Nelson's seminal treatise on the world of computers

Type: Oversize trade paperback book

First Developed: 1973

Price Range: $24.95

Key Features: Amazing prescience

Ages: 10 and up

Obsolescence: Low

Further Information: The original is exceedingly rare. The Microsoft Press version is less hard to find. Other books and articles by Ted Nelson are more abstruse.

For more on Nelson's contribution to the history of computing, see
✳ *http://www.netvalley.com/ netvalley/intvalxan.html*

CAN IT BE DONE?

I dunno.

Licklider, one of computerdom's Great Men, estimated in 1965 that to handle all text by computer, and bring it out to screens, would cost no more than what we pay for all text handling now. (But of course there is the problem of what to do with the people whose lives are built around paper; that can't be taken up here.)

The people who make big computers say that to get the big disk storage to hold great amounts of text, you have to get their biggest computers. Which is a laugh and a half. One IBM-style computer person pompously told me that for large-scale text handling the only appropriate machine was an IBM 360/67 (a shamefully large computer). Such people seem not to understand about minicomputers or the potential of minicomputer networks— using, of cburse, big disks.

There are of course questions of reliability, of "big brother" (see Canons, p.   ), and so on. But I think these matters can be handled.

The key is that people will pay for it. I am sure that if we can bring the cost down to two dollars an hour— one for the local machine (more than a "terminal"), one for the material (including storage, transmission and copyrights)— there's a big, big market. (And that's what the Xanadu network is about; see p. DM57.) My assumption is that the way to do this is not through big business (since all these corporations can see is other corporations); not through government (hypertext is not committee-oriented, but individualistic— and grants can only be gotten through sesquipedalian and obfuscatory pompizzazz); but through the byways of the private enterprise system. I think the same spirit that gave us McDonald's and kandy kolor hot rod accessories may pull us through here. (See Xanadu Network, p. DM57.)

Obviously, putting man's entire heritage into a hypertext is going to take awhile. But it can and should be done.

EVERYTHING IS DEEPLY INTERTWINGLED.

In an important sense there are no "subjects" at all; there is only all knowledge, since the cross-connections among the myriad topics of this world simply cannot be divided up neatly.

Hypertext at last offers the possibility of representing and exploring it all without carving it up destructively.

Arthur C. Clarke wrote a book entitled The Lost Worlds of 2001 (Signet, 1972), about the variants and alternatives of that story that did not find their way to the screen.

In a hypertext version, we could look at them all in context, in collateral views, and see the related variants— with annotations.

→ Computer Lib/Dream Machines *continued*

THE WORLD ACCORDING TO TED NELSON

Today's Horrible Computer World: A work in progress

"The computer world is like a great big toy store. But all the toys are broken." –Steve Witham

"Microsoft is not the problem. Microsoft is the symptom." –Eric S. Raymond

"If houses were built the way computers are built, the first woodpecker would bring down civilization." –Anon.

Note that these are not empty criticisms thrown out without alternatives. In my designs over the years I have proposed principled alternatives. Finally it is possible to see some of my designs in preliminary implementations.

The dirty little secret: The computer world is an incredible uphill mess. Nobody's life has been simplified by computers.

When I published *Computer Lib* in 1974, computers were big oppressive systems off in airconditioned rooms. In the 1987 edition of *Computer Lib—the Microsoft edition!*—I wrote, "Now you can be oppressed in your own living room!" It has gotten far worse.

The Mercedes and Your Family
THE GOOD NEWS: They say: "If cars had improved as much as computers, a Mercedes-Benz would cost ten dollars, go ten thousand miles on a liter of gas, and go a thousand miles an hour."

THE BAD NEWS: …and if you had such a Mercedes-Benz, it would stop unexpectedly, and your family would be missing from the back seat. Forever.

THE DREAM WE ALL SHARED: Computers would make it easy to save information, keep track of things, and manage creative work.

THE REALITY: A nightmare.

©1998 T.Nelson

Above, a superfreak detail from the Computer Lib/Dream Machines *cover.*

Index

INFORMATICA 1.0

INDEX

INDEX

INDEX

INDEX

INDEX

The Contributors

Ravi Desai is a Managing Director at Scient, and one of the founders of theStreet.com. He is one of those few people who seems to be able to keep the whole calculus of the Net in his mind.

Terry Irving is the producer of Don Imus' show on MSNBC. Before that he was a senior producer for Nightline. I met him when he took a sabbatical to learn the multimedia business. The natural cynicism of his trade is tempered by an unbounded enthusiasm for all things new and interesting.

Tom Bradford Executive Produces the CBS overnight news broadcast, and has been with CBS for two decades. He is smart, thoughtful, and has had a watchful eye on high tech for as long as I have known him.

Matt Devost works for a beltway firm called Infrastructure Defense. He is one of the small cadre of folks who understand - really understand - what infrastructure warfare will mean to the United States in the next century.

David Ellis is one of the principals of Vigon/Ellis, a very sophisticated design firm in Los Angeles. He has an excellent grasp of mnemonics—how you make stuff stick in peoples minds.

Dan Kempler is Director of the Communication Disorders Division and Professor in the Department of Otolaryngology—Head and Neck Surgery at the University of Southern California. He is also, as it happens, an ordained minister so he can conceivably marry you and check your tonsils at the same time.

Frank Tyneski is the lead designer of the Motorola Talkabouts, and has won a bushelful of awards for same.

About the Author

Peter McNaughton Black founded and is CEO of XIPHIAS Corporation, a Los Angeles-based publisher of reference products on disk and the Net. He has a Master's Degree in Sanskrit and Linguistics, and has run XIPHIAS Corporation since 1979. He is the publisher of *Encyclopedia Electronica*™, and is a recognized authority on Infrastructure Warfare.

Mr. Black lives with his wife, Patricia and three children in West Los Angeles.

About the CD-ROM and Updates

Informatica 1.0 on CD-ROM

Informatica 1.0 comes in two versions—one, the meatspace version rendered on paper alone in book form; the other version is the book with a CD-ROM bundled on the inside back cover.

The CD-ROM contains *Informatica 1.0* in bits and bytes. We have rendered it in two forms: one for reading and printing (in Adobe Acrobat™-compatible .pdf files), and one for linking (using The Brain software as an index to a set of Microsoft Word files).

Using the advanced capabilities of The Brain (we also discuss The Brain software on page 242), the entire book is organized dynamically with Web site URLs hot-linked to your Net browser. The individual articles and essays are in files small enough to attach to e-mails and you are welcome to do just that, as long as it is not for commercial purposes, and not to more than three e-mail addresses. Same limitations apply to printing the .pdf files—not for commercial purposes, and no more of the material than would be allowed under generally recognized standards for fair use.

All rights, title, and interest in *Informatica 1.0* are retained by Xiphias Corporation. *Informatica 1.0* © 2000.

Obtaining the CD-ROM

If you purchased the book-only version, you can order the CD-ROM version over the Net at www.etronica.com. There, at our master Web site you will also be able to:

1) Use Encyclopedia Electronica™ and it's Brilliant Search capabilities
2) Order supplements to *Informatica*, which will keep you posted on the best stuff you can find on the Web